Cinderella of the New South

Cinderella of the New South

A History of the Cottonseed Industry, 1855–1955

Lynette Boney Wrenn

The University of Tennessee Press • Knoxville

The paper in this book meets the minimum requirements of the
American National Standard for Permanence of Paper for Printed
Library Materials. ∞   The binding materials have been chosen
for strength and durability.

Library of Congress Cataloging-in-Publication Data

Wrenn, Lynette Boney, 1928-
      Cinderella of the new South: a history of the cottonseed industry, 1855-1955/
Lynette Boney Wrenn. —1st ed.
         p.   cm.
      Includes bibliographical references and index.
      ISBN 0-87049-882-7 (cloth: alk. paper)
  1. Cottonseed—Southern States—History—19th century.
  2. Cottonseed—Southern States—History—20th century.
  3. Cottonseed oil—Southern States—History—19th century.
  4. Cottonseed oil—Southern States—History—20th century.
  I. Title.
HD9093.U6S688   1995
338.1'735121'0975—dc20   94-18733
                                                 CIP

This book is dedicated to my husband, Earle.

Contents

Illustrations

Tables

Preface

Nineteen ninety-three marked the two-hundredth anniversary of Eli Whitney's cotton gin, the engine that by mechanizing seed removal helped make cotton king in the South. Cottonseed furnished the raw materials for cottonseed milling, an industry that developed during the second half of the nineteenth century and became an important component of the southern economy. The current concern with dietary fats makes the cottonseed industry a timely subject. In the past decade Americans have increasingly switched from animal to vegetable fats in their diets as evidence has mounted that highly saturated fats contribute to heart and circulatory diseases. Because soybean oil currently dominates the market, few people realize that the modern vegetable oil and shortening industry originated in the continuing efforts of cottonseed crushers and oil refiners to improve and market their product as a less-expensive substitute for olive oil, butter, and lard.

The inspiration for this book came from Pete Daniel's *Breaking the Land,* in which he said that no one had yet written a history of the cottonseed industry nor studied the role of ginners in cottonseed transactions. My gratitude to Pete Daniel goes beyond providing me with an absorbing project; he also read and made thoughtful comments on this book in its early manuscript form.

Staff members of the National Cottonseed Products Association, located in Memphis, made a desk available, where I read trade journals and other materials, and the association's executive vice president, Lynn Jones, reviewed the manuscript.

Questions raised by Harold Woodman and David Carlton, who read the manuscript for the University of Tennessee Press, strengthened the book in innumerable ways. I am grateful for their insights and the time they spent reading and thinking about the manuscript. Remaining errors and misjudgments are solely my responsibility.

Karin Kaufman's careful copyediting of the manuscript and the work of Acquisitions Editor Meredith Morris-Babb, Managing Editor Stan Ivester, and others at the University of Tennessee Press who helped to launch this book are much appreciated.

My thanks go to Dun & Bradstreet and the Baker Library of the Harvard University Graduate School of Business Administration for permission to use material in the R. G. Dun & Company Collection.

I wish to thank James E. Kolar of Moulton, Texas, for a tour of his oil mill, one of the last two hydraulic oil mills still in business in the United States, and Brian R. Lundgren, who explained the various operations of the screw-press mill at Elgin, Texas, that his family has owned since the 1930s.

With little secondary literature available on the history of cottonseed processing, the quest for primary materials has involved a voluminous correspondence with librarians and archivists in all of the cotton-producing states and in key northern cities, as well as visits to many of their institutions. Only with their aid could this study been completed, and I wish to thank them all. Several individuals and institutions that proved to be especially helpful in terms of the quantity and quality of their records and the assistance provided by their staff members are singled out for special thanks.

Carol Smith of the Area Resource Center and members of the history and business departments of the Memphis–Shelby County Public Library and Archives; the Southern Historical Collection staff at the University of North Carolina, Chapel Hill; William R. Erwin Jr., manuscript department of the Perkins Library at Duke University; Maurice C. York, local history librarian with the Edgecombe County Memorial Library in Tarboro, North Carolina; members of the manuscript department of the J. Y. Joyner Library at East Carolina University in Greenville, North Carolina; the staff of the Spangler-Robinson Room of the Charlotte, North Carolina, Public Library; librarians and staff at the Mississippi Department of Archives and in Special Collections at the Mitchell Memorial Library of Mississippi State University; staff of the Oklahoma Department of Libraries in Oklahoma City; archivists at the DeKalb County Historical Society, Decatur, Georgia, and at the University of Alabama's Stanley Hoole Special Collections Library; librarians at the Cincinnati Historical Society and Dayton, Ohio, Public Library; staff of the New Orleans Public Library and at the Howard-Tilton Memorial Library of Tulane University; personnel at the Boston Athenaeum and the manuscript division of the Baker Library at the Harvard University Graduate School of Business Administration; Michael R. Green, Reference Archivist at the Texas State Library and Archives; local history librarians at the public libraries of Dallas, Fort Worth, Houston, and Galveston; researchers at the National Archives and Library of Congress in Washington and staff at the National Agricultural Library in Beltsville, Maryland; the Southern Regional Research Center of the Department of Agriculture in New Orleans; and Professor William H. Phillips, University of South Carolina.

My greatest thanks go to my husband Earle, who has been my granting agent, a willing listener, a wonderful companion, and since his retirement, an assistant on research trips. Without his support and encouragement this book would not have been possible.

Introduction

Aided alone by actual worth and intrinsic value, this ugly
duckling has assumed the splendid plumage of the swan,
this despised Cinderella of the Kitchen has become the radi-
ant belle of the ball, this neglected stepchild has become the
sturdy heir of the house, and stands today as the most valued and important representative of the South's manufacturing progress in the markets of the world.

John W. Allison, *Proceedings of the Interstate
Cotton Seed Crushers' Association,* 1905

When I read my Bible more diligently perhaps than I do now,
I was wont to believe that the children of Israel were the
chosen people of God. But since the development of the
cottonseed to its present commercial status, since that poor
little Cinderella has been lifted from the dust heap and en-
throned the royal consort of King Cotton, I have changed
my views, and now firmly believe that He has chosen the
dwellers in this beautiful Southland as the especial objects of
His favor.

Aaron D. Allen, *Proceedings of the Interstate
Cotton Seed Crushers' Association,* 1909

Like sawdust piles around lumber mills, mounds of cottonseed accumulated near southern gins before large-scale processing developed after the
Civil War. Excess seed was either fenced to keep out livestock, burned,
or dumped into streams and gullies. Only a fraction of the seed produced
each year was required for planting, and surplus cottonseed had little
utility except as feed for cattle or as fertilizer on depleted cotton and corn

fields. Rotting cottonseed produced an offensive odor that people considered unhealthy, and cottonseed killed hogs and other nonruminants when eaten in large quantities. Unused seed became a problem of such magnitude that Alabama, Georgia, and Mississippi passed laws to regulate its disposal.

The metamorphosis of commercially worthless cottonseed into valuable raw materials for a leading New South industry seemed like a fairy tale to some pioneer oil millers.[1] During the early twentieth century, writers frequently described cottonseed as an "economic Cinderella,"[2] and cottonseed crushers used the Cinderella theme to remind farmers dissatisfied with low seed prices that processors had turned a waste product into the second most valuable cash crop in the South. The magic wand that transformed "lowly" cottonseed was its manufacture into marketable commodities. Seed and labor came from the South, as did much of the capital and entrepreneurial initiative during the early days of cottonseed processing, but full development of the industry involved people and resources from many parts of the United States.

Cottonseed crushing became an integral part of the cotton South after Reconstruction. As oil mills expanded throughout the cotton-growing states during the last two decades of the nineteenth century, more and more farmers found a market for their cottonseed. Fluctuating from about one-fifth to one-eighth the value of lint, cottonseed helped to compensate for slumping cotton prices.[3] The sale of cottonseed paid for ginning the cotton and baling the lint and pumped money into the economy at the end of the long growing season. Generally exempt from the crop liens or mortgages that covered lint sales in the postbellum South, cottonseed brought many small growers the only cash they saw from one year to the next. Money from cottonseed sales supported numerous farm families while they harvested the crop, and larger farmers generally used their cottonseed earnings to buy fertilizer or pay cotton pickers. With cottonseed prices having a direct impact on the purchasing power of so many people, it is no wonder that oil mills were the frequent object of political denunciations and price-fixing investigations.

Public cotton gins appeared in thousands of southern communities after the Civil War as landowners subdivided their plantations and cotton cultivation became more widespread. Ginners served as the principal middlemen in the transfer of cottonseed from producers to processors. Most of the money needed to purchase seed came from southern banks in the form of short-term loans to oil mills and independent cottonseed buyers. Cottonseed buying and selling became an important component of the complex of businesses associated with cotton ginning in many small southern towns of the late nineteenth and early twentieth century. Countless southern entrepreneurs combined farming, merchandising, ginning, and buying cotton and cottonseed. In order to control seed supplies, many oil mill companies owned cotton gins and loaned money to finance the building of new gins and the modernization of old ones. The close relationship that existed between cottonseed oil mills and cotton gins in the New South has not been fully understood.

Between 1880 and 1920 cottonseed-oil mills dominated the economic life of hundreds of market towns in the Cotton Belt. The rapid growth of southern towns during those years was in part a result of the cottonseed-processing industry. Before the First World War, smaller mills located near cotton fields could compete with larger and more efficient crushing operations. Because cottonseed crushing and cotton ginning, both seasonal operations, had to be combined with other activities, oil mills operated a variety of auxiliary enterprises, such as cattle feeding, feed and fertilizer mixing, and ice making.

A small number of largely northern-owned refining and manufacturing companies stood at the top of the cottonseed-processing pyramid composed of farmers, seed buyers, crushers, and manufacturers of cottonseed products. Their research and development and aggressive advertising of cottonseed oils and shortenings helped create the demand that fueled the expansion of cottonseed crushing in the cotton-growing states. Most of the refining and manufacturing companies eventually acquired crushing mills in order to ensure adequate supplies of cottonseed oil. Full-line companies that bought cottonseed at unprofitably high prices in order to produce set quotas of crude oil for manufacturing purposes angered independent operators whose mills could not survive unless they crushed cottonseed on a profitable basis.

By neglecting the cottonseed industry, historians have overlooked an important facet of life in the Cotton Belt of the late nineteenth and early twentieth centuries. The crushing industry touched the lives of cotton farmers who produced the seed, ginners and cottonseed buyers who purchased seed for the oil mills, bankers who financed seed purchases and mill construction, merchants whose sales rose and fell with cottonseed prices, investors, managers, and laborers in crushing plants, and most others in the cotton South.

Because little has been published about cottonseed processing in half a century, apart from government and technical bulletins, this book traces the history of an almost forgotten industry during its first century, 1855–1955. I also analyze cottonseed crushing, the distinctively southern phase of the processing industry, in the context of the New South, defined as the former Confederate states and Oklahoma. My aim is to show the impact cottonseed milling had on the Cotton Belt and how the time and place of its development shaped the crushing industry. The emergence of large, cottonseed-processing companies, the role they played in developing, manufacturing, and marketing finished products, and the tensions that existed between them and the independent crushing mills is a third focus of this book. Finally, I expand on a subject that has been treated by a number of historians in recent years, the economic and social revolution that began in the South during the 1930s and 1940s, in this case, the impact of the New Deal and World War II on the cottonseed-processing industry.[4]

The fifth most valuable class of manufactured products in the South by 1890, the crude cottonseed oil, cake/meal, hulls, and linters produced by crushing mills moved into fourth place a decade later, and ranked third in the value of its products and sixth in value added by manufacturing in 1909 and 1919.[5] It is impossible to calculate the value of shortening, salad oil, soap, fertilizer, mixed animal feeds, rayon, and other goods manufactured from the four basic cottonseed products during the same period, but Ivory Soap, the Gold Dust Twins washing powder, Wesson Oil, Crisco, Spry, and Snowdrift were all popular cottonseed-oil products, and some V-C fertilizers contained cottonseed meal as a source of nitrogen. Manufacturers of cottonseed oils and shortenings pioneered the edible vegetable oil industry in the United States; fertilizer and mixed-feed manufacturers incorporated cottonseed meal into their products; and during the early decades of the twentieth century, the infant cellulose industry found important new uses for linters, the short fibers that remain on American upland cottonseed after it has been ginned.

For half a century cottonseed crushing ranked among the leading industries of every former Confederate state except Virginia and Florida, yet the cottonseed industry receives little attention in historical accounts of the New South written since the First World War. Published in 1934, Emory Q. Hawk's *Economic History of the South* contains two misleading sentences about the manufacture of cottonseed oil in a chapter on antebellum southern industry and an abbreviated reference to cottonseed processing after the Civil War. In *Origins of the New South*, C. Van

Woodward allocated considerably more space to iron and steel manufacturing than to cottonseed processing, even though cottonseed products had a higher value added by manufacturing than iron and steel during most of the period covered by the book. George B. Tindall ignored cottonseed crushing completely in *The Emergence of the New South,* although cellulose made from cottonseed linters proved to be an ideal raw material for the new rayon industry he describes. Two contemporary encyclopedias of southern history and culture make only a passing mention of cottonseed. *King Cotton and His Retainers,* Harold D. Woodman's groundbreaking account of financing and marketing the cotton crop from 1800–1925, does not discuss cottonseed or the crushing industry.[6] Reflecting the state of secondary literature in general, college textbooks either ignore cottonseed milling altogether or merely list it among "other New South industries."

With a few exceptions, such as cottonseed processing and cotton ginning (apart from its mechanical aspects), most of the leading industries of the New South have been the subject of historical investigation, although southern business and industry have not been of major interest to historians. In the 1920s a professor wrote of the North Carolina cottonseed industry, "While we rightly emphasize our progress in textiles, in tobacco, in lumber and in furniture, we often forget the little cottonseed and its economic significance not only to the state but also to the South and to the nation." On the eve of World War II, a writer for *Fortune* described cottonseed processing as "the biggest unknown industry in the country." More recently, Pete Daniel has called attention to the neglect of cottonseed marketing and processing.[7]

Before the Second World War, cottonseed processors, economists, popular writers, scientists, and government officials wrote extensively about the cottonseed industry and most histories of the South contained short sections on cottonseed crushing. Why has this industry received so little attention from writers and scholars in recent decades? Unlike the textile, tobacco, iron and steel, sugar, rice, and petroleum industries, each of which operated on a large scale in a limited number of southern states, cottonseed crushing went on in all of the cotton-producing states, but with more modest results on the state level than the highly concentrated industries. Many of the oil mills were small, and manufacturing added little to the value of cottonseed. The labor force was almost wholly black and insignificant in size compared to the manpower employed in saw mills and textile factories. Companies located throughout the United

States manufactured a wide variety of articles from crude cottonseed products, but the raw materials used were rarely known to the public. As an industry spokesman pointed out in 1911, cottonseed processors could "make edible oil without olives; medicinal oil without codfish; butter without cows; ice cream without cream; lard without hogs; fertilizers without blood; mattresses without hair; stock feed without corn or oats and explosives without powder."[8]

Because the primary crushing industry was decentralized and corporations in both the North and South made use of crude cottonseed products in manufacturing dissimilar goods, the impact of the cottonseed-products industry has been obscured. Moreover, as the dominant economic enterprises in the Cotton Belt, cotton growing and lint marketing and manufacturing have overshadowed most other activities. A preoccupation with industrial winners probably contributes to historians' neglect of cottonseed processing. In the 1929 Census of Manufactures, the four primary cottonseed products dropped in value to fifth place in the New South, and ten years later were left far behind by textiles, tobacco, and petroleum refining. Beginning in the 1930s soybeans were grown on a large scale, and by the end of World War II had passed cottonseed as the leading source of vegetable oil in the United States. Reflecting the changed status of cottonseed processing, the 1947 Census of Manufactures ceased to treat cottonseed oil, meal, hulls, and linters in a separate section as the census had done with only one exception since 1880. With the accelerated consolidation of cottonseed crushing and the increased production of cotton in the Far West following the Second World War, many southern towns lost their oil mills. Even the mills' characteristic odor disappeared with the adoption of new technologies. Thus, the industry faded in importance and ceased to be a subject of interest to reporters and scholars as the twentieth century progressed.

The history of cottonseed processing, from its commercial beginnings on the eve of the Civil War to the end of its first phase in the mid-twentieth century, falls into three periods. From 1855 to 1879, cottonseed crushing was concentrated primarily in the lower Mississippi Valley, the number of mills grew very slowly, and much of the mills' oil and cake went overseas. Beginning in 1880 and lasting until the First World War, mills multiplied rapidly in all parts of the Cotton Belt, and the American shortening industry increasingly used cottonseed oil. Finally, the period from World War I to the mid-twentieth century was a time of tribulation and change for cottonseed crushers as they faced postwar deflation, the loss of export markets, short crops due to boll weevil damage, aggressive competition for seed, business depression, federal intervention, and competition from other vegetable oils. The number of mills shrank materially as larger companies acquired many of the smaller, less-efficient crushing plants.

During the first century of cottonseed processing, the hydraulic press dominated crushing technology, many small oil mills operated wherever cotton grew in quantity, and cottonseed reigned supreme in the vegetable oil industry. The New Deal and the Second World War initiated the changes that eventually brought that period to an end. Implementation of minimum-wage legislation after 1938, together with the imposition of social security and other taxes, made the labor-intensive hydraulic process more expensive than alternative technologies. Wartime shortages created a greater demand for vegetable fats than could be satisfied by domestic cottonseed oil alone. Because the amount of cottonseed available for crushing depended on the amount of cotton harvested and the aim of New Deal policy was to cut cotton production in order to raise lint prices, an opportunity existed for soybeans and other oleaginous crops to fill the gap.

Other conditions that had once favored the construction of hundreds of small oil mills also began to change during the 1930s and 1940s. As southern states improved their roads and trucks replaced farm wagons, mills located near cotton fields ceased to have a natural monopoly of the seed in their immediate territory. To be cost effective, technologies such as solvent extraction had to be carried out on a large scale. Thus, more expensive labor, a cut in cotton production, the necessity for economies of scale, and the increasing use of trucks had destroyed the rational for small crushing operations by the mid-twentieth century.

I have examined the first century of cottonseed processing because no full-length historical study exists and memory of the industry's role in the New South is dim. The term *New South* is used, as it was by Woodward and Tindall, despite reservations, to indicate the period that began in the late 1870s with, in Woodward's words, a "sudden quickening of life in commerce and investment in certain areas of the South" and ended with the Second World War, after which came a succession of rapid changes. The cottonseed-processing industry had its maximum impact on the South during that span of time. New South describes an attitude or outlook receptive to industry among a segment of the southern population during the late nineteenth century, and southern cottonseed crushers could be counted among the most ardent proponents of industrialization. Recently, some historians have begun to refer to the period from the Civil War to the First World War as the "first New South," to distinguish it from the "genuine New South" of changed racial relations that had emerged by the 1980s.[9]

I have adopted the classification system that divides manufacturing into processing and fabricating industries. Carrying out the first stages of production, processing industries tend to cluster in areas rich in natural resources. The term *processing* has been applied to the cottonseed industry as a whole, as well as to the initial stage. *Crushing* and *milling* describe the primary phase of processing carried on in the South's oil mills, and *refining-manufacturing* refers to the secondary stage, transforming crude oil into marketable products.[10]

Chapter 1 of *Cinderella of the New South* provides a brief history of the origins of cottonseed processing in the United States. Expansion of the crushing industry after 1880 and its general development until World War I are traced in chapter 2. Cottonseed buying and selling and the many connections that developed between the cottonseed processing and cotton ginning industries after the Civil War are the focus of chapter 3. The fourth chapter treats cottonseed crushing, the primary and wholly southern phase of the industry. The emphasis is on technology, improvements in machinery and methods, and labor and management. Chapter 5 is devoted to cottonseed-oil refining and the manufacture of cottonseed-oil products by a few national companies and a larger number of regional companies. The pioneering achievements of oil-mill chemists in steadily improving edible cottonseed oil and shortening is chronicled here. Organization of the cottonseed industry is the subject of chapter 6. The formation of large, integrated cottonseed companies was one method entrepreneurs used to bring order to their industry. Operational methods of the giant corporations provoked distrust among independent oil men, and crushers not affiliated with the refining and manufacturing companies took the lead in creating state and national trade associations as a means of solving common problems and providing some protection against their powerful corporate competitors.

Chapter 7 discusses cottonseed pools and cartels created by crushers, principally before 1917, for the purpose of restraining cottonseed prices. The suspicions of cotton farmers and cottonseed buyers whenever seed prices dropped made price-fixing a fertile political issue in the first New South and led to repeated investigations of the industry. Chapter 8 analyzes how the First World War and postwar economic crises changed the cottonseed industry. Federal regulation of the industry during America's involvement in the war was followed by free-for-all competition at a time of short crops, declining exports, and deflation. The unrestrained quest for cottonseed between the world wars and efforts to moderate competition through cooperation and trade associations are discussed in chapter 9. Mergers, codes of fair trade, and a stronger trade association were three methods processors employed in their attempts to stabilize the industry in the face of strong competition among processors. Chapter 10 looks at the effects of federal policies on the oil mills during the New Deal years, the Second World War, and the immediate postwar period, and shows how government programs helped to launch a new phase of cottonseed processing. More efficient oil-extraction technologies and greater centralization of crushing have characterized the cottonseed industry since the second half of the twentieth century. Finally, chapter 11 examines the impact of the milling industry on the Cotton Belt before the Second World War.

To avoid repetition, cottonseed processing has been treated as a whole, although the industry was far from monolithic. Until the Second World War, three distinct oil-milling areas existed: the Southeast, the lower Mississippi Valley, and the Southwest. The Far West processed less than 7 percent of all cottonseed before 1944, and most mills in the area employed solvent- or screw-press extraction technologies. Because hydraulic pressing dominated the industry and most oil mills were located in the New South, California and Arizona are not included in this study.[11]

Other variations characterized the cottonseed-crushing industry. At the end of the nineteenth century, cottonseed production ranged from five or six bushels per acre to as high as fifty bushels. Differences in weather, soil, and cotton variety produced seed with different properties in each area and in the same area in different seasons. In the dryer sections of the Cotton Belt, such as West Texas and Oklahoma, cottonseed generally produced more cake and less oil, whereas in the Mississippi Valley cottonseed tended to have a higher oil content. Although western manufacturers considered their "butter" oil superior to that produced in other parts of the South, cottonseed oil from different regions varied little in chemical composition. Southeastern crushers had to pay more for cottonseed, because farmers in the region used the whole seed for fertilizer and feed when seed prices dropped below the cost of comparable commercial products, but lower wages helped to compensate for higher seed costs. Wages increased from east to west. Large mills in the Mississippi Valley and Southwest often had massive cattle feeding operations that used much of the cottonseed meal they produced. In the Southeast, cottonseed meal was more likely to be used as fertilizer, and mills in that region commonly had fertilizer-mixing operations. The Southeast had the largest number of small mills and, eventually, the greatest overcapacity. The Southwest was a stronghold of independent oil mills, as the crushing plants unaffiliated with the major corporations were called. Thus, the interests of oil mills in different regions of the Cotton Belt did not always coincide, and that, added to the distrust that existed between independent milling companies and large cottonseed corporations, resulted in an industry that spoke with many voices.[12]

It will become evident to readers that the spelling of *cottonseed* has not been uniform. During the nineteenth century most people made two words of the term. Sometime after the turn of the century usage changed, and I have adopted the later practice of writing cottonseed as a single word.

A final note relates to the secrecy that characterized the cottonseed-processing industry during its first century. The reluctance of crushers to reveal what they paid for cottonseed, the number of tons they crushed, the amount of cottonseed products they produced, and the prices they received for those products makes it difficult or impossible to provide precise price information. When the United States government began to publish annual cottonseed prices in 1909, they were the average prices paid to farmers across the Cotton Belt for an entire crushing season. Cottonseed prices differed from day to day, season to season, and place to place. Only since the initiation of a Department of Agriculture price reporting service at the end of the 1930s has it been possible to know fairly precise figures for any given time.

Cottonseed's eclipse by competing oil seeds after the Second World War should not obscure its importance in the first New South. The "economic Cinderella" added to the income of most Cotton Belt residents and influenced the ginning and marketing of cotton for more than half a century.

CHAPTER 1

Beginnings of the American Cottonseed Industry

I believe our cotton seed, which has hitherto been used only as manure, may be converted into oil and sold at great profit; certain I am, if you will instruct the cotton planter how he may add ten dollars value to the labor, which now produces him a bale of cotton, you will do him a great favor, and be, moreover, the conductor of a reasonable reward, to the inventors of a [hulling] machine which will probably rank, in the cotton country, second only to Whitney's ginn [*sic*].

A Cotton Planter [David R. Williams], 1829

The time will come when a man will just as soon think of throwing away his corn as his cotton seed.

Judge A. S. Clayton, 1833

It is known to all, that the cotton seed of the entire cotton crop, is annually thrown away, as useless. . . . That oil can be manufactured from cotton seed in large quantities, there can be no doubt; and that the oil is of great value, we are equally certain. The only question to be tested is whether the cost of manufacture will be sufficiently low to place the oil in fair competition with other oils. We hope that the experiment will be tried, for the purpose of settling the question—a question which involves millions of dollars.

DeBow's Review, 1854

Despite the antiquity and widespread use of vegetable oils, more than seventy-five years elapsed between the first experiments in extracting oil from American cottonseed and the successful establishment of commercial processing in the United States. Eli Whitney's 1793 invention of a gin to remove seed from short-staple cotton and the westward expansion of cotton cultivation provided an abundance of oil-rich seed, stimulating the interest of various entrepreneurs, but demand for cottonseed products lagged. The new nation's sparse and predominately rural population had limited need for vegetable oil or cake, and inadequate transportation facilities made the cost of moving cottonseed and cottonseed products from farm to mill to market prohibitively high. Technical problems of crushing and refining also had to be overcome before commercial processing became efficient enough to be profitable.

In most parts of the world, vegetable oils have supplemented animal fats in the diets of human beings for thousands of years. They have been used as lubricants, paint bases, perfumes, and medicines, and have provided sources of light and been used for various industrial purposes. In some cultures people anointed themselves with oil during special rites and ceremonies. The ancient Chinese, Egyptians, Indians, and Hindus pressed oil from a variety of seeds, and the Hebrews, Greeks, Romans, and other inhabitants of the Mediterranean basin relied primarily on oil from olives. From as early as the fourteenth century, mills in England crushed rape and other seeds to obtain oil for lamps and for working wool. The cake that resulted from the crushing process could be used as either fuel or animal feed.[1]

The industrial revolution that began in eighteenth-century England and spread to western Europe generated demand for vegetable oils. The new machines had to be lubricated, and iron structures of all kinds required oil-based paints to prevent corrosion. Rapid population growth and urbanization increased the market for soap, candles, lamp oil, and edible fats. The expanding textile industry required more soap, and those living in large cities needed soap to wash off the grime produced by coal-burning steam engines. Since supplies of fats and oils did not increase as rapidly as the population, some Europeans had no more than occasional meat drippings to supply essential fat and supplement their staple diet of potatoes and bread.

Because olives require special soil and climate conditions, their cultivation could not be expanded enough to meet the demand for vegetable oil in southern Europe, nor could cattle and hog populations be enlarged sufficiently to satisfy the preference for butter in northern Europe and lard and bacon fat in other parts of the continent. Cheaper and more plentiful substitutes needed to be found. The European vegetable-oil industry expanded and modernized during the first half of the nine-teenth century primarily to satisfy the growing demand for illuminating and industrial oils; production of edible fats became increasingly impor-tant as the century progressed.[2]

As a predominately agricultural people, most North Americans had adequate supplies of edible fats and sufficient corn, oats, and forage for their livestock, but increasingly used whale and lard oil for illumination. Many North Americans made linseed, castor-bean, and other kinds of oils on a small scale for their own use or for sale locally, just as some people ground corn into meal and wheat into flour for themselves and their neighbors. In about 1770 some Pennsylvania Moravians demonstrated that cottonseed hulled by hand and processed like flaxseed yielded as much as six pints of oil per bushel of seed. In the years that followed, Americans in both the North and South periodically expressed oil from cottonseed, studied its properties, and compared it favorably with linseed oil, which northeasterners began to produce commercially in the second half of the eighteenth century by crushing flaxseed.[3]

Excess supplies of seed rather than demand for cottonseed products stimulated most of the interest in cottonseed crushing during the late co-lonial and early national periods. The mechanization of spinning and weaving in the eighteenth century had caused demand for cotton to ex-pand, and ever-increasing amounts of unused oil-rich seeds challenged people to think of new commercial uses. The London Society of Arts in 1783 and the South Carolina Agricultural Society several years later of-fered prizes for the manufacture of cottonseed products.[4]

In 1790 Edward Rutledge, a signer of the Declaration of Independen-ce and future governor of South Carolina, considered building an oil mill. Cottonseed sent to Connecticut by a South Carolinian had reportedly yielded eight pints of oil per bushel. Rutledge wrote to Phineas Miller, the Yale-educated plantation overseer for General Nathanael Greene's widow and future partner of Eli Whitney in the manufacture of cotton gins, in-quiring where he might find a person capable of running a mill, how many laborers would be needed to operate it, if Negroes could do the work, and how much processing would cost. If cottonseed oil were suit-able for lamps and could be manufactured cheaply enough to undersell imported whale oil, Rutledge believed that Charleston public officials would buy large quantities of it for lighting city streets.[5]

Whitney's invention of the cotton gin in 1793 cleared the way for greatly increased cotton production in the southern states. Seed could easily be removed from long-staple Sea Island cotton with roller gins, but in the United States that variety thrived only in the humid coastal regions of the South. The short-staple cotton suitable for cultivation elsewhere had seed that resisted separation from the lint. The time-consuming process of removing seed by hand made it impractical to grow short-staple upland cotton in large quantities. With that hurdle overcome by Whitney's invention, cotton production soared and seed accumulated.[6]

William Dunbar, a Scottish-born immigrant who grew cotton in the vicinity of Natchez, Mississippi, during the 1790s, became interested in the manufacture of cottonseed oil about the turn of the century. Hoping to help pay for a screw press he had purchased for baling cotton, Dunbar expressed oil from the seed in about 1801 but found little market for it.[7] It would be more than half a century before cottonseed oil was sold on a commercial scale in the lower Mississippi Valley.

Although nothing resulted from Edward Rutledge's inquiry about the feasibility of manufacturing cottonseed oil for Charleston street lamps, another South Carolinian became the first American to produce the oil commercially. Sometime before 1802, Benjamin Waring built a mill in Columbia, South Carolina, where he made oil from cottonseed, castor beans, and benne seeds. For some time after Waring's death in 1811, his son carried on his oil-milling business.[8]

A mill built in about 1814 by planter and political leader David R. Williams of Society Hill, South Carolina, failed, because Williams tried to press oil from the whole seed as flaxseed processors did.[9] Williams must have been working with seed from short-staple, or upland, cotton. Seed from long-staple cotton could be crushed whole because ginning left the seed completely free of lint. Seed from upland cotton, even after ginning, are covered with short fibers and fuzz, which absorb too much oil. The tough, lint-covered hulls must be removed from the kernels before pressing. Once the seed had been hulled, techniques for making linseed and other vegetable oils from whole seed could be applied to the manufacture of cottonseed oil.

The first practical cottonseed huller was designed by Francis Follett and Jabez Smith of Petersburg, Virginia. Follett patented a huller in 1829, and Smith patented an improved huller the same year. With financial backing from Follett, Smith built and marketed hullers and an improved oil press during the late 1820s and early 1830s. In an 1829 letter describing the machines, David Williams said that it had not occurred to him fifteen years earlier that the seed "might be hulled, like rice, so as to separate the kernels which contain all the oil." That year Williams, James Chesnut, and another South Carolina planter invested in a Follett and Smith huller for the water-powered oil mill on Williams's plantation. They had no one experienced in oil making to advise them, yet found the huller easy to operate.[10]

Hullers invented by Lancelot Johnson of Edgecombe County, North Carolina, were being used in the manufacture of lamp oil at several locations in 1833. Johnson's huller was said to be similar to a coffee mill. A vertical block with steel teeth revolved inside a circular hopper also lined with teeth, and when properly adjusted the two sets of teeth cut cottonseed into pieces. Later hullers would employ the cutting principle, but not Johnson's particular design.[11]

Follett and Smith hullers and presses, powered in most cases by horses, were installed in cottonseed-oil mills in Virginia, the Carolinas, Alabama, Georgia, and Mississippi between about 1829 and 1834. The huller patented by Smith consisted of "a heavy stone cylinder, turning within a semi concave circle, brought so near together as to crack the seed." Air from a fan and a wire sieve separated the hulls from the kernels. After being hulled, cottonseed kernels were crushed like olives by millstones on edge running over them in a space hollowed out of a flat rock. Follett and Smith derived their press design from that used to create linseed oil. Crushed cottonseed kernels were enveloped in haircloth, placed in a mortar, and mashed with a heavy pestle, moved by animal or water power, until the oil flowed out.[12]

European and American oil mills of the period also used screw and lever, or wedge, presses. The latter were sometimes referred to as stamper presses, because vertical rods, or stampers, provided the force for driving in and releasing the wedges. The more primitive French oil mills employed a vertical wooden screw attached to a heavy beam. Manually operated wooden screw and wedge presses had long been used in southern Europe to extract the residual oil from crushed olives and juice from grapes. The drawback to the screw press was its tendency to break under the pressure of steam operation. By the middle of the nineteenth century, most oil millers considered the hydraulic press invented at the end of the previous century to be the strongest and most efficient oil press available.[13]

During the 1820s and 1830s the *Niles' Register* provided a forum for those interested in cottonseed processing. Writers recommended cottonseed oil for a variety of uses. The oil had been mixed with pigments and used to paint barns and houses, reported a correspondent. At least one man had substituted cottonseed oil for lard in cornbread, but edible applications were rare before the Civil War. Promoters advocated cottonseed oil as a lubricant for machinery and for medicinal purposes, but the major use envisioned was in lamps, as a substitute for increasingly scarce and expensive whale oil. Cottonseed cake was recognized as an excellent feed for cattle.[14]

The first large mill organized to produce cottonseed oil on a commercial scale was constructed at Natchez, Mississippi, in 1834. The principal backers were J. Hamilton Couper (Cooper), who had built a steam-powered mill for making sugar and pounding rice on his Georgia plantation about 1830, Samuel Plummer, also of Georgia, Anderson Miller of Louisville, Francis Follett of Virginia, and Archibald Dunbar of Mississippi. A number of Natchez-area residents invested in the project. The *Natchez Journal* reported that the mill had a steam engine, eight hullers, five sets of stones for crushing the kernels, eight kettles for heating the meats, and seven lever presses. It had the capacity to produce one to two thousand gallons of oil a day, suitable for paints, lamps, woolens, and machinery. For its day, the Natchez mill was a large-scale undertaking.[15]

The cottonseed-oil mills constructed during the late 1820s and early 1830s did not survive. A Nashville, Tennessee, mill shown on an 1831 map went out of business within several years. The ambitious Natchez venture also failed, as did a cottonseed-oil mill erected around 1834 near Mobile by former mayor Samuel H. Garrow, who offered to pay for the bagging and rope to bale all cotton whose seed were delivered to his mill. The Cotton Seed Oil Factory and Insurance Company chartered in 1835 by the Louisiana legislature probably never built its projected factory in New Orleans, even though the city council voted to require the mayor to purchase cottonseed oil as a substitute for whale oil.[16]

J. H. Couper attributed the Natchez mill's financial problems primarily to wasteful refining methods. Couper concluded that the Follett and Smith huller and Flemish machinery designed for heating and pressing rapeseed had worked well in the cottonseed-oil mill. Others considered the Follett and Smith huller "imperfect," because in the process of cracking the hulls it crushed too many seeds to permit efficient separation of the meats from the hulls. In applying for a patent on an improved huller in 1845, Smith admitted that 10 to 15 percent of the cottonseed kernels had been lost in the company's earlier hullers, because the matted hulls prevented them from being recovered.[17]

Besides the technical difficulties of refining and hulling, limited demand for cottonseed products and high freight costs impeded the devel-

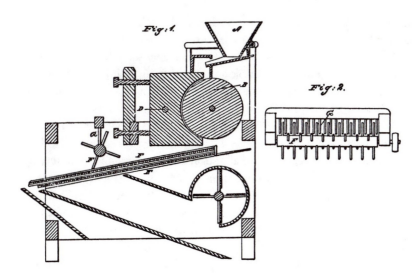

Drawing, Jabez Smith, cottonseed huller, patented 15 March 1845, U.S. Patent Office. Courtesy, Library of Congress.

opment of commercial cottonseed processing during the first half of the nineteenth century. Cottonseed and cottonseed products are bulky commodities of comparatively low value. In a given amount of cotton, the seed weigh twice as much as the considerably more valuable lint. Until the First World War, hulls, always the third or fourth least valuable cottonseed product, accounted for close to 50 percent of the weight of cottonseed. It takes one and a half times as much space to carry a ton of cottonseed as a ton of flaxseed, corn, or wheat. Heavy freight charges made it difficult for cottonseed oil and cake to undersell whale oil and other well-established products. Poor roads and a paucity of railroads in the antebellum cotton-growing areas also hampered the collection of seed. For those reasons, the first successful cottonseed oil mills would be located near the Mississippi River and other waterways.[18]

Failure of the Natchez mill and other crushing operations, financial panic in 1837, and several years of economic depression dampened interest in commercial cottonseed processing. It began to revive in New Orleans during the late 1840s and early 1850s. Several Crescent City residents and *DeBow's Review* in New Orleans publicized the potential rewards of processing cottonseed. In about 1852 wealthy New Orleans drygoods merchant Paul Aldigé visited Marseilles, the great center of European oil and soap making, to study French methods of processing Egyptian cottonseed. Aldigé also may have viewed oil-mill machinery at the Crystal Palace Exhibition in London. A hydraulic box press was among the inventions on display there.[19] In his travels Aldigé would have seen the latest advances in pressing and refining technology, but nothing helpful in the critical area of cottonseed hulling. Ginning left Egyptian cottonseed, like seed from the Sea Islands, bald, and European mills crushed the seed whole.

Frederick Good and William Wilbur formed a partnership in New Orleans in 1853 for the purpose of manufacturing cottonseed oil and soap. Wilbur improved traditional cottonseed processing machinery and methods, and Good, a manufacturer of lard oil, supplied most of the capital. Their enterprise failed, though their cottonseed oil won a silver medal at a New York exhibition. Charles W. Bradbury bought Good's interest in 1854, but the new partnership lost money as well.[20] Nonetheless, cottonseed processing on a commercial scale was about to begin.

In 1855 Paul Aldigé and P. J. Martin in New Orleans and Lyman Klapp and associates of the Union Oil Company in Providence, Rhode Island, began to manufacture cottonseed products. Aldigé's mill earned little profit initially, but the company survived, as did the Union Oil Company, which moved its crushing facilities from Providence to New Orleans after the Civil War. By 1860 there were at least seven oil mills crushing cottonseed, three in New Orleans, and one each in Memphis, St. Louis, New York, and Providence. All of the early plants were located near waterways, and ships that had discharged their freight transported seed to the mills in the Mississippi Valley and on the Atlantic coast at moderate rates.[21]

Some of the antebellum cottonseed-processing plants had originally been linseed-oil mills. New Orleans entrepreneur A. A. Maginnis manufactured linseed oil from flaxseed before he began crushing cottonseed in 1856. A St. Louis company organized to make linseed and castor oils began processing cottonseed in 1857. For several decades flax cultivation had been declining in the United States because of the widespread availability of inexpensive, easy-to-clean cotton textiles. Linseed-oil mills began to experiment with various oil seeds in their search for additional raw materials.[22]

Linseed-oil manufacturers in western Ohio, the center of flax growing during the middle decades of the nineteenth century, could buy cottonseed and have it shipped up the Mississippi and Ohio Rivers in boats that had carried goods from Cincinnati to southern plantations and ports. In 1857 Cincinnati resident William R. Fee, a partner in a company that operated a linseed-oil mill, patented the first efficient cottonseed huller and an improved hydraulic press. Another Cincinnatian, Charles Cist, promoted cottonseed processing. *Debow's Review* published Cist's report on "Cotton Seed Oil—Its Manufacture, Uses, and Profits" in 1859. Primarily for southern readers, Cist's article stated that cottonseed would eventually be processed near the cotton fields. In his *Sketches and Statistics of Cincinnati in 1859,* Cist said that cottonseed milling would take place for the most part in progressive manufacturing centers such as Cincinnati.[23] The other major area of flaxseed milling was in and around New York City, and it, too, became one of the early centers for cottonseed processing and oil refining. Like the oil mills of Cincinnati, those in New York and Providence could also get reasonable freight rates from ships returning from southern ports.[24]

Companies in Memphis and St. Louis that called themselves "white lead and oil works" produced cottonseed oil before the Civil War. The Southern Oil Mill organized in Mobile in 1860 planned to make both cottonseed oil and turpentine. The manufacture of pigment or turpentine in conjunction with cottonseed oil suggests that a few paint manufacturers on the eve of the Civil War experimented with cottonseed oil as a substitute for linseed oil. Because cottonseed oil lacks the drying properties necessary for paints, that would have been a dead end.[25]

The petroleum boom of the Civil War era ended hopes that cottonseed oil would replace whale and lard oil in the nation's lamps. In 1860, one year after Edwin Drake had successfully drilled for oil in Pennsylvania, a reporter for the *Scientific American* described a New Orleans cottonseed-oil business as profitable and added that "unless the coal oil should master it, it might grow rapidly into one of our very largest manufactures." Apart from its use as a smokeless oil in miner's lamps during the late nineteenth century, cottonseed oil would have no future as an illuminant. Instead, cottonseed oil produced by the first generation of American crushing mills became an ingredient of inexpensive soaps and was secretly added to olive oil and sold as the higher priced article at home and abroad.[26]

After half a century of intermittent and unsuccessful efforts to establish cottonseed milling on a commercial basis, oil mills organized in New Orleans and Providence in 1855 managed to survive. The Civil War closed all but three of the seven mills operating in 1860, but soon after Lee's surrender, the industry began to revive in the lower Mississippi Valley. During the 1870s mill construction proceeded slowly, but in 1880 a period of rapid expansion began and did not come to an end until the First World War.

CHAPTER 2

Expansion of Cottonseed Milling
in the South

Every cross-road in Alabama has got a mill.
George O. Baker, 1883

The prosperity of nearly a thousand towns and villages
throughout the South is more or less determined by the pres-
ence and active operation of a Seed-crushing, Oil-producing
and fertilizer manufacturing plant within its borders.
Andrew M. Soule, president,
Georgia State College of Agriculture, 1914

By 1867 the number of cottonseed oil mills in the United States had again
risen to seven, the prewar total. During the following two years, crushing facilities nearly quadrupled in number as cotton cultivation recovered
and river and rail lines were restored in the aftermath of the war. Between 1869 and 1879 the number of oil mills increased from twenty-six
to forty-five. Thereafter, the cottonseed-processing industry grew rapidly
in all parts of the expanding Cotton Belt.

Before 1880 cottonseed processing had gone on principally in the
lower Mississippi Valley, the center of cotton cultivation and of an extensive river network. Most oil mills were located in Louisiana, Tennessee, Mississippi, and Arkansas. New Orleans and Memphis were the leading centers of cottonseed processing. East Texas and Alabama had a few
mills, but in 1879 there was only one in the South Atlantic states, the
Augusta Cotton Seed Oil Company in Georgia. In a region with few roads
and railways, boats provided the most economical means of transporting
the bulky seed and seed products. Most of the cottonseed oil and cake
exported to Europe was shipped from the port of New Orleans.[1]

The economic advantages of crushing cottonseed close to where it grew soon limited preliminary processing almost entirely to the Cotton Belt. As a writer for a business journal had predicted in 1859, "If small establishments for the manufacture of cotton-seed oil were so located in the South as to be convenient to the seed, and also readily accessible to market, capital prudently invested and carefully managed might obtain some reasonable reward." Otherwise, the writer believed, the seed should be left on the fields as manure, "the only really profitable use ever yet made of cotton-seed."[2] By 1880 very few cottonseed-oil mills could be found outside the cotton-growing states. Cincinnati, St. Louis, Chicago, Providence, and Brooklyn became major centers of refining, and much oil-mill machinery came from western Ohio and the New York City area, but crushing was an almost wholly southern industry. The commercial success of cottonseed processing depended to a great extent on developing markets for the new products. Lack of demand had been a major reason for the failure of mills before 1855, and an analyst of the industry writing in 1868 concluded that finding new uses for cottonseed oil was "the first and great necessity" of the industry.[3]

Crushers and brokers did most of the work of developing markets for cottonseed oil and cake. Initially, they pushed cottonseed products as cheaper and better substitutes for established vegetable oils and cakes. American cottonseed cake found a sizable market in England after Parliament passed an act putting cottonseed cake on the same footing as linseed cake for feeding purposes. In most cases, cottonseed oil masqueraded as olive oil or was "quietly" added to lard. "We dare not call it cotton-seed oil," said an early manufacturer, "for fear it might prejudice the sale." The American consul in Naples reported in 1880 that cottonseed oil was selling as olive oil even in isolated parts of Italy that produced only olive oil. In France cottonseed oil displaced turnip-seed and poppy-seed oils as cheap substitutes for olive oil.[4]

One of the most vigorous early promoters of cottonseed meal was Lyman Klapp, whose Union Oil Company began operations in Providence, Rhode Island, in 1855, and after the Civil War established a branch in New Orleans. Klapp personally introduced his company's cottonseed cake in England and on the Continent. Klapp also acquired a farm in Connecticut to demonstrate the value of cottonseed meal as a fertilizer for tobacco and conducted cattle feeding experiments in Massachusetts that showed the superiority of cottonseed meal to corn and rye.[5]

F. M. Fisk, one of the pioneer crushers in New Orleans, also shipped cottonseed cake to England before the Civil War and went there himself to talk to farmers about using it as cattle food. Jules Aldigé, another New Orleans processor who developed European markets, used family ties in France to spur the sale of cottonseed products there. Emanuel Steinhard and Moses Frank, German immigrants who engaged in cottonseed processing after the Civil War, helped promote cottonseed products in their native land. Other processors at great expense opened the Spanish and Italian markets for cottonseed oil. Knowledge of European languages and personal contacts abroad aided some crushers and brokers in making marketing arrangements overseas.[6]

From the outset brokers handled the bulk of cottonseed products. Some specialized in crude oil, others in meal, and still others in linters. The Boston brokerage firm of J. E. Soper received its first consignment of cottonseed cakes in 1869. The Union Oil Company of New Orleans sent the cakes by ship, informing the company that they made good cattle feed. Soper had the cakes ground to meal at a local linseed-oil mill but could not sell it. Finally, Soper persuaded a Massachusetts farmer to feed the meal to his cattle. Very slowly demand for southern cottonseed meal increased, and in 1887 the Soper company sold forty thousand pounds. Brokers throughout the Cotton Belt sent cottonseed meal to the J. E. Soper Company for resale in New England.[7]

F. W. Brode became one of the largest dealers in cottonseed meal after the Civil War. Born in Saxony in 1843, Brode moved with his family to Memphis in 1856. Having begun his business career as a broker of sugar and molasses, Brode used his contacts with sugar planters to sell cottonseed meal as a fertilizer for cane fields after scientific fertilizer studies carried out in about 1875 greatly increased the demand for cottonseed meal. The value of cottonseed meal as high-protein animal feed was just beginning to be recognized in the United States, and Brode soon played a major role in promoting its use for that purpose in New England and abroad. As a result of numerous visits to Europe, Brode built up an extensive export business. When he died in 1931, he had been brokering cottonseed meal for more than fifty years.[8]

Edward Flash of New York also dealt in cottonseed products for more than half a century. Flash began his brokerage business in 1879 after a friend in Germany suggested that they sell cottonseed meal to German farmers as cattle feed. At that time many of the big brokers were located in New Orleans, still the major center of cottonseed processing and the export trade. In 1882 Flash went to Europe to find agents to sell meal for him. Realizing that people in northern Europe had little knowledge of cottonseed oil, Flash made arrangements with firms there and in the Mediterranean countries to handle it. Deciding to limit his business to trading in crude and refined cottonseed oil, Flash established his headquarters in New York City, which was rapidly becoming the leading center of the cottonseed-oil trade. The Rotterdam broker who convinced one of Europe's largest margarine manufacturers in 1884 to substitute cottonseed oil for more expensive peanut oil doubtless worked for an American brokerage firm such as Flash's.[9]

The advertisement and promotion of name-brand cottonseed-oil products became primarily the province of several large refining and manufacturing companies, all organized in the last decade and a half of the nineteenth century. With far fewer financial resources, cottonseed crushers individually and through their trade associations promoted cake and meal sales. A Houston, Texas, mill manager in the 1880s persuaded his company to buy land and to feed cottonseed meal to steers in order to convince farmers and cattle feeders of its superiority. Through bulletins describing feed and fertilizer trials, state agricultural colleges and experiment stations also helped publicize the value of cottonseed meal.[10]

Crushing mills either sold their crude oil directly to refiners or relied on brokers to arrange sales. The relatively low cost of shipping oil meant that it tended to go wherever there was a price advantage. Independent cottonseed crushers chafed at having to sell their crude oil to refiners during the busy autumn crushing season, when full storage tanks had to be emptied to make room for additional oil. Not only did abundant supplies of crude oil depress prices, but the tendency of crude oil to deteriorate rapidly, as compared to the refined product, restrained crushers from constructing additional tanks. Operators of small mills believed that large refiners took advantage of their inability to hold crude oil off the market. The New York Produce Exchange organized a futures market in cottonseed oil in 1904, but, if later evidence is any indication, independent crushers rarely protected themselves by hedging their transactions.[11]

Both southern entrepreneurs and outside capitalists invested in crushing facilities. The ownership of two Memphis oil mills established about 1870 illustrates the diverse sources of capital in the early years of the crushing industry. The large Southern Oil Works had eighteen hydraulic presses capable of producing as much as two thousand gallons of oil a day and a steamboat to transport cottonseed to the mill and oil and cake to New Orleans for export. Stockholders of the company resided in New York, Connecticut, Wisconsin, Memphis, and Liverpool, England. Lacking the capital to complete its ambitious plans, the company borrowed money. Some of its backers suffered reverses in the Panic of 1873, a year the company's stock was reported to be worthless. In contrast, most of the men who bought stock in the Panola Oil and Fertilizer Company of Memphis were "substantial" local residents, although at least one New Yorker was an investor. Panola paid a 10 percent dividend in 1873 and expected to double its dividend the following year.[12]

Because venturing into cottonseed processing on a small scale required relatively little money, oil mills were attractive investments. Two Irish immigrants built what was believed to be the first interior cottonseed-oil mill. Following the Civil War, Michael O'Shaughnessy moved south to go into business with his brother James, who operated a grain and cotton commission business in Nashville. In about 1867 they established the Nashville Cotton Seed Oil Company. The company began on a very modest scale, with a single screw press turned by hand, but by 1870, according to the Census of Manufactures, the company possessed four hydraulic presses and five thousand dollars in capital. Throughout most of the 1870s its owners struggled to keep the business solvent; by the end of the decade, the company was almost out of debt. In 1881 the O'Shaughnessy brothers were said to be "very prosperous" and part-owners of a Huntsville, Alabama, crushing mill.[13]

An initial five-thousand-dollar investment in the new industry paid off for an Alabama mercantile firm. G. O. Baker & Company, commission merchants in Selma, invested in a local oil mill in the early 1870s. In 1872 a Selma representative of the R. G. Dun credit rating firm described G. O. Baker and associates as being willing to "take up anything they think there is money in." Six years later the company had a large interest in cottonseed-oil mills. Their crushing facilities were considered to be among the most efficient and up-to-date before the mid-1880s.[14]

In Mississippi the Meridian Oil Mill & Manufacturing Company began with local capital and expanded with the help of outside money. Organized in 1876 with a capital stock of twenty-five thousand dollars, the mill doubled its stock within a year. John A. Lewis, the longtime president, was part owner of a Meridian drug firm. In 1879 the company incorporated with a capital of one hundred thousand dollars; Cincinnati investors owned half of the stock. The John V. Lewis Company of Cincinnati, one of the major refiners of cottonseed oil, invested in the Meridian Oil Mill & Manufacturing Company, as well as in several other southern oil mills, after crushing ceased to be economically viable in Cincinnati.[15]

The year 1880 marked the beginning of a period of rapid growth in the cottonseed-oil industry. The depression that followed the Panic of 1873 lifted in 1879, and, as a consequence, capitalists in England and the United States began to invest in the South on a large scale. Substantial mill profits during the 1870s attracted the interest of new investors. The relatively small number of crushing mills in the lower Mississippi Valley had enabled operators to keep raw material prices low during the early postwar years through cooperative agreements. Overseas demand for cottonseed oil increased tenfold during the 1870s, resulting in profits of as much as 50 percent.[16]

An upsurge in cotton cultivation made more cottonseed available for crushing after the mid-1870s, although production fluctuated from season to season. The westward movement of cotton continued after the Civil War, bringing all of Texas and Oklahoma into the Cotton Kingdom. Southeastern cotton fields that had been abandoned for richer soils or depleted by extensive cropping during the antebellum period were restored by massive applications of fertilizer. Fertilizers also enabled farmers to produce cotton on marginal lands. After the Civil War many small farmers gave up partially self-sufficient economic practices and shifted from corn and food crops to cotton production. The crop lien system that developed in the postbellum South tied many small farmers in the Cotton Belt to the production of the region's leading cash crop.[17]

Rapid railway expansion during the 1880s contributed to the proliferation of oil mills in the four decades before the United States entered World War I. By bringing more farmers within reach of world markets, railroads stimulated greater cotton production. As the rails spread across the South, entrepreneurs established oil mills in towns and cities along their routes wherever sufficient cotton grew.[18]

More money available for investment, increased railroad mileage, greater cotton cultivation, and growing demand for cottonseed products created the conditions for rapid expansion in the industry after 1880. Capital invested in cottonseed-oil mills tripled between 1880 and 1885, according to a survey by the *Manufacturers' Record*. Capitalization in 1885 ranged from $5,000 to more than $500,000. Of the eighty oil mills reporting their capital in 1885, ten were capitalized at $20,000 to $25,000, fourteen at $45,000 to $50,000, and fifteen at $100,000.[19]

The Port Gibson Oil Works in Mississippi, believed to be the oldest cottonseed-oil mill in continuous operation today, began life in the early 1880s. The enterprise was organized by six men, including a father and son who were "Dealers in Dry Goods, Groceries and Plantation Supplies." Two other investors managed the business at different times. The major pieces of machinery purchased initially cost under $5,000, and the enterprise began with an operating capital of only $285. That level of investment was the minimum reported by the *Manufacturers' Record* in 1885. Among the larger oil mills established during the boom of the early 1880s was the Hanauer Oil Works of Memphis. It began operations in 1882 with a paid-up capital of seventy-five thousand dollars. Investing in the Hanauer were prominent Memphis cotton merchants and businessmen.[20]

Major infusions of outside capital into the oil-milling industry came after 1880, as was the case with textiles, railroads, iron, and some other southern industries.[21] During the last decade and a half of the nineteenth century, northern capitalists largely financed several cottonseed companies that carried on substantial crushing, refining, manufacturing, and marketing operations. The major meat-packing and soap-making companies added cottonseed processing to their activities at the turn of the century.

Although most of the capital for creating large, integrated cottonseed corporations came from northern investors, southern entrepreneurs raised money to build hundreds of small oil mills between 1880 and 1914. A South Carolina trade journal reported in 1894 that twenty-four of twenty-seven oil mills in the state had been built by local capital, much of it subscribed by farmers. In 1911 industry leaders estimated that southerners owned more than six hundred of the approximately eight hundred oil mills and refineries.[22]

Sometimes machinery salesmen misrepresented the amount of money required to build, equip, and operate oil mills, and when the work had proceeded too far to stop, companies without adequate capital had to borrow to complete their plants. If the first crushing seasons proved to be unprofitable, undercapitalized companies often lost their property to the banks or sold out for less than they had invested.[23]

The history of the Kathwood Manufacturing Company of Beech Island, South Carolina, illustrates the problems faced by small, undercapitalized oil mills at the turn of the century. In an 1896 report to the Department of Agriculture, Henry Hammond described the prospects for small crushing mills in optimistic terms. That same year the Hammond family built a modest oil mill and cotton gin across the Savannah River from Augusta, Georgia. Evidently, members of the community who had promised to support the project backed out, for in 1896 only $3,500 in property and $2,875 in cash had been paid of the $8,275 promised. The

Table 1
Capital Invested in Three
Southern Industries, 1890

State	Lumber[a]	Cotton Goods	Cottonseed
Alabama	$7,460,108	$2,853,015	$592,408
Arkansas	7,778,792	NA	1,488,690
Georgia	6,697,515	17,664,675	992,131
Louisiana	6,662,150	NA	1,082,752
Mississippi	4,591,790	2,053,743	1,497,746
North Carolina	5,865,577	10,775,134	743,675
South Carolina	2,198,626	11,141,833	565,372
Tennessee	9,542,758	2,928,657	1,833,204
Texas	12,344,996	NA	2,358,615
Total	63,142,312	47,417,057	11,154,593

[a]Lumber includes timber and planing.
SOURCE: Bureau of the Census, *Census of Manufactures*, pt. 2, Reports by States, 1890.

amount subscribed represented only about half of the capital considered necessary for the project to be launched. At the end of the first year of operation, the company had lost one thousand dollars on its operations and owed five thousand dollars for machinery, construction, and supplies. The president managed to secure a loan and negotiate more favorable terms with creditors, which enabled the company to limp along for several more years. In 1901 the Southern Cotton Oil Company purchased the Kathwood Manufacturing Company for five thousand dollars less than the oil mill and gin had cost. The mill ceased to operate and served only as a seed collection point for the Southern Cotton Oil Company.[24]

A comparison of the capital invested in cottonseed-oil mills, lumber and timber operations, and cotton-textile mills in the former Confederate states during the late nineteenth century shows the cottonseed industry trailing the South's two leading industries by a considerable margin (see tables 1 and 2).

Cottonseed-oil mills came to be divided into two categories, *terminal* and *interior,* based on their size and location, although some mills

Table 2
Capital Invested in
Three Southern Industries, 1900

State	Lumber[a]	Cotton Goods	Cottonseed
Alabama	$13,020,183	$11,638,757	$1,607,674
Arkansas	22,940,721	NA	2,484,794
Georgia	13,876,942	24,222,169	4,098,668
Louisiana	21,133,079	NA	4,622,569
Mississippi	17,969,091	2,209,749	3,711,930
North Carolina	14,751,920	33,011,516	1,841,856
South Carolina	5,599,945	39,258,946	1,959,872
Tennessee	14,243,976	3,767,726	1,996,791
Texas	20,094,125	NA	7,986,962
Total	144,054,381	114,108,863	30,705,966

[a]Lumber includes timber and planing.
Source: Bureau of the Census, *Census of Manufactures,* pt. 2, Reports by States, 1900.

defied classification. The two types of mills were described and compared for several decades before being labeled. Large terminal mills, in many cases owned by the leading refining and manufacturing companies, acquired seed in railway carloads from great distances, and offset high freight charges through economies of scale that lowered crushing costs. Terminal mills generally earned more on crude-oil sales because of their larger, more efficient production and multiple rail connections, but less on cake and meal, which they usually disposed of in bulk at discounted prices to brokers who sold it in the northern states and overseas.

In addition to substantial crushing facilities in major railway centers, individuals and stock companies built hundreds of smaller oil mills, as well as a few large ones, in river and railroad towns located as close as possible to the cotton fields. Interior, or country, mills competed with the more efficient terminal mills by saving money on freight. They crushed seed from their immediate territory and disposed of most of the meal and hulls, about 75 percent of the weight of cottonseed products, locally. By selling meal directly to farmers, interior mills could charge more than terminal mills for their second most valuable product.

Interior mills had other advantages over their large competitors, such as close supervision from owners or major investors. Personal acquaintance with area farmers and ginners gave local mill personnel an edge in the competition for seed from the surrounding territory. By acquiring much of their seed from local cotton gins as they ginned the crop, interior oil mills did not have to invest in large amounts of storage space nor incur the expenses of insuring and protecting massive supplies of seed. In working seed that had not been damaged by long hauls and processing it shortly after it arrived from the gins, small mills could turn out products comparable in quality to those manufactured by terminal mills. Labor costs also tended to be lower at country mills, where farm labor could be more readily used.[25]

During the early 1880s, some people thought that every gin or neighborhood should have a small oil mill, just as most communities had their own grist and saw mills. In 1883 the Cardwell Machine Company of Richmond, Virginia, began to manufacture equipment for tiny oil mills. By 1890 the company had equipped twenty-one oil mills ranging in capacity from five to twenty-four tons daily. Most presses in 1890 had a fifteen-ton capacity. Cardwell officials considered the five-ton mill ideal for use on plantations in conjunction with a cotton gin. A purchaser of Cardwell machinery for a five-ton mill in Wateree, South Carolina, wrote that he ran the mill with farm laborers and that his neighbors exchanged their seed for meal and hulls, which meant that he did not have to pay freight on seed or the heaviest products.[26]

Although many small (one to three presses) mills were built in southern towns close to cotton fields, plantation mills did not multiply. A change in the method of shipping cottonseed oil probably did more than anything else to end the building of farm mills. By the 1890s most cottonseed oil was being transported in railway tank cars rather than in barrels. The only mills not located along rail lines were a few adjacent to waterways, and crude oil was held in storage tanks until a sufficient amount accumulated to be shipped in bulk. Rural or farm mills, with their small output, would have been at a disadvantage in disposing of their oil.

Between 1885 and 1895 the average interior mill constructed by the D. A. Tompkins Company of Charlotte, North Carolina, had two presses and a crushing capacity of thirty tons in twenty-four hours. Terminal mills built by the firm crushed on the average of one hundred tons daily. Writing in 1911, South Carolina crusher B. F. Taylor characterized small mills as those having one to four presses capable of crushing fifteen to sixty tons in twenty-four hours and being located in towns served by one or two railroads. Large mills in major railway centers operated six or more presses, according to Taylor.[27]

Southeastern mills tended to be smaller than those in other parts of the Cotton Belt, where more cottonseed was produced and sold at lower prices. In his 1896 survey of the crushing industry for the U.S. Department of Agriculture, Henry Hammond reported that oil mills in the Southeast crushed in the range of twenty-one to forty-four tons a day and that most western mills crushed between sixty-two and seventy-seven tons daily. South Carolina had an unusually high percentage of small mills. In 1909 nearly half of the Palmetto State's oil mills crushed less than two thousand tons annually, compared to the average of 28 percent in that category for all cotton-producing states. A Texas crusher estimated that the average mill in his state during the 1890s and early twentieth century operated four presses with a sixty-ton daily capacity.[28]

At the beginning of the twentieth century a few giant mills at major railway junctions crushed as much as 150 to 200 tons of cottonseed a day, or from twenty to fifty thousand tons a season. At the other end of the scale, close to 11 percent of the mills processed fewer than one thousand tons of seed during 1909. The largest number of mills in 1909 processed from twenty-five to fifty tons daily for seasonal totals of two to five thousand tons. More than 65 percent of all oil mills in 1909 crushed less than five thousand tons of seed annually and employed from six to twenty workers. Eighty-three percent of the mills had fewer than fifty wage earners.[29] It is clear from these statistics that most of the cottonseed-oil mills in operation in the early twentieth century were relatively small.

By the twentieth century, overcapacity, or "misplaced capacity," plagued the crushing industry. The relatively unsophisticated, inexpensive crushing technology prevalent until after the Second World War fostered mill building, and the New South drive to industrialize encouraged numerous communities to organize their own crushing facilities. Oil mills sprang up wherever sufficient cotton grew. If cotton production declined in an area because of poor prices, crop failures, or other reasons, oil mills could not buy enough seed to operate at full capacity. They closed when adverse conditions persisted but reopened if seed supplies increased. The level of cotton production more than anything else determined the fate of oil mills, although management was an important factor.[30]

Terminal and interior mills competed for seed so aggressively during the early twentieth century that B. F. Taylor believed one type would eventually dominate the other. What Taylor forecast in 1912 came to pass gradually in the years after the First World War as changing conditions made milling on a larger scale essential. The distrust that operators of interior oil mills and officials of large companies with terminal mills came to feel toward each other had its origins during the 1890s, when independent mills multiplied and the quest for cottonseed intensified.[31]

Neither vigorous competition among the proliferating mills nor boll weevils, which migrated into Texas from Mexico during the early 1890s and began to move north and east through the Cotton Belt, slowed the building of mills before 1914. Despite the fierce competition, interior and terminal mills remained in equilibrium until the First World War. In 1916–17 three large companies with 123 mills produced 27.1 percent of the crude cottonseed oil in the United States, eight other companies manufactured 16.2 percent of the crude oil, and hundreds of small mills accounted for the remaining 56.7 percent. Before the war price-fixing and seed-sharing agreements, as well as low freight costs and other advantages enjoyed by interior mills, helped independent crushers to hold their own against larger competitors in the scramble for raw materials.[32]

Increased cotton production and railroad building, in addition to the growing demand for cottonseed oil as a substitute for more expensive oils in soaps and edible fats, fueled a rapid expansion of the crushing industry from 1880 to 1914. As oil mills appeared in hundreds of southern towns during those years, they developed close relationships with cotton gins and other institutions that linked mills to the countryside.

CHAPTER 3

Cottonseed Buying and Selling

I don't think there are as big fools in other businesses as there
are in cottonseed. They seem to be unable to sit down and
say, "I am not going to take that seed because I am unable
to see the profit in it." It is largely due to a lack of an adequate supply of raw material.

Secretary of the
South Carolina Division
of the National Cottonseed
Products Association, 1930

The shortage of seed in our mills is the thing that keeps us
awake at night.

Supervisor of Southern
Cotton Oil Company
mills in Georgia, 1930

Aggressive competition for cottonseed made acquisition of raw materials
the major task facing crushers. As a by-product of cotton lint, seed production could not be expanded to meet demand. Oil mills rarely got as
much seed as their operators considered desirable, particularly after boll
weevils invaded cotton fields after 1892 and the number of mills continued to grow rapidly until the First World War. Short cotton crops during
the early 1920s further intensified competition. Managers had to scramble
to buy the tonnage they needed to operate near capacity. With seed accounting for more than two-thirds of the total cost of processing, high
raw-material prices eroded mill profits.

Cotton ginners acquired most of the seed removed in the ginning process, although people outside the ginning industry also engaged in cottonseed buying and selling.[1] By concentrating the seed produced by many farmers into larger lots, ginners and other cottonseed buyers made it possible for oil mills to acquire their raw materials more efficiently. Because ginners moved most of the cottonseed from producers to processors, gins and oil mills developed a symbiotic relationship. Neither institution can be fully understood without considering the other. Seed purchases for oil mills became an important component of the ginning business, and many ginners relied on oil mills rather than banks to provide them with short- and long-term credit. Because of the pivotal role played by cotton gins in consolidating cottonseed supplies and the intense competition among crushers for seed, oil mills acquired cotton gins, obligated many ginners through commission contracts and loans to supply them with seed, and developed additional methods of controlling seed supplies from gins. Despite the emergence of common practices in cottonseed buying and selling, infinite variety characterized the cottonseed exchanges that took place during the harvest season in thousands of communities across the Cotton Belt.

The first oil-mill operators had a difficult time securing seed. An agent sent out on horseback in 1857 by pioneer New Orleans processor Paul Aldigé managed to buy only 1,764 tons of cottonseed from planters in eighteen months, an amount the smallest turn-of-the-century oil mill could have crushed in a third that time. Unlike Southeastern planters, Mississippi Valley cotton growers did not need to return cottonseed to the soil to restore its fertility. They consequently considered the seed a nuisance to be disposed of rather than saved in good condition for the valley's new cottonseed oil mills. Because of limited demand for cottonseed oil and cake during the industry's early years and their interchangeability with similar products, processors did not earn enough to be able to raise seed prices materially as an inducement to planters to collect and sell their seed.[2]

The paucity of roads and railroads in the Cotton Belt during the middle years of the nineteenth century added to the difficulties the first commercial crushers had in acquiring cottonseed. Plantations located more than ten or twelve miles inland from waterways were inaccessible.[3] It is true that planters got their lint to market in spite of obstacles to transportation, but cotton prices were high during the 1850s and lint could be compressed and stored until roads became dry enough for hauling. Cottonseed needed to be processed more rapidly in order to prevent overheating and deterioration. Moreover, the bulkiness and relatively low value of cottonseed and cottonseed products compared to lint made the cost of transportation a critical factor in the operation of cottonseed-oil mills at all times.

Decentralized ginning further hampered seed collection. Before the Civil War, slaves harvested cotton on plantations on sunny days and ginned it on wet days. With some exceptions, antebellum farm gins processed at most three or four bales of cotton a day, and few public gins existed. As tenant farming and sharecropping spread after the war, planters had trouble mobilizing laborers to gin their cotton. Cotton growing also became more prevalent in upcountry areas dominated by small farmers. Public, or custom, gins that charged set fees for their services opened in thousands of communities, whereas private gins continued to handle the cotton grown on many large plantations. The addition of labor-saving machinery such as feeders and condensers doubled the capacity of cotton gins after the Civil War, but improved gins still did not generate adequate seed for efficient processing in some areas.[4]

In the southeastern states, small-scale ginning and the widespread custom of fertilizing the soil with cottonseed combined to retard development of the processing industry. An oil mill established in Columbia, South Carolina, in 1869 failed, because not enough cottonseed could be purchased to make the venture profitable. The promoter had hoped to sell stock to farmers who would supply the mill with seed. Nearly a decade later, two oil mills in Montgomery, Alabama, could only operate intermittently because of lack of seed. As late as 1881 New South prophet Henry Grady lamented that the uneven distribution of cotton gins and the limited quantity of cotton ginned at any one place made seed "too expensive and difficult for oil mills to acquire." [5]

The first cottonseed processors relied on commission merchants, cottonseed buyers, and steamboat companies to acquire seed from farmers. Cotton factors sold lint for planters on commission, and so it was natural for them to collect and market much of the cottonseed in areas served by oil mills. Crushers gave commission merchants the number of bags they wanted filled with seed, and employees of the commission houses took care of all details. As their role in the marketing of cotton diminished following the Civil War, factors and commission merchants ceased to handle seed.[6] Cotton factors and commission merchants had been liable for short weights, lost seed sacks, and poor quality seed. Their disappearance as purchasing agents made it almost impossible for mills to hold anyone responsible for such losses. If a mill deducted for missing sacks or trashy, dirty, rotting seed, sellers could easily find other buyers, so great was the demand for seed wherever crushing mills existed. In areas without access to oil mills, cottonseed could hardly be given away.[7]

Besides sending their own buyers into the countryside to purchase seed, crushers acquired their raw materials from steamboats and independent buyers. Employees of steamboat companies and other middlemen, regarded as "scalpers" by oil men, bought seed from producers. They offered it for sale on the river banks, where seed could not be weighed accurately and often suffered damage from bad weather. Crushers bought seed "on the bank" from middlemen who had paid farmers low prices and charged crushers considerably more.[8] Middlemen, crushers claimed, were to blame for high seed prices.

In the early years of the industry, steamboats dropped sacks off at towns and plantation landings along the Mississippi River and other waterways before the cotton harvest began. On return trips, boats picked up the seed-filled sacks and carried them to the mill towns. Missing bags were a constant headache and a heavy expense for the oil mills. Many farm families turned cottonseed bags into saddle blankets, bed covers, coats, pants, and other pieces of clothing, just as thrifty farm wives made flour-sack dresses. Carelessness and misuse of sacks by steamboat crews compounded the problem. One crusher saw hundreds of sacks being used as a walkway for steamboat passengers. Mill agents sometimes bought seed that had already been put into sacks belonging to other mills, repacked the seed in their own bags, and abandoned the empty ones. As many as 1.5 million cottonseed sacks disappeared annually during the early 1890s, according to the president of the nation's largest cottonseed processing company.[9]

Changes taking place in the South after 1880 had a significant impact on the cottonseed industry and on the way crushers collected their raw materials. The postbellum increase in cotton production and the expansion of railroads made more cottonseed available for crushing and reduced transportation costs. Railway freight cars supplanted boats as the main carriers of cottonseed and cottonseed products. Because loose seed could be loaded directly into cars, rail transportation eliminated the expensive and time-consuming process of sacking and unsacking seed. Large oil mills in major cities shipped most of the seed they purchased by railway car, sometimes for great distances. Small interior mills located close to the cotton fields received seed by wagon from nearby farms and gins, as well as by railway, and along the Mississippi and other rivers, cottonseed continued to be packed in sacks and carried to oil mills by boat. Crushers paid about one dollar less per ton for sacked seed to off-set the greater expense of handling.[10]

A third change that made it easier for oil mills to buy sufficient seed for profitable crushing was the revolution in cotton ginning that began with the introduction of the Munger system in the mid-1880s. Largely automated, steam-powered ginning plants transformed the scale of the industry. Productivity increased from about six bales a day in improved postwar gins to as much as twenty-four to thirty bales per day. As gins became more efficient, consolidation began to take place in the ginning industry.[11] The increased production of cotton, extension of the railway system, and greater productivity of cotton gins during the late nineteenth century made more seed available for processing and concentrated the seed at fewer points.

During the late nineteenth century, ginners became the principal agents in the acquisition of cottonseed for the crushing mills. Street buy-ers not affiliated with cotton gins also bought seed from farmers and gin-ners in towns without oil mills, but they handled much less cottonseed than ginners. Ginners and street buyers either purchased seed with a mill's money on commission or salary and according to its instructions or used their own funds to buy seed as independent agents.

The majority of cotton farmers sold their seed to the gins that pre-pared their cotton for market because it was convenient. Selling to the gin made it easier for a busy grower or the driver of his cotton wagon to get back to the fields and continue harvesting cotton and doing other chores. Those who decided to seek better prices had to take the time to collect their seed from the gin and haul it to other buyers.[12]

The need for cash experienced by many cotton farmers at the end of the growing season provided another strong incentive for them to sell their seed without delay. "I will tell you the truth," one cotton grower said around 1930, "the farmer . . . cannot take his seed home; he has got to have a little seed money, no matter what the price may be." Follow-ing the long-established custom of grain and corn millers, cotton ginners usually took a portion of the seed as their toll to cover the cost of gin-ning, bagging, and ties. After paying the toll for ginning and saving some seed for the next year's planting and possibly some for stock feeding or fertilizer, small producers generally sold the rest of their seed for cash at the time of ginning.[13]

Most sharecroppers had to divide the seed they produced with their landlords, which also increased the likelihood that they would sell their seed at the time of ginning. As a rule, planters pooled their tenants' seed with their own and sold it for more money per ton than individual farmers could have realized on small lots. Most landlords kept the difference of several dollars a ton that came from selling to the mills in large lots, but others gave their tenants the carlot price for their seed.[14]

In some communities cotton growers had access to only a single gin, whereas in other places several ginners vied with one another for business. Also bidding for the farmers' cottonseed in many towns were street buyers unaffiliated with gins who intercepted cotton wagons on their way to the gins. Sometimes called "snipers," street buyers acquired seed for crushers in towns where oil mills did not have ginners to act as their purchasing agents, or they bought seed on their own account as a speculative venture. At the turn of the century, D. A. Tompkins of Charlotte, North Carolina, described the frenzied bidding for seed that went on in many localities during the cotton harvest: "The competition of the different local seed buyers is sometimes very keen, to the extent of much excitement. It is not uncommon to see two or more young white men—runners for seed agents or buyers—mount the wagon of a negro or white farmer, as he comes from the country into the market town. These press upon the farmer offers for the seed. Sometimes the drummers, or runners, even get into personal encounters."[15]

Street buyers found out what local gins were paying for seed on a given day and matched it or advanced the price. A farmer might sell at the gin price to a street buyer who was his friend or to one who paid him well for hauling his seed from the gin, but street buyers often had to pay more for seed than local ginners if they expected to acquire any. The number of street buyers declined as telephones became more widespread after the First World War and much of a mill's seed buying could be done from the central office.[16]

Oil mills decided what to pay for cottonseed on the basis of factors such as the size of the cotton crop, the probable earnings of cottonseed products, the prices of lard and other competing products, and the current market rate for seed. Accurate, up-to-the-minute crop and market information helped managers to make more informed seed-buying decisions. Operators of terminal mills and mill chains were more likely to stay abreast of market news than managers of small, interior plants. The size of cotton crops was the single most reliable indicator of cottonseed price trends, because the value of seed varied inversely with the amount produced. Knowing the size of the corn crop and corn prices aided crushers in estimating more precisely the number of hogs likely to be raised in a year and, consequently, the approximate amount and price of lard, which had a greater influence on cottonseed-oil prices than any other factor, because vegetable-oil shortening served as a less-expensive substitute.[17]

Crushers purchased most of their seed during the three or four months of the fall cotton harvest, and then bid for the large lots of higher-priced seed held by speculators in order to continue crushing as long as possible. Small oil mills often adopted the prices set by the largest crushing plants in their territory. The secrecy surrounding mill operations and seed bids made it easy for a seed seller to pit one mill man against another by reporting that he had received higher offers elsewhere. "I don't believe that there has ever been a ginner born that would not lie to you about what he had been offered for seed," one mill manager stated in about 1930, and that was a widely held conviction.[18]

Seed generally went to the mills paying top prices or bonuses, but when crushers offered equal prices, friendship and personal ties usually determined who got a load of seed. Mill managers and buyers thus cultivated close ties with ginners, brokers, and seed dealers, visiting them regularly and telegraphing or telephoning information and offers for seed. An Arkansas farmer-ginner who had sold his seed to the Gayoso mill in Memphis for thirty-five years switched to the Perkins mill when a friend became its traveling seed buyer. "There's not any difference in the mills," he said. "It is just knowing the man."[19]

Whatever factors entered into seed pricing, there was always an element of speculation, because no one could forecast whether the prices of cottonseed products would go up or down. Crushers had to decide what to pay for seed based on estimates of what the manufactured products would earn. Sometimes crushers paid more for seed than cottonseed products were bringing at the time, on the gamble that product values would advance enough to yield a profit. Generally, product prices rose as the crushing season progressed, but the pattern did not always hold true after the First World War, and sometimes crushers who counted on rising product prices to cover high-priced seed came to grief.[20]

Mill managers notified ginners of changes in their price for seed. Once ginners posted their seed prices for the day they might advance them, but those who faced competition seldom reduced prices until the following morning to avoid losing customers. The difference between what the mill paid and what the farmer received for cottonseed constituted the dealer's spread, from which he had to pay the costs of handling cottonseed. Where strong competition pushed up seed prices or ginners incurred extra expenses in hauling seed to railheads, they often had to settle for smaller margins. Larger returns could be earned in less-competitive locations by paying farmers as little as possible. Ginners who sold large volumes of cottonseed and those who kept in close touch with the market or were more "capable and skillful" often got higher prices for their seed at the expense of those not as well informed or as advantageously located.[21]

Anyone who bid more for seed than his competitors generally set off a price war. At such times oil mills had little control over prices. It was to everyone's advantage, except cottonseed producers, to keep prices stable. Thus, seed prices would remain unchanged for days, then shoot up quickly when a buyer thought he could get a large amount of seed, and finally return to a lower level. The greater the competition for seed among mills and gins, the more unstable cottonseed prices tended to be. By agreement or tacit understanding, cotton ginners and oil-mill operators in some communities paid farmers identical prices for cottonseed. In those places and in isolated country districts served by a single mill, seed prices might change very little during the course of a crushing season.[22]

Because raw materials required by far the largest outlay of operating capital, the great majority of mills borrowed money to finance all or part of their seed purchases. When the cotton harvest began in late summer, local banks made short-term loans to oil mills for seed purchases. Payable in three to six months, seed loans generally required the endorsement of mill directors rather than collateral, because stored seed might deteriorate. During the late nineteenth century a number of oil mills adopted the system common among textile mills of arranging for buyers to be reimbursed by a bank once they had shipped cotton. Many banks permitted ginners and cottonseed buyers to draw drafts on them when they presented evidence that cottonseed had been shipped to a mill. During the 1920s banks loaned money for cottonseed based on promissory notes and granted credit based on bills of exchange, or used a combination of the two methods.[23]

The small Tar River Oil Company near Tarboro, North Carolina, spent from forty-five to sixty thousand dollars a year for seed between 1888 and 1903 and crushed a minimum of twenty-five hundred tons of seed annually. A Texas Federal Reserve agent estimated that a mill buying six to eight thousand tons of seed per season before the First World War needed to borrow about $120,000 annually, but that by 1917 inflation had caused that figure to double. The largest buyer of cottonseed between the world wars, the Wesson Oil & Snowdrift Company, borrowed $8.45 million in 1937 and $10 million in 1938 to finance seed purchases. Banks expected to be repaid by season's end, but in bad years they had to carry over seed loans and sometimes found themselves owning oil mills.[24]

Numerous mills, particularly in the Southeast, reduced the amount of money they needed to borrow for seed purchases by bartering meal or fertilizer for seed. Some mills exchanged as much as a ton of meal for a ton of seed when farmers hauled the seed to the mill and took away the meal or when they ginned their cotton at a mill-owned gin. Although it took about two tons of seed to produce one ton of meal, processors did not have to pay freight on seed delivered directly to the mill and on meal carried home by farmers. They also saved interest that would have been paid on money borrowed to buy the seed. When mills paid freight costs and commissions on meal, exchange rates fluctuated from one thousand to fifteen hundred pounds of meal for two thousand pounds of seed, depending on the market value of meal and seed.

Ton-for-ton swaps of seed for meal declined during the late 1920s, when meal prices rose and seed values remained the same or declined. In some cases seed producers refused to sell seed to a ginner unless he made an even trade, and swapping ton-for-ton when meal cost more relative to seed was sometimes done as a way of paying more than the market rate for seed. An increasing use of ammoniates other than cottonseed meal reduced fertilizer exchanges toward the end of the 1920s.[25]

Over time oil mill operators worked out various strategies for keeping a fairly steady flow of cottonseed coming into their mills. One of the earliest methods used by crushers to tie up seed supplies was to pay ginners and buyers either a monthly salary or a commission on each ton of seed they acquired for the mill. Those ginners and seed dealers were known as wagon-lot buyers, because they bought the seed from wagonloads of cotton brought to the gins by farmers. Some crushers had verbal understandings with particular ginners that they would get all of a gin's seed they wanted at a set commission. In other cases mill managers made contracts with the ginners and street buyers who regularly acted as their major seed suppliers. Large mills and mill chains tended to use written contracts more than small mills, which bought seed principally from the farmers and ginners in their immediate territory. From their commissions buyers paid for storage and the loading of cottonseed into railway cars, absorbed weight losses above about 1 percent, and defrayed other expenses involved in the accumulation of many small lots of seed into railway carlots of about forty tons or truckloads of approximately twenty tons. Crushers paid handling charges on seed purchased by their salaried buyers.[26]

Wagon-lot commissions varied from year to year and place to place depending on local custom, the state of the economy, the general level of prices, and the competition for cottonseed. During the first decade and a half of the twentieth century, commissions ranged from one to two dollars a ton. By 1918 wartime inflation had caused commissions to rise to three dollars. Although seed prices fell after the war, wagon-lot commission rates did not decline, probably because short cotton crops in the immediate postwar period made it a sellers' market. During the 1920s commissions sometimes ran as high as four, five, and six dollars a ton, despite efforts by crushers to enforce uniform commissions of three dollars. At the depths of the Great Depression, commissions of seventy-five cents to two dollars were the rule.[27]

Other cottonseed buyers, known as carlot buyers, acquired railway carloads of seed for mills, which before the First World War paid them a commission of twenty-five cents or more a ton in addition to the full carlot price paid to the seed seller by the mills. After the United States entered the war, the Food Administration set fifty cents as the commission for buying carloads of seed, and that figure remained customary, although crushers paid more than fifty cents at times. In the Southeast during the 1920s, wagon-lot buyers might also be fifty-cent buyers, but that was frowned on elsewhere, because it enabled ginners to sell some of the seed they had bought in wagon lots for a higher commission. The commission ginner with a fifty-cent provision in his contract who persuaded customers to sell carloads of seed to the mill was supposed to receive his commission after the planter had shipped his seed to the mill and been paid the carlot or mill price.

A person with a financial interest in the seed being offered for sale, such as the relative of a large cotton grower or ginner, was considered ineligible to be a carlot buyer. In reality, a man's influence with large farmers or ginners had more to do with his selection as a fifty-cent buyer than any other factor. Crushers expected their fifty-cent buyers to use political, religious, and kinship connections to acquire carloads of seed.

Moreover, they realized that commissions would often be split between the parties involved.[28]

Seed brokers also arranged deals between oil mills and sellers with carloads of seed and collected from twenty-five cents to one dollar per ton from the mills. Brokers and fifty-cent carlot buyers performed essentially the same service. The difference was that brokers pitted one mill against another in order to get the best possible seed prices for their customers, and fifty-cent buyers theoretically worked for a single mill. In reality, they sometimes bought seed for several companies.

A cotton planter or other person with one or more cars of seed to sell who made a sale through a broker or fifty-cent buyer received the mill price or higher for his seed, that is, the equivalent of the farm price plus the wagon-lot commission per ton. The broker or fifty-cent commission buyer who arranged the sale got an additional fifty cents or so per ton from the mill, which made seed acquired by fifty-cent buyers and brokers more expensive than that purchased by wagon-lot commission buyers. Crushers considered the acquisition of large lots of seed worth the additional cost.[29]

Terminal mills and oil-mill companies that acquired their seed from a wide area hired traveling seed agents who supervised commission buyers and bought seed from other sources. Independent crushers in eastern North Carolina at the turn of the century had to compete with traveling seed buyers sent into their territory by several large milling companies in the state and from Virginia.[30]

At railway stops that did not have seed-processing plants, the larger oil mills maintained seed houses and wagon scales, where the ginners and street buyers working for them on commission or salary accumulated and stored seed. Major companies owned as many as fifty to seventy-five of the "small and cheaply constructed warehouses, capable of holding one to three or four carloads of seed." After the turn of the century, warehouses at major seed concentration points gradually replaced the flimsy seed houses. Buyers could also lease railway cars and pay farmers to load seed directly into them. Sometimes several mills maintained storage facilities at favorable collection points, and in those towns competition often became quite fierce, unless oil men arranged for one person to buy all the seed and divide it among the mills according to a prearranged plan.[31]

In the early days of cottonseed processing, oil mills generally advanced money to the men buying seed for them on commission. The "novelty" of cottonseed processing and the "uncertainty of any gain" had made it necessary for oil mills to pay salaries and commissions and to supply cash to their seed agents. During the decade and a half before the First World War, crushers advanced their agents sums ranging from $150 to $500.[32] As a rule, mills told their buyers the maximum price they could pay for a ton of seed. Crushers communicated with their agents by letter and telegram during the early years of the industry, later by telephone. Oil mills had to keep their buyers "in the market." That is, a mill either had to take a gin's seed at the market price if it had a contract or understanding with the ginner, or permit him to sell to the highest bidder.[33]

Despite contracts and strict instructions from mill managers, the highly competitive seed market gave contract buyers many opportunities to manipulate seed prices. One way they persuaded mill officials to sanction higher buying limits was by falsely informing them that other buyers had made higher offers for desirable lots of seed. Crushers often complained that buyers under contract to one mill and using its money to buy seed contacted other mills and pocketed the difference whenever they made better deals, or shipped lower-grade seed and less seed than mills had paid for. Some ginners buying seed on commission reported that they had paid the limit fixed by the mills when they had actually paid farmers less and kept the extra mill money. Other critics charged that seed agents used money that processors had borrowed at 6 to 8 percent interest to finance their own businesses.[34]

Efforts to reduce the amount of cash held by seed buyers began early in the twentieth century. In 1907 Alabama cottonseed crushers were warned not to give a buyer cash, because "he uses your money and then dictates prices to you." Attributing most of the evils associated with seed buying to the practice of supplying cash to seed-purchasing agents, a speaker at the 1912 convention of the Interstate Cotton Seed Crushers' Association recommended that oil mills give each of their buyers a book of blank seed drafts to be filled out in triplicate when the agent purchased seed for the mill. The person selling the seed to the ginner or buyer got the original draft, which alone could be cashed at the bank, once the mill had made the necessary arrangements. The mill received a copy and the seed buyer kept another copy of the transaction for his records.

Eventually, many processors avoided the problems associated with advancing cash to ginners by arranging for farmers to take gin tickets that recorded the weight and price of the seed to a bank or the mill and cash them like checks. That cut down on the amount of surplus mill money in the hands of seed buyers and eliminated the opportunity for agents to misrepresent prices and weights. The practice of advancing money to seed buyers persisted, but it became less widespread. During the 1920s merchants and banks routinely cashed the gin tickets farmers received from commission ginners.[35]

Having commission contracts tied up seed in advance, but too often buyers on commission paid more than the limit set by their companies, did not ship seed promptly, failed to account for all the money advanced to them, and split their commissions with growers. After the First World War, fewer ginners and buyers had commission contracts or agreements, although buying on commission persisted longer in parts of the Southeast than in Oklahoma, Texas, and the Mississippi Valley.[36]

Independent ginners and seed buyers used their own resources or borrowed money to buy seed. Their scale of operations ranged from a single carload of seed a season, which might represent the total capital of an individual, to major investments by groups of capitalists. Independents either sold the seed they had purchased to a single mill that they regularly did business with or offered it to several mills hoping that competition among them would increase seed prices. Independent buyers were the bulls in the cottonseed market.[37]

Southerners with capital frequently speculated in cottonseed. Because it cost less to buy and store seed, people could invest in cottonseed more easily than in cotton lint. Bankers, merchants, lawyers, doctors, real estate brokers, and farmers were among the businessmen, in addition to independent ginners, who bought and stored cottonseed anticipating that prices would increase as seed became harder to find and mills sought to extend their crushing season. Independent seed buyers reportedly earned larger profits at times than the oil mills. In 1931 a Texas cottonseed buyer said that by forcing oil mills to pay "more for those seed than they were worth," speculators like himself were partly responsible for the mills' financial problems.[38]

Most of the independent seed buyers were ginners. Although some independent ginners sold seed as fast as they acquired it, many tried to wait for a price rise before selling. Few people stored the immature, damp seed frequently encountered early in the season, because it deteriorated too rapidly and caused spontaneous combustion. Those who took the risk of buying large quantities of less-expensive early seed had to watch it carefully and turn it frequently. With proper care, clean, dry seed could often be kept for long periods, although there was always the possibility that overheating would cause damage.[39]

Ginners sometimes switched back and forth from buying on commission to buying on their own account. An independent buyer who had a bad year might become a commission buyer, or a dealer on commission might be tempted to buy for himself if independent buyers were prospering. Sometimes the same person bought both on commission and as an independent. When the mill that commissioned him stopped buying seed, the ginner was free to buy on his own account. Even when his mill stayed in the market, a ginner might acquire some seed for himself on the side. Changing from one kind of buying to another was probably more common among seed dealers during the turbulent 1920s than earlier.[40]

Independent ginners had a better chance of earning more money on a carload of seed if they offered it to several mills, but other factors sometimes made it advantageous for them to sell to a single mill. Crushers frequently felt obligated to take all of the seed that loyal ginners offered to sell, even sometimes at unprofitable prices, in order to keep them as regular suppliers. Street buyers generally refused to purchase early seed, which tended to be immature and damp and subject to overheating, and they did not want to bother with a few loads of seed at the end of a crushing season. As a rule, they only purchased prime, high-quality seed in the heart of the season.[41]

Oil mills had negative as well as positive methods of inducing independent ginners to do business with them. Those that owned cotton gins could bring pressure on independent ginners by lowering charges at the oil mill gin or by paying high prices for seed. One Texas ginner who had sold seed to outside mills reported that the local mill "liked to put him out of business." If a gin wouldn't sell seed at a satisfactory price, an oil mill might put in another gin or threaten to do so.[42]

To gain greater control over raw-material supplies, many oil mills built, leased, or bought stock in cotton gins. Despite the widespread custom among cottonseed crushers of not buying seed in another mill town, a North Carolina oil mill company in 1904 secretly helped to finance a cotton gin in a nearby community where the local oil mill had been getting most of the seed. A crusher who built a gin in another oil mill's territory ran the risk of a competing gin being erected in a town where he enjoyed a seed monopoly. "When you build a gin at Aliceville, I will build one at Columbus," wrote one Mississippi crusher to another in 1909. "I will not be run over," he concluded.[43]

"For many years the oil mills have had to control a large percentage of cotton gins in their territory in order to get a full share of cotton seed," stated a trade journal in 1917. An Arkansas man writing in 1929 declared that oil mills had constructed gins whether they were needed or not just to obtain cottonseed and that cutthroat competition among ginners had been the result. The number of cotton gins had actually declined since the late nineteenth century. From 1902 to 1929 the number of gins decreased by half, but ginning capacity more than doubled. Although oil mills probably never owned more than about 10 percent of all cotton gins, mill gins had a significance greater than their numbers, for they were among the largest, most up-to-date, and best located gins, particularly those associated with mills in major market towns.[44]

The practice of mills owning multiple cotton gins became very unpopular among farmers, because it reduced competition. In 1913 the Texas attorney general ruled that oil mills had to get out of the ginning business, but the ruling could not be upheld because many mill charters specifically included the right to gin cotton. The following year a bill that would have barred Texas cottonseed-oil mills from owning cotton gins failed to pass in the state legislature. Mississippi legislators succeeded in 1914 in prohibiting mills from owning more than one gin, which had to be in the same town as the mill. Some Mississippi mills sold their cotton gins at a loss; others evaded the law by making various arrangements to hide gin ownership. The Texas attorney general tried again in 1920 to separate oil mills and cotton gins, but the three bills introduced for that purpose did not become law. Despite the meager success of efforts by some state governments to divorce cotton gins and oil mills, gin ownership by oil mills declined in most cotton-growing states after the First World War. Crushers found that they were less vulnerable to retaliation by other oil mills when they did not own cotton gins.[45]

In 1929 Senator Heflin of Alabama introduced resolutions requesting the Federal Trade Commission to find out if cottonseed-oil companies owned or controlled gins in order to destroy competition and lower cottonseed prices. After a lengthy investigation, FTC agents concluded that mills in most states owned an insignificant number of cotton gins. The percentage of cotton gins owned by 431 of 495 oil mills reporting to the FTC were: Oklahoma, 44.2 percent; Tennessee, 17.62 percent; Texas, 12.16 percent; Georgia, 5.46 percent; Louisiana, 4.6 percent; South Carolina 3.83 percent; Alabama, 2.95 percent; Mississippi, 2.54 percent; North Carolina, 2.51 percent; and Arkansas, 1.86 percent.[46]

Special circumstances in western Oklahoma and Texas fostered gin ownership by oil mills at a time when the trend was being reversed in other parts of the Cotton Belt. In the early twentieth century, boll weevil infestation caused a westward shift in cotton cultivation to areas where dry, hot summers, cold winters, and treeless plains provided a less hospitable environment for the insects that were steadily moving east and north. R. K. Wootten of the Chickasha Cotton Oil Company campaigned aggressively among western Oklahoma farmers during the early twentieth century to persuade them to plant cotton, even furnishing many of them with seed. Because the scarcity of gins in the area made farmers reluctant to grow cotton, Wootten began building gins. When frost killed much of the cotton before the bolls opened, Wootten equipped his company's gins with newly invented machinery capable of breaking and cleaning bolls. At one point, the Chickasha Cotton Oil Company owned 175 gins and eleven oil mills. Wootten, J. W. Simmons, and other investors built 125 cotton gins and five oil mills in West Texas, because weevils did not thrive there.[47]

The unusually high percentage of gin ownership attributed to Tennessee oil mills in the Federal Trade Commission report is misleading, as is the extremely low figure for Arkansas. The Tennessee cottonseed industry was concentrated in Memphis, where crushing went on in some of the largest mills in the South. The National Cottonseed Products Corporation, a sizable enterprise created by the merger of mills in Tennessee, Arkansas, and adjacent states, had its headquarters in Memphis. All but ten of the eighty-nine cotton gins attributed to Tennessee mills in 1929 were the property of the National Cottonseed Products Corporation. After its formation in the mid-1920s, the corporation operated nearly one hundred gins, a large number of which had belonged to Arkansas oil mills. Over a period of several years the company sold all but six or eight of its gins. In 1930 Tennessee oil mills owned very few cotton gins.[48]

Federal Trade Commission statistics probably understated the actual level of gin ownership by oil mills in Mississippi and possibly in other states. Because of the 1914 law making it illegal for Mississippi mills to own more than one gin, trusteeships and other arrangements had been created to hide gin ownership. The Lee County Gin Company was one of several bogus corporations organized by the same people who had previously owned and operated the gins. Mississippi mills did not report such gins when they completed the FTC questionnaire in 1929.[49]

Cottonseed crushers made loans to cotton gins as another way of obligating ginners to sell them seed. Ginners, in turn, sometimes loaned money to farmers in order to get their ginning business. Oil mills routinely loaned small unsecured sums to gins annually to enable them to make repairs and to buy coal or fuel oil, bagging, ties, and other items necessary to start up operation when the harvest began. Bagging and ties constituted a major expense. Sometimes oil mills bought bagging and ties and supplied them to cooperating gins at low prices, even below cost, although other mills sold bagging and ties as a profitable sideline. Some of the state cottonseed crushers' associations bought bagging and ties for their members at bulk rates. The 1914 Texas bill forbidding oil mills from owning gins would also have prohibited cottonseed crushers from selling bagging and ties to gins had it passed. Gins customarily repaid short-term or "open-account" loans with seed or in cash at the end of the crushing season. At times ginners succumbed to the temptation of selling seed to other mills for cash instead of erasing their debt with seed deliveries.[50]

Oil mills with sufficient capital also made major loans to finance gin construction in places where they wanted to acquire new sources of seed. Large construction loans were usually secured by mortgages on the gin property, and gin companies paid interest on their debts. In some cases oil mills waved interest payments in order to induce gins to accept loans. When gins defaulted, ownership eventually passed to the mills, although they frequently carried gin loans over from year to year without foreclosing.[51]

Gins borrowed large sums of money to buy modern equipment and upgrade facilities. From the mid-1920s to the end of the decade a number of ginners who had let their plants deteriorate during the period of short crops after the First World War borrowed money from the mills in order to modernize or build up-to-date gins. Farmers wanted their cotton ginned by companies that had machinery for cleaning and handling cotton with minimum damage to the fiber. The number of gin loans increased dramatically during the late 1920s. In the case of a new gin it was customary for the company that supplied the machinery to take a first mortgage on the machinery and a second mortgage on the building and grounds and for the oil mill to take a first mortgage on the property and a second mortgage on the equipment.[52]

Some ginners claimed that accepting loans did not obligate them to sell their seed to the mills loaning them money, but crushers expected to have the first opportunity to bid on those seed. Sometimes oil men were disappointed. In 1930, Texas crusher W. A. Sherman denied that his company required seed delivery when making loans, but he said the loans were made for the purpose of getting seed. J. W. Simmons, general manager of a large group of Texas mills, said, "If he doesn't give us the seed we don't loan to him any more."[53]

Although mills in all of the cotton-growing states made gin loans, the practice seems to have been more pervasive in the Mississippi Valley states and the Southeast than in the Southwest. That was undoubtedly because the mills of the two companies loaning the most money, Buckeye and the Southern Cotton Oil Company, were concentrated in the eastern and central sections of the Cotton Belt. In 1929–30 cotton gins owed Buckeye Cotton Oil Company, a subsidiary of Procter & Gamble, close to $3 million, and the Southern Cotton Oil Company had outstanding gin loans of $1.75 million. It was conservatively estimated at the First Annual Convention of Mid-South Ginners in 1929 that at least half of all cotton gins were either owned by oil mills or were financially obligated to them through loans.[54]

Crushers looked for opportunities to lend in order to tie up seed, and ginners sought loans from mills because of the easy terms and availability of money. Gin companies found it difficult to borrow money from other sources. Much of the limited capital of southern banks was necessary to finance cotton lint transactions. Preferring the liquidity of short-term loans based on commercial paper, many banks in the South either could not or would not make long-term mortgage loans to cotton gins.[55]

The widespread custom of the larger mill companies loaning money to gins and the difficulty of collecting on them caused some cottonseed crushers during the 1920s to try to curb gin loans. Loans tied up a great deal of mill money and increased operating costs when the interest and principal could not be collected. Most crushers disliked gin loans but considered them a necessary evil, because of the aggressive competition for cottonseed. With the onset of the Depression, gin property values and incomes declined, making it more difficult for oil mills to recover their money. Nevertheless, the practice of mills loaning money to cottons gins persisted.[56]

Besides using commission contracts, gin ownership, and gin loans as ways of lining up specific ginners as regular suppliers of seed and of employing various positive and negative inducements to influence independent ginners to send them seed, oil mill operators developed strategies for acquiring large tonnages of seed held by speculators. Storing seed was one way some gins and mills got large lots of seed after the peak of the harvest and ginning season had passed. A number of gins and oil mills stored seed for their major customers without charge until prices rose and owners of the seed decided to sell. People in the cottonseed industry referred to the practice as "storing on call." Once an individual had stored seed for longer than a day or two, he was obligated in some sections to sell to the company storing his seed. That was not the case in other parts of the Cotton Belt, and if producers sold their seed elsewhere, they expected to get back sound seed even if their seed had deteriorated in storage.[57]

Although a farmer might save a sack of cottonseed to sell before Christmas in order to buy gifts, most small cotton producers could not afford to hold their seed for higher prices. Generally, only independent farmers and large planters were in a position to wait for the higher seed prices that tended to come in the late winter and spring. Ginners stored seed for their farmer customers in order to establish a strong claim to them. Ginners, as a rule, did not charge for storing seed, but there were exceptions. In North Carolina, where the custom of seed storage was particularly entrenched, some gins rented separate rooms to large customers and deposited seed in them each time a farmer had his cotton ginned.[58]

Because most ginners had limited storage space, those that held seed for their customers or wanted to wait for a price rise before selling their own seed generally asked oil mills to store the seed. Mills that stored seed on call usually did not keep the actual seed in storage. Unlike bales of cotton, specific lots of cottonseed could not easily be kept separate. Mills crushed seed as rapidly as possible to prevent damage, sold the products, and settled with those storing on call at the price for seed in effect at the time. That permitted a mill to acquire seed without borrowing money and to pay for it after selling the products, although crushers risked financial losses on such transactions if seed prices rose to levels higher than anticipated.[59]

Mills had to pay more for stored cottonseed, because the purpose of storing was to sell when seed ceased to be a glut on the market. If cottonseed prices declined instead of rising, mills and gins notified those storing seed of the impending change and gave them an opportunity to sell at the higher price. The practice was referred to as "buying on the decline," and farmers and speculators holding seed in their own warehouses expected to be accorded similar protection. As a rule, seed owners did not sell if prices were rising, and some charged that when mills needed seed, they put out the word that prices were about to go down. It was common for seed dealers to sell short when they received word of an impending decline. That is, they sold more cottonseed than they had on hand in order to take advantage of the higher price.[60]

Mills and gins carried insurance on seed and incurred other expenses in storage, yet growers expected them to store seed free of charge. The seed may have been crushed long before a financial settlement took place, but the company accepting the seed remained responsible for it. A few gins and oil mills collected a fee to cover insurance and other expenses, and some required farmers to settle on stored seed by a given date at the price in effect at that time, but most charged nothing for storage. Seed shrank as much as 5 to 10 percent in storage. Some gins and mills deducted for shrinkage, but the amount was arbitrary because they rarely kept one farmer's seed separate from all the rest. A crusher who deducted for insurance, loss of weight, and deterioration on seed taken out of storage by the owner and sold to other mills found that he lost the sellers' future business and therefore felt obligated to match the high prices offered by competing mills.[61]

Little information on the actual cost of storing cottonseed has come to light. In 1918 an Oklahoma mill manager stated that insurance and seed shrinkage made the cost of storing cottonseed about one dollar a ton, presumably for the entire storage period. Seed delivered to mills at that time was about seventy dollars a ton or more because of wartime inflation. In 1930 a Texas mill manager who refused to store seed explained that storage cost two dollars a ton and the farmer wanted to leave his seed at the mill's gin free of charge. For the 1929–30 season, trade association officials estimated that the average cost of a ton of cottonseed delivered to the mills was $35.88. In 1933, when deflation had shrunk prices generally, cotton ginners proposed that where seed from different farmers could be kept separate, the monthly cost of storing cottonseed and insuring it against loss from fire be set at twenty-five cents a ton.[62] That storage costs and higher seed prices due to storage became increasingly burdensome to gins and oil mills is evident from the persistent efforts made by ginners and crushers after the First World War to eliminate free storage.

The not-uncommon practice among ginners of adding trash to cottonseed to increase its weight and price was an irritation for crushers that defied solution until oil mills began to buy seed on grade in the 1930s. Ginners were tempted to add trash because they paid for a high proportion of waste when they bought the seed. Gin operators weighed seed cotton on wagon scales before ginning it. Because few gins had seed scales, ginners either estimated the weight of the seed or subtracted the weight of the lint from the total weight of the cotton to arrive at the number of pounds of seed in a farmer's cotton. State laws forbidding the addition of sand and trash to cottonseed could not be enforced, as crushers did not want to risk losing seed by docking sellers for excess trash.[63]

In 1929 the Memphis Merchants Exchange established a futures market for cottonseed trading in conjunction with its reorganized cottonseed-meal futures market. There had been a futures market in flaxseed since the end of the nineteenth century, and with about twenty-two times as much cottonseed being produced as flaxseed, the promoters expected a successful outcome. At first Memphis was the only delivery point for seed, and that limited the number of traders who could take advantage of the service. Despite the addition of other places of delivery and changes in the rules, seed futures did not attract enough customers. Unlike the cottonseed-meal and oil futures markets in Memphis, New York, and New Orleans, seed trading never became broad enough for processors to hedge their purchases. Poor timing undoubtedly contributed to the demise of the cottonseed futures market.[64]

Cottonseed purchasing became more concentrated after the First World War as consolidation took place in the crushing industry. In 1930–31 the ten leading seed-milling groups controlled 178 of 504 mills and about 45 percent of the total crushing capacity. The Southern Cotton Oil Company and Procter & Gamble's subsidiary, Buckeye, each purchased and processed approximately 10 percent of the seed crushed annually. Unlike Anderson-Clayton's domination of cotton-lint buying during the first half of the twentieth century, however, no single firm made cottonseed buying its principal interest.[65]

Oil mills depended on cotton gins to supply most of their raw materials. To ensure regular and predictable supplies of cottonseed, oil mills paid some ginners and dealers commissions to buy seed, acquired cotton gins, loaned money to ginners, and stored seed free for planters and ginners until prices rose. The methods devised by oil mills to control gins and their seed supplies increased the interdependence of cotton gins and cottonseed-oil mills.

CHAPTER 4

Cottonseed Crushing

[Laborers] no longer bring meat for their dinners, but put their bread under the press, where the sweet, warm, fresh oil is trickling out, and eat it with a relish, finding it healthful and nutritious.

Henry Hammond,
"The Cotton Seed Industry"

This type of labor—negro laborers and Mexican laborers in Southwest Texas—seem to be well adapted to this seasonal work. The milling industry seems to have a special attraction for them, and they never tire of the long twelve hour shifts.

F. W. Hobbs, "The Cotton Seed
Oil Industry with Particular Reference
to the Farmers and Ginner's
Cotton Oil Company"

Cottonseed crushing, the initial stage of processing carried out in the Cotton Belt, fit the traditional pattern of southern manufacturing, which was to process natural resources and agricultural staples such as timber, coal, iron, cotton, corn, tobacco, sugar, and rice. In a region where workers in industries, or departments within industries, were primarily of the same race, cottonseed-oil mills employed low-paid black workers for the most part. Although some African Americans worked as oil-mill mechanics, they could not move into administrative or managerial positions.

Cottonseed processing resembled other New South industries, apart from timber and cotton goods, in the comparatively small size of its work force. Nevertheless, hydraulic pressing, the dominant means of oil extraction during the industry's first century, required more labor than alternative methods. Milling added little value to the cost of cottonseed and produced generally modest profits. The more remunerative secondary stages of oil refining and manufacturing went on in northern states or in southern plants controlled to a large extent by outside capital. Most of the machinery in crushing mills came from northern factories.[1]

The technology used in crushing cottonseed came principally from that used to mill flaxseed, rape seed, castor beans, grain, sugar, and rice, and the basic principles involved in the primary stage of manufacturing changed little during the first century of cottonseed processing in the United States. Until the 1870s American oil mills relied for the most part on methods worked out in England and on the Continent. Thereafter, American companies took a leading role in developing mill machinery and processes.[2]

During the fall cotton harvest, seed poured into oil mills, principally from cotton gins. Crushing operations went on for twenty-four hours a day, six days a week until seed supplies had been exhausted. Around-the-clock crushing reduced the amount of storage space and insurance on seed needed by gins and crude-oil mills and minimized heat damage to the massed seed. It also cost less to keep mills operating day and night than to interrupt processing. Efficiency declined at the beginning of the work week as the kettles and machines were heated. Laborers worked twelve-hour day or night shifts for sixty to seventy-two hours a week.[3]

The crushing season began as early as July in the warmest parts of the Cotton Belt but generally in late August or early September and lasted until March or April, unless short crops reduced the crush. After cotton-seed had been cleaned, delinted, and hulled, the kernels were crushed or rolled into flakes, cooked, and subjected to great pressure to express the oil. By that process, crushing mills produced crude oil, the seed residue known as cottonseed cake, hulls, and short cotton fibers called linters.

Seed arrived at oil mills by steamboat, wagon, and railway car until trucks became common in the 1920s and 1930s. Laborers unloaded the seed, at first by hand and later by power tools, and stored it on the mill premises or in separate seed houses until needed. Growing awareness of the danger of spontaneous combustion from damp or dirty seed and from sparks igniting lint and dust eventually made separate storehouses the rule, except in dry parts of the Southwest, where cottonseed could be piled up in the open air. The wooden seed houses of the late nineteenth century were gradually replaced by steel warehouses and tanks. In the "tunnels" of twentieth-century seed houses, laborers shoveling seed into conveyors worked in suffocating dust and dirt and risked losing life or limb if they stepped into a conveyor. Air-circulation systems developed after the First World War helped to cool and preserve stored cottonseed.[4]

To eliminate some of the manual labor involved in handling cottonseed, early mills installed wooden conveyors and other elevating equipment similar to that employed in the automated rice and flour mills of the late eighteenth century. Because lint caused cottonseed to clump rather than flow freely like wheat or corn, manufacturers produced spiral conveyors. By the end of the 1870s, seed at various stages of processing were moved vertically by bucket elevators and horizontally by screw conveyors inside metal troughs, perforated to facilitate sand removal.[5] Before being processed, seed had to be cleaned of sand, bolls, trash, and metals by a series of moving screens, beaters, blowers, and magnets. Dirty seed damaged mill machinery and reduced the quality of products. Because trashy, hot seed deteriorated rapidly, some mills cleaned seed prior to storage.[6]

Steam engines, which began to be used widely in the United States during the mid-nineteenth century, powered all but a few of the cottonseed-oil mills built after 1855. For several decades mills burned cottonseed hulls to fuel the engines, but when demand for hulls as roughage in animal feed increased their price, mills switched to coal. During the Great Depression some companies found that it was again economical to use hulls in the boilers.[7]

In steam-powered mills, belts connected all of the machinery to a drive shaft powered by a large engine housed in a separate building and requiring attendance. In the early decades of the twentieth century, some mills switched at least partially to electric and diesel motors. The change may have been delayed by the need for steam in cooking cottonseed meats, but the transition to newer power sources was virtually complete by the end of the 1930s.[8]

A much more efficient power source than steam engines, electric motors made power instantly available when and where it was needed at the flick of a switch. Electric motors cost less than a steam outfit and required neither an additional engine house nor constant attention from a crew. In adopting electric power, mills had several options. Engineers recommended installing motors with individual drives, but it was possible to use motors to power different groups of machines or a single large motor connected to the line. Individual-drive motors eliminated the need for cumbersome belts and shafts, which permitted more-flexible

Drawing, W. R. Fee,
cottonseed huller, patented
11 August 1857, U.S. Patent
Office. Courtesy, Library of
Congress.

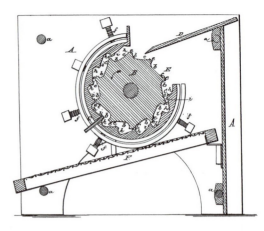

arrangements of machinery. It was also advantageous to be able to turn
a single motor on and off for cleaning and repairs, or for moving seed to
prevent decomposition, without affecting the entire power system.[9]

About 1867 oil mills started ginning cottonseed for a second or third
time to remove as much as possible of the remaining cotton fiber. The
delinting machine, known as a linter or delinter, resembled a regular gin
stand, but the saws had more and finer teeth and were placed closer together. Linter saws had to be sharpened every day. The delinting process required so much power that it usually cost mills more than they
earned from the sale of the short fibers or linters. Removing most of the
linters, however, minimized loss of oil during the hulling process, when
bits of oily kernels came into contact with lint-covered pieces of hull that
soaked up oil like sponges. Better separation of the hulls and meats
could also be achieved after lint removal, and it made the hulls and cake
less linty and more desirable to cattle feeders.[10]

The first delinting machines had to be fed by hand. Lint blown into
a separate room was manually collected several times a week and put
into a baling press. Later delinting equipment automatically brushed or
sucked linters from the saw teeth, formed them into sheets similar to cotton batting, pressed, and baled them in a continuous operation. The price
of linters determined the amount removed above the minimum required
for efficient processing.[11]

The dusty linters rooms left workers covered with a white film and
subject to colds, coughs, and other respiratory diseases, making delinting
one of the most dangerous oil-mill jobs. One writer referred to the linters room as "the Hades of the mills." On the eve of the Second World
War, progressive companies took steps to cut down the amount of dust

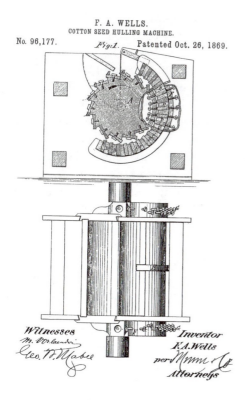

F. A. WELLS.
COTTON SEED HULLING MACHINE.
No. 96,177.   *Fig.1.*   Patented Oct. 26, 1869.

Witnesses
M. Worlaender
Geo. W. Mabee

Inventor
F. A. Wells
per Munn & Co
Attorneys

Drawing, F. A. Wells, cottonseed hulling machine, patented 26 October 1869, U.S. Patent Office. Courtesy, Library of Congress.

and encouraged workers to wear masks. Sparks hitting the highly flammable lint caused numerous fires.[12]

Reginned seed next had to be hulled. During the first half of the nineteenth century, the lack of an efficient cottonseed huller had been the greatest technological barrier to successful cottonseed crushing. The variable size and condition of seed made it difficult to design a machine suitable for hulling all types. Dry, mature seed hulled easily, but the hulling process frequently mashed damp, immature seed. In 1857 William R. Fee of Cincinnati invented the most successful of some sixteen hullers patented before the Civil War. Fee's bar huller cut cottonseed into pieces, rather than hulling by "a grinding action." Seed fell between a revolving cylinder and a stationary concave surface, each equipped, according to Fee, "with cutting edges with deep intervening furrows." The force of the cutting blows knocked the kernels from the hulls, making it easier to separate the two parts of the seed.[13]

Cottonseed hullers would be improved many times during the coming years, but the cutting or cracking principle employed by Fee became the standard for the industry. F. A. Wells of Memphis patented a knife huller in 1869 that was widely used during the late nineteenth century. A huller of that type was described in 1877 as "a heavy cylinder, provided with knives that pass between teeth so close together that the seeds are cut in two or three pieces." Huller knives with multiple cutting edges had to be sharpened frequently and reset at just the right angle. "It required eighteen hours for us to change the knives," said one mill superintendent, "keeping us away from Sunday school and church." The pneumatic hullers of the 1930s, which cracked the hulls and sucked them off the meats by air, could be changed in two hours. A man who had worked for an Oklahoma cottonseed-oil mill before the Second World War described hulling as "the most difficult thing in an oil mill."[14]

Following decortication, meats and hulls were separated by another series of screens. Hulls went into storage for later use. The pieces of kernel were crushed to a finer, more uniform texture in preparation for cooking. A Texas mill of the late 1860s had a crusher similar to an olive press that "used large hollowed out stones in which heavy stones on edge rolled over the bed and crushed the seed thrown on it." Other pioneer mills had two iron rollers that mashed the kernels into flakes as they fell between them. Eventually, three, four, or five sets of chilled iron rollers placed one on top of the other came to be standard crushing equipment in oil mills. Rolling produced thin flakes like oatmeal that cooked more rapidly and uniformly.[15]

The crushed or flaked meats went into large steam-heated cooking pans or kettles equipped with mechanical stirring paddles. Cooking coagulated some of the albuminous waste matter and facilitated the removal of oil by making it more fluid. During the early years of the cottonseed industry, proper cooking required great care and judgment on the part of the cook because the moisture content of seed varied from year to year, at different times during the same season, and from place to place. Cooks frequently sampled the hot mixture. "Some say they cook by smell, some by feeling, and others by time," reported the writer of a manual for mill superintendents. He advised using all three methods, because there were no "set rules" for cooking. The cook had to add moisture to dry kernels before cooking them. Meats that had not been crushed uniformly or cooked sufficiently to remove excess moisture formed hard balls that tore the press cloth and left green spots in the cake. During the 1930s automatic processes replaced "cooking by feel" in many mills.[16]

Early kettles contained about seven hundred pounds of meats, an amount that filled one press. The "cooker" or "heater man" sampled a batch by withdrawing some of the mixture through an opening in the side of the kettle. After each batch of meal had been cooked, a kettle had to be emptied, cleaned out, and reloaded. Because cooking time varied depending on the amount of moisture in the meats, bottlenecks could occur during the cooking process. Eventually, manufacturers developed more efficient methods that involved the use of several kettles stacked one on top of the other. Stack cookers minimized delays, because they could be programmed to complete a batch at fixed intervals in coordination with press-room schedules. After cooking for a set period of time, the meal dropped from the top kettle to the one beneath it and so on until cooking had been completed. The cooked meats then went into a holding kettle that kept them at the proper temperature until the batch was needed for the next stage of processing.[17]

Stacked kettles could also be used to cook meal continuously instead of in batches, but the process had to be monitored carefully. When an operator removed meal from the bottom cooker, an equal volume automatically moved down from each of the kettles above it. Unless properly controlled, meal sometimes failed to move through the cookers at a uniform rate, resulting in undercooked or overcooked meal.[18] A pressure cooker developed at the University of Tennessee during the late 1930s reduced cooking time to twelve to fifteen minutes, which eliminated the need for multiple kettles that cooked meats a total of one and a half to two hours but completed batches at shorter intervals. Automatic controls reduced the amount of labor needed in the cooking process. By more thoroughly destroying oil cells, pressure cooking also facilitated the removal of additional oil from the meats.[19]

Once the meal had been heated to the proper temperature, the press crew formed it into rectangular shapes and enveloped it in a porous material that would permit oil to drain out under pressure but prevent most of the meal particles from contaminating the oil. For many years that was a laborious and time-consuming task.[20] Several descriptions of cottonseed crushing in 1881–82 provide detailed accounts of cake forming just before the process became more mechanized. First, large bags had to be sewn to a uniform size following a template. The handmade sacks were hung beneath the six spouts or holes of a revolving stand called "the Devil." Laborers dipped hot meal from troughs underneath the cookers and put it into the porous bags hanging from the stand. Because meal expanding under pressure might rupture the bags, workmen placed them between hinged boards or inside horsehair mats whose leather backs sometimes had fluted inside surfaces to permit oil to escape under pressure.[21]

A steam-powered cake former invented in about 1883 eliminated the old process of filling bags with cooked meats. English patents for molding machines had been issued in 1856 and 1872, the first being hand operated and the second power driven. The American machine used light pressure to mold cakes into a standard size and to make them more compact so that additional cakes could be put into each press. Even though the early cake former had to be loaded by hand, it increased the efficiency of preparing cooked meats for the presses and paved the way for more automated processes. By 1900 an operator pulled a lever that deposited a fixed amount of meats on a six-foot-long strip of camel's hair press cloth spread on a steel plate. After the ends of the thick cloth had been manually folded over the meats leaving the sides uncovered, the mixture was lightly pressed between the steel lower plate and an indented upper plate, producing a cake twelve inches wide and forty inches long.[22]

The boxes of late-nineteenth-century hydraulic presses had open ends, perforated or channeled bottoms, and solid sides, which is why the ends but not the sides of preformed cakes had to be covered by press cloth. Substituting strips of press cloth for handmade meal bags reduced the amount of labor needed, even though mills still had to hire women to repair tears in the cloth on special sewing machines. Press cloth constituted one of the most expensive items used in hydraulic-press mills. One writer called it the "evil genius of the oil-mill business." Treated carefully, a cloth could be used six to seven hundred times, but improperly cooked meats or rough handling shortened the life of press cloths. The search for a less-expensive substitute for camel's hair after the decimation of Russian camel herds during the First World War resulted in the widespread use of human hair from China and Japan in press cloth.[23]

Extracting oil from the meats was the major function of crushing mills. Although some of the mills built just before and after the Civil War used screw presses similar to those that compressed cotton into bales or pressed apples for cider, the hydraulic press dominated the first century of American cottonseed processing. Based on principles of Pascal and invented in England in 1795, the hydraulic press began to replace older methods of pressing in English and French vegetable-oil mills during the first half of the nineteenth century.[24]

Before the steam-powered cake former became available, hydraulic presses contained no more than five or six compartments. A six-box press had the capacity to crush only five tons of seed every twenty-four hours. Because bags of meal enclosed in wooden or leather mats were four or five inches thick, a press with more than six boxes would have been too tall for anyone to reach the top compartments. With preformed cakes only one and a half inches thick, press capacity increased. Some mills began to put two cakes separated by a metal plate into each press box, and machinery manufacturers followed their lead by developing boxes with perforated plates to replace the thick leather-backed hair mats.

The steel box-frame hydraulic press used in most American mills after its development in the late nineteenth century had four vertical supports, an iron plate on top, and the hydraulic unit at the bottom. The frame held up to fifteen moveable, perforated or channeled, steel plates with sides. Once the preformed cakes had been placed in the boxes, the hydraulic piston in the cylinder at the bottom pushed one plate or box against another toward the top of the press, thus compressing the meats and forcing out the oil. To prevent leaking hydraulic fluid from contaminating the oil, crushers used cottonseed oil in the cylinder. Hydraulic pressing required considerable labor and created difficult working conditions. Leaking oil and scattered bits of meal created a dirty environment, and press-room temperatures rose as high as 110 degrees.[25]

Hydraulic presses became more reliable and powerful and press capacity tripled from five to fifteen tons during the late nineteenth century. Cakes made at a New Orleans mill in 1860 weighed approximately seven pounds. By the end of the century, presses contained twelve to fifteen compartments instead of five or six, and produced cakes weighing from twelve to fourteen pounds. In the 1930s cakes weighed twenty pounds. In the 1880s D. A. Tompkins believed that a yield of thirty gallons of oil per ton of seed was a "fair" result. In 1928 a Department of Agriculture official estimated that on the average a ton of cottonseed yielded about forty gallons of oil.

Because the light presses of the early 1880s rarely had gauges, operators had to guess the amount of pressure being exerted. To avoid damaging the presses and the brittle cast-iron boxes, pressmen tried not to exceed twenty-five hundred pounds of pressure per square inch. A high percentage of oil remained at those relatively low pressures, so that cakes tended to be light yellow, soft, and oily.[26] Stronger presses with steel boxes enabled operators to increase pressures. By the early twentieth century more than four thousand pounds of pressure per square inch could be applied. As pressure went up, the amount of residual oil de-

Cottonseed-oil mill, West Memphis, Arkansas, 1936. LC-USF 6336-D. Carl
Mydans, photographer. Courtesy, Library of Congress.

clined from 12 or 13 percent at the end of the nineteenth century to as
low as 6 or 7 percent in the most-efficient mills on the eve of World War
I, although the average was closer to 9 percent. In 1941 meal produced
by hydraulic presses still contained from 5 to 8 percent oil. The harder,
darker, less-oily cakes produced by the plate presses and higher pressures
caused dissatisfaction among animal feeders. Grinding the cake into meal
or breaking it into pellets made the residue easier for animals to eat.[27]

The small profit margins generally characteristic of cottonseed crushing meant that time lost in the press room could cause a mill to fail. Managers placed great emphasis on speed and keeping up the level of production. At the turn of the century, a press had to sit for fifteen or more
minutes after the maximum pressure had been applied while the oil
drained out. Between the world wars presses were operated on fifteen-
or twenty-minute schedules with presses arranged in groups of four or
three. Mills allowed twelve to fifteen minutes for pressing, approximately
eighteen minutes for draining, and up to five minutes for loading and
unloading presses. Some crews could load and unload a press in two
minutes. In one- and two-press mills, crews had free time between charg-

A truckload of cottonseed coming into a cottonseed-oil plant, Clarksdale, Mississippi, 1939. LC-USF 34-52492-D. Marion Post Wolcott, photographer. Courtesy, Library of Congress.

ing and discharging the presses, but with three or more presses they worked almost continuously.[28]

After pressing had been completed, cake strippers removed the press cloths and set cakes aside to dry. They became as hard as boards and resembled strips of carpet. A mill engineer who began his career in 1882 recalled that "skinning the cake" was "the hardest work in the press room," and that "if the cakes became cold it was beyond human power to skin them." In time, manufacturers developed automatic cake-stripping machines. The dark red crude oil that flowed over the sides of the presses and into settling tanks on the floor below had to be handled carefully or much would be lost in the refining process. Bits of meats remaining in the oil formed a sediment that soured in hot weather if the oil were not pumped into fresh tanks or filtered.[29]

Although hydraulic pressing dominated the first century of cottonseed crushing in the United States, other extraction technologies existed. Solvent extraction was suggested by an Englishman in 1843, proposed by a French chemist in 1876, and used in England as early as 1885. In

Unloading cottonseed, Waco, Texas, 1939. LC-USF 33-12505-M3. Russell Lee, photographer. Courtesy, Library of Congress.

1880 an Atlanta resident called solvent extraction "a new process" but added that "our best authorities, in the South, do not regard it as likely to prove successful." The only American cottonseed-oil mill known to have adopted solvent extraction before the mid-twentieth century was a Wilmington, North Carolina, plant that employed naphtha as early as 1883 and persisted in its use at least until 1906. During the second half of the nineteenth century, mills in Germany, France, Italy, and other European countries tried solvent extraction on a variety of oil seeds and materials.

More oil can be recovered from cottonseed by solvent extraction than by any other method, but the early process had serious drawbacks. Besides being expensive, solvents could explode. Traces of solvent also remained in the oil and meal. In 1930 David Wesson reported that chemists were overcoming the difficulties of refining cottonseed oil produced by solvent extraction, but the solvent process did not become economically feasible in the United States until labor costs went up during the 1940s.[30]

The screw press or oil expeller developed by the V. D. Anderson Company of Cleveland, Ohio, and patented in 1903 became available to American cottonseed-oil mills about 1905, after being used in linseed and corn-oil mills. A prototype, described as "a conical screw rotating within a perforated hollow cone," had been patented in England thirty years earlier.

Unloading cottonseed, Waco, Texas, 1939. LC-USF 3434724-D. Russell Lee, photographer. Courtesy, Library of Congress.

Anderson expellers improved oil extraction and, operating in a nearly continuous fashion, required considerably less labor than hydraulic presses. The work normally done by twenty-one men in the press rooms of large hydraulic mills could be done by three men. Expellers eliminated the need for preformed cakes and press cloth. Flaked meats went from the rolls into the expeller, which was constructed like a giant sausage grinder with a rotating worm shaft or screw and slits in the barrel or outer covering to allow oil to flow out. High pressure resulted from the seed being compressed into a progressively smaller space and egress being restricted by the small size of the opening at the end of the barrel. The residual meats were extruded in the form of large flakes rather than as cakes.[31]

Used initially in Texas, Oklahoma, and Louisiana, where much cottonseed meal was fed to livestock, the first expeller mills pressed cottonseed without hulling or cooking it. The resulting "cold press cake," which actually became hot from the friction of grinding, made a good feed, its advocates claimed, and could be manufactured more cheaply than sepa-

Cottonseed in storage, Waco, Texas, 1939. LC-USF 34-3429-D. Russell Lee, photographer. Courtesy, Library of Congress.

rate meal and hulls. Southeastern cottonseed mills, by contrast, sold most of their meal as fertilizer, and hulls had to be kept to a minimum to achieve the levels of ammonia required by state laws. Hulling and heating were consequently incorporated into the expeller process.

By 1912 more than eighty U.S. mills employed expellers. American expeller mills formed their own trade association in 1910 after hydraulic-press users rebuffed them. Subsequently, the number of screw presses declined sharply in the United States as the first generation of expellers experienced metal fatigue and other difficulties. A man who had worked in an Oklahoma expeller mill recalled that "it had to be the best steel in the world to work it through." Early expellers did not operate efficiently unless a certain proportion of hulls had been mixed with the meats, but considerable oil was lost when seed was pressed whole and uncooked. Currently all screw-press mills hull and cook cottonseed.[32]

In the beginning, expeller oil and meal proved to be inferior to that produced by hydraulic methods. Moreover, the low wages paid to southern labor before the Second World War more than offset the relatively expensive initial investment and power required for expeller operation.

Pushing cottonseed onto a conveyor, Waco, Texas, 1939. LC-USF 34-34748-D. Russell Lee, photographer. Courtesy, Library of Congress.

Even after labor costs rose, cottonseed crushers were slow to turn to alternative technologies. The fact that screw presses could not be easily incorporated into existing hydraulic mills and that the oil had to be handled differently by refiners retarded their adoption. Declining raw material supplies and increasing labor costs hastened the adoption of more efficient oil removal processes. Since the 1950s solvent extraction and screw pressing, in that order, have been the preferred extraction technologies for new mills.[33]

As Nathan Rosenberg emphasized in *Technology and American Economic Growth,* many factors affect the rate of change to new technologies. Abundant supplies of cheap labor and raw materials and scarcity of capital in the Cotton Belt together with the seasonal nature of crushing and the small size of many mills combined to retard the adoption of more efficient but costly extraction methods until the second half of the twentieth century. In western Europe, on the other hand, the relatively higher costs of labor and oleaginous materials made it economically feasible to

Sweeping up around
the machines that
remove linters from
the seed, Waco, Texas,
1939. LC-USF 34-
34753-D. Russell Lee,
photographer.
Courtesy, Library of
Congress.

invest in more-efficient extraction technologies several decades earlier
than in the United States.

The first American crushers acquired mill equipment from abroad,
adapted machinery from other American industries, or had it made by
local foundries. New Orleans, one of the two cities where commercial
cottonseed milling began in 1855, had good local foundries by that date,
because of their patronage by sugar makers. During the 1870s American
iron and machinery companies, located for the most part in northern
states with strong machine tool establishments, began to meet the needs
of the growing cottonseed industry.[34]

The Carver Gin Company of East Bridgewater, Massachusetts, dominated the market for delinting machines at the end of the nineteenth century. In 1869 W. F. Pratt of East Bridgewater patented a machine for
delinting cottonseed that became known as the Carver linter. Although
southern companies manufactured most cotton-gin machinery, Carver
was strong in the New Orleans area, where commercial cottonseed milling began. Later, the Carver Gin Company made other types of cotton-

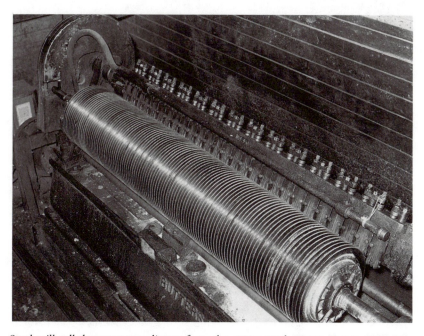

Steel mill roll that separates linters from the cottonseed, Waco, Texas, 1939. LC-USF 34-34802-D. Russell Lee, photographer. Courtesy, Library of Congress.

oil machinery and after the turn of the century ceased to supply cotton gins altogether.[35]

In western Ohio and the New York City area, the two major centers of flaxseed milling in the United States, makers of equipment for linseed-oil mills manufactured cottonseed hullers and adapted linseed press-room machinery to cottonseed processing. Until the mid-1880s the major supplier of press-room equipment in the United States was the Columbian Iron Works of William Taylor & Sons in Brooklyn. More than half of the presses owned by cottonseed-oil mills in 1885 had been manufactured by the Taylors. The W. P. Callahan Company of Dayton, Ohio, sold the second largest number of cottonseed presses. Smith & Vaile, also of Dayton, ranked third. During the 1880s the Buckeye Iron & Brass Company of Dayton made rollers and press plates and subsequently expanded into other lines of oil-mill machinery. The Cardwell Machine Company of Richmond and the Van Winkle Company of Atlanta and Dallas were among the few southern firms to make and sell press-room machinery outside their local markets. During the 1880s they lagged far behind Taylor, Callahan, and other leading machinery makers.[36]

Laborer stuffing linters into a baling machine, Waco, Texas, 1939. LC-USF 34-34771-D. Russell Lee, photographer. Courtesy, Library of Congress.

Easy credit terms provided by machinery firms, as well as the willingness of some companies to invest in oil mills that used their equipment, encouraged the building of hundreds of oil mills from 1880 to 1914. The leading promoter of a Demopolis, Alabama, oil mill described himself as "being associated with parties largely interested in the construction and operation of cotton seed oil mills, and in the manufacture of new and improved machinery for working up cotton seed." He and his associates proposed to take one-third of the shares.[37]

The Van Winkle Company of Atlanta and Dallas, manufacturers of machinery for cotton gins, oil mills, and saw mills, aggressively competed for cottonseed machinery and building contracts during the late nineteenth century. Edward Van Winkle, the son of a New Jersey textile-machinery manufacturer, founded the company in Atlanta in 1870. By selling half of the business to W. W. Boyd a decade later, Van Winkle had the resources to establish a branch in Dallas in the mid-1880s. The selling tactics of the company are evident in the following announcement from the *Manufacturers' Record:* "Messrs. Strand And Van Winkle, of Hillsboro, Texas, and Atlanta, Ga. intend to erect a cottonseed-oil mill at

Workman pushing a hand-truck of linters, Waco, Texas, 1939. LC-USF 34-34758-D. Russell Lee, photographer. Courtesy, Library of Congress.

San Marcos, Texas. They have made the citizens a proposition for the erection of a $35,000 plant, which will doubtless be accepted and its conditions met." As a result of such promotional campaigns, the Van Winkle company organized, financed, and equipped a number of oil mills during the 1880s and 1890s. The Murray Gin Company of Dallas purchased the western branch of the Van Winkle Company in 1897 and the Atlanta branch in 1912.[38]

The rapid growth of cottonseed-oil mills after 1880 stimulated machinery companies to improve their products. Many of the innovations had been patented in some form years earlier in England or on the Continent. The W. P. Callahan Company developed the first successful American steam-powered cake former and one of the earliest plate-box presses before being surpassed by the still more innovative Smith & Vaile Company at the end of the 1880s. A Texan who entered the crushing business in about 1884 recalled that users of Callahan's "so-called first improvements bore the brunt of experimentation," for the cast-steel boxes his company manufactured broke under pressure, and Callahan declined to buy at least one patent that might have made his boxes more durable. For

Oil mill belts and the machinist, Waco, Texas, 1939. LC-USF 34-34823-D. Russell Lee, photographer. Courtesy, Library of Congress.

the next decade or more, cottonseed crushers considered Smith & Vaile the most progressive American manufacturer of oil-mill machinery.[39]

In 1900, A. W. French, an MIT graduate in civil engineering, established the French Oil Mill Machinery Company in Piqua, Ohio. Manufacturers regularly visited their clients and demonstrated their products at meetings, but French concentrated more than most on solving practical problems. French worked on machinery problems with oil men at meetings and in their mills and eventually established a model oil mill in Piqua to test equipment scientifically. As a result of the steady stream of inventions and improvements that flowed from the company, it became the largest of its kind in the world. When oil-mill machinery makers organized an association in 1918, they made A. W. French their chairman. Several machinery companies went out of business in the 1920s, but the French Oil Mill Machinery Company survived, despite the accidental death of its founder in 1925.[40]

Beginning in the 1880s the processes of cottonseed-oil production also underwent significant improvement. In 1884 D. A. Tompkins, one of the New South's most ardent promoters of industrialization, con-

Working on the hydraulic presses, Waco, Texas, 1939. LC-USF 34-34822-D. Russell Lee, photographer. Courtesy, Library of Congress.

structed a mill in Charlotte, North Carolina, that he described as "the first cotton seed oil mill ever built from designs made by the modern type of educated and practical American engineer." Before that date crude-oil mills had generally been constructed by millwrights and carpenters.[41]

Finding the classical curriculum offered by the University of South Carolina inadequate for what he perceived to be the needs of the post–Civil War South, Tompkins had transferred to the Rensselaer Polytechnic Institute in Troy, New York. Following his graduation in 1873, Tompkins went to work for engineer Alexander Lyman Holley, who had adapted the Bessemer process to the mass production of steel in the United States. Through his plant designs Holley sought to minimize rehandling and to facilitate "as continuous a flow as possible of materials within the works." In 1882, after acquiring additional practical experience in the North, Tompkins established an engineering business in Charlotte. When asked by Fred Oliver, a New York state capitalist, to design a cotton-oil mill in Charlotte, Tompkins specified the most modern machinery available and applied Holley's "continuous process" ideas.

In 1887 Tompkins planned and built for the newly incorporated Southern Cotton Oil Company eight large, modern oil mills. Over a period of two decades, the Tompkins Company built wholly or in part more than 250 oil mills across the Cotton Belt, as well as fertilizer plants, refineries, and one hundred textile mills. Its well-equipped foundry manufactured cleaning, separating, and hulling equipment for oil mills. The company acted as agent for Smith & Vaile and other machinery companies, and like the machinery manufacturers and other individuals and firms associated with cottonseed processing, the Tompkins Company provided plans and specifications for those wishing to hire their own builders.[42]

During the last two decades of the nineteenth century, when mechanical improvements were steadily increasing, the analysis of cottonseed products remained largely a matter of guesswork, except in mills owned by the major corporations. "We had no analysis to scratch our heads about," commented one mill superintendent about "days gone by." Chemical studies began to replace rule-of-thumb estimation in most mills during the first decade of the twentieth century. Early tests measured the amount of oil that remained in cakes, and as a result, oil loss during the extraction process declined and the protein content of cake and meal became more standardized. Laboratories serving oil mills provided standards of expected yields of oil and cake and comparative information about the performance of other mills. By the 1920s in the larger mills the managerial staff customarily met each morning to hear the chemical analysis of the previous day's production as a guide for that day's work.[43]

As the crushing industry expanded after 1880, construction, equipment, and manufacturing costs declined. In 1881 a Louisiana mill owner estimated that his small, ten-ton-capacity mill had cost more than twenty thousand dollars to construct, or about two thousand dollars per ton for plant and machinery. A 50 percent reduction in building and equipment costs occurred before the decade ended. In 1887 D. A. Tompkins estimated that a plant capable of crushing one hundred tons of seed in twenty-four hours could be built and equipped for about one hundred thousand dollars, half the cost of older one-hundred-ton mills with their smaller capacity presses. Actual construction figures for the original Southern Cotton Oil Company mills ran slightly higher than Tompkins's estimates, but one thousand dollars per ton for a mill in working order was the accepted industry figure at the turn of the century. Even taking into account the late nineteenth-century deflation of more than 1 percent annually, the cost of building and equipping crude-oil mills declined sig-

Removing Chinese hair mat from cottonseed cake, Clarksdale, Mississippi, 1939. LC-USF 34-52503-D. Marian Post Wolcott, photographer. Courtesy, Library of Congress.

nificantly, and that must have contributed to the proliferation of cotton-seed-crushing plants in the South.[44]

The cost of processing cottonseed underwent a similar decline during the late nineteenth century. Average manufacturing costs per ton of seed dropped from about $5.00 to $6.00 during the early 1880s to from $2.50 to $3.50 at the end of the century. Those figures did not include the cost of raw materials, which remained the same or increased. Inflation caused operating costs to escalate during the First World War. The estimated cost of processing a ton of cottonseed in 1917–18 was thirteen dollars. From 1927 to 1930 the cost of converting a ton of seed into crude products ranged from about eight dollars in the largest mills to nearly fourteen dollars in the smallest.[45]

Black males provided most of the labor in cottonseed-oil mills, as they did in southern saw mills, sugar houses, blast furnaces, mines, tobacco-redrying plants, and leaf-stemming departments of chewing tobacco factories. Many of the manufacturing jobs held by blacks went on in dangerous or unpleasant environments and required great physical strength.

Hydraulic presses and machine for removing cottonseed cake from mats after oil
has been removed, Waco, Texas, 1939. LC-USF 34-34783-D. Russell Lee, photographer. Courtesy, Library of Congress.

Because the South had a large pool of unskilled black workers in the
major cotton-growing areas and most of the work was physically de-
manding, black men made up the work force from the outset. Southwestern mills hired some Mexicans and whites; it is not known whether in
those situations the races worked together or were segregated into crews
doing different jobs.[46]

Black men dominated the oil-mill labor force to a greater extent than
any other industry in the southern states. A 1927 Labor Department survey of 4,586 male workers showed that 83 percent of them were black,
14 percent white, and 3 percent Mexican. Because only 67 out of a total
of 547 oil mills reported, the study may have underrepresented blacks.
Country mills using farm labor probably employed the highest percentage of black laborers. Mill photographs uniformly show black workers.
As late as 1939 close to 90 percent of all wage earners at Southern Cotton Oil Company mills were black. By comparison, the highest percentage of black workers in southern saw and planing mills was about 63
percent in 1910 and 1920. Between 1890 and 1930, 60 to 79 percent of

Oil being pressed from cottonseed, Clarksdale, Mississippi, 1939. LC-USF 34-52498-D. Marion Post Wolcott, photographer. Courtesy, Library of Congress.

the workers in southern tobacco factories were black, and in the southern iron and steel industry in 1930, 81.8 percent of the common laborers were black.[47]

For most of the first century of cottonseed processing, mill workers had little prospect of bettering their economic position, because the South had an abundance of low-wage, unskilled workers. Cottonseed-oil mills paid lower hourly wages than most other southern manufacturing enterprises, and the cost of mill labor as a proportion of total operating expenses generally fell below 7 percent before the Second World War. In 1943, after minimum wage laws and social security taxes had increased hourly wages, the U.S. Department of Labor calculated that labor costs represented only 7.9 percent of the value of cottonseed products in the Southeast and 8.2 percent in the Southwest.[48]

Black "cooks" and press-room workers earned more than their unskilled co-workers. In the 1880s mills tried to retain skilled cooks by paying them as much as $2.50 a day. The going rate for most other oil-mill jobs and for much unskilled industrial labor at the time was $1.00 or $1.25 a day, although South Carolina textile workers reportedly earned

Removing cottonseed cake from hydraulic presses after the oil has been removed, Waco, Texas, 1939. LC-USF 24-34825-D. Russell Lee, photographer. Courtesy, Library of Congress.

an average of 78 cents per day. Daily wages on cotton farms in 1880 ran around 40 or 50 cents with rations or 75 cents without them. Because the work was seasonal, oil mills had to pay slightly more than the wage for year-round jobs.[49]

Deflation and other factors reduced mill wages and labor costs materially during the last two decades of the nineteenth century. The per ton cost of labor in 1896 varied from 75 to 95 cents. A decade earlier labor costs had fluctuated from $1.84 to $2.04 per ton. Henry Hammond reported in 1896 that labor's proportion of operating expenses had declined because of the increased automation of machinery, the greater experience of workers, and the lower wages being paid. Oil-mill wages across the Cotton Belt averaged 60 to 70 cents a day during the crushing season, or from 5.0 to 5.8 cents an hour. Hourly rates would have been lower for unskilled laborers and higher for cooks, press men, and linterroom crews. By way of comparison, adult male textile workers in North Carolina during the 1890s earned 40 to 50 cents a day, southeastern cotton mills paid adult spinners 2.3 to 4.5 cents an hour for seventy hours a

Stacks of cottonseed cake, Clarksdale, Mississippi, 1939. LC-USF 34-52499-D.
Marion Post Wolcott, photographer. Courtesy, Library of Congress.

week between 1890 and 1900, and tobacco stemmers, leather tanners, and unskilled construction workers in the Southeast during the same period averaged 10, 11, and 8 to 12 cents an hour, respectively.

Before the First World War, the Farmer's and Ginner's Cotton Oil Company of Austin, Texas, paid unskilled labor $1.00 and skilled labor $2.00 a day. Wartime inflation caused daily wages of the company's unskilled and skilled oil-mill workers to jump to $2.25 and $4.50. In a study of oil-mill wages for 1927 the Department of Labor found the average to be 24 cents an hour, or $2.88 for a twelve-hour day. The Depression brought a marked drop in wages. The Southern Cotton Oil Company commonly paid an average of 20 cents an hour before the Fair Labor Standards Act went into effect in 1938, but some small country mills paid as little as 5 cents an hour in 1933.[50]

Poignant letters and petitions sent to President Roosevelt and federal officials in 1933 and 1934 reveal the hardships endured by oil-mill employees during the Depression. In some places authorities would not permit unemployed and underemployed cottonseed workers to get public jobs at forty cents an hour. Many reported that they could not feed their families on what they earned. Most communications came from white machinists and other skilled workers, in some cases speaking on behalf of their fellow workers, black and white. Generally, the writers asked that their names not be revealed. "We are afraid to put our name," explained an anonymous black writer, "for they will kill us Before night."[51]

The lowest pay in the cottonseed industry went to laborers who worked in mills with one to three presses in small towns in the Carolinas, Georgia, Alabama, Mississippi, and Louisiana. Farm workers generally manned these "cotton-patch" mills and returned to farm labor or other seasonal work when the crushing season ended. In England, too, workers in small-town mills sought agricultural jobs after the crushing season. Urban oil mills were less likely to use agricultural labor. Crushers claimed that the cost of living was lower in small communities and that most of the workers received housing and other benefits that city laborers lacked. In 1933 it was estimated that fifty-eight small mills, about 13 percent of the total, were still in operation.[52]

Workers fell into three general categories: temporary, normal, and dormant. Mills acquired as much as three-quarters of their seed during the fall cotton harvest. At that time extra men had to be hired to unload and move seed. Temporary unskilled laborers lost their jobs as soon as the volume of seed coming into a mill diminished to the point that the normal crew could handle operations. The number of workers steadily declined as the season progressed. When crushing ended, operations managers discharged most of the remaining unskilled workers.[53]

Mills increasingly retained a skeleton crew throughout the year in order to avoid competition for skilled cooks and pressmen at the beginning of each season. Some of these dormant workers weeded the grounds, did repairs, and cleaned the buildings after the crushing season. Gradually, many crushing mills added auxiliary enterprises suitable for their off-season months or made arrangements with companies doing a large summer business to employ a few cottonseed workers. Fertilizer mixing became an early adjunct to oil milling in the southeastern states, where tobacco and cotton farmers during the late nineteenth century applied large amounts of fertilizer to their fields. Ice making was an important sideline by the turn of the century, as activity peaked when oil mills would otherwise be idle. Crushers also engaged in cotton ginning, feed mixing, cattle feeding, coal selling, and other enterprises that often proved to be more profitable than milling.[54]

Until 1914 cottonseed crushers had little difficulty finding enough workers to man the mills at modest wages. At their annual conventions oil men discussed all of the troubling aspects of their industry in detail, but until the draft and better-paying jobs caused acute labor shortages during the First World War, crushers almost never mentioned labor. Labor questions again came to the forefront of crushers' concerns during the early New Deal, when National Recovery Administration officials sought to reduce hours, create more jobs, and increase wages.[55]

Like most other southern industrial workers, those in oil mills had no organization to represent them during most of the years covered by this study. Attempts by the Knights of Labor to organize unskilled southern laborers in the 1880s proved to be premature. A Cotton Oil Helpers Association organized by the Knights of Labor in Memphis in 1882 collapsed following a strike for higher wages. During the 1890s, and to an even greater extent after the outbreak of World War I, oil-mill workers joined thousands of African Americans who went North in search of better-paying jobs. Peter Gottlieb concluded that many who moved to Pittsburgh between 1916 and 1930 had first acquired a measure of independence and job information by working in seasonal southern industries such as cottonseed processing, cotton ginning, and fertilizer production, or in lumber, mining, railroad building, and other nonagricultural work. When the right to organize was written into National Recovery Administration labor codes, there was renewed interest in oil-mill workers among union officials. During and after the Second World War, several unions affiliated with the CIO organized some cottonseed-oil mills, but widespread unionization of the industry did not take place.[56]

Most managers, superintendents, plant engineers, and other salaried employees and skilled workers learned cottonseed milling on the job. At least some machinists served apprenticeships. During the late nineteenth century a few engineering companies offered short courses in oil-mill operation, but it is doubtful that a significant number of oil men got their training that way. Typically, a young man began work in a low-level position in the office or plant and worked his way to a supervisory job.[57]

A mill superintendent speaking to cottonseed crushers in 1911 attributed the failure of most oil mills to the lack of "competent" superintendents. They needed to know steam and electrical engineering and chemistry, have building skills, and understand cotton ginning, yet no training courses existed in the South. Moreover, the superintendent's job paid only about twelve hundred dollars a year, not enough to attract people with the requisite technical skills. The larger companies could afford to employ trained engineers to improve manufacturing efficiency, but their smaller competitors could not. After the First World War, a firm of cottonseed chemists in Memphis added an engineer to its staff to provide consulting services to area mills. During the 1920s Texas A&M and North Carolina State College began offering short courses and degrees in oil-mill engineering and chemistry.[58]

In a 1927 talk to oil-mill superintendents, "Why Oil Mills Cannot Get Good Young White Men in the Mills to Learn the Business," the president of the Interstate Cotton Seed Crushers' Association pointed out that even college graduates had to have experience before they could run an oil mill, but they hardly received enough money to live on while learning the ropes. Why, he asked, would they want to work twelve hours a day, not counting the time it took to go and come, six or seven days a week, in dirty, dusty, unheated mills that couldn't afford to pay people after crushing stopped?[59]

Except for the added step of hulling seed from short-staple cotton, American cottonseed-oil mills relied on techniques commonly used in processing other oil seeds. With the multiplication of oil mills and their spread across the Cotton Belt after 1880, machinery manufacturers began to improve their products. The cost of manufacturing declined and yields of oil and cake improved. In the twentieth century, regular chemical analysis of cottonseed products further increased productivity. An abundance of cheap labor in the Cotton Belt, the seasonal nature of the crushing industry, and the small size of many mills retarded the adoption of more efficient but expensive processing technologies. The hydraulic press dominated cottonseed crushing until the second half of the twentieth century.

Although now all but forgotten, cottonseed milling was widespread in the Cotton South for more than half a century. Cottonseed processing also stimulated a number of modest auxiliary enterprises in the cotton-growing states. The increasing demand for cottonseed oil that fueled the crushing industry's expansion between 1880 and 1914 was in large part a result of refining improvements made by several large northern companies during the late nineteenth and early twentieth centuries that enhanced the flavor and quality of their products.

CHAPTER 5

Cottonseed-Oil Refining
and Manufacturing

They make olive-oil out of cotton-seed oil, nowadays, so
that you can't tell them apart. . . . There now, smell them,
taste them, examine the bottles, inspect the labels. One of
'm's from Europe, the other's never been out of this country.
One's European olive-oil, the other's American cotton-seed
olive-oil. Tell 'em apart? 'Course you can't. Nobody can.
People that want to, can go to the expense and trouble of
shipping their oils to Europe and back—it's their privilege;
but our firm knows a trick worth six of that. We turn out the
whole thing—clean from the word go—in our factory in
New Orleans: labels, bottles, oil, everything.

Mark Twain, *Life on the Mississippi*

There is no line of argument to justify the sending of cotton
oil or any of its manufactured products into the world under
false names. . . . This adulterating practice has been carried
entirely too far.

C. W. Burkett and C. H. Poe, *Cotton*

Dark red in color and often unpleasant in flavor and odor, crude cottonseed oil must to be refined before it can be used for most purposes. The
goal of refining is to produce a neutral oil with a nearly perfect balance
between glycerin and fatty acids combined as glycerides. Free fatty acids
and nonfatty substances such as pigment and bits of hull are removed
from crude oil during the refining process. Following the commercial
beginnings of American cottonseed processing in 1855, more than half a
century elapsed before chemists through research and experimentation
developed the clear, bland, odorless cottonseed oil and creamy white

shortening that set the standard for all edible fats of vegetable origin produced in the United States. A chemist writing in 1904 summed up the progress that had been made in refining cottonseed oil:

> The real advancement of the last twenty years in the cottonseed-oil industry has been made by the refinery. While there have been many improvements in the machinery of the crude-oil mills, the process is today practically what it was many years ago, but when we turn to the refinery, the tremendous strides which have been made in the improvement of the refining methods result in a product so superior to the article produced years ago, that industries utilizing the oil, on account of this improvement, can use greater quantities of the oil than ever before.[1]

During the infancy of the industry a number of crushing mills refined the crude oil they produced. Although a few mills carried on refining operations, consolidation took place rapidly. Technological advances in the late nineteenth century made refining a complex and expensive process; it proved to be more economical to refine crude oil on a large scale. Most of the improvements came from the laboratories of large northern corporations, whose trained chemists worked on refining problems. The leading refineries were located in cities with mass markets for cottonseed products and access by rail to large crude-oil supplies.[2]

Within the notoriously secretive industry, nothing remained more closely guarded than refining methods. Unlike the Louisiana sugar planters described by John Alfred Heitmann, who shared ideas and technology, cottonseed-oil men rarely exchanged information during the early years of the industry. "The oil is clarified by a secret process," said a visitor to the New Orleans mill of F. M. Fisk in 1860. Twenty years later a speaker describing the industry told his audience that "every oil refiner has his own peculiar process—supposed to be known only to himself." The early history of cottonseed-oil refining is thus shrouded in mystery.[3]

Since the late eighteenth century, when the new science of chemistry was being established in western Europe, two processes for purifying fats and oils had been known. One used sulfuric acid and the other a caustic alkali to combine with extraneous substances and facilitate their removal. Alkalies proved to be more satisfactory for refining crude vegetable oil. Many of the techniques later applied to the refining of oils for edible purposes grew out of chemists' efforts to improve illuminating oils, soaps, and candles before the middle of the nineteenth century.[4]

James Hamilton Couper (Cooper), the leading promoter of the large cottonseed-oil mill erected at Natchez, Mississippi, in 1834, attributed its failure primarily to inefficient refining methods. Although the best refining technology available had been adopted, the process had been difficult to use and caused considerable oil to be lost. When Cooper outlined the prospects for manufacturing cottonseed oil in the United States to the U.S. Patent Office in 1844, he pointed out that organic chemists were on the brink of discovering less expensive and more effective refining methods. Couper could have been referring to research on the use of caustic alkalis for purifying fats and oils, which led to French and English patents in 1842 and 1846, or to an American patent granted in 1844 for a new method of refining oils.[5]

The open-kettle method dominated American cottonseed-oil refining until the 1930s. The first generation of refiners used a variety of vessels, including sugar kettles, for purifying the oil. The method required skill and judgment. Refiners decided how much alkali to use in a batch of crude oil by tasting it, then adding caustic soda to a sample until it produced the desired color.[6]

The rapid spread of railroads during the last two decades of the nineteenth century revolutionized the transport of cottonseed oil and paved the way for large-scale refining. At first oil was shipped in barrels, many of which had held kerosene, whiskey, or varnish. Early refiners complained that crude cottonseed oil absorbed strange flavors from improperly cleaned secondhand barrels. In 1882 New Orleans refiner Jules Aldigé described having seen hundreds of barrels of cottonseed oil in France and Italy that had been ruined by being shipped in coal-oil containers. About that time T. R. Chaney of the Howard Oil Company in Dallas and Houston contracted with a Standard Oil Trust subsidiary in Texas to fill its empty tank cars with cottonseed oil for the return trip north. Large companies that refined and manufactured products from cottonseed oil acquired fleets of railway tank cars. By the turn of the century most cottonseed oil was moved within the United States by rail, although barrels were still used to ship it overseas.[7]

When chemist David Wesson visited refineries in 1887 he found that practices had altered little since the industry's beginnings. Subsequent years brought rapid changes. Mass production transformed all of the late-nineteenth-century refining industries—petroleum, sugar, and lard, as well as vegetable oil. Leading cottonseed-oil refineries installed kettles large enough to hold sixty thousand gallons of oil, the capacity of a railway tank car. Some later kettles held double that amount. The increased scale required far greater investment in capital goods, and that limited the number of companies that could afford to engage in refining.[8]

At the end of the nineteenth century, cottonseed oil chemists learned that the amount of free fatty acids present in a given batch of crude oil provided a good indication of its quality. The more free fatty acids there were, the greater the loss of oil during the refining process. During the late 1880s, chemists began to perform laboratory tests to determine the acidity of crude oil, and refiners made price reductions or rejected crude oil with high levels of free fatty acids. The probably apocryphal story was told about a crusher who, when informed that a shipment of crude oil from his mill contained excessive free fatty acids, wired the refinery: "Never had any fatty acids in the mill. Must have been put in tank by railroad. Claim declined."[9]

With the inauguration of chemical analysis, refining became more precise and less a matter of individual judgment. When crude cottonseed oil arrived at turn-of-the-century refineries, it was weighed and tested for acidity to see how much caustic soda or lye would be needed. Refiners heated the oil in large steam-jacketed kettles equipped with mechanical agitators or pipes that delivered compressed air for stirring the mixture and bringing all parts of the oil into contact with the alkali. Caustic soda dissolved in water was sprayed on top of the oil, and the mixture was agitated for thirty or forty minutes. Rapid heating to 120 or 130 degrees caused the alkali to combine with the free fatty acids, coloring matter, and other impurities in the crude oil to form brown soapy flakes or particles that clumped together and settled to the bottom of the kettle. This mass, known as foots, formed a soap stock. After settling for up to twenty-four hours, the refined oil would be pumped into clean tanks and washed to remove all remaining caustic soda. Care had to be taken in the use of heat to remove moisture, lest it injure the flavor of the oil.[10]

Refining losses varied, depending on the quality of the seed from which the crude oil had come, the acidity of the oil, and the volume being refined. In 1881 the average loss of oil during the refining process was believed to be about 18 percent. Refining on a small scale tended to increase the amount of oil lost. A Charleston refinery soliciting business from oil mills in 1892 warned that refining losses would run from 8 to 25 percent, depending on the grade of crude oil, but losses might be considerably higher than that in the case of lower grade oils. By 1919 refining losses averaged 9 percent.[11]

Much of the oil produced by refineries through the 1880s went to southern Europe, where it was sold as a cheap substitute for olive oil or was used to adulterate olive oil exported to the United States and South American countries. A mixture of 75 percent or more of cottonseed oil and 25 percent or less of olive oil frequently passed for the genuine article before the passage of pure food laws during the late nineteenth and early twentieth centuries. The smaller amounts of oil sold in the United States were used primarily for soap making.[12]

The foots, or soap stock, that remained after refined oil had been drawn off the settling tanks became the raw material for industrial and laundry soaps. Those soaps tended to have a disagreeable odor. Refined cottonseed oil went into higher grade toilet soaps as a less-expensive substitute for the olive oil traditionally used by soap makers. Some of the soap manufacturers who experimented with cottonseed oil just after the Civil War experienced serious problems. A large Philadelphia soap maker reported that a gummy brown substance oozed from his cottonseed oil soap after it had been stored. Nevertheless, a number of early oil mills manufactured soap as a side line.[13]

As personal cleanliness came to be associated with middle-class status during the second half of the nineteenth century, soap sales increased in the United States and soap manufacturing became the specialty of a few large companies. Soap making ceased to be an auxiliary enterprise of cottonseed-oil mills, but refined cottonseed oil became an important ingredient in many soaps. In 1878, after trying a variety of oils as a replacement for olive oil, Procter & Gamble succeeded in manufacturing an all-purpose soap from cottonseed oil that the company marketed as Ivory. The American Cotton Oil Company, producer of the Gold Dust Twins washing powder, Lever Brothers, the makers of Lifebouy, and other soap companies used large amounts of cottonseed soap stock and oil in their products during the late nineteenth and early twentieth centuries.[14]

Cottonseed oil commanded higher prices when used for edible purposes, but refining techniques had to be improved considerably before the American public fully accepted it as food. In turning refined cottonseed oil into edible products, manufacturers had to conform to established preferences of color, taste, and texture. Consumers expected oil to be light green or straw colored, butter to be a golden yellow, and lard to be white.

Resistance to trying new food products explains why cottonseed oil first entered the marketplace disguised as olive oil, lard, and butter.

Greatly increased production of cottonseed oil after 1880 lowered prices, and by the end of the century much of the refined oil sold in the United States went into the manufacture of compound lard, or compound, as it was often called. Generally composed of a mixture of animal and vegetable fats, compound did not always contain lard. Demand for lard was especially great in the United States because American breads, unlike most European varieties, incorporated shortening to make them light and flaky. Because hog supplies did not keep pace with demand for shortening, lard prices remained relatively high during the second half of the nineteenth century.

It was common to adulterate lard by mixing it with water and beef fat or tallow, so the addition of cottonseed oil was a natural step. Because tallow made lard stiff, manufacturers used cottonseed oil to soften their shortening mixtures, as well as to reduce their cost. With the availability of large supplies of cheap cottonseed oil, the compound industry grew six or sevenfold from the late 1880s to 1914. More influenced by lower prices than by food prejudices, bakers and other industrial users accepted the new shortenings, and the large volume of their business caused the rapid growth of compounds.[15]

Few people realized that cottonseed oil was being added to shortening. When the N. K. Fairbank Company began to adulterate lard with cottonseed oil, it transported the oil in tank cars labeled "Garden City Dairy Company of Chicago" to keep people from finding out its secret. An attempt to corner the lard market in 1883 made the general public more aware of the practice of adulteration. Knowing that hog production had declined, Milwaukee resident Peter McGeogh bought future contracts for the delivery of a larger amount of lard than could normally have been made from the available swine. For a short time McGeogh was known as the Lord of Lard, and lard prices escalated. As a larger volume of deliveries than expected poured in to fulfill the contracts McGeogh had bought, someone suggested that the lard might have been adulterated. McGeogh subsequently refused to accept a shipment of lard on the grounds that it was not the pure prime steam lard his contract called for. At the request of McGeogh, the Chicago Board of Trade undertook to settle the matter by asking a number of chemists to examine samples and render a judgment. Lacking adequate tests for determining adulteration, the expert witnesses failed to reach an agreement, and the Board of

Trade exonerated the packing company. Lard prices plummeted, McGeogh was financially ruined, and the reputation of Chicago lard suffered.[16]

Widespread publicity of the attempted lard corner gave the American pure-food movement a boost. Massachusetts enacted a food-labeling law in 1886 and other states followed its lead, with a national pure food and drug law being passed in 1906. Congressional hearings on an 1888 bill to require proper branding of shortenings elicited much testimony concerning the wholesomeness of cottonseed oil. The lard substitute Cottolene, a yellow-colored shortening composed of 80 to 85 percent cottonseed oil plus beef stearine as the stiffening agent, was the first cooking fat made with large amounts of cottonseed oil that advertised its major ingredient. In 1893 Swift introduced Cotosuet and Armour launched Vegetal.[17]

Improved refining methods paved the way for cottonseed oil to become the principal ingredient of various shortenings. Early refining methods had left an acrid flavor and an unpleasant odor in much cottonseed oil, which limited its acceptance by consumers. "There is a great deal of very mean oil put upon the market" for cooking purposes, one cottonseed crusher complained in 1882. "Families . . . buy it and throw it away, and afterwards refuse to use cottonseed oil." Cottonseed crushers urged refiners to treat prime crude oil with extreme care and label it for cooking purposes.[18]

Refineries produce what is known in the trade as summer yellow, or butter, oil. Besides being used as an adulterant of olive oil, it became a major ingredient in European and American margarine during the late nineteenth century as manufacturers began to substitute cottonseed oil for some of the animal fat in margarine. French chemist Hippolyte Mège-Mouriès created oleomargarine in 1869 after Emperor Napoleon III offered a prize for a good butter substitute for his soldiers. Limited supplies of butter had made it a luxury item. Mège-Mouriès made an acceptable spread by churning melted beef fat with milk. Dutch butter traders became the leading European manufacturers of margarine, which they sold principally to residents of British and German industrial cities. Cottonseed oil lowered the cost of margarine, or butterine, and helped to give it the color of butter, although color had to be added as well.[19]

Because people expected lard to be white, the cottonseed oil used to adulterate lard and as an ingredient of most compound lards and shortenings had to be colorless. Initially, refiners bleached summer yellow cottonseed oil by exposing it to sunlight for long periods. The method had first been used during the early nineteenth century to take the orange color out of palm oil. Cincinnati refiners bleached vegetable oils in the sun before the Civil War. The N. K. Fairbank Company of Chicago had large, shallow bleaching vats on its factory roof up to 1879. Bleaching in sunlight had serious drawbacks: the lengthy process tied up capital for months and caused deterioration. Refiners of cottonseed oil thus began to experiment with bleaching agents, such as carbon, and with different kinds of white clays that had been used for centuries to absorb grease.[20]

In about 1880, major changes in bleaching methods resulted from the work of several chemists, among them W. K. Allbright. Following his graduation from MIT, Allbright went to work for the N. K. Fairbank Company, which hired the young chemist in 1879 to improve its refined lard. At the time, most meat packers sold their fat by-products to other companies, which then refined and marketed lard. N. K. Fairbank was one of the leading lard refiners in the United States. Soon, Armour, Swift, and other meat packers added the lucrative sideline to their meat-packing businesses.

During the 1870s, N. K. Fairbank and other lard producers lost much of the firmer types of pork fat to the new margarine industry, but they gained a hardening agent, oleo stearine, a by-product of oleo-oil manufacture. Meat packers made oleo oil for the margarine trade by separating the liquid and solid components of beef fat. Lard refiners reduced costs by secretly adding cottonseed oil to their products and stiffening it with oleo or beef stearine. An early N. K. Fairbank lard formula called for about eight parts oleo stearine, thirty-two parts cottonseed oil, and sixty parts lard. The proportion of cottonseed oil could not be increased until bleaching and deodorizing processes were improved.[21]

Because MIT had not offered a course in vegetable-oil refining, Allbright proceeded by trial and error to try to upgrade the quality of the cottonseed oil used in Fairbank's compound lard. Half a century later, David Wesson said that "an Oriental gentleman," from Morocco he thought, had explained to Allbright that olive oil was bleached in his country by being mixed with clay and allowed to settle. Allbright obtained satisfactory results with fuller's earth, which English and European refiners had used in the early nineteenth century to take the color out of vegetable oils. The American patent for bleaching with fuller's earth went to Alexander W. Winter in 1880. Six years later Allbright secured a patent for fuller's earth applied with steam to facilitate removal of oil from the used earth.

Allbright also invented cooling rolls to harden lard products and prepare them for shipping. The practice of European manufacturers, following the invention of refrigeration in the United States, was to spray iced water on margarine to cool and solidify the emulsion. Rapid cooling prevented shortenings from crystallizing, and beating gave them a creamy texture. Both the bleaching and cooling processes enabled manufacturers to add more cottonseed oil to lard compounds. Within a few years after Allbright joined the company, N. K. Fairbank substantially increased the amount of cottonseed oil in its products and became the world's largest producer of lard compounds. Chemistry had enabled Fairbank to outdistance its competitors.[23]

Before being marketed as a salad oil, cottonseed oil must be "winterized." That is, the stearines that begin to solidify and give the oil a milky or cloudy color as it gets colder than forty to forty-five degrees Fahrenheit are removed. Glycerin, an alcohol, combines with three fatty-acid molecules to form triglycerides. The principal glycerides in edible fats are stearine, palmitin, linolein, and olein. All have about the same amounts of carbon and oxygen but different proportions of hydrogen. The solidity of a fat varies according to the amount of hydrogen contained in its predominant glycerides. Stearine and palmitin, found principally in solid fats, have the most hydrogen, whereas linolein, the major component of oil, and olein have the least. To produce cottonseed oil that will remain clear and liquid at cold temperatures, refineries cool the oil until the stearine precipitates. The stearine is then pressed or centrifuged out, leaving a clear salad oil. Producing winter oils required an ice plant and expensive equipment, which smaller refineries could not afford.[24]

The winterization process was developed in France during the early nineteenth century, when much effort went into the refining of vegetable oils for use in lamps. Winterization was achieved by placing oil in outside tanks during cold weather. It is possible the French took the lead in refining and using vegetable oils because the English blockade during the Napoleonic Wars reduced the amount of whale oil available in France. In the interior of the United States, where whale oil was expensive, companies used the winterization process to produce lard oil by taking the stearine out of melted animal fat. The stearine removed in the process went into tallow candles to make them harder, so that they could be sold as cheaper substitutes for beeswax candles.[25]

It took several decades for refiners to learn how to deodorize refined cottonseed oil satisfactorily. Frying with cottonseed oil produced a disagreeable odor, and many people found edible cottonseed-oil products objectionable. Some fats had been deodorized since the 1840s by being boiled in water and having steam blown through them. In about 1891, Henry Eckstein, a chemist at the N. K. Fairbank Company, discovered in England that blowing steam through hot oil in an enclosed vessel or still caused fatty acids carrying unpleasant odors, flavors, and coloring material to volatilize and escape with the steam through holes in the top of the kettle. Deodorization enabled manufacturers to increase the amount of cottonseed oil in lard substitutes to 80 percent or more. Further improvement in deodorization came from James Boyce of the American Cotton Oil Company laboratory.

At the beginning of the twentieth century, David Wesson perfected the deodorization process in his private laboratory by exposing cottonseed oil to superheated steam in a vacuum. Carrying out the deodorization process in a vacuum minimized oxidation and made it possible to lower the temperature and prevent the oil from acquiring a cooked taste. Wesson Oil, produced by the Southern Cotton Oil Company, commemorated Wesson's achievements in the chemistry of fats.[26]

Hydrogenation enabled manufacturers to produce shortenings made exclusively of vegetable oils. As long as American and European compound lard and margarine manufacturers had to depend on oleo stearine as the stiffening agent for their products, they remained at the mercy of the meat packers who supplied it and charged high prices. As noted earlier, solid and liquid fats differ chemically in the amount of hydrogen they contain; lard has more hydrogen, oil less. Molecules of the fatty acids that predominate in solid fats have absorbed all the hydrogen they can; they are saturated and have a relatively stable molecular structure. The fatty acids in liquid vegetable oils, on the other hand, are largely unsaturated and less stable. One of the double bonds between each of the carbon atoms is capable of taking up more hydrogen or oxygen. Absorption of oxygen is undesirable because that causes a fat to become rancid, but the addition of hydrogen raises the melting point and makes the fat harder.[27]

At the turn of the century, European chemists learned to saturate oils with additional hydrogen by introducing the gas into heated oil using nickel as a catalyst. By that process, oil could be either partially hydrogenated to the desired consistency or hardened until it became completely brittle and more cottonseed oil had to be added to make it pliable. Procter & Gamble bought the right to use the 1903 patent of a German chemist, Dr. Normann, from Joseph Crossfield & Son, a British soap-manufacturing firm. Much work had to be done before the practical application of hydrogenation could be achieved. In 1911 Procter & Gamble unveiled the first all-vegetable shortening produced for the retail trade. It was called Crisco, short for crystallized cottonseed oil. When the U.S. Supreme Court invalidated Procter & Gamble's exclusive use of the Normann patent after the First World War, the way was cleared for other companies to manufacture all-vegetable shortenings.[28]

Hydrogenation made it possible for almost the total output of refined cottonseed oil to be used in the production of shortening, for saturation with hydrogen made even lower grade oils more stable and less likely to become rancid. Besides enabling manufacturers to create more stable and uniform vegetable shortenings, hydrogenation also gave them the ability to create specialized shortenings for bakery products. Crackers made from hydrogenated shortening keep better and can be stored longer than those made from lard, and fried foods need to be cooked in fats that do not solidify on the surface when they cool. As commercial baking expanded and became more scientific, all-vegetable shortenings tailored to meet a wide range of specific needs became more desirable, and sometimes even more expensive, than the lard they replaced. The properties of hydrogenated cottonseed oil can be controlled, whereas the consistency of lard varies according to the time of year, the variety and age of the hogs used, and the type of feed they have eaten.[29]

Cottonseed-oil chemists made many valuable contributions to the development of their industry, yet most of the pioneers have been forgotten. Because his name still appears on the label of a popular salad oil, David Wesson is the best-known oil chemist. Born in Brooklyn the year the Civil War began, Wesson attended Brooklyn Polytechnic Institute and graduated from MIT in 1883 with a degree in chemistry. The N. K. Fairbank Company hired Wesson in 1884 to work on its soap products, but after the company became part of the American Cotton Oil Trust (a merger of many oil companies) in 1887, Wesson was given the job of analyzing cottonseed and cottonseed products at the company's oil mills in different parts of the Cotton Belt. Wesson considered his analytical work to be the first systematic chemical analysis of cottonseed products carried out by a cottonseed oil company. Wesson also worked on the development of Cottolene, the popular butter-colored shortening produced by Fairbank.

The American Cotton Oil Company transferred Wesson to its Wilcox Lard & Refining Company in Guttenberg, New Jersey, in 1890 and made him chief chemist. There Wesson set up a laboratory and studied cotton-

seed oil and other edible fats. In 1898, after being away from the industry for several years, Wesson started his own research laboratory and
worked on the problem of removing the unpleasant odor and taste that
still characterized much cottonseed oil. By 1899 Wesson was ready to
market an improved oil that he named for himself but never patented.
The Southern Cotton Oil Company agreed to manufacture and distribute
the oil, and Wesson accepted a job as manager of the company's technical department. In 1900 Wesson supervised the establishment of a Southern Cotton Oil Company refinery at Savannah, Georgia, where he guided
the development of Snowdrift shortening. He also set up laboratories for
the Southern Cotton Oil Company at Bayonne, New Jersey; Marburg,
Germany; and Manchester, England, between 1908 and 1912. Wesson
held the position of technical adviser with the Southern Cotton Oil Company until his death in 1934.

Wesson worked on a number of projects related to cottonseed—hydrogenation, making paint from cottonseed pitch, extraction of glycerin
from soap stock, stabilization and standardization of oils and shortenings,
and a centrifugal method of removing oil from soap stock. With beef steaks
costing forty cents a pound and cottonseed meal only about six cents a
pound in the 1920s, Wesson thought the time would come when ham-
burger made from cottonseed would find a market. He developed flour,
steak, and a sausage called "Wessona" from cottonseed meal, and according to one writer, dinner guests "eagerly awaited courses" that Wesson
"concocted with his own synthetic products." Wesson correctly forecast the
use of vegetable proteins, but acceptance came much later than he anticipated, and they are made from soybeans rather than cottonseed.[30]

Between 1911 and 1930, Wesson wrote a number of articles about
the cottonseed industry and his experiences as a chemist that are an important source of information about the state of crushing and refining
during the late nineteenth and early twentieth centuries. In a 1920 article, Wesson summed up the achievements of cottonseed-oil chemists.
They took the guesswork out of refining by standardizing the process
and helped crushers and refiners reduce manufacturing losses through
analyses of cottonseed products. But most important, by developing hydrogenation and improving bleaching, deodorization, and other processes,
they transformed cottonseed oil into edible foods of great commercial value.
Chemists helped demonstrate the feeding value of cottonseed meal and
developed new industrial products from cottonseed hulls and linters.[31]
Chemistry made the modern cottonseed-oil industry possible.

American chemists, drawing on basic scientific research carried out by European scientists, transformed the cottonseed-oil industry from one that relied primarily on rule-of-thumb methods and the experience of skilled employees to one based on analysis and scientific investigation. In his account of the modernization of the Louisiana sugar industry, John Alfred Heitmann characterized the embrace of science by Louisiana sugar makers during the late nineteenth century as "rather remarkable for the times." But the N. K. Fairbank company hired its first chemist in 1879, and the large cottonseed corporations that came into existence during the 1880s also engaged in the "organized industrial research" by "university-trained experts" that Heitmann considered insignificant elsewhere in American industry before the pre–World War I decades and that A. Hunter Dupree in *Science in the Federal Government* described as "rare" before the 1920s.[32]

On the eve of the Second World War, nine-tenths of the cottonseed oil manufactured in the United States went into food products. Large-batch refining in open kettles and other traditional processes were discontinued as researchers developed more continuous methods of refining, which saved time and plant space, reduced oil loss, and improved odor and color. With continuous refining, the skill of individual refiners is of less importance.[33]

In contrast to the widespread proliferation of crushing plants after 1880, refining and manufacturing became highly concentrated during the late nineteenth century. The economics of cottonseed processing meant that oil mills located near cotton fields could save money on freight, whereas for maximum efficiency, refineries needed to operate on a large scale and be located at major shipping points within reach of both crude-oil mills and large consumer markets. The number of mills refining their own crude oil and making soap and oils for edible and industrial purposes declined, and a small number of refineries, principally under northern control, came to dominate the industry. Large-batch refining, which transformed the secondary phase of processing during the last decades of the nineteenth century, resulted in significant economies of scale but required such expensive equipment that few companies could marshal the resources. Organization of the cottonseed industry during the late nineteenth century reflected the different directions being taken by crushing and refining.

CHAPTER 6

Organization of the
Cottonseed Industry

It is best, gentlemen, that we should assemble together once
a year, to compare notes, and talk with one another as to what
is best for our common interest, as well as for purposes of social intercourse, which tend to smooth our respective paths,
bury any asperities which may exist, and produce better and
more harmonious understandings among us.

Col. T. A. Nelson,
president, Cotton Seed
Crushers' Association, 1879

The structure of the cottonseed industry of the United States
roughly resembles a pyramid. At the base are over 1 1/2 million
cotton growers, above whom are successively some 12,625
active cotton gins, 471 cotton-seed crushing mills, and about
70 cotton-seed oil refineries.

George Marshall,
"Cottonseed—Joint Products
and Pyramidal Control," 1938

Organization of the cottonseed industry followed a pattern common to
many manufacturing industries in the United States during the late nineteenth century. Oil men formed price-fixing pools and a trade association in the 1870s as their first response to common problems. These voluntary organizations worked well as long as the industry remained small,
but they failed to cope with the crisis that enveloped cottonseed processing during a period of rapid growth and increased competition for
seed during the early 1880s.[1]

Higher raw material costs and lower product prices caused a merger of most of the crude-oil mills and refineries between 1884 and 1886. The resulting American Cotton Oil Trust, reorganized as a holding company in 1890, rapidly transformed itself from a horizontal combination of mills and refineries into a vertically structured company that controlled every stage of processing, from raw material purchases to the manufacturing and marketing of well-differentiated cottonseed products. Through the integration of mass production and mass distribution, the American Cotton Oil Company became one of the first modern industrial corporations in the United States. By the early twentieth century, a few large companies dominated cottonseed-oil refining and manufacturing. Their expensive refining technology, chemical research, sales networks, and popular name-brand products created powerful barriers against new entries.

The modest expense of building small oil mills and the high cost of transporting cottonseed, meal, and hulls produced a different outcome in the crushing stage of the industry—the multiplication of crude-oil mills throughout the Cotton Belt between 1880 and 1914. Because most of the acute problems of the industry occurred during the initial phase of processing, crushers took the lead in forming cottonseed price-fixing pools and state and national trade associations.[2]

The Cotton Seed Crushers' Association, the first general organization of cottonseed processors in the United States, formed in Cincinnati in 1878. Creation of a trade association is usually a signal that an industry is experiencing difficulties. The Cotton Seed Crushers' Association grew out of a meeting oil men held in New Orleans in 1876 to discuss high cottonseed prices and other problems. Refiners were not permitted to join the association unless they also owned crude-oil mills.[3]

In 1879 crushers representing twenty-seven mills met at the association's first annual convention in Memphis. Seven mills each from Louisiana and Tennessee were represented, four each from Arkansas and Mississippi, two apiece from Alabama and Texas, and one from Georgia. Despite the building of a number of new mills after 1879, membership in the association remained static through 1881 and came primarily from mills in the lower Mississippi Valley, where crushing on a commercial scale began. The number of mills involved in the association jumped to fifty in 1882 and sixty-three in 1883. At its maximum strength, the Cotton Seed Crushers' Association enrolled about 60 percent of the operating oil mills—28 of 46 mills in 1880 and 63 of 104 mills in 1883—and it probably represented an even higher proportion of total crushing capacity.[4]

As Louis Galambos observed in his study of the textile industry, trade associations, like medieval guilds, sought to achieve stability through cooperation, a goal people in the United States regarded with suspicion because of the national commitment to competition.[5] During the life of the first cottonseed trade association, 1878–87, its members focused primarily on drawing up trading rules to govern transactions between buyers and sellers of cottonseed products and promotion of cottonseed oil and cake at home and abroad. Two problems that preoccupied crushers were the enormous loss of seed sacks suffered by the mills annually and the deliberate addition of trash to cottonseed by many ginners.

The Cotton Seed Crushers' Association resembled the "loose" organizations being formed by many industries in the United States after the Civil War. It paid a secretary to keep records but had no employees to administer affairs between annual meetings. The executive board seldom met, except during yearly conventions. To pursue the association's interests, the president appointed committees to investigate problems and plan responses. The association reimbursed them for any expenses. A few members took committee responsibilities seriously and worked on them between meetings, but many did not. Although some crushers wanted the association to set maximum cottonseed prices, there is no evidence that it attempted to control prices, unlike many trade associations of the late nineteenth century that fixed both product prices and production quotas.[6] During the early 1880s, serious problems of overproduction, lagging demand, and cutthroat competition for seed convinced many that the industry's salvation required measures stronger than voluntary association.

Between 1880 and 1885 the number of oil mills tripled. Production of cottonseed products exceeded demand and prices declined. In 1881, following the lead of Spain, the Italian government imposed an "almost prohibitory" tariff on American cottonseed oil. Exports to Europe dropped from a high of 147,241 barrels in 1879–80 to only 12,186 barrels in 1881–82. After reaping "extremely gratifying" returns during the previous decade, oil men began to see their profits squeezed between high seed costs and low product prices. During the 1883–84 crushing season, few Mississippi Valley mills earned a profit.[7] That made many crushers receptive to the idea of a merger, as neither cottonseed buying pools nor the trade association had been effective in checking competition from new mills. In the long run, abundant supplies of cheap cottonseed oil made it attractive to shortening and soap manufacturers and created a large domestic market for "Dixie olive oil," but the short-term crisis prompted an attempt at monopolization of the industry.

John Van Houten Lewis of Cincinnati urged his fellow cottonseed processors as early as 1881 to form "a more systematic and binding association for the general good of all engaged in the crushing business." Three years later Lewis took the lead in bringing about a merger of more than a dozen cottonseed companies to form the American Cotton Oil Trust. According to later testimony, the original organizers included John V. Lewis and his Cincinnati associates, F. H. Baldwin and W. H. Anderson; John W. Cochran, Lewis's Memphis partner; Zebulon Ward, Edmund Urquhart, James W. Miller, and Logan H. Roots of Little Rock; Jules Aldigé of New Orleans; J. F. O'Shaughnessy of Nashville; J. J. Green of Mississippi; Moses Frank of Atlanta; George O. Baker of Selma, Alabama; and Judge Howard of Texas.[8]

John V. Lewis, who spearheaded the drive to consolidate cottonseed-oil mills and refineries, became involved in cottonseed processing soon after the Civil War, when the industry began to revive in the Mississippi Valley. Born in Cincinnati in 1839, Lewis joined the Quartermaster Department of the United States Army in 1861 as a civilian and the following year enlisted in the department. Captain Lewis arranged transportation for Union troops operating in the Memphis territory. After his resignation in 1865 with the rank of major, Lewis worked as the Memphis agent for the Atlantic and Mississippi Steamship Company. He moved to St. Louis in 1867 and the next year became the partner of J. Bonnell Smith in a Cincinnati cottonseed-oil business. Smith supervised the technical details of cottonseed processing and Lewis handled business matters. Lewis could have become interested in cottonseed processing either in Memphis or in Cincinnati, because both cities had milling operations before the Civil War, and the steamship line that employed Lewis as its Memphis agent may have transported cottonseed to Cincinnati for processing.[9]

Sometime during the early 1870s Lewis withdrew from his partnership with Smith and formed John V. Lewis & Company. Within a few years Lewis's company operated crushing mills in Arkansas, Mississippi, and Tennessee. By the late 1870s John V. Lewis & Company ranked as one of the three largest refiners of cottonseed oil in the United States, the other two being the Aldigé Company of New Orleans and the Union Oil Company of Providence, Rhode Island. In 1881 John V. Lewis & Company bought the Future City Oil Works of St. Louis. Most accounts of the American Cotton Oil Trust give Lewis the major credit for its formation.[10]

At the end of the 1870s, businesses engaged in both mass production and mass distribution hardly existed in the United States. In *The Visible Hand,* Alfred Chandler noted that modern American industrial corporations took one of two routes to growth. Some large corporations developed when individual companies installed continuous-process machinery or otherwise speeded up the flow of goods through their factories and then moved into advertising and sales in order to dispose of the increased production. That avenue was taken by manufacturers of breakfast cereals, matches, cigarettes, canned foods, and soaps. Similarly, some manufacturing firms grew by offering new or specialized services, such as the repair shops and sewing demonstrations provided by the Singer Sewing Machine Company. The second path to industrial growth, taken by cottonseed processors, was for a number of small companies producing similar products to merge and subsequently engage in mass distribution and mass production.[11]

In order to merge businesses in different states without attracting the publicity that would have surrounded efforts to secure incorporation by private legislative act in each of those states, the cottonseed-oil men borrowed the trusteeship idea from John D. Rockefeller's Standard Oil Trust created in 1882. The American Cotton Oil Trust thereby became the second organization of its kind in the United States. Owners of enterprises that merged to form the trust surrendered their stock to nine trustees in return for trust certificates, or in a few cases for cash. The nine trustees managed all of the properties as a whole. The American Cotton Oil Trust came into existence between 1884 and 1886, during the first wave of business mergers in the United States. Following consolidations in the petroleum-refining and cottonseed-processing industries, trusts were formed in the sugar, whiskey, lead, cordage, and linseed-oil industries later in the decade. A second and larger wave of mergers occurred between 1895 and 1904.[12]

From her analysis of turn-of-the-century mergers, Naomi Lamoreaux concluded that the conditions predisposing firms to consolidate were rapid growth of an industry engaged in the mass production of undifferentiated products followed by a period of economic depression leading to price wars in which no firm managed to achieve dominance. The pattern of "expansion, depression, and consolidation" identified by Lamoreaux applies to the cottonseed industry. Beginning in 1880 cottonseed-oil mills multiplied rapidly, production of cottonseed products exceeded demand, and cottonseed price-fixing agreements that had functioned reasonably well broke down, causing the price of raw materials to rise. The general business depression underway by 1884 aggravated all of the industry's problems. Even though price wars took place in the area of seed purchasing rather than product sales, the results were the same for the cottonseed industry as for other troubled businesses: drastically reduced incomes for the competing firms and an interest in consolidation.[13]

Initially, organizers of the American Cotton Oil Trust offered the owners of productive, debt-free mills and refineries trust certificates worth more than three times the value of their businesses. Trustee John Scott testified at a New York Senate hearing in 1888 that the stock had been watered about 400 percent. Watered stock encumbered the trust with a heavy debt at the outset, but such inflation seemed necessary to attract other participants as rapidly as possible. It became common practice in the United States for promoters to offer large stock bonuses as inducements to merge even though that caused the consolidated companies to be overcapitalized. One of the properties acquired by the trust in 1884 was the United States Cottonseed Cleaning Company owned by some of the trustees. Although it had assets of only $19,000, the company had been capitalized at $1.5 million, and its stockholders received $5 million worth of trust certificates. The company's patents for a new method of cottonseed cleaning made it seem valuable at the time, but the process proved to be virtually worthless.[14]

Working with great secrecy, the promoters of the American Cotton Oil Trust accumulated considerable property, thanks to the generous inducements offered. Aggressive competitive practices helped to persuade holdouts to join the trust, or financially ruined some of them. Owners of a Fort Worth, Texas, oil mill blamed its failure in the 1880s on the trust's use of its near monopoly of cottonseed products to obtain reduced freight rates. Rockefeller and the Standard Oil Trust had shown how size could be used to force concessions.[15]

By 1886 the American Cotton Oil Trust reputedly controlled all desirable mills west of the Mississippi River and approximately 60 percent of all cottonseed-crushing plants in the United States. At that point so many mill owners clamored to join that trustees could acquire property at closer to its market value. When questioned about the trust in 1886, Louis Hanauer of Memphis replied that the pool of six mills he headed did not want to get into the oil trust, but that it might become too strong for them to "stand against it." Hanauer's group of mills soon became part of the trust.[16]

It has been estimated that at its peak the American Cotton Oil Trust embraced more than 80 percent of the total crushing capacity of the

United States and nearly all of the refineries. When the Cotton Seed Crushers' Association met in Memphis in 1887 for its tenth convention, only twelve mills sent representatives. They voted to adjourn and the organization died. Because everyone expected the trust to monopolize cottonseed processing, there seemed to be no reason to maintain a trade association. Petroleum refiners had also let their association lapse following the organization of the Standard Oil Trust.[17]

Organizers of the American Cotton Oil Trust undertook to rationalize production. They closed unprofitable operations and appointed superintendents, generally former owners or managers, to run the remaining businesses. Reduction of expenses became a major goal of the trust. Its officers required uniform bookkeeping and reporting practices, and mills annually turned their net profits over to the trust. A chemical laboratory was created to check cottonseed products and provide production standards and controls. In the opinion of a Memphis reporter, the trust "rescued the industry from impending disaster and developed it" by using every part of the seed.[18]

Several policies adopted by the first trustees created ill will among some trust certificate holders, oil users, and cottonseed producers and resulted in a shakeup of the board of trustees and bad publicity for the trust. Failure to pay dividends in 1885 caused trust certificates to depreciate in value. The *St. Louis Republican* attributed the decline to a policy of selling oil below cost for the purpose of forcing independent mills to join the combine. Other contemporaries charged that the reason for lowering oil prices, and thus certificate values, had been to induce small holders to sell their trust certificates. Low oil prices may simply have resulted from the excess of supply over demand, which had initially prompted the formation of the trust. Whatever the cause, trust certificates that had traded as high as sixty dollars dropped to thirty dollars. Standard Oil certificates had been held rather than traded, which American Cotton Oil trustees had assumed would be the case with their company's certificates, but Wall Street reportedly "tempted" some of the small investors to sell.[19]

A number of certificate holders objected to the veil of secrecy that covered everything the trustees did. Frederick and John Oliver turned two profitable mills in the Carolinas over to the American Cotton Oil Trust in exchange for certificates and then could learn nothing about the conduct of business. The trustees managed the company "to suit themselves," Frederick Oliver told a reporter. "They are at liberty to vote themselves any salaries they choose, sell themselves seed if they wish, and absorb all the profits of the enterprise if they so incline."[20] The management did not issue detailed annual reports until 1891. In 1887 the Olivers and other entrepreneurs whose enterprises had been absorbed by the trust took the lead in forming a second major cottonseed-processing corporation, the Southern Cotton Oil Company. The new company attracted the support of several large users of cottonseed oil, who feared that the merger of oil mills would result in higher prices.[21]

At the end of the 1880s, the Armour meat-packing company of Chicago purchased about one-fifth of all the cottonseed oil produced in the United States as an ingredient for its compound lard. After the American Cotton Oil Trust absorbed the rival lard- and soap-making company, N. K. Fairbank, and offered to buy out the Armour lard division, P. D. Armour and his associates threatened to buy stock in the new Southern Cotton Oil Company or to build their own cottonseed-oil mills. Armour had been given an opportunity to become a stockholder in the Southern Cotton Oil Company but had declined because the other parties would not permit him to own a majority of the stock and name a majority of the directors. Instead, Armour used rumors of his involvement in the new company to negotiate a contract with the trust that permitted him to buy cottonseed oil at cost. That caused trust certificates to rise in value but did not add to the company's earnings.[22]

At the annual meeting of the American Cotton Oil Trust in July 1887, officers informed certificate holders that the company had a capital worth of nearly $42 million and had earned a profit of about $2.5 million during the previous year. In August the trust would begin paying quarterly dividends. The management announced plans to list the certificates on the New York Stock Exchange. In 1887 leading promoters of the original enterprise dominated the board of trustees.[23]

Before the end of the year, the trust's top management changed, and men connected with the Standard Oil Trust secured the top positions. Standard Oil had provided the organizational model for the American Cotton Oil Trust and there had been hauling arrangements between the two companies, but the principal investors of Standard Oil had not been interested in the cottonseed combination initially, despite rumors to the contrary. Because certificate values remained depressed, the trustees aggressively courted Standard Oil partners, several of whom decided to invest in the cotton-oil trust. News of the association caused the value of certificates to rise.[24]

The annual meeting of American Cotton Oil Trust certificate holders in October 1887 was a stormy one. The Southern Cotton Oil Company had appeared on the scene, and the November dividend promised by trust officials could not be paid. Henry M. Flagler, Jabez A. Bostwick, and other Standard Oil associates who had invested in the trust chose three new trustees. J. H. Flagler, a relative of Henry M. Flagler, replaced John V. Lewis as president. Following his ouster as president, Lewis ceased to be connected with the trust or the cottonseed industry and appears never to have successfully established himself in another line of business.[25]

A New York Senate committee investigating trusts compelled several American Cotton Oil trustees to testify in 1888. Although few in number, trusts had become synonymous with monopoly in the public mind, and as such they received a great deal of unfavorable publicity, which culminated in the passage of the Sherman Antitrust Act in 1890. Investors consequently preferred industrial stocks to trust certificates. In 1889 the trustees decided to change the American Cotton Oil Trust into a holding company under the New Jersey general incorporation law, which had recently been amended to include companies with property in several states.[26]

As the American Cotton Oil Trust wound up its affairs preparatory to becoming a holding company, its certificates dropped in value from nearly forty-two dollars to thirty-three dollars between 30 October and 1 November 1889. Trading in American Cotton Oil certificates was so heavy during those three days that little other business could be transacted on the New York Stock Exchange. Leaks about the annual report scheduled for release on the first of November caused the panic. Instead of the $2.5 million profit projected six months earlier, actual earnings had shrunk to $1.5 million. Certificate holders learned that nature and human error had caused the million-dollar loss. After the trust had purchased crude oil from "rival" mills, oil prices declined. A crop of inferior cottonseed had also resulted in products of poor quality. Later, the company revealed that President J. H. Flagler and Treasurer J. O. Moss had lost more than half a million dollars by speculating in the trust's certificates. On the advice of Winslow, Lanier, & Company and two other investment banking firms, Flagler and Moss had attempted to boost the value of American Cotton Oil Trust certificates before the reorganization, but the plan had backfired. The First National Bank of New York and the Richmond Terminal Company, as large owners of American Cotton Oil Trust certificates, helped to arrange a compromise so that reorganization as a holding company could proceed. Flagler agreed to pay back $150,000 and Moss $100,000, leaving a stock market loss of $277,511. Some of the certificate holders demanded restitution of the remaining sum by the bankers, who reportedly offered to pay $75,000.[27]

At the time of the trust's conversion into a holding company, some "water" was wrung out of the stock. Directors of the reorganized American Cotton Oil Company elected Jules Aldigé of New Orleans president. Aldigé, whose father had founded one of the pioneer oil mills in 1855, had been an early proponent of merger in the cottonseed industry. Winslow, Lanier & Company, the firm that had helped to secure financing for the original merger and for the reorganization, probably in return for a block of stock, also participated in the company's management at the highest level. Charles Lanier served a term as president of the company, and Edward D. Adams, a firm member who had been on the reorganization committee, became chairman of the board of directors.[28]

Like many large U.S. corporations at the end of the nineteenth century, the American Cotton Oil Trust and its successor company adopted the "staff-and-line" management structure developed principally by the Pennsylvania Railroad Company during the middle decades of the nineteenth century to administer its far-flung properties. Because the investment bankers who organized the merger had been involved in railway finance and John V. Lewis had early experience with railway transport, it is not surprising that the American Cotton Oil Company followed railway management policies.

A hierarchy of managers at the top, middle, and lower levels directed the diverse activities of the country's largest cottonseed corporation. Managers at staff or company headquarters in New York made general decisions that line officers carried out at the operational level. American Cotton Oil Company managers also organized the business along functional lines. Separate departments supervised purchasing, crushing, refining, research and development, transportation, and sales. Department heads reported directly to the president. To comply with state laws and avoid further litigation, the company consolidated its mills in each state and chartered separate corporations, each receiving its instructions from headquarters. The Georgia Cotton Oil Company, for example, embraced all of the American Cotton Oil Company mills in that state.[29]

Through centralized coordination of every phase of cottonseed processing, the closing of outmoded facilities, more efficient processing, accounting, and management practices, the American Cotton Oil Company achieved significant economies of scale and became one of the pioneer industrial corporations in the United States. Between 1884 and 1889 the company closed a number of outmoded mills and refineries and built some new facilities. In 1894 the organization operated 49 of the 72 crude-oil mills it owned, 10 of 15 refineries, 8 of 9 soap factories, 11 of 15 cotton gins, only a fraction of the gins controlled by the company, 2 of 3 compresses, 4 lard and Cottolene plants, 2 fertilizer-mixing plants, 1,112 seed storage houses, 355 railway tank cars, 23 box cars, plants in Rotterdam and Canada, and a chemical laboratory. Its foreign holdings made the American Cotton Oil Company one of the early multinational corporations in the United States.[30]

Not all of the company's efforts to streamline its operations succeeded. Plans to ship cottonseed oil overseas in bulk went awry. The tank steamer *Arco,* constructed for the American Cotton Oil Company in Glasgow, made its maiden voyage to Rotterdam in 1894. Knowing that officials would reduce prices rather than bring the oil back to the United States, prospective customers waited until the price of oil went down before buying. The company then sold the steamer to a petroleum company and resumed the practice of sending cottonseed oil to Europe in barrels.[31]

An 1891 article on the American Cotton Oil Company stated that its profits came not from crushing but from the development and marketing of new products. Under the brand name Gold Dust, the company produced, advertised, and marketed a yellow washing powder. It also manufactured vegetable oil and lard substitutes, such as the popular Cottolene. "If our company is a monopoly it lies in our brands," said the president in 1896. As Alfred Chandler observed, creating and successfully marketing name-brand products strengthened a company's competitive position even more than expensive technology and exclusive patents.[32]

Although the American Cotton Oil Company had strong competitors, it remained the dominant cottonseed-products company until the First World War. When Chauncey Depew compiled his *History of American Commerce* in 1895, he turned to American Cotton Oil Company president Thomas R. Chaney for a chapter on "The Cotton-Seed-Oil Industry." By 1917 the company ranked 126th in size among all U.S. industrial corporations.[33]

The Southern Cotton Oil Company organized in 1887 prospered despite the head start and near-monopoly position of the American Cotton Oil Company. At the time of its incorporation in New Jersey, the company had at least $2.5 million in paid-up capital. Henry C. Butcher, whose Philadelphia meat-packing firm of Washington Butcher's Sons had been acquired by the American Cotton Oil Trust, headed the corporation and owned about a quarter of the stock. Other officers included Frederick Oliver of New York and Charlotte, North Carolina, general manager; John Oliver of New York, treasurer; D. A. Tompkins, of Charlotte, engineer; and Richard H. Edmonds, editor of the Baltimore *Manufacturers' Record*. Several packing interests that invested heavily in the Southern Cotton Oil Company insisted that their participation be kept secret lest the American Cotton Oil Trust deny them oil.[34]

D. A. Tompkins and Fred Oliver had been among the first people to perceive the vulnerability of the American Cotton Oil Trust. Its organization in 1884 came a year after the invention of the steam cake former, which paved the way for larger and more-efficient cottonseed presses. Having designed "modern" cottonseed-oil mills in Charlotte, North Carolina, and Columbia, South Carolina, for Fred and John Oliver, Tompkins and the Olivers realized that a new venture could successfully compete against the trust. Because most of the trust's properties were old, Tompkins concluded that new mills could pay farmers more per ton for seed and sell crude oil to customers for less than the trust and still make a profit. Tompkins's assumptions proved to be correct; the Southern Cotton Oil Company earned a modest profit in its first year of operation and increased its earnings during the next several years.[35]

D. A. Tompkins built eight large crude-oil mills for the Southern Cotton Oil Company and had all of them in operation by 1 October 1887. Normally it took about two years to complete a mill and have it functioning successfully. Tompkins finished the job in approximately six months. Three-hundred-ton mills in Houston and New Orleans, two-hundred-ton mills in Little Rock, Memphis, Montgomery, and Atlanta, and one-hundred-ton mills in Savannah and Columbia gave the Southern Cotton Oil Company the capacity to process about half the tonnage of cottonseed crushed by all of the American Cotton Oil Trust mills at a fraction of the investment. As rapidly as possible, refineries were added at each of the Southern Cotton Oil Company's mill sites. The Smith & Vaile Company of Dayton, Ohio, supplied all press-room equipment in return for giving the Southern Cotton Oil Company sole access for several years to its machinery, "considered the best made of its time." Agreeing to buy all of the machinery produced by a manufacturer was how some companies sought to erect barriers against new entries.[36]

The Southern Cotton Oil Company underwent a major expansion at the beginning of the twentieth century. In 1901 it was bought by the Virginia-Carolina Chemical Company, the so-called "fertilizer trust" organized in 1895 with American Tobacco Company backing. In buying the oil company, the fertilizer giant eliminated a strong competitor in the fertilizer business and gained control of cottonseed-meal supplies, which the company used as a source of nitrogen in some of its fertilizers.[37]

At the time of its purchase, the Southern Cotton Oil Company owned the eight large mills constructed in 1887 and the refineries, gins, and other facilities associated with them. Cottonseed-oil mill properties belonging to the Virginia-Carolina Chemical Company became part of its Southern Cotton Oil Company subsidiary. Under its new ownership, the company pursued an aggressive policy of buying financially troubled oil mills at bargain prices. In 1914 the Southern Cotton Oil Company owned eighty-two crude-oil mills, eight refineries, ninety-four cotton gins, three compound-lard manufacturing plants, and numerous seed houses. Located principally in the southeastern states, most of the new crushing mills acquired by the company were relatively small interior mills. Like its larger competitor, the Southern Cotton Oil Company developed and marketed name-brand products such as Wesson Oil and Snowdrift shortening. Much of the cottonseed meal produced by company mills went into commercial fertilizers. In developing its manufacturing and marketing network, the Southern Cotton Oil Company built plants in Marburg, Germany, and Manchester, England, to take advantage of the large urban markets in the two most highly industrialized countries of Europe. By 1917 it ranked 223d in size among American industrial corporations.[38]

At least one other company attempted to enter the field of cottonseed processing on a large scale at the turn of the century. Financed largely by Liverpool capitalists associated with British vegetable-oil refiners and soap manufacturers, the Continental Cotton Oil Company of Philadelphia could not overcome the head start of the American and Southern Cotton Oil Companies. Continental planned to build a chain of mills from Texas to the Atlantic but got no farther than Jackson, Mississippi, before going out of business in about 1911. The Southland Cotton Oil Company of Texas took over at least some of the mills.[39]

Several large meat-packing and soap-manufacturing firms successfully entered the cottonseed crushing and refining business during the late nineteenth and early twentieth centuries. In 1893 G. F. Swift of Chicago and Edward Morris of Maine purchased several cottonseed-oil mills in Texas. They believed they could save money by producing part of the cottonseed oil consumed by their packing houses in the making of compound lard, but neither felt that his company could afford to venture into crushing on its own. To avoid antitrust actions against the Swift and Morris companies, the two men secretly formed the Consumers' Cotton Oil Company, which sold its output of oil to the parent companies. From time to time the Consumers' Cotton Oil Company added mills to its Texas holdings. Armour became associated with Swift and Morris in 1902. Michael Cudahy also bought stock in the company, but sold it to Swift in 1909. By that date the associated meat packers owned fourteen crushing mills and a number of cotton gins and seed houses in Texas. The packers divided the output of crude oil in proportion to their investments.[40]

During the early twentieth century, Swift also began to acquire mills in other parts of the Cotton Belt. By 1930 Swift owned mills in Columbia, Augusta, Atlanta, Macon, Montgomery, Memphis, and Little Rock, in addition to its Texas mills, and operated refineries in Atlanta, Jacksonville, Charlotte, Memphis, Chicago, Houston, and Fort Worth. By that date Armour, with the East Saint Louis Cotton Oil Company and two crude-oil mills in Arkansas, was the only other meat-packing company engaged in cottonseed crushing. In 1943 Armour also owned the Lookout Oil & Refining Company in Chattanooga and crushing mills in Jackson and Memphis, Tennessee, as well as shortening plants in Arkansas, Florida, and Virginia. Swift had closed some mills and added others in Cairo, Illinois; Portageville, Missouri; Vernon, California; and elsewhere in the South.[41]

Procter & Gamble organized the Buckeye Cotton Oil Company in 1901, the same year the Virginia-Carolina Chemical Company bought the Southern Cotton Oil Company and launched a major expansion program. Begun in 1837 as a partnership to produce soap and candles, Procter & Gamble used large amounts of fats and oils in its manufacturing. The company went more heavily into soap making after the Civil War, because kerosene produced by the new petroleum industry decreased the demand for candles and the growing emphasis on cleanliness among middle-class Americans caused the soap industry to boom.[42]

Requiring large amounts of cottonseed oil for its soap products, Procter & Gamble freed itself from dependence on the American and Southern Cotton Oil Companies at the end of the nineteenth century by arranging to buy the total crude cottonseed-oil output of several independent crushing mills. In 1901 Procter & Gamble organized the Buckeye Cotton Oil Company as a subsidiary to acquire and operate cottonseed crushing mills. During the next four years Buckeye bought three mills and built five more. The company set up its first cottonseed-products laboratory in 1910.[43]

With a supply of crude cottonseed oil assured, Procter & Gamble began to produce refined cottonseed oil for bakeries and restaurants. Later the company moved into the vegetable-shortening business after it became more profitable to use cottonseed oil in edible products than in soaps. In 1909 the company unveiled the first hydrogenated cottonseed-oil shortening, and two years later Crisco made its appearance. By the First World War, Procter & Gamble was the largest user of cottonseed oil in the world. It operated eleven large terminal mills in Georgia, Alabama, North Carolina, South Carolina, Mississippi, Tennessee, and Arkansas. All but two had sixteen presses. For the five seasons between 1912 and 1917, the total tonnage of seed crushed by Buckeye oil mills ranged from 197,041 to 326,903. By contrast, small country mills operating two to three presses generally processed only a few thousand tons of seed annually.[44]

British and European firms that manufactured soap, margarine, and other fat-based products diverged from their American counterparts in several respects before the First World War. Powerful owner-managers of Lever Brothers in England and of the Jurgens and Van den Bergh operations on the Continent exerted tight control over their companies long after most large American companies had come to rely on professional managers. As those companies acquired related businesses during the late nineteenth and early twentieth centuries, they rationalized their holdings more slowly than American corporate leaders. William Lever, for example, believed that the good will enjoyed by small soap firms with name-brand products offset the greater efficiency of production that could be achieved by closing small firms and concentrating manufacturing in a few large facilities. Rationalization of Lever Brothers' operations did not take place fully until after the First World War.

Lever Brothers, Jurgens, and Van den Bergh decided earlier than American companies involved in cottonseed crushing that vertical organization had drawbacks. They concluded that it did not pay to subordinate companies providing raw materials to those manufacturing consumer products. Buckeye Cotton Oil Company frequently provided oil at a loss to its parent company, Procter & Gamble, whereas Lever Brothers, Jurgens, and Van den Bergh decided after the First World War that affiliated oil mills and raw materials companies had to stand on their own feet and compete in the world market.

The antitrust legislation that placed limits on mergers in the United States after 1890 either did not exist in Western Europe or was interpreted in ways more favorable to corporate growth. The creation of Unilever in 1929 by the merger of the three giant soap and margarine manufacturing companies brought together under one management some six hundred companies in different parts of the world. A holding company on that scale could not have been created in the United States.[45]

The emergence in the United States during the late nineteenth and early twentieth centuries of several giant corporations engaged in all phases of cottonseed processing did not result in the oligopolistic domination of the entire industry. Consolidation took place at the level of refining, research and development, manufacturing, advertising, and sales, but not in crushing. The relatively small amount of capital needed to go into the cottonseed milling business made it impossible for the big companies to keep other investors out, and the high cost of freight and perishability of cottonseed made small "cotton-patch" mills economically viable. In 1896 the *Oil, Paint and Drug Reporter* estimated that although the American and Southern Cotton Oil Companies controlled a majority of the refineries, they owned less than half of all cottonseed presses. The American Cotton Oil Company's share of cottonseed crushing declined from a high of about 80 percent before the appearance of the Southern Cotton Oil Company in 1887 to approximately 50 percent in 1891, 20 percent in 1901, and slightly more than 8 percent in the early 1920s. On the eve of World War I, fewer than two hundred of the more than eight hundred crude-oil mills belonged to the principal cottonseed-processing companies.[46]

As independent mills multiplied and competed vigorously with one another and with the large cottonseed corporations for finite raw materials, some crushers began to feel the need for organizations to represent their interests. With the largest number of independent crude-oil mills and fierce competition for cottonseed, Texas crushers organized a state association in 1894. Working together, they hoped to control the cost of cottonseed and to secure lower insurance and freight rates.[47]

Three years later, forty or fifty industry representatives met in Nashville, Tennessee, and formed the Interstate Cotton Seed Crushers' Association (ICCA). Unlike the first trade association, which enrolled only crushers, the ICCA included representatives of crude-oil mills, refineries, brokerage firms, and related businesses. Although crushers dominated the association, some oil men refused to attend conventions because they could not openly discuss seed prices and other problems with brokers present.[48]

Among the large corporations that engaged in cottonseed crushing, only the Southern Cotton Oil Company actively participated in the affairs of the ICCA. The company's ownership of many small country mills tended to align it with independent mills on many issues, whereas companies with large terminal mills often found themselves at cross-purposes with the independents. In the 1890s crushers used the term *independent* to indicate a mill with no ties to the American Cotton Oil Company, which had attempted to monopolize the industry; consequently, from the outset the company considered the trade association unfriendly to the larger interests. Swift and Buckeye, following the latter's organization in 1901, also had little to do with the national trade association. By the early twentieth century, an independent oil mill was a crushing facility unaffiliated with any of the refiner-controlled companies.[49]

During the early years of the twentieth century, crushers in all of the major cotton-growing states followed the example Texas had set in 1894 and formed state associations. Some state groups, such as those in the Carolinas, were more successful than others in rallying the support of their members for statistical reporting and other programs. No formal connection existed between the interstate association and the state associations, although most state leaders participated actively in the national organization. Only cottonseed crushers could become voting members of the state groups.[50] As the largest cotton-producing state, Texas had the strongest and most active of all the state associations. It functioned much as an equal partner of the ICCA. Nonetheless, many Texas mills joined the national organization, and Texans were among its most energetic leaders.[51]

The Interstate Cotton Seed Crushers' Association had more members and greater financial resources than the first industry trade association, but like the earlier Cottonseed Crushers' Association, the ICCA had no full-time employee until 1917. For years it shared a part-time secretary-treasurer with the Texas association. The ICCA's president recommended in 1914 that an assistant be employed because no chief executive could spare sufficient time from his occupation to carry on the work of the association.[52]

The Cotton Seed Crushers' Association had begun the process of drawing up trading rules in the late 1870s. The Memphis Merchants Exchange had a set of rules governing the cottonseed trade by 1883, and other commercial associations adopted similar regulations for cottonseed trading. The lack of uniformity increased disputes among buyers and sellers until the ICCA codified trading rules. Most state associations other than Texas, which maintained its own slightly different rules, adopted those of the interstate organization. Keeping the rules up-to-date and providing arbitration committees in different parts of the Cotton Belt to resolve disputes between buyers and sellers were the most important services the ICCA performed, for that saved thousands of dollars in court costs annually during the early years of the twentieth century.[53]

The association's legislative committee endeavored to put the views of the cottonseed industry before congressmen and state legislators. Unfavorable tariff rates, for example, were a major concern of cottonseed processors. Austria placed a very high tariff on American cottonseed oil, and the United States taxed imported press cloth, caustic soda, fuller's earth, and other materials used by cottonseed crushers and refiners. Members of the legislative committee worked for the passage of a reciprocal tariff as an instrument for negotiating an end to prohibitive tariffs against cottonseed products. Following the creation of a tariff commission, which the association favored, legislative committee members eventually succeeded in getting duties lifted from materials used in their industry. The other great legislative matter that concerned cottonseed processors was federal and state taxation of colored margarine. In that area the dairy interest proved too strong, and heavy taxes and license fees continued to retard the margarine industry until after the Second World War.[54]

The publicity committee created in 1905 at the urging of Texan Jo Allison worked hard with limited funds to advertise cottonseed products. Some of the large companies that promoted their own brands of cottonseed oil, shortening, and soap objected to paying higher dues to the ICCA for advertising. When several refiners resigned in protest, collections had to be made voluntary for a time. The association never managed to raise the sums for publicity that its leaders considered necessary to increase the demand for cottonseed products. The publicity committee prepared a series of bulletins and paid to have articles on the merits of cottonseed oil and meal inserted in farm and religious journals as news items rather than as advertisements. Oil mills were urged to buy booklets published by the committee for distribution among farmers to increase their consumption of cottonseed products.[55]

Before 1918 less than three hundred of the more than eight hundred crude-oil mills belonged to the ICCA. All mills paid the same dues regardless of size. Because a company could use the association's arbitration services if only one corporate officer joined, some of the large companies did not buy memberships for their crude-oil mills. When the United States entered the First World War, those companies increased the number of their mills belonging to the association, because the Food Administration regulated the industry in cooperation with it. After the conflict ended, large companies dropped many of their individual mill memberships.[56]

The two stages of cottonseed processing, crushing and refining, followed different organizational patterns before the First World War. A small number of large, vertically integrated companies dominated refining and manufacturing, and loosely organized state and national trade associations provided services for those mills and companies engaged in crushing that elected to become members. Where there was general agreement on matters, such as the need for uniform rules and arbitration rather than litigation, trade association members worked together and strengthened their industry. Serious disagreements between crushers and refiners, which intensified with the multiplication of mills, or among oil men in different geographical sections, revealed the shortcomings and weaknesses of voluntary associations. Even when processors agreed in principle about the desirability of a common course of action, such as controlling seed prices, aggressive competition limited the effectiveness of the cartelistic organizations they created.

CHAPTER 7

Cottonseed Price Fixing
and Politics

We might just as well be frank, because if you don't buy a carload of Seed, however rotten it may be, your neighbor in the
next town is going to do it. . . . it is the demagogue and the
crook between the mill and the farmer that plays the mischief.
[cheers] When you attempt to have a general co-operation to
buy Seed on grade, as intelligent men and intelligent Crushers
ought to do, someone like the Attorney General of Texas or
Mississippi will dump you the first crack out of the box, and
use you as a stepping-stone to the Governorship.

> N. T. Blackwell,
> Interstate Cotton Seed Crushers'
> Association convention, 1915

Long ago we should have taken the producers of our raw
material into our confidence and acquainted them with our
difficulties and gotten their confidence; had we done this we
would not have been the door mat over which many small
politicians have tried to walk into popular favor.

> President of the Texas Cotton
> Seed Crushers' Association, 1921

After cotton lint prices began their long decline in the 1870s, growers
depended on seed money to augment farm incomes. As the number of
cottonseed-oil mills increased during the last two decades of the nineteenth century, seed sellers in search of higher prices learned to play one
mill against another. Competition for seed drove up prices, especially
around the turn of the century, when mills multiplied at a very rapid rate

and boll weevil damage drastically reduced seed supplies in some areas. By the early twentieth century, expenditures for seed represented about three-quarters of the cost of producing crude cottonseed products and added approximately $60 million a year to the income of cotton growers.[1]

Beginning about 1875, during a depression that spawned an unprecedented number of cartels among beleaguered American businesses, cottonseed processors formed price-fixing combinations for the purpose of exercising some control over the prices of their raw material.[2] Because crude oil, cake, hulls, and linters had to compete with a wide array of similar and interchangeable products, crushers could not increase the prices of goods they manufactured by limiting production or dividing up markets as many cartels did. By cooperative buying or price setting, however, they could sometimes restrain cottonseed prices.

At the beginning of a crushing season, when seed poured into the mills, oil men set prices as low as they dared, as competition for the remaining seed almost inevitably caused prices to rise. The larger the crush per press that a mill obtained, the more profitable the plant's operations tended to be. Managers thus competed aggressively for raw materials. The most seed pools could do when the market for cottonseed oil remained strong was to retard the rate of price escalation. When oil prices declined, cartels could usually lower seed prices, because their members exercised greater caution in seed buying.[3]

Price-fixing agreements seldom lasted longer than a few months, because violations of the purely voluntary compacts could not be punished. Their widespread use provoked angry reactions from cotton farmers, ginners, and other seed sellers, who attributed every seed price decline, regardless of the cause, to secret agreements among the oil mills. Politicians in the cotton states capitalized on the growing antipathy toward monopoly by lambasting oil mills and other companies suspected of price fixing. Most southern states passed antitrust laws during the 1880s and 1890s, after pools and mergers were formed in the cotton-oil, jute-bag, tobacco, and fertilizer industries; and in Louisiana, Arkansas, Mississippi, Oklahoma, and Texas, officials investigated and prosecuted oil mills for restraining trade in cottonseed. By the end of World War I, it had become too risky to fix prices on a regular basis. Cottonseed processing had created demand for a once-unsalable commodity, but competition for scarce and expensive raw materials became the crushers' biggest headache every season.[4]

In 1875, when New Orleans was still the leading center of cottonseed processing, the city's major oil mills formed the New Orleans Cotton Seed Association to centralize seed buying. The association purchased seed at a set price from as far away as Texas and divided it among pool members according to the number of press boxes operated by each participating company. Memphis mills soon made a similar arrangement, and the two groups agreed to a division of territory. Crushers in each section set their own seed prices. In the Memphis district, mills were said to be subject to a fine of one hundred dollars if they exceeded the fixed price. Near the Red River in Louisiana, planters believed that steamboat companies and oil mills had combined to set seed prices.[5]

Pools maintained relative harmony among Mississippi Valley crushers until a mill-building boom began. Between 1880 and 1885 the number of cottonseed-oil mills tripled, and some of the new competitors refused to honor prior agreements and territorial divisions. During the 1881–82 crushing season, thirty-four mills belonging to the Cotton Seed Crushers' Association reported that they had averaged less than five months of operation due to lack of seed. In Texas that year fierce competition among a growing number of mills convinced crushers to organize a seed pool for the following season. To keep the New Orleans Cotton Seed Association from bidding in its territory, the Texas pool arranged to ship a portion of its seed to New Orleans.[6]

During the 1882–83 crushing season, competition caused seed prices to rise to new levels in the mid-South, but overproduction and the temporary loss of major export markets due to unfavorable tariffs depressed oil prices. More than forty Mississippi Valley cottonseed crushers met in Memphis during the spring of 1883 to deliberate on a course of action. At the Cotton Seed Crushers' Association convention a few weeks later, members discussed the seed situation at length without coming to a meeting of minds. A Memphis member urged the association to set a maximum price per ton for seed, but a Little Rock crusher insisted that because conditions varied from place to place, seed prices had to be negotiated by mills in each locality. Geographic isolation still protected most mills outside the Mississippi Valley from excessive competition. Unable to get a general seed price agreement for 1883–84, Mississippi Valley mills organized separate pools.[7]

At the 1884 Cotton Seed Crushers' Association meeting, representatives of the Mississippi River mills were "gloomy" but hopeful that they could agree on an "equitable division of seed" and "uniform prices." Valley mills reorganized their seed-buying pools, and a general agreement went into effect on 1 September 1884. Memphis bankers had forced local mills to join the combination before they would advance money for seed buying. That arrangement did not end the scramble for seed, however. Circulars sent out by the newly formed American Cotton Oil Trust announcing that it would pay top prices for seed touched off a bidding war with the valley pools that had refused to provide ten thousand tons of seed to the trust as requested.[8]

The New Orleans seed-buying agreement collapsed in the spring of 1885. One company had requested and received allocations of seed on the basis of 410 press boxes, even though the mill containing half of the boxes had been destroyed in a fire. With extra seed the company was able to continue crushing after other mills in the combination had closed. Another New Orleans mill announced that it would have an additional ninety boxes in operation by the following season, thus reducing the amount of seed available for the remaining members of the cartel. The practice of adding press boxes in order to get larger shares of seed frequently undermined pools.[9]

Four separate groups of New Orleans mills purchased seed in the autumn of 1885. Memphis mills also began crushing in 1885 without a seed pool. Near the end of October some of the Memphis mills joined forces. Calling themselves the Independent Cottonseed Oil Company, five of the eleven Memphis mills bought seed cooperatively in 1885–86 and reported a profitable season. The other six had become part of the American Cotton Oil Trust.[10]

By 1886 the trust had acquired 80 percent or more of the total U.S. crushing capacity. With little competition and the supply of cottonseed products exceeding demand, the new colossus lowered seed prices. As a result, the trust soon came under attack from a Louisiana state senator and farmer. In 1887 the attorney general of Louisiana sought to bar American Cotton Oil Trust mills from operating in the state, on the grounds that the trust had not organized under the laws of Louisiana. Although several writs of injunction against the trust remained in effect permanently, the state lost its suit to liquidate the business.[11]

The Southern Cotton Oil Company, which began processing seed at eight efficient new mills in the fall of 1887, was able to pay more for seed and sell products for less than its large rival, which owned many antiquated mills. Soon feeling the effects of competition for seed, the trust negotiated an agreement with the new company. In 1889 the two agreed to cooperate in the purchase of seed. According to an Alabama oil-mill prospectus, the two companies bought seed in that state "at their own price" and distributed 45 percent of the seed to the American Cotton Oil Trust mill in Mobile, 20 percent to its mill in Demopolis, and 35 percent to the Southern Cotton Oil Company mill in Montgomery.[12]

Undaunted by the existence of two powerful corporations, independent mills multiplied during the late nineteenth century in response to increased cotton production in the South and greater demand for cottonseed oil at home and abroad. As the number of mills grew, competition for seed intensified and prices became much more difficult to control. A number of men whose mills had been acquired by the American Cotton Oil Trust built new facilities in Texas. "You never saw anything in your life like this scramble in Texas to build mills," one resident said. Independent producers in Texas constituted the American Cotton Oil Company's fiercest competition at the end of the nineteenth century.[13]

As a rule, intense competition for seed for any length of time led to collusion among mills. Little Rock mills combined to set raw-material prices in 1891. Georgia farmers complained that the state's oil mills had conspired to set a limit on the price of seed in 1893. The spirited bidding of Memphis mills pushed seed prices so high in 1893 that Tennessee oil men met in November to form a price-fixing pool. The following year the attorney general of Tennessee sought to void the charters of six oil mills for antitrust violations.[14]

In 1893 some of the Texas country mills engaged in a cottonseed war with agencies buying seed for Galveston and Houston oil mills owned by the American Cotton Oil Company and other "outside" companies. The Southern Cotton Oil Company owned a mill in Houston and the Consumers' Cotton Oil Company acquired its first Texas mills in 1893. Attractive prices offered at Brenham, Texas, brought fifteen hundred farm wagons to town on a single day. So many wagons clogged the streets of Brenham that other vehicles could not move. Although cotton growers generally hauled lint or seed no more than about ten or twelve miles round trip by wagon,[15] farmers traveled as far as forty miles in order to take advantage of the prices in Brenham.

Texas cottonseed crushers formed a state association in 1894, the year after the cottonseed war in the Lone Star state, in order to control seed prices and protect themselves from "outside influences and interests." Following a 50 percent reduction in seed prices, the state attorney general prosecuted the Texas Cottonseed Crushers' Association for violating state antitrust laws, and the organization was enjoined from fixing seed and product prices. A dozen years later the president of a Texas cottonseed-oil mill said that members did not discuss seed prices at meetings of the Texas Cottonseed Crushers' Association, but after meetings ended, "they would have their smokers, and drink Champaign [*sic*], and there they would discuss most everything."[16]

In the Southeast, crushers made various cooperative arrangements for controlling raw material costs. Carolina and Georgia mills worked in harmony during the 1893–94 season to hold down seed prices. By 1896 crushers in the Carolinas had begun to meet annually, and Alabama, Georgia, Mississippi, and Tennessee mill men gathered in Chattanooga regularly to discuss seed buying and other problems. At the end of the nineteenth century, L. W. Haskell, a Southern Cotton Oil Company executive based in Savannah, said that he belonged to several organizations that had been effective in regulating local markets. In 1900 a combination of oil mills in North and South Carolina divided their territory and placed one buyer in each division. To hold down freight costs, the mill closest to any lot of seed purchased for the pool had the option of buying it. Mississippi mills also had a seed-pricing arrangement in 1900, and the following year Mississippi and Louisiana mills cooperated in fixing prices.[17]

The inner workings of seed pools in North and South Carolina during the first decade of the twentieth century are described in the correspondence of E. V. Zoeller, secretary and treasurer of a cottonseed-oil mill near Tarboro, North Carolina. Independent crushers in eastern North Carolina had their own organization whose leader negotiated on their behalf with representatives of the American and Southern Cotton Oil Companies and whenever possible combined with them to set seed prices. Cheating by individual crushers and their seed buyers limited the effectiveness of the pools; nevertheless, price increases brought some kind of agreement during each of the five years for which letters exist. The head seed buyer for the American Cotton Oil Company directed operations from his headquarters in Columbia, South Carolina, whenever combinations embraced the large companies as well as the independents. Price information was routinely transmitted by coded telegrams, and participants were requested to keep all transactions secret.

During the 1903–4 season, most of the mills interested in buying cottonseed in eastern North Carolina formed a pool that allocated seed among the members on a per press basis and set maximum prices for seed each week. The purpose of giving mills a weekly quota and requiring them to sell excess seed to competitors was to keep outside mills from bidding up prices. The allocation scheme worked so poorly that it was not attempted again during the period covered by the Zoeller letters. In subsequent years the mills made repeated efforts to control prices, always reaching an agreement when raw material costs got so high that production threatened to become unprofitable.[18]

The Sons of Plato, a secret society that set seed prices and divided seed-producing territories among mills, operated in a number of southern states for a decade or more. Jo Allison, a popular and influential member of the Texas and Interstate Cotton Seed Crushers' Associations, took the lead in organizing the Sons of Plato in Texas in 1905. Thereafter, he helped to form chapters in other states. As the Plato, or head, of the SOP in Texas, Allison's task was to resolve price and territorial disputes among the state's crushers.[19]

Many forms of price manipulation went on in Texas during the years the Sons of Plato existed. Some mills shared seed with buyers for outside mills who agreed not to bid for seed in their territory. Other mills paid buyers cash to stay out of their buying area. A witness charged that each mill was assigned a specific tonnage of seed it could crush. Sometimes all the mills in a single town or region boycotted cotton ginners and independent buyers who refused to abide by prices set by local mills and gins. A cottonseed buyer alleged that mills purchasing seed outside their area incurred a penalty. Every effort was made to restrict seed buyers to their designated territories. In 1913 ginners and buyers in several towns testified that only one mill bid for their seed, and that unless they dealt with a single mill they could not find a buyer. Oil mills also had an agreement in 1913 not to market cottonseed meal and hulls outside their own territories.[20]

Mississippi crushers quickly followed the lead of Texas oil men. By February of 1906 the Mississippi Academy of the Sons of Plato had established a fixed price for cottonseed. Its secretary encouraged members to adhere to this price and get "some cheap seed." General meetings of the Mississippi SOP took place in New Orleans and Memphis, and members in the eastern, central, and western divisions of the state met monthly to decide matters in their territories. Between meetings they reported violations of agreements to "Plato," E. M. Durham, president of the Refuge Cotton Oil Company of Vicksburg and a founding member of the Interstate Cotton Seed Crushers' Association. Durham's chief role was to investigate and resolve complaints of unauthorized price increases and invasions of others' territories in search of seed. Because Memphis mills purchased much of their seed in North Mississippi, chapters of the Sons of Plato in the two states negotiated agreements and met from time to time.[21]

To insure harmony, Mississippi Sons of Plato members sometimes leased or traded seed storage houses to one company at each seed collection point, and that company shared all the seed with its competitors at the fixed price. When the system worked smoothly, sellers had only one party to deal with, which made it easier for the mills to keep prices under control. Letters exchanged by Mississippi crushers during those years, and later used as evidence against them in an antitrust suit, show that disagreements and misunderstandings frequently developed among the crushers.[22]

Members of the Mississippi Sons of Plato reportedly deposited money with a grievance committee that was subject to forfeiture in case a mill violated SOP agreements. It is more likely that leaders of the organization relied on persuasion rather than fines to retain the allegiance of mills. Each member was also expected to pay a fixed amount per press to support a statistical bureau. Some mill men dragged their feet about complying with the reporting requirement.[23]

Cotton growers reacted to seed pools and low seed prices in a variety of ways. In the southeastern states, where fertilizers were essential, large farmers returned much of their seed to the land if oil mills offered less for seed than commercial fertilizers cost. For that reason, southeastern oil mills always had to pay more for seed than mills in other regions. Higher oil yields, better prices for meal, and lower labor costs generally enabled eastern mills to pay several dollars more per ton for seed than western processors. Oil mills and state agricultural departments and experiment stations waged an increasingly successful campaign in the late nineteenth century to convince farmers that cottonseed meal made a better fertilizer than whole seed. Nonetheless, if prices dropped significantly, larger growers tended to hold seed off the market.[24]

In a few instances groups of cotton planters contemplated operating their own oil mills, and some actually ventured into the crushing business. The Planters Oil Mill of Memphis began operations in 1883, and alone among Mississippi Valley mills refused to join the price-fixing pool that year. By the following season it had become a regular joint-stock company and ceased to function as a farmers' cooperative. Low seed prices in 1885 caused widespread dissatisfaction among cotton growers. The following year Greenville, Mississippi, planters built another cooperative crushing mill.[25]

The Southern Farmers' Alliance movement, a product of the agricultural distress of the late 1880s and early 1890s, spawned a variety of short-lived cooperative enterprises that may have included one or more oil mills. Alliancemen in Kaufman County, Texas, made plans to establish a crushing mill in about 1885. Several years later a Richmond County, North Carolina, alliance group attempted but failed to organize an oil mill. The alliance chapter of Griffin, Georgia, operated an oil mill, gin, and fertilizer factory around 1890.[26]

The impetus for at least some of the "cooperative" mills came from large planters who joined the alliance movement along with many impoverished small farmers and tenants. The Farmers' Cooperative Manufacturing Company organized in eastern North Carolina in 1888 listed Elias Carr as its first incorporator. One of the most prosperous agriculturists of his day and the descendent of a distinguished North Carolina planter family, Carr joined the alliance in 1887 and soon became state president. Despite its name, the mill appears to have been organized by relatively prosperous members of the farming and professional class in and around Tarboro, North Carolina. Twenty-eight individuals, five of them bearing the same family name, signed the articles of agreement, which stipulated that twenty-five thousand dollars in capital was to be raised by selling five hundred shares of stock at fifty dollars a share. The high price of shares would have barred most alliance members from participating in the so-called cooperative. In 1895 the company changed its name to the Tar River Oil Company.[27]

A prospectus entitled *The Plan and Scope of the Alabama Alliance Oil Company* was circulated among "Planters and Citizens" of the Demopolis area in the summer of 1889. A number of Alabama commercial ventures used "alliance" in their names to capitalize on the organization's great popularity. The Alabama Alliance Oil Company proposal stipulated that two-thirds of the stock be paid for in seed, which would have helped to solve the perennial problem of insufficient raw materials, as well as the difficulty of finding farmers able to buy shares. The promoter stated that the mill would "be run in the interest of the planters and producers of cotton seed" who had been forced to sell at the low prices dictated by the American Cotton Oil Trust and the Southern Cotton Oil Company. He warned farmers that seed prices would be temporarily raised by the two corporations in order to try to wreck the proposed mill. A few years later an oil mill in Demopolis bore the name of the man who had instigated the project, which suggests that alliancemen either had little to do with the mill's organization or that they soon lost control to the promoter.[28] Several cooperative oil mills would be organized by cotton growers after the First World War, but during the first century of cottonseed processing, cotton producers rarely took the cooperative route to higher seed prices. A sizable number of farmers invested in joint-stock companies before the mill-building boom ended with America's entry into the war.[29]

Another response to unsatisfactory lint and seed prices was the organization of protective associations by cotton growers. Believing that prices would be higher if cotton and cottonseed could be marketed over a longer period of time, groups of cotton farmers frequently proposed "holding the crop" as the surest method of increasing commodity prices. During the late nineteenth and early twentieth centuries, major growers tended to hold their seed for higher prices when cotton or tobacco sold well and to sell seed even at low prices when the value of lint or tobacco declined. With the cash earned from their cottonseed, large producers could afford to store their more valuable lint or tobacco and wait for better prices.[30]

The Mississippi Valley Cotton Planters' Association, which claimed to have members in Alabama, Arkansas, Louisiana, Mississippi, and Tennessee, held its first convention in Vicksburg, Mississippi, in 1880. Resolutions passed by the association recommended that cottonseed be used as a fertilizer or exchanged for meal rather than being sold to the mills, and that a committee be appointed to seek higher seed prices from oil mills and publicize them in farm papers. There is no evidence that the association survived, but during the years that followed, farmers in different parts of the Cotton Belt held seed off the market periodically while they bargained for higher prices.[31]

During the 1893 crushing season, for example, some Georgia farmers presented a united front to seed buyers. In many parts of the Cotton Belt that year seed prices ranged from sixteen to twenty dollars a ton, but farmers around Sandersville, Macon, and Augusta, Georgia, could get only eleven dollars. A committee appointed at a protest meeting recommended that Georgia farmers hold their seed or sell them in other states. At a second meeting planters and seed sellers organized the Georgia Cottonseed Growers and Dealers' Association. The leadership urged farmers not to sell their seed until the association could complete plans for soliciting sealed bids from mill companies and arrange to sell seed to the top bidder. Sometimes cotton growers organizing seed boycotts promised loans to those who could not afford to hold their cottonseed for future sale.[32]

The Farmers' Union, following its organization in Texas in 1902, had some success in helping members hold their lint and seed for higher prices. In Mississippi forty-two warehouse companies cooperated with the Farmers' Union, making it possible for farmers to store their lint and seed and sell them more advantageously to manufacturers in large lots. Returning prosperity killed the Farmers' Union in Mississippi before the

First World War. The largest postwar membership was in Oklahoma, where the union held seed from time to time and sold it in large lots for higher-than-market prices.[33]

During the early twentieth century, several organizations of cotton growers sought agreements on minimum seed prices that would be fair to both farmers and mills. The Georgia Cotton Growers Association invited the South's cotton producers to meet with them in November 1900 for the purpose of "obtaining a fair and just price for our cotton and cotton seed products." Following the example of Georgia, some of the major planters in North Carolina organized in 1900.[34]

An aggressive mill-buying campaign by the Southern Cotton Oil Company the following year alarmed southeastern cotton farmers. Rumors that the Southern and American Cotton Oil Companies would soon control 90 percent of the Carolina crushing mills and be in a position to dictate seed prices prompted the North Carolina Farmers' Alliance in 1901 to plead with its members to sell their seed to the state business agency. Later that year the North Carolina Cotton Farmers State Association advised farmers not to sell seed below a certain price but to use it on their farms. That threat and advances in crude-oil values caused a combine of oil mills in the Carolinas to raise seed prices in their territory. In 1903, when crushers reduced seed prices in the Carolinas, Farmers' Alliance leaders again urged members not to sell seed to the mills.[35]

When cotton prices fell in 1904, the Southern Cotton Growers' Protective Association was revived. In 1907 the association asked the Interstate Cotton Seed Crushers' Association to appoint a committee to meet with their representatives and discuss "the best method of maintaining stable and satisfactory prices of cotton-seed in the different states." The planters wanted to set a minimum price for seed and advise farmers not to take less. Oil men refused to authorize a discussion of specific seed prices with the growers even though they recognized the importance of trying to win the good will of farmers. The two committees met, but representatives of the Interstate Cotton Seed Crushers' Association would only talk about the factors that influenced seed prices and caused them to fluctuate. Conferees agreed that uniform seed prices could not be set, because of differences in freight rates, the variable condition of seed, and fluctuations in supply and demand.[36]

Farmers' frequent dissatisfaction with seed prices made price fixing by the crushing industry a perennial political issue in the Cotton Belt before the Second World War. "A fellow wants to get in politics," said a

Mississippi businessman in 1915, "will commence cussing and flim-flamming the Cotton Oil Industry." Describing cottonseed prices in 1931 as "nothing short of highway robbery," and threatening to close every gin and mill until Mississippi farmers received a "decent price" for their seed, Governor Theodore Bilbo was one of a long line of politicians who capitalized on low seed prices to win votes. Eugene Talmadge, Georgia's commissioner of agriculture in 1930, used well-publicized attacks on seed prices as one stepping stone to the governorship.[37]

Investigations of the cottonseed industry occurred frequently during the fifty years before the Second World War. In about 1900 Mississippi's attorney general instituted proceedings aimed at revoking the charters of sixteen oil mills believed to be engaged in fixing the prices of seed, mill insurance, and railway freight rates. A county judge dismissed the case on a technicality. Price-fixing activities of the Sons of Plato provoked legal attacks in several states. During the first two decades of the twentieth century, Mississippi, Texas, Oklahoma, and Arkansas prosecuted mills for conspiring to fix prices, and the Louisiana attorney general and U.S. Department of Justice investigated charges of price fixing. Many Mississippi mills paid fines for belonging to the Sons of Plato, and several corporations in Texas and Arkansas were banned from doing business in those states. The American Cotton Oil Company organized the Union Seed and Fertilizer Company to operate its crushing mills following legal attacks in several states.[38]

The widespread publicity surrounding the trials and investigations of the early twentieth century heightened the suspicion and mistrust of farmers and the general public by confirming what many had long suspected, that oil mills had indeed collaborated for the purpose of depressing cottonseed prices. When the Mississippi Cotton Seed Crushers' Association was formed in 1912, many people assumed it had been created for the purpose of manipulating cottonseed prices, and the grand juries of several counties investigated those charges. The last chapters of the Sons of Plato disappeared around 1917 as legal attacks made the risks of cottonseed pools unacceptable. There would be collusion and price fixing after that date, but never as persistently, or on the same scale, as existed before the First World War.[39]

Although cotton lint was considerably more valuable than seed, low lint prices did not provoke investigations as frequently as declines in the price of seed. Henry C. Hammond explained that farmers usually sold lint through brokers to distant textile mills, but they knew the cottonseed crushers, and the oil mills were located in their midst. When cottonseed prices fell, farmers and ginners immediately suspected the oil mills of fixing prices. Before the First World War their suspicions would have been justified, even though seed prices followed cottonseed product prices up and down. The prices of fats and oils have historically been subject to great fluctuation. The instability of cottonseed prices frustrated producers, who tended to believe that the mills took advantage of them in seed transactions. "When I was a farmer," said a ginner whose mill stock had paid few dividends, "I thought the oil mill man made all the money, but I have decided I would rather be a ginner."[40]

In addition to fighting antitrust suits, crushers in the western and central sections of the Cotton Belt had to contend with virulent boll weevil attacks before the First World War. In the early 1890s boll weevils crossed the Rio Grande River from Mexico and invaded Texas cotton fields, adding to the shortage of seed in some areas. Moving inexorably east and north, weevils devastated first one area and then another. Farmers sometimes lost a half or more of their cotton crop to the pests. Between 1905 and 1915 the boll weevil spread over much of Oklahoma. Around 1908 farmers east of the Mississippi River began to experience the consequences of weevil infestation. Some mills in Louisiana closed as farmers temporarily switched from cotton to rice in the afflicted areas. Boll weevils caused heavy damage to the cotton crops of 1915 and 1916. Overall cotton production did not suffer, but wherever boll weevils appeared, oil mills closed their doors for lack of seed or paid higher prices because of seed shortages. Unabated mill building and the seed crisis in areas invaded by weevils intensified competition for raw materials and made control of seed prices seem more necessary than ever, yet antitrust prosecutions had made price-fixing schemes too costly.[41]

High seed prices caused by unrestrained competition created a desperate situation for many independent mills in the fall of 1916. In Texas the number of oil mills had almost doubled during the first decade of the twentieth century.[42] Louisiana and Texas crushers turned to their state governments in 1916 for a means of restoring public confidence in the industry and of suggesting seed prices that would be fair to producers and processors alike. With seed supplies reduced by boll weevils, independents in those states feared they would be swallowed up by the big corporations unless seed prices could be controlled. The "Louisiana Plan" proposed that the governor appoint a "Cotton Seed Quotation Committee" consisting of the commissioner of agriculture, the president of the

Farmer's Union or some other farmer representative, and a respected cottonseed crusher. The function of the committee would be to set a minimum price for cottonseed each week based on the average costs of crushing and transportation and the value of products sold during that period. The minimum price was to serve as a guide, not a constraint. Texas crushers agreed to fund a state committee, but in order to avoid any suspicion of industry influence wanted no mill representation. Publicity about the Sons of Plato had given oil men in Texas and other states a bad name.

With seed pools discredited, emphasis fell on the importance of publicizing all the factors involved in arriving at a "just price" for seed, so that farmers would be aware of the reasons seed prices declined and crushers would have some guidelines for seed buying. Adoption of the Louisiana Plan would have ended the secrecy that had surrounded crushing operations for so long. Mills would have been forced to open their books to auditors employed by the "Cotton Seed Quotation Committee," so that they could determine the aggregate costs and tonnages on which to base suggested seed prices. Desperate Texas and Louisiana oil men wanted an official committee similar to an insurance commission and other state advisory bodies. Apart from the information that a committee was appointed in Louisiana, no evidence has been found of cottonseed committees operating in Louisiana and Texas in 1916 or 1917.[43]

Finding adequate supplies of cottonseed at prices that would permit profitable manufacturing was the major challenge faced by crushers during the industry's first century. Raw-material costs far exceeded other processing expenses, and demand for seed always outran supply. Although both cotton production and the percentage of cottonseed crushed rose steadily until well into the twentieth century, mill building also proceeded at a rapid pace.

It is impossible to assess the effectiveness of price fixing by the mills, but market forces appear to have had a far greater impact than collusion on raw-material costs. Cottonseed prices generally rose when supplies were small and fell when production increased. As long as agreements worked, they must have contributed to a more equitable sharing of raw materials, the supply of which could not be expanded to meet mill demand. They probably made it possible for some of the weaker mills to resist being absorbed by strong competitors. At best, cartels could only retard the rate of price increases, because there were usually crushers willing to offer more than the fixed price for a large supply of seed.

By World War I repeated antitrust prosecutions had convinced crushers to all but abandon price-fixing cartels. Beginning in 1916 the idea of "fair" seed prices being determined by official committees gained support and was put into effect under federal supervision in 1917 and 1918. With the return of peace, efforts to continue cooperation among the diverse groups interested in stable cottonseed prices collapsed. Ahead of the mill operators lay several decades of ruthless competition.

CHAPTER 8

World War I
and Postwar Shocks

The war and inflation, after the war deflation, plus the ravages of the boll weevil, further aided by non-cooperation in the industry, have nearly bankrupted a business that is essential to the well being of our whole people.

T. J. Kidd, general manager,
Farmers & Ginners Cotton Oil Company, 1925

Something has been radically wrong in the cotton-oil business for the last ten years.

Harry Hodgson, president,
Hodgson Oil Refining Company, 1930

World War I brought cottonseed processors both frustrations and opportunities, and aftershocks of the conflict permanently altered the cottonseed industry in the United States. The rapid proliferation of oil mills that had begun in the 1880s came to an end with World War I. Consolidation of processing became the wave of the future as crushers confronted deflation, small cotton crops, high raw-material costs, oil prices that rose less than comparable products, loss of export markets, and other problems. The 885 cottonseed-oil mills operating in 1914 shrank to 711 in 1919, 553 in 1929, 447 in 1939, and 214 in 1958.[1]

A severe labor drain caused by the lure of job opportunities in war-related industries and by the draft was one of the most serious difficulties faced by mill operators during the war years. Shortages of coal used to fuel steam engines and of railway cars needed to haul supplies, seed, and products also plagued crushers. Inflated wages and freight charges, and higher prices for fuel, press cloth, and cottonseed, added to the wartime woes of oil mills. Counterbalancing the adverse effects of war on the industry were more welcome consequences. Cottonseed-oil prices went up about 200 percent, and the demand for gun cotton, or nitrocellulose, enhanced the value of cottonseed linters, which normally cost more to remove than could be recovered through their sale. Between 1914 and 1916 alone, the value of linters quadrupled.[2]

In May of 1917, with the Allies desperate for fats and other foods, President Wilson authorized Herbert Hoover to initiate a food conservation program. Following passage of the Food and Fuel Control Act of 10 August 1917, Hoover's agency became the United States Food Administration. To encourage self-regulation, Hoover requested associations of food producers to appoint committees to work with the new Food Control Board. The executive board of the Interstate Cotton Seed Crushers' Association formed the War Service Committee to fulfill this request. J. J. Culbertson, a prominent Texas crusher and former president of the trade association, served as the industry's chief representative in Washington for several months.[3]

The Food and Fuel Control Act of 1917 empowered President Wilson to regulate and license industries considered vital to the war effort. The Cottonseed Division, embracing all groups involved in cottonseed processing, was created in October 1917. Hugh Humphreys, a Memphis cottonseed-meal broker, became the division's first head. Following consultation with representatives of the different groups involved in cottonseed processing, the Cottonseed Division issued rules aimed at controlling speculation, hoarding, excess profits, and wasteful practices in the cottonseed industry. All cotton gins, cottonseed-oil mills, vegetable-oil refineries, persons handling more than 150 tons of cottonseed annually, and dealers in cottonseed products had to have a license to operate. Violations of the rules could be punished by fines or cancellation of a company's license. Although the Cottonseed Division sent numerous warning letters to violators threatening to deprive them of markets or to withdraw their licenses, the agency appealed to patriotism and relied principally on cooperation to achieve its goals.[4]

The rules prohibited anyone from having more cottonseed or cottonseed products on hand than could be stored properly. Whole cottonseed could no longer be used for feed or fertilizer. The common practice among ginners of adding trash to cottonseed to increase its weight and price was forbidden. No dealer could hold cottonseed in excess of twenty tons for longer than sixty days. Mills were not permitted to store more seed than their average crush for sixty days and no more crude oil than they normally produced in thirty days. Dealers in cottonseed meal and refiners of vegetable oils were likewise restricted in the amounts of those products they could have in their possession.[5]

Limiting the amount of seed and products that licensees could have on hand curbed speculation in the industry by speeding up the movement of raw materials and manufactured goods. Storing seed and products in anticipation of rising prices had been a common practice, because prices tended to advance as the crushing season progressed. To further discourage speculation in cottonseed products, the New York futures market in cottonseed oil and the Memphis futures market in cottonseed meal were suspended.[6]

Rumors that cottonseed prices might be fixed by the Food Administration brought a flood of letters to congressmen in the fall of 1917 from cotton growers and seed speculators who objected to the idea of capping prices. Cottonseed had increased from less than twenty dollars a ton in 1912 to more than seventy dollars in 1917, and some people expected the price of seed to reach one hundred dollars. Although some crushers advised the Food Administration not to regulate prices, many oil men squeezed by high raw material and labor costs were disappointed when Hoover declined to set prices at the beginning of the 1917 season.[7]

Most crushers large and small believed that only the government could save the industry from ruin. Following meetings held in early December at the request of the Food Administration, oil men agreed on maximum prices for crude cottonseed oil and meal in different sections of the Cotton Belt. Refiners accepted a 3 percent limit on profits, ginners agreed to handle cottonseed for two dollars a ton plus loading charges, and shortening manufacturers set a maximum price per pound on lard substitutes. Although the Food Administration did not "officially" fix seed prices, it mandated a spread of thirteen dollars a ton between seed and product prices. Crushers in the various states worked out the maximum prices mills could pay for seed and still maintain the differential. Controlling the spread rather than fixing prices was the principal method used by the Food Administration to stabilize prices, and the strategy was largely successful.[8]

Federal administrators viewed payment of higher seed prices as evidence of lack of cooperation and threatened to punish offenders. Following an investigation, T. F. Justiss, president of the Ginners' Association and head of the cotton-ginning section of the Food Administration, charged that many of his fellow ginners and other cottonseed dealers had reaped excessive profits when the war effort required that the seed speculation "previously prevailing" be eliminated.[9]

Other violations came to the attention of Food Administration officials. To keep cottonseed purchases below the 150 tons that made a license necessary, a dealer could have other people buy smaller lots of seed for him. Some mills sold lower grades of cottonseed meal at the price set for the highest grade. Other mills stored more than a sixty-day supply of seed. Despite the prohibition against adding trash to cottonseed, one mill claimed to have on its premises "a good car load of rocks, sticks, bricks, glass, scrap iron and . . . possibly three car loads of sand and dirt" that had been removed from seed processed that season. Crushers repeatedly accused cotton ginners of making excess profits on cottonseed.[10]

During the spring of 1918, the Cottonseed Division sought advice from the different interests involved in cottonseed processing about appropriate prices and regulations for the coming year. The maximum amount of seed that could be handled without a license was reduced from 150 to 20 tons. Prices fixed for the 1918–19 crushing season had to be increased to compensate for inflation. Seed buyers' commissions were set at $1.50 a ton plus handling expenses, and maximum gross profits allowed to independent cottonseed dealers rose from $2.00 to $3.00 per ton. The spread between the cost of seed and the price of products went from $13.00 to $18.50. Food administrators in the cotton states calculated seed prices that would enable crushers to realize the new margin. Mills were expected to be able to earn a maximum net profit of about $3.00 per ton, or slightly better than 3 percent. However, high hull prices that inhibited sales and poor oil yields in the West due to drought reduced the income of some crushers.[11]

After the armistice, leaders of the cottonseed industry labored successfully to keep the Food Administration program of stabilized prices in place for the remainder of the crushing season, because all seed had been purchased on that basis. The Food Administration then rescinded the rules that had governed the industry and closed the Cottonseed Division in May 1919. Unfortunately for cottonseed processors, the government waited so long to permit the unrestricted export of cottonseed oil that mills in the Far East satisfied most of the overseas demand for vegetable oil.[12]

Because of their importance in the manufacture of munitions, cottonseed linters came under the control of the War Industries Board headed by Bernard Baruch. George R. James, a Memphis wagon manufacturer, supervised the production, sale, and distribution of linters for the board. As the principal raw material for nitrocellulose, known as smokeless powder or gun cotton, linters were in great demand at home and abroad. Before the war most mills made one cut of linters, which removed about forty pounds of lint per ton of seed. That was less than half the amount of linters the War Industries Board estimated would be needed in 1918–19.

The Linters Section decided that linters should be used only for munitions and other war-related purposes and that production should be significantly increased. George James informed the Interstate Cotton Seed Crushers' Association in the spring of 1918 that all linters requested by the Allies, the United States government, and private munitions firms would be allocated among members of a buying pool. The U.S. Army Ordnance Department contracted to buy all linters at a fixed price from 1 August 1918 to 31 July 1919. Crushers expanded production by a second cut or a single "mill run" to a total of about 145 pounds per ton. A number of oil mills purchased additional delinting machinery, because the government threatened to seize mills that failed to meet production goals. Moreover, the fixed price on linters guaranteed that they would be a source of profit.[13]

Breach of the linter contracts soon after the termination of fighting resulted in a long struggle by cottonseed crushers for payment of the full amount the federal government owed them under the terms of their original contracts. Mills had been ordered to cut the maximum amount of linters, and they had been promised payment at a fixed rate through July of 1919. When the Linters Section failed to devise a plan satisfactory to all interested parties and the War Industries Board went out of existence, the Ordnance Department undertook to dissolve the linters pool and settle accounts with buyers and producers.[14]

The Interstate Cotton Seed Crushers' Association appointed the Linter Committee to negotiate with the Ordnance Department. It won a promise from the War Department not to dump its linters on the market and depress prices further. Federal officials also agreed to promote research into new ways of using linters. In return for those concessions and an agreement to maintain fixed cottonseed oil and meal prices for the remainder of the crushing season, the association and individual crushers reluctantly accepted a "supplemental linter contract." By its terms the Ordnance Department agreed to take all linters the mills had on hand at the end of 1918 at the stabilized price and to buy an additional 150,000 bales before the end of July 1919 at prices set for each grade by the department. Because crushers had paid the high fixed price for all of their seed, they continued to insist that mills be paid the guaranteed price for the remainder of the linters cut under their initial contracts and that they be reimbursed for purchases of new equipment.[15]

The Linter Committee filed a claim with the Board of Contract Adjustment created at the end of the war on behalf of every mill that had been licensed by the Food Administration. Although board members recognized a "moral responsibility" toward the mills, they upheld the legality of the modified linter contracts, which members of the Linter Committee claimed the industry had been forced to accept in order to get a federal guarantee that cottonseed oil and meal prices set by the Food Administration at the beginning of the 1918–19 crushing season would remain in effect until season's end. When industry representatives appealed to the secretary of war for a reversal of the decision, he replied that "the government couldn't keep taking war materials," and he denied that crushers had been coerced into accepting the supplemental contracts.[16]

In 1920 former South Carolina senator Christie Benet, counsel for the Interstate Cotton Seed Crushers' Association's Linter Committee, sued in the United States Court of Claims for the balance due the mills under their original contracts. Five years later the court rejected the claims. In 1927 Benet brought a new suit in the Court of Claims on behalf of the Hazlehurst Oil Mill and Fertilizer Company in Mississippi and won a favorable verdict in 1930. When the Justice Department declined to appeal, Congress appropriated money to satisfy the claim. The successful outcome of the test case cleared the way more than a decade after the end of the war for other mills to seek restitution for breach of their linters contracts.[17]

The availability of large amounts of relatively cheap linters at the end of the war, as well as supplies of cotton cellulose not yet manufactured into gun powder, and chemical cotton plants for sale at a fraction of their cost, stimulated the expansion of cellulose-based industries in the United States during the postwar years. Most of the basic chemical research that prepared the way for the cellulose industry had been done in England and Western Europe. Treated with different chemicals, cellulose became the base of a wide range of products. By the mid-1920s cellulose made from linters was being used in the manufacture of artificial leather for car seats, imitation French ivory for combs and brushes, film, cellophane, plastics, lacquer for automobiles, and artificial silk or rayon.[18]

Cellulose exists in varying degrees in all plants, but some forms are more useful for manufacturing purposes than others. Cotton linters have

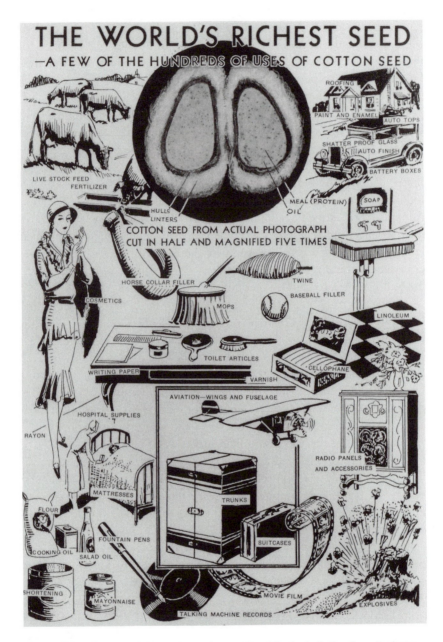

The world's richest seed, from *Facts about a Great Exclusively Southern Industry* (Memphis: National Cottonseed Products Association, 1930), 6. Courtesy, National Archives.

a high percentage of pure cellulose and are easy to clean and process. From the early twentieth century, linters, particularly the fuzz obtained on second cuttings, proved to be the most desirable source of cellulose in the United States. Longer cotton fibers became matted when wet and delayed the chemical reaction necessary to transform cellulose into different products. Procter & Gamble's Buckeye Cotton Oil Company and two other large companies purified and bleached most of the linters that were transformed into chemical cotton.

Although demand for cottonseed linters multiplied with the development of the cellulose industry, the increasing availability of wood pulp and other less-expensive sources of cellulose checked the price of linters when it got too far out of line. Rising prices, fluctuating supplies, seasonal availability, and other negative characteristics of linters stimulated companies to experiment with wood pulp, the most abundant source of cellulose. Much research and development had to be done before wood pulp could be substituted freely for linters in the manufacture of rayon and other products. As the quality improved, wood pulp could more readily be substituted for linters.[19]

Disposal of surplus linters and the long fight to win a favorable settlement of wartime claims was just one of several matters that preoccupied the cottonseed-processing industry during the difficult 1920s. To continue the cooperation of the war years and defuse the suspicions and hostility of cotton producers, processors in several states attempted to set up official state cottonseed committees in 1919 to collect statistics and fix seed prices that would be fair to all parties. Under the proposed postwar cooperative plan, committees representing growers, ginners, brokers, crushers, and the railroads, working with their state agricultural or marketing commissioners, would determine the fair price of cottonseed in different areas based on the chemical analysis of seed, crushing costs, and income from products. The "fair price plan" went into effect briefly in Alabama, Mississippi, Louisiana, and Arkansas in 1919, but growers rejected the proposal in Texas and South Carolina. The Arkansas committee, composed of a crusher, a ginner, a farmer, and a representative of the agricultural commission, decided each week what the price of seed should be and publicized it. After about two months the market declined and the commissioner of agriculture for Arkansas withdrew his support.[20]

Attempts to suspend antitrust laws and revive the cooperative price fixing of the war years proved short lived, but the idea continued to appeal to many processors. A decade later, A. K. Tigrett, president of the

International Vegetable Oil Company, said that his mills would "welcome" a commission to fix cottonseed prices. "We assume that under no conditions would they give us a narrower margin to work upon than the existing competition forces us to work upon."[21]

The sharp deflation of 1920–21, which caused a 35 percent fall in the general price level, created much distress in the crushing industry. Diminished federal spending, the inability of Europeans to buy American goods after the government terminated war credits in June of 1919, and high discount rates imposed by the Federal Reserve Board in the summer of 1920 contributed to the slump in prices. The total value of crude cottonseed products dropped by more than 55 percent between 1920 and 1921. Although the decline in product prices was offset by an even greater fall in cottonseed prices, the sudden deflation, together with an unusually small cotton crop, destabilized the crushing industry. Numerous mills closed, and the F. W. Brode Company of Memphis, one of the oldest and largest cottonseed-meal brokerage firms in the United States, declared bankruptcy in 1921.[22]

Steep freight increases in August 1920 exacerbated the problems of farmers and processors, who had been hit by price declines a year earlier than those in most industries. In the cotton states, railway freight rates went up about 25 percent overnight. Large oil mills that relied on the railroads to transport their seed were particularly hard hit. Freight was a major expense for the American Cotton Oil Company, which owned many of the large terminal mills that depended almost entirely on trains to move seed and products. Railway companies needed the rate increases to remain solvent, but the freight hikes came at an unfortunate time for the producers and processors of American farm products. In response to their complaints, the Interstate Commerce Commission reduced freight rates about 10 percent at the beginning of 1922.[23]

World War I had interrupted overseas trade patterns, but contrary to expectations, exports of cottonseed oil and meal did not rebound when the fighting ended. In the past sales of surplus cottonseed products abroad had helped to maintain higher prices at home. At first industry leaders blamed the weak export market on European financial problems and unfavorable exchange rates. As exports continued to decline, refiners attributed the loss of European markets to the tax on imported vegetable oils that had been included in the Emergency Tariff Act of 1921 at the request of the dairy industry and most cottonseed crushers.

To meet wartime demand for fats, both the United States and European countries had imported coconut, soy, peanut, palm, and other oils and oleaginous materials from the Far East. Some American cottonseed-oil mills crushed peanuts, copra, and a variety of oil seeds during the war years. When the fighting ended, cotton farmers, ginners, other cottonseed dealers, and crushers asked the United States Food Administration to halt the importation of Asian vegetable oils and raw materials.[24]

Republicans came to power in 1921 determined to restore protective tariffs that had been removed in 1913 following the election of Woodrow Wilson. In a departure from agriculture's traditional free-trade position, many farmers demanded protective tariffs, believing that they would bring higher prices for agricultural products as they had in the past done for manufactured goods. Farmers had been converted to the principle of protection after the sudden price deflation of 1920–21. President Harding called an emergency session of Congress to enact a temporary measure that would serve until permanent tariff legislation could be prepared.[25]

The small but growing volume of cheap imports of vegetable oil and oleaginous materials from Asia alarmed many American cottonseed crushers and convinced them to support the Emergency Tariff Act even though edible vegetable oil imported into the United States after the First World War actually amounted to only about 1.5 percent of the cottonseed oil produced domestically. The pro-tariff memorial sent to Congress by cottonseed crushers maintained that they could not compete with Asian oils produced by "half-starved, unsanitary, disease-ridden labor, requiring a hand-full of rice as a daily ration and living under conditions which no American would regard as tolerable." [26]

Passage of the Emergency Tariff Act brought retaliation from Italy and France in the form of much higher duties on American cottonseed oil. By 1922 cottonseed oil exports had fallen to a quarter of their pre-war volume. The Interstate Cotton Seed Crushers' Association called a special meeting to reconsider the question of taxing foreign vegetable oils. After hearing persuasive speeches by John Aspegren and other refiners, a majority of the members present voted against a permanent tariff on imported vegetable oils.

Oil men supporting the tariff charged that those in the opposing camp had secured enough proxies from cottonseed brokers and dealers to run roughshod over the crushers. Although it is impossible to know exactly how processors lined up on the tariff issue, independent oil men in Texas, Oklahoma, and to a lesser extent Georgia, took the lead in the fight for protection. A number of independent mill operators withdrew from the Interstate Cotton Seed Crushers' Association to protest the methods used by refiner-manufacturers to get their views adopted by the association. The tariff issue caused bitterness between independent crushers and refiners and reinforced divisions that had originally appeared during the period of rapid mill building that began in the 1880s and lasted until the outbreak of World War I.[27]

Following the anti-tariff vote at the Interstate Cotton Seed Crushers' Association convention, representatives of the association told members of the Senate Finance Committee that with no competition from the United States, European vegetable-oil producers could buy oil and oleaginous materials from the East at very low prices, especially as no anti-trust laws barred European mills from forming buying pools. Lift the duty on Asian oils, association spokesmen argued, and permit the oils to be used by U.S. soap manufacturers. Then surplus cottonseed oil would once again find markets abroad. Despite their pleas, the Fordney-McCumber Tariff Act of 1922 imposed high duties on imported vegetable oils and oleaginous materials, as well as on a wide range of American industrial and agricultural products. The president of the Interstate Cotton Seed Crushers' Association blamed the outcome on the dairy lobby, but "a considerable number" of cottonseed crushers joined the "farm bloc" in support of prohibitive duties. As some cottonseed-oil refiners had predicted, British and European soap and margarine manufacturers formed a Soya Bean Oil Pool in the mid-1920s that very successfully held down oil prices.[28]

Those who attributed the loss of overseas markets for cottonseed products to high tariffs overlooked other factors that discouraged Europeans from buying the products of American farms and factories. Because of growing domestic demand, food produced in the United States became more expensive around the turn of the century and therefore less desirable to foreign buyers. The First World War transformed the United States from a debtor to a creditor nation. In order to buy American goods, Europeans had to be able to sell their products in this country. United States postwar policy made that difficult. Besides imposing protective tariffs, the United States demanded that its former allies promptly repay the money they had borrowed to finance the war. That left even fewer dollars for purchasing American goods. European countries thus had many reasons for becoming more self-sufficient in agriculture and industry. The United Kingdom and other formerly large consumers of American agricultural products bought in the cheapest possible markets, preferably from countries that purchased their manufactured products in return.[29]

Some European countries had begun to free themselves from dependence on American cottonseed oil and meal before the erection of an
American tariff wall. The modern German oil-seed industry dates from
the first decade of the twentieth century. Solvent extraction mills processed copra, palm kernels, peanuts, and other materials with a high oil
content. The experience of wartime blockades made Germans more aware
than ever of the importance of having a large domestic vegetable-oil industry. By the fall of 1917 most German oil mills had closed for lack of raw
materials, but processors erected new solvent extraction and hydrogenation
plants in anticipation of strong postwar demand.[30]

The British seed-crushing industry expanded very rapidly during the
First World War in order to supply vitally needed fats, animal feed, and
glycerin for munitions. The most important product of prewar British
mills, generally called cake mills, had been linseed and cottonseed cake
for cattle feeders. When the blockade diverted oleaginous materials from
Germany to England, British cake mills began to process a greater variety of raw materials and became primarily interested in the edible oil
market. The amount of peanut oil manufactured by British mills increased
eightfold during the war years. After the war British and European producers of vegetable oil and cake expanded their domestic capacity.[31]

Growing demand for cottonseed products in the United States and
declining demand abroad caused the postwar drop in exports. During
the early years of the crushing industry most cottonseed oil and cake had
been shipped overseas. Rapid expansion of oil mills to all parts of the Cotton Belt after 1880 depressed prices and made cottonseed oil attractive to
domestic shortening manufacturers. Increased volume and cheaper prices
also stimulated large sales of oil and cake overseas during the 1890s.
Between 1900 and 1914 the percentage of exports declined as continued
improvements in oil refining and the development of hydrogenation increased domestic demand. Only about 8 percent of the cottonseed oil
produced in the United States was exported in 1914. Postwar declines in
cotton production left little surplus oil to be exported. Although refiners
made the protective tariff their scapegoat, a number of factors interacted
to cause exports of cottonseed products to shrink.[32]

Three small cotton crops during the early 1920s hurt many mills. The
high cost of combating boll weevils speeded the shift of cotton growing
to dryer areas of the Southwest, which were less subject to infestation. A
number of southeastern mills closed during the early 1920s for lack of
seed. Memphis processor William H. Jasspon estimated that all the seed

from the 1924 crop could have been crushed in three months. In the scramble for raw materials, numerous crushers paid more for seed than their manufactured products earned. A large surplus of lard in 1922 and 1924 kept the price of cottonseed oil low despite the smaller production. The lower seed prices that resulted from increased cotton production in 1925–26 and the record cotton crop of the succeeding year did not bring relief to the crushing industry. Jasspon believed that the loss of export markets was in large part responsible for the low prices received by cottonseed crushers in those years of large crops.[33]

Postwar changes in transportation that accelerated the marketing of cottonseed brought new expenses to processors. Before World War I many small gins had been necessary to process cotton grown in remote areas. Dependent on roads that often became impassable in winter or on streams that could be navigated only at times of high water, ginners sometimes had to wait for weeks to move seed to the mills. A Louisiana crusher said that when he went into the business early in the twentieth century, ginners marketed cottonseed over a seven- or eight-month period. Dramatic growth of the automobile industry during the 1920s spurred the development of good roads and that in turn contributed to the demise of many country gins. Modern gins could handle much more seed and transport it to mills without delay. Most cottonseed poured into mills within three months, and crushers had to build more storage houses, tie up larger sums of money in seed, and pay more for interest and insurance.[34]

The problems faced by cottonseed crushers after the war overwhelmed the American Cotton Oil Company and forced a reorganization of the Southern Cotton Oil Company. The combination of high seed and freight costs, low oil and shortening prices, loss of export markets, and, according to some critics, financial mismanagement destroyed the American Cotton Oil Company. Immediately after the war the company built at Memphis a twenty-four-press mill, the largest in the world, which some people considered evidence of poor judgment. Operating losses ranged from $1.5 million in 1919–20 to about $3 million in 1922–23. Between 1921 and 1924 the American Cotton Oil Company sold its crushing mills and gins at nearly $4 million less than their book value. In September 1923 the heavily indebted company scrapped all but its profitable soap-making operations and reorganized as the Gold Dust Corporation.[35]

The Southern Cotton Oil Company was also hurt by adverse conditions in the crushing industry during the early 1920s, although not as severely as the American Cotton Oil Company, which had not kept pace with Buckeye and the Southern Cotton Oil Company in developing popular vegetable oils and shortenings. Before the war the bulk of the Southern Cotton Oil Company's exports had gone to margarine manufacturers in northern Europe. That market collapsed in the aftermath of war, and high seed prices and low oil prices squeezed the company's cottonseed-oil mills. After three difficult years, the Virginia-Carolina Chemical Company and its subsidiary, the Southern Cotton Oil Company, went into receivership in 1924. In order to survive, the Virginia-Carolina Chemical Company decided to sell the Southern Cotton Oil Company. Bernard Baruch, New York capitalists, and Virginia-Carolina Chemical Company stockholders put up 40 percent of the approximately $9 million paid for the company, and a group of New Orleans businessmen headed by Rudolph Hecht and A. D. Geoghegan supplied 60 percent of the purchase price. Geoghegan, president of Southport Mill Ltd., a manufacturer of cottonseed products, and operator of the Southern Cotton Oil Company under the receivership committee, became president of the new Wesson Oil and Snowdrift Company. Both the Southern Cotton Oil Company and Southport Mill became subsidiaries of Wesson. The Southern Cotton Oil Company thus became the first major full-line cottonseed-products company to be principally owned by southern capitalists.[36]

The difficulty of earning "fair profits" because of increased raw-material costs after the First World War hastened the consolidation of oil mills. Between 1914 and 1940 the number of cottonseed-oil mills declined by almost half. The need to operate more efficiently and the opportunity to acquire bankrupt mills at cut-rate prices during the early 1920s contributed to the formation of small chains of mills within the same general geographical area. Successful independent operators took the opportunity offered by depressed mill prices to add to their holdings, often in collaboration with former officials of the American Cotton Oil Company. Mississippi crusher G. W. Covington bought the Jackson, Mississippi, mill of the American Cotton Oil Company in 1923. His partner in the purchase was a former manager of the mill and a vice president of the American Cotton Oil Company. Three years later Covington, John B. Perry of Grenada, and other Mississippi crushers and bankers formed the Mississippi Cottonseed Products Company, which owned thirteen mills with a total of eighty-three presses.[37] Among the other horizontal mergers that took place during the immediate postwar years was that of John T. Stevens of Kershaw, South Carolina. Beginning with three mills in South Carolina, Stevens and a partner acquired several American

Cotton Oil Company mills in the southeastern states in 1922. The company had twenty-four presses in South Carolina, twenty in Alabama, and seventeen in Georgia.[38]

A successful merger of Oklahoma mills inspired Tennessee and Arkansas mill owners to organize the National Cottonseed Products Corporation in 1924. Two years later several Tennessee and New York companies that dealt in securities invested heavily in the venture. With about twenty mills in five contiguous states, the new company expected to save money on freight and increase operating efficiency by buying seed in common and shipping it to the nearest mill. The National Cottonseed Products Corporation was said to have the second largest crushing capacity in the industry, but overvaluation of its properties and disagreements among the principal stockholders on opposite sides of the Mississippi River started the company on a downward slide toward insolvency.[39]

To eliminate excess crushing capacity in the southeastern states, where the problem was greatest, officers of the Southern Cotton Oil Company, Procter & Gamble, Swift, and other leading cotton-oil companies in 1927 began to investigate the possibility of buying independent mills and closing many of them. The Southern Cotton Oil Company studied North and South Carolina, Georgia, and Alabama and reported that those states had 887 presses and produced only enough seed to crush fourteen hundred tons per press. The big companies hoped to increase the annual crush per press to twenty-five to thirty-five hundred tons or more. A single press could handle forty-five hundred tons in three hundred days, but no one considered that a practical goal. The cost of the planned consolidation was estimated to be approximately $15 million. In 1929 President Geoghegan of the Southern Cotton Oil Company instructed the heads of several large mill groups in the Southeast to get as many options as they could on independent mills, most of whose owners appeared anxious to sell. At that point the plan foundered, because of the questionable legality of forming a corporation for the sole purpose of buying excess mills and scrapping many of them.[40]

The two major companies involved in the plan to reduce southeastern crushing capacity individually acquired oil mills and took a number of them out of operation. The Southern Cotton Oil Company bought eight Georgia mills in 1928 for about 20 percent of their book value from the bankrupt Empire Cotton Oil Company and closed all but two of them. During the late 1920s Buckeye purchased, and in some cases closed, mills in Corinth, Mississippi; Memphis; Milledgeville, Georgia; Raleigh, North Carolina; and Decatur, Alabama. In acquiring the last two mills, the com-

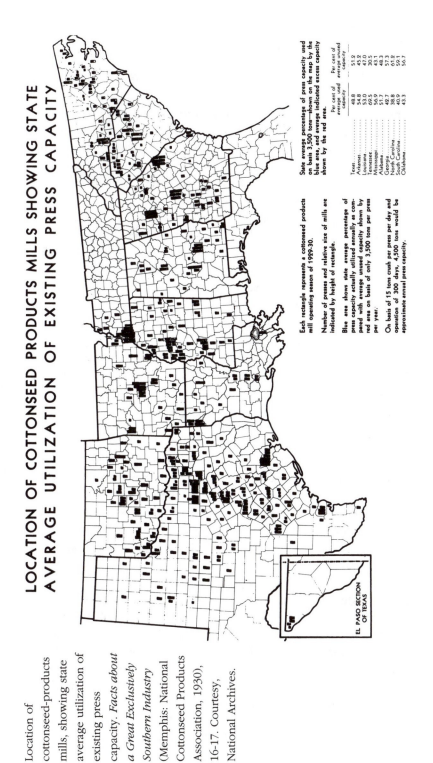

LOCATION OF COTTONSEED PRODUCTS MILLS SHOWING STATE AVERAGE UTILIZATION OF EXISTING PRESS CAPACITY

Location of cottonseed-products mills, showing state average utilization of existing press capacity. *Facts about a Great Exclusively Southern Industry* (Memphis: National Cottonseed Products Association, 1930), 16-17. Courtesy, National Archives.

Each rectangle represents a cottonseed products mill operating season of 1929-30.

Number of presses and relative size of mills are indicated by height of rectangle.

Blue area shows state average percentage of press capacity actually utilized annually as compared with average unused capacity shown by red area on basis of only 3,500 tons per press per year.

On basis of 15 tons crush per press per day and operation of 300 days, 4,500 tons would be approximate annual press capacity.

State average percentage of press capacity used on basis 3,500 tons—shown on the map by the blue area, and average indicated excess capacity shown by the red area.

	Per cent of average used capacity	Per cent of average unused capacity
Texas	48.8	51.2
Arkansas	54.8	45.2
Louisiana	53.0	47.0
Tennessee	69.5	30.5
Mississippi	56.9	43.1
Alabama	51.7	48.3
Georgia	42.7	57.3
North Carolina	38.8	61.2
South Carolina	40.9	59.1
Oklahoma	43.3	56.7

EL PASO SECTION OF TEXAS

pany used aggressive tactics. The International Vegetable Oil Company reportedly did not wish to sell its profitable Raleigh operation, but Buckeye purchased land close by and began to prepare the site for a new mill. As part of its sale's agreement with Buckeye, the International Vegetable Oil Company promised to not operate or buy seed within a hundred mile radius of Raleigh for seven years. Buckeye apparently also used the threat of building a competing mill as a lever to acquire the Decatur mill.[41]

In 1929 the Buckeye Cotton Oil Company bought nine oil mills from the financially troubled National Cottonseed Products Corporation with the promise that oil milling would not be carried on in any of them for at least a decade. Altogether, seventy-one presses, principally in Tennessee and Arkansas, were eliminated. In return for financial assistance, the National Cottonseed Products Corporation had to sell its crude oil, and a large amount of its cottonseed, to Buckeye.[42]

During the 1920s large companies bought and often "junked" mills to squeeze out excess capacity and increase their crush by acquiring new sources of seed. They also tried to eliminate or change the management of mills that consistently bid up prices. Two companies that controlled close to 40 percent of South Carolina's crushing capacity, the John T. Stevens chain based in Kershaw and another group in the area of Hartsville, acting independently and jointly, leased and purchased other mills, which they used only for collecting seed and selling cottonseed products. Among the mills they acquired were several that had kept the seed market in turmoil. Four Dallas mills purchased the city's fifth crushing operation, because it refused to work with them in holding down seed prices. A Swift and Company officer at Montgomery, Alabama, said about two similar purchases: "It looks now as if we will have a steady seed market and much better conditions since the Buckeye is in control of Chattanooga and Louisville, both of which disturbed us previously by raids and secret prices."[43]

By 1930 ten companies with 178 mills owned about 45 percent of the cottonseed-crushing capacity in the United States. They were the Southern Cotton Oil Company of New Orleans; Buckeye Cotton Oil Company of Cincinnati; Swift and Company of Chicago; the R. K. Wooten group of Chickasha, Oklahoma; the P. A. Norris interests of Ada, Oklahoma; the Mississippi Cottonseed Products Company; Anderson-Clayton Company of Houston; the National Cottonseed Products Corporation of Memphis; Southland Cotton Oil Company of Paris, Texas, soon to be acquired by the Southern Cotton Oil Company; and the J. W. Simmons chain of Dallas. The Wootten, Norris, and Simmons groups had a working relationship. All of the top ten crushing companies except Buckeye and Swift were predominantly owned by southern investors. Contrary to the situation before the First World War, autonomous mills had become a minority by 1930. Large and small mill chains controlled a major portion of the total crushing capacity.[44]

In a number of ways World War I constitutes a watershed in the history of cottonseed processing. 1914 saw the largest number of oil mills in the industry's history, marking the climax of a half-century trend of building numerous small mills close to the cotton fields in addition to large terminal mills in the major market towns. After the war consolidation became the rule, and fewer and larger mills processed most of the annual crush. The economic shocks of the postwar period reinforced the new trend, because some bankrupt mills remained closed permanently. Finding labor to man the mills became an industrywide problem for the first time after 1914, and the difficulty persisted for several years following the war.[45] Secret price-fixing and seed-sharing agreements had been the dominant strategy for moderating seed prices before the First World War, whereas after the conflict crushers faced fierce competition for seed with fewer opportunities for collusion due to vigorous antitrust activities by state and federal governments. World War I created an enormous demand for cottonseed linters in the production of gun cotton, and the availability of large supplies of cheap linters and surplus powder plants at the end of the war helped American companies take the lead in developing the chemical cellulose industry. The market for cottonseed products became primarily a domestic one as exports ceased to be a significant factor after the war. Finally, the First World War stimulated government-industry cooperation and self-regulation, which became ideals of the cottonseed processing industry during the difficult postwar era.

CHAPTER 9

Competition and Cooperation
between the World Wars

The obsolete slogan that "Competition is the Life of Trade"
should be relegated and the one of 'Co-operation' should
take its place.

> J. J. Culbertson, *Cotton Oil Press,* 1918

Competition was believed to be the life of trade, but we are
beginning to see that beyond certain limits competition be-
comes disastrous. Co-operation in all phases of life is necessary for common growth and development, where competition often breaks down of its own attrition.

> William H. Jasspon,
> "What a Large Crop Does to
> the Cotton Oil Industry," 1927

Industry at the Cross Roads, One Way by the Bridge of Hon-
est Cooperation Leads to Prosperity—the Other Is the Free-for-
All Route, by Short Cuts and Devious Trails, to the Slough of
Despond and Bankruptcy.

> Cover of *Cotton Oil Press,*
> March 1933

After the First World War, many cottonseed processors looked back nos-
talgically on the years of wartime regulation, believing them to have been
a time when "distrust" among farmers, ginners, crushers, and refiner-manufacturers diminished. They hoped to preserve the spirit of cooperation that
had existed briefly during the final months of the conflict. The guaranteed
spread between the cost of seed and the prices of cottonseed products

negotiated by representatives of all groups involved in cottonseed processing and enforced by the federal government during the 1917 and 1918 crushing seasons became a goal for many in the industry.[1]

The commitment to cooperation among cottonseed processors during the postwar years came at a time of heightened competition within the industry. Boll weevil damage contributed to several years of short cotton crops and high seed prices; yet the more seed a mill processed, the more likely it was to operate at a profit in the highly competitive postwar crushing industry. With price-fixing pools subject to antitrust prosecution and many oil mills seeking to enlarge their seed-buying territories, the quest for raw materials intensified after the First World War. Rules of fair trade drawn up by industry members during the 1920s and 1930s describe the competitive practices processors employed to acquire cottonseed.[2]

Seed shortages increased the resentment that many crushers felt toward the powerful refining and manufacturing companies. The rivalry began during the late nineteenth century, when several large cottonseed, meat-packing, and soap-making corporations engaged in cottonseed crushing and oil mills not aligned with those companies multiplied. The tariff fight of the early 1920s, in which refiners objected to and crushers generally supported a proposed tax on foreign vegetable oils, aggravated divisions within the industry.[3]

The financial ability of major companies to tie up seed supplies by controlling gins through ownership and loans and to buy seed at unprofitably high prices when it was in short supply further heightened tensions between crushers and refiner-manufacturers. Full-line companies could make up for mill losses through sales of manufactured products, but independent mills had to make a profit on their crushing operations or go out of business. Independent operators also resorted to "unfair competition" at times in the annual contest for seed, but they felt besieged by their larger rivals. A federal official observed in 1933 that for a decade independent mills had been "fighting" Procter & Gamble, Swift, and the Southern Cotton Oil Company.[4]

Despite the distrust that existed between many independent crushers and refiners, processors made modest progress toward cooperation and stabilization during the postwar years. Working through its national trade association, the industry sought to moderate competition for seed by grading it and publicizing prices, standardizing buying practices, and proscribing so-called unfair dealings that contributed to the high cost of seed. All of those initiatives required cooperation among crushers.

Cottonseed processors shared their enthusiasm for cooperation or "open competition" with other American entrepreneurs. Despite the wave of business mergers that took place during the late nineteenth and early twentieth centuries, savage competition persisted in many branches of American industry, especially those that processed raw materials such as timber, petroleum, and cotton. State and federal antitrust laws made traditional price-fixing pools too risky and widespread cheating by participants limited the cartels' effectiveness. At the turn of the century a number of leading businessmen called for federal regulation of American industries and full disclosure of financial information. Some business leaders even suggested that the government fix prices based on analyses of costs and earnings in highly competitive industries.

In 1912 Arthur Jerome Eddy proposed in *The New Competition* that companies in highly competitive industries form "open price associations" that would collect and publicize a wide range of statistics. Individual manufacturers could then make informed decisions about prices, and the need for secret price fixing would disappear. The act creating the Federal Trade Commission in 1914 outlawed "unfair competition." Cooperation became the battle cry of many American businessmen in the fight against "destructive" and "wasteful" competition.

Throughout the 1920s many business leaders, including those in cottonseed processing, worked through their trade associations and as far as possible with federal officials to lessen the impact of antitrust legislation. In Secretary of Commerce Herbert Hoover, American industry found a strong ally in its campaign to eliminate inefficient business practices, but changing personnel and attitudes in different departments of the federal government made efforts to achieve greater cooperation within highly competitive industries more difficult.[5]

The role trade associations played in mediating between industry and government during and after the First World War resulted in their accumulating new powers. Cottonseed processors transformed the Interstate Cotton Seed Crushers' Association from what Louis Galambos has called "a dinner club association" that relied on its officers and committee members to transact limited business between annual conventions into a "service association" with a larger income and full-time, salaried employees who carried on a wide range of activities year round. The association hired Louis Geldert as its first full-time executive in 1917. Geldert assisted the president and edited the *Cotton Oil Press,* a new publication designed to keep members informed about their industry. The only previous salaried official had been the secretary-treasurer, who principally handled membership matters. Because of its central location and prominence as a crushing center, Memphis became the site of the association's permanent office. At their 1925 convention, members approved the hiring of a general manager and the creation of the Bureau of Markets and Bureau of Research.[6]

Price publicity became the top priority of cottonseed industry leaders following the First World War, but Justice Department hostility to open price associations and publicity plans delayed implementation. Disapproval of price publicity dissipated at the top levels of government following the election of Calvin Coolidge as president and the departure of Attorney General Daugherty in the spring of 1924. The Supreme Court ruled in the Maple Flooring Case of 1925 that price publicity did not in itself contravene federal antitrust laws. As a result of that decision, Christie Benet, general manager of the Interstate Cotton Seed Crushers' Association, announced that he intended to "stabilize the value of cottonseed by each day giving publicity in the widest sense to the prices paid for cottonseed all over the belt and the value of products thereof."[7]

In reality, the trade association lacked the means to implement price reporting on an industrywide basis. Instead, state crushers' associations took the lead in publicizing seed prices west of the Mississippi. In 1924 the Dallas Cotton Exchange began to post cottonseed prices reported to its office daily by a committee of the Texas Cottonseed Crushers' Association and based principally on what Dallas mills paid for seed. The exchange posted the prices reported to them without further investigation. Prices posted by the Houston Cotton Exchange served mills in south Texas. From 1924 to 1929 the New Orleans Cotton Exchange performed a similar function for mills in its area, and in 1926 the Little Rock Cotton Exchange began posting cottonseed prices. Crushers hoped to stabilize cottonseed values by posting prices that would permit profitable operation.[8]

Some crushers east of the Mississippi reported prices to their trade association secretaries, who analyzed the information and communicated it to members along with advice on appropriate prices for different sections. The North and South Carolina crushers' associations pioneered price reporting early in the twentieth century and were the only crushers in the Southeast to report prices on a regular basis.[9]

Prices quoted on the cotton exchanges were supposed to be the highest paid for seed on a given day. The Federal Trade Commission later charged that posted prices represented the "general" or "average" price paid by a mill, and that higher than average prices paid to meet competition in isolated places did not receive publicity. The FTC also found evidence that both price posting and price reporting had been used to discourage competition for seed. At times oil men agreed to buy seed at posted or reported prices and brought pressure to bear on those who did not conform.[10]

If price publicity were to be of real value, companies needed to use identical accounting methods. Being able to compare the costs of different units in an industry also contributed to increased efficiency. For those reasons uniform cost accounting became a crusade among businessmen after the First World War, and Interstate Cotton Seed Crushers' Association leaders got on the band wagon. In 1922 the ICCA president appointed a committee to develop standard cost-accounting procedures for the crushing industry. He argued that adoption of uniform accounting methods could prevent seed speculation by making it clear to oil men when they paid more for seed than product prices warranted. The association's Uniform Cost Accountancy Committee prepared standard forms for compiling statistics on operating costs and made them available to oil mills in 1923. That year more than one hundred trade associations embraced uniform cost accounting.[11]

The Interstate Cotton Seed Crushers' Association adopted the committee's cost accounting plan in 1924 and urged state associations to follow suit. Several years later the president reported that the subject of uniform cost accounting had not been pursued for several years. Buckeye and other large firms employed sophisticated accounting procedures, but many small mills continued to rely on old-fashioned bookkeeping methods that did not make adequate provision for depreciation, losses incurred at different stages of production, and similar items. Some mills kept only one set of books for all their business enterprises, so that it was difficult for operators to determine the earnings of their different activities, such as ginning, milling, fertilizer or feed mixing, and ice manufacturing.[12]

Cottonseed grading was another item on the agenda after the First World War. Without some means of judging the oil and protein content of cottonseed, all raw materials had to be purchased at the same price. The high seed prices and reduced profits of the postwar years made it highly desirable for processors to pay less for seed of lower quality.[13] The difficulty of determining the value of different lots of seed delayed the adoption of cottonseed grading. The first grading system devised by the Department of Agriculture, known as "cut and count," although easy to use, proved to be unreliable. The grader decided how much moisture was present by shaking seed to see if they were dry enough to rattle. He determined the amount of trash in a carload of seed by visual examination. The grader then cut open one hundred seeds and counted the number of abnormally colored and immature ones. Based on moisture content, the amount of trash, and the color and maturity of seed, the grader decided how much to deduct from the price of "prime cottonseed." Further study revealed that seed color has virtually no bearing on oil quality. Moreover, one hundred seeds could hardly represent the two hundred million in a freight car.

Chemical analysis of cottonseed samples provided the basis for a more reliable method of cottonseed grading at the end of the 1920s. Chemists at the Department of Agriculture discovered that the oil content of cottonseed varied from as little as 150 pounds to more than 400 pounds per ton of seed. The protein content of different batches of seed, also varied widely, as did the staple length of linters. Even cottonseed from the same farm or gin might be quite different. The condition of seed affected the quality and amount of oil a mill produced. Much higher losses occurred during the refining of crude oil made from wet, dirty, or rotting seed. In 1928 the Department of Agriculture presented a grading plan to the industry that combined quantity and quality indexes. The quantity index measures the amounts of oil and protein, which accounted for 77 to 90 percent of the total value of cottonseed products in a ton of seed; the quality index measures moisture, foreign materials, and free fatty acids, the amount of which indicates the degree of deterioration.

A mathematical formula based on the quantity and quality indexes is used to calculate cottonseed grades. Cottonseed that contains specified amounts of oil and ammonia and does not exceed fixed levels of free fatty acids, foreign matter, and moisture receives the "basis grade" of one hundred. Processed efficiently, basis cottonseed should yield given amounts of oil and cake. Grades above and below one hundred are classified as "high" and "low," and premiums and discounts are applied to seed prices for these grades at a predetermined rate. The new form of grading, known as the Meloy system for the Department of Agriculture official who guided its development, was introduced in Georgia in 1928 following a hurricane that badly damaged seed.[14]

During the first two years of grading under the new system, seed dealers frequently complained that samples from identical lots of seed that were tested by different chemists gave varying results. Finding that to be the case, a committee of chemists worked for several years to stan-

dardize laboratory equipment and procedures. Satisfied that more uniform results were being achieved, the Department of Agriculture made
its grading system an "official standard of the federal government" in
1932. With modifications based on additional information and experience, the method is used today.[15]

The complexity of cottonseed grading made it unpopular with ginners and farmers. Most of them could determine the approximate grade
of cotton lint by visual examination, but cottonseed analysis had to be
carried out by trained chemists. "When they tell you all that stuff about
protein, and dirt and trash," said a ginner, "it is all dutch to me anyhow."
It frustrated independent ginners and seed sellers, who had to purchase
seed with their own money, not to know in advance the grade of their
seed and what sums might be deducted from the purchase price.[16]

A problem that defied resolution was the impracticality of grading
seed in amounts smaller than railway carlots or large truckloads. At from
two to five dollars an analysis, it was too expensive to test samples from
individual wagonloads. Furthermore, ginners believed that they could not
pay farmers different prices for seed, even though quality varied, and still
retain their business. Thus, although in theory ginners could afford to pay
more for seed in prime condition, small farmers received no direct reward for producing high-quality seed. When the Meloy system first went
into effect, short-lived efforts were made in several states to analyze
samples and determine the average grade of cottonseed in different agricultural districts as a basis for buying seed. Such plans had little impact
on the problem of compensating small farmers for superior cottonseed.[17]

Another cause of dissatisfaction with the Meloy system was its application only to seed sold by independent ginners. Crushers explained that
there was no reason to grade seed purchased from ginners buying on commission, because the mills told them what to pay, supplied the money, and
owned the seed from the moment of purchase. Because independent
ginners tended to delay selling for weeks or months, their seed was more
likely to be damaged and to be in greater need of grading. The large
number of discounts on seed during the first season of grading worked
a great hardship on independent ginners, who had to pay as much for
seed as their competitors buying on commission. They viewed grading
as the crushers' method of forcing independent cottonseed dealers to sell
on commission.[18]

The national trade association defused some criticisms of seed grading by lowering the oil content for basis cottonseed in 1931. Instead of

losing money on the seed they sold because of deductions, as had been common during the first seasons of grading, independent cottonseed shippers received premiums on much of their seed. Bonuses reconciled many of them to the grading system. Later adjustments resulted in about 90 percent or more of the graded cottonseed bringing the basis price.[19]

Aggressive competition for seed after the First World War made crushers receptive to the idea being promoted by the U.S. Chamber of Commerce during the 1920s of preparing a "code of good trade practice." Rules proscribing unfair practices were first implemented under the auspices of the Cottonseed Division of the Food Administration during World War I. The Federal Trade Commission created the Trade Practice Conference Division in 1926 to assist industries in framing rules of fair competition. Such rules became legally enforceable if the commission sanctioned them.[20]

Before the opening of the 1926 crushing season, the trade associations of the southeastern states compiled "Trading Rules Governing the Buying and Selling of Cottonseed." That year the Cotton Belt produced a record crop, which lessened the need for rules to protect against aggressive competitors. The average farm price of cottonseed per ton dropped from $30.88 in 1925–26 to $21.63 the following season. Not understanding the inverse relationship between the size of the cotton crop and the prices of cottonseed and cottonseed products, farmers charged that prices had been fixed. As a result of complaints from farmers, Representative John Rankin of Mississippi introduced a resolution, which the House of Representatives passed on 2 March 1927, directing the Federal Trade Commission to determine whether cottonseed crushers and refiners had combined to fix cottonseed prices. The FTC reported a year later that it had discovered too little evidence of collusion to justify proceeding further. Examination of mill records showed that profit margins had been low or nonexistent for much of the decade.[21]

The Federal Trade Commission finding that lack of price reporting and grading made it impossible for people to know the market price of cottonseed encouraged trade associations to ask for the agency's help in formulating and enforcing rules of good business practice. In 1928, with assistance from officials of the Trade Practice Conference Division, the Interstate Cotton Seed Crushers' Association prepared a "Suggested Memorandum of Business Principles for Cottonseed Oil Mills," a proposed code that drew on earlier cottonseed trading rules.[22] The memorandum's first principle called for immediate publication of all prices bid or paid for cottonseed and cottonseed products. Based on that information, individual crushers would theoretically make their own decisions about prices without any obligation to adhere to those being paid by other oil men. Another principle demanded that cottonseed purchases be based on quality, moisture, and cleanness, that is, that they be graded.

The code specified that no contract for seed or products should be canceled except for legal reasons, that contracts should be for specific quantities at specified prices and not predated or postdated. Another principle stated that "the entire consideration should be included in the price paid or bid, and no [secret] commissions, bonuses, rebates, or subsidies of any kind are to be paid or allowed to sellers of seed or buyers of products." Requiring contracts to be for specific amounts was to stop crushers from agreeing to buy all the seed of a farmer or ginner at a fixed price, which took that seed off the market. The stipulation that seed contracts be uniform and binding and that they include every payment was intended to make price reporting more accurate. A crusher who paid more than the prevailing price for seed but did not want it to be known that he had disturbed prices might ask the seller to put a date on the contract when the higher price was in effect, or he might buy more seed than the tonnage specified on a higher-price contract after reporting that he had begun to pay lower prices for seed. When mills paid secret subsidies for seed, reported prices became meaningless.

Storing cottonseed free for owners until the price went up and they chose to sell and buying seed slated for delivery more than two weeks after purchase were forbidden by the code. Both practices resulted in higher seed prices. Notified of an impending price decline, seed dealers frequently contracted to sell at the current price more seed than they had on hand. Two weeks gave seed sellers ample time to load and ship the seed they had on their premises but discouraged them from contracting to sell seed they did not have.[23]

Under the 1928 rules, mills were not to loan money to ginners without requiring proper security and interest payments. Many crushers considered gin loans unfair, unethical, and discriminatory because they tied up seed and only well-financed companies had large sums of money to lend. Moreover, some processors believed that loans encouraged the overbuilding of gins and greater competition among them for cotton to gin, which frequently led to higher seed prices being offered as an inducement. Oil men discussed gin loans in off-the-record sessions, but the code did not prohibit them, as many desired, because other powerful individuals and companies supported gin loans.[24]

Another rule would make sellers rather than crushers responsible for paying brokerage fees on seed, as mill operators did when selling cottonseed products through brokers. Seed prices tended to go up when brokers encouraged processors to bid against one another for large lots of seed. Brokers believed, with reason, that the purpose of the rule was to eliminate them from cottonseed buying and selling. By the early 1930s few seed brokers remained in business because sellers with large lots of seed dealt directly with mills rather than pay brokerage fees.[25]

Hauling allowances for trucks carrying cottonseed caused much dissension among crushers, yet the 1928 code was silent on the subject. Without uniform hauling allowances, accurate reporting of seed prices could not be carried on, but crushers were too divided on the subject in 1928 to agree on a general rule. The matter had to be resolved state by state.

As roads improved after the First World War, farmers and ginners increasingly used trucks to transport cottonseed to interior mills, whereas the terminal mills continued to rely principally on the railroads. Trucks increased the seed-buying range of small mills and intensified the competition between interior and terminal mills. It also cost mills less to have seed and products moved by truck than by rail, and larger hauling allowances could be used to pay dealers more for seed without increasing reported prices.

The custom had long been for mills to pay freight on seed from the railway point nearest a seller. The obligation of hauling seed to the railroad rested with the ginner, seed dealer, or planter, and the farther away he was from the railroad, the more he had to pay for hauling. Some interior mills began to pay ginners to truck their seed from locations off the railroad to their final destination. Operators of terminal mills considered that unfair competition. Most crushers agreed that compensation for truck transportation should be based on railway freight rates and the most direct routes, but disagreed about whether hauling allowances should begin at the point of origin of the seed or at the railroad station closest to the gin or plantation. In order to hold down transportation costs, terminal mills insisted that those shipping seed by truck be paid in lieu of railway freight only.

To offset the advantages trucks gave country mills, some of the larger companies sought reduced freight rates on incoming seed when they shipped finished products out by the same rail line, an arrangement known as milling-in-transit. One of the arguments made by Buckeye, Swift, Armour, and other proponents of milling-in-transit was that it would help eliminate "the small illogically located and inefficiently operated mill." Although operators of interior mills strongly objected to milling-in-transit, the railroads agreed to a modified form in the early 1930s. Some large processing companies acquired trucks and collected seed at gins, but transporting cottonseed to the oil mills remained primarily the responsibility of ginners. As roads improved, rail lines would lose most of their cottonseed business to trucks, but that was not yet the case in the 1920s. At the end of the decade, 75 percent of seed still moved by rail.[26]

Some industry members wanted the 1928 proposed code to require a uniform spread between seed and product prices at all times, as the Food Administration had done during the First World War. A uniform spread would have kept seed prices down by curbing the widespread custom of paying more for raw materials after overhead costs had been paid. Those who bought seed on a lower margin or a break-even basis at the end of the season defended the practice as a way of keeping their labor employed longer. If product prices went up, the mills earned a profit. Here again, opinion was too divided to make a uniform spread requirement acceptable in 1928.[27]

At meetings in Atlanta, Columbia, Montgomery, Memphis, Hot Springs, and New Braunfels, Texas, processors discussed the proposed rules. Those conferences resulted in the addition of two more principles. One forbade the furnishing of bagging and ties to cotton gins at less than market prices, which had the effect of obligating an independent ginner to sell the mill his seed and of raising the prices of that seed. The second principle stated that seed in railway carlots should be bought only according to weight and quality as determined by the mills that received it, not by the sellers. It had been common practice for many years to base seed contracts on mill weights, as mill scales tended to be more accurate than those available to ginners and seed dealers. To secure more seed, some crushers during the 1920s permitted the weight and quality of seed to be determined at the sellers' warehouse. Those mills were said to be buying cottonseed "as is" and "where is." Calling for mill weights reinforced earlier practice.[28]

Members of the Interstate Cotton Seed Crushers' Association adopted the principles at their annual convention in June 1928. Before the crushing season began a trade practice conference was held in Memphis to further revise the rules and make them acceptable to all parties. Judge Edgar A. McCulloch of the Federal Trade Commission presided, and the head of the Trade Practice Conference Division attended. At the insistence of Judge McCulloch, the word "bid" was removed from the requirement for price publicity, because the Department of Justice objected to the reporting of bids. Only prices actually paid for seed could be publicized, even though processors considered bidding information the key to buying cottonseed.[29]

Provisions added to the code following the conference further addressed the problem of how to control the speculative profits and destabilizing influences of middlemen in the cottonseed market. Oil men had long complained that seed brokers and speculators earned too large a proportion of the profits. Studies made by the trade association during the early 1930s demonstrated that on the average, seed merchants profited more per ton of seed than oil millers.[30]

Processors sought to return commissions to the levels sanctioned by the Food Administration during the First World War and to eliminate kickbacks to farmers and ginners. High commissions increased raw-material costs, and splitting commissions with sellers obscured the true price of seed. The 1928 code limited commissions to three dollars per ton on purchases of wagonloads of seed and fifty cents a ton on railway carloads of seed. The code prohibited as an "unfair practice" the payment of fifty-cent carlot commissions to relatives, business associates, or friends of seed sellers who performed no service for their fee but merely passed part or all of the commission to the seed dealer. According to the code, the names of all fifty-cent carlot buyers were to be publicized, and carlot buyers could work for only one mill instead of being free agents in a position to play one mill against another.[31]

With the permission of the Federal Trade Commission, crushers added an enforcement clause to the code. After the commission approved the fair-trade principles and a sizable majority of crushers had indicated their willingness to abide by them, the FTC was supposed to prosecute those guilty of unfair practices. Some crushers expected the commission to regulate oil mills the way the Food Administration had done in 1917 and 1918, and a number of mill men informed ginners that they couldn't pay higher commissions, store cottonseed free, or do other things prohibited by the rules, because the government would not permit them to do so.[32]

Most state cottonseed associations adopted the code, and set up special price-reporting bureaus, but all did not go smoothly. Crushers in Louisiana stopped reporting seed prices after several months, because of competition from Texas mills. Few North Texas mills ever reported prices. Western crushers also dragged their feet about grading for several reasons. Excess moisture was not a problem for them. Western seed also had a lower oil content than that from other regions, and many oil men believed they would grade lower. Moreover, the seed from the "bolly," or immature cotton, so prevalent in western Texas and Oklahoma because of early frosts gave misleading results on chemical tests. By June of 1929 the president of the Interstate Cotton Seed Crushers' Association had to admit that the state associations had failed to secure compliance from a majority of their members. Texas, Oklahoma, California, Arizona, and Nevada, states that crushed more than 40 percent of the total, either never adopted or never enforced the code.[33]

The cottonseed industry reorganized its national trade association in 1929 for the primary purpose of making the 1928 rules more effective. A trend toward stronger trade associations had been underway in the United States for several years, the least-profitable postwar industries taking the lead in trying to moderate competition. Officials of the major processing companies believed that the loosely organized Interstate Cotton Seed Crushers' Association working through independent state associations lacked the power and funds to implement the code. To secure the support of the larger interests, power had to be centralized in the national organization despite reservations on the part of a number of crushers.

A joint committee composed of representatives of the interstate and Texas associations worked on a plan of reorganization that would harmonize the trading rules and services of the two groups. Following the plan's approval at the interstate convention and, afterward, the Texas convention, members attending a second session of the interstate convention in July 1929 adopted the final plan and renamed their organization the National Cottonseed Products Association. Most of the state cottonseed associations quickly transformed themselves into divisions of the national association, as provided by the reorganization plan. The national organization collected all dues and returned a portion to the divisions to cover operating expenses.[34]

At the opening of the 1929 crushing season, the new National Cottonseed Products Association sent rules governing price publication to its state divisions. Mills were instructed to inform their division secretaries by telegram daily of the prices they paid for cottonseed and received for cottonseed products. Price changes were to be reported without delay. After being summarized, the information was to be disseminated by radio, newspaper, and a bulletin sent to subscribers. Division secretaries were enjoined not to analyze market conditions, as some had done in the past. Despite the prohibition in the 1928 code against publicizing bids, mills reported them for several months until the Justice Department threatened to prosecute association officials.[35]

The reorganized national association still lacked the power to fully implement grading, price reporting, and other items on its agenda. For a brief period state divisions functioned in North and South Texas, but Oklahoma processors never gave up their independent state association. The Louisiana division went out of existence after a few months, because of competition from Texas mills not buying seed according to the rules. Thus, the attempt to centralize power in the national association succeeded only partially. Regional differences made it impossible to impose uniform rules and grading standards on the entire industry. Moreover, the Southwest had long been a stronghold of independent cottonseed-oil mills and regional mill chains suspicious of the larger companies.[36]

During the months the national association tried to implement grading and price reporting there had been numerous abuses. Some crushers didn't report price changes until their competitors ferreted out the information. Others reported one price but secretly paid their biggest suppliers a higher one. Some selected the best seed in a carload for laboratory analysis and paid for all on that basis, or let a sample dry before sending it to the laboratory so that there would not be discounts for excess moisture. Others did not report and deduct as much as they should have for excess trash in the seed they bought. Sometimes a mill got options on several large lots of seed at a price higher than the prevailing one, hurriedly bought them all, and only then reported that it had paid a higher price. Crushers accused Buckeye in particular of violating the spirit of the code by engaging in a number of such "seed raids" in 1928 and 1929. To undercut criticism of grading and price-reporting abuses and to bring about greater compliance, industry leaders urged that an impartial government agency take over or supervise the two activities they considered critical to the stabilization of the cottonseed crushing industry.[37]

Creation of the National Cottonseed Products Association in 1929 and its efforts to carry out price reporting, grading, and rules of fair trade aroused great hostility among cottonseed producers and dealers. Many ginners, seed brokers, buyers, and other middlemen objected to rules that strictly regulated their activities. Believing that adoption of the trade practices code and creation of the new and more-powerful trade association had caused cottonseed prices to drop in 1929, seed producers and sellers appealed to southern members of Congress for redress. At the end of the year, the United States Senate adopted a resolution introduced by Senator J. Thomas Heflin of Alabama that asked the Federal Trade Commission to investigate the allegation that "certain cottonseed crushers and oil mills have entered into a combination for the purpose of fixing prices on cottonseed in violation of the antitrust laws."[38]

The Senate authorized the FTC to investigate the cottonseed industry at a time when official Washington had become less receptive toward the idea of business cooperation. President Hoover's unwillingness to be considered lax on antitrust enforcement created an attitude toward trade-association codes more cautious than had existed under President Coolidge. The Justice Department cracked down on "cartelistic" practices. Changes in the composition and policy of the Federal Trade Commission and its investigation of collusion in cottonseed buying diminished the agency's interest in punishing code violations. With no way to enforce the 1928 rules and with lack of compliance in the Southwest and other areas, the National Cottonseed Products Association could only encourage the state divisions to carry out grading and price reporting.[39]

For many months in 1930 and 1931, the Federal Trade Commission conducted an intensive state-by-state investigation of the cottonseed industry. The commission issued a report of its findings in May 1933 that charged processors with multiple violations of the 1928 rules of fair trade and withdrew its approval. More than a year later, officers of the National Cottonseed Products Association and of the independent Texas and Oklahoma associations received word of the agency's intention to prosecute them unless they ceased to carry out practices the commission judged objectionable. The National Cottonseed Products Association responded to the charges in mid-August of 1934, and the FTC subsequently dropped its proceedings against the association's officers.[40]

The Federal Trade Commission's investigation of the cottonseed-processing industry took place while the nation spiraled deeper and deeper into financial depression. Cottonseed oil, the most valuable product of the crushing mills, suffered the greatest price decline among crude cottonseed products as increased hog and lard production and decreased consumer buying power sharply reduced demand for vegetable shortenings. Cottonseed prices reflected the downturn in oil prices. During the early months of the 1931 crushing season, seed prices dropped so low that they hardly paid for the cost of ginning, leaving many small farmers with no cash for living expenses during the cotton harvest. According to the director of the Mississippi Agricultural Service, farmers realized only about 31 percent as much for cottonseed in 1931–32 as they had from 1926 to

1930. Mill wages declined precipitously, and mill closings left many job-
less. According to an industry survey, mill losses averaged close to seventy
cents a ton during the two crushing seasons between 1930 and 1932.[41]

When the Roosevelt administration came into office in the spring of
1933, cottonseed processors looked to the federal government for relief.
At their convention in June, members of the National Cottonseed Products Association empowered their president and executive secretary to
appoint a committee of nine to recommend a plan for stabilizing the industry. Undeterred by the Federal Trade Commission's withdrawal of
support from its 1928 rules, the committee drafted a similar "code of fair
competition," which it sent to federal administrators following ratification
by state committees. Membership in the National Cottonseed Products
Association rose to nearly 100 percent of all oil mills in 1933, because
the Roosevelt administration, following World War I precedent, intended
to work on recovery plans for industries through their trade associations.
Cottonseed processors hoped to have new government regulations in
place before the 1933 crushing season began.[42]

As an industry based on an important farm commodity, cottonseed
processing fell under the jurisdiction of both the Agricultural Adjustment
Administration (AAA) and the National Recovery Administration (NRA).
The Agricultural Adjustment Act authorized the secretary of agriculture
to develop codes or marketing agreements with processors of farm products and to license them as a means of enforcing compliance. The NRA
had responsibility for the labor provisions of marketing agreements.[43]

During the summer of 1933, members of the National Cottonseed
Products Association committee charged with drawing up a code met frequently with NRA and AAA staff members in Washington. In August industry and government representatives held an informal conference to
review the code that had been prepared. Many people believed that if
businesses could be protected from destructive competition, they would
have the financial resources to increase wages, reduce hours, and employ
more workers, who in turn would have greater buying power. The major
objective of the proposed code was to stabilize cottonseed prices at a level
that would permit profitable crushing, in other words, to reduce competition for seed and thereby lower raw-material prices. The goal of cheaper
cottonseed was not shared by cotton growers, and ultimately Department
of Agriculture officials placed the interests of farmers first.[44]

A public hearing on the code took place in Memphis on 11 and 12
September 1933, under the auspices of the AAA. Representative Wright
Patman of Texas denounced many features of the code, calling grading,

uniform seed contracts, cost accounting, a prohibition against building new crude-oil mills, and other provisions a "scheme" to fix cottonseed prices. Patman told the more than one thousand people at the hearing: "I am against a fixed return for the oil mill, the refiner and the ginner, with no fixed return for the farmer."[45]

A majority of the processors attending the hearing voted to recast the code in the form of a marketing agreement. Believing that marketing agreements would enable agricultural producers and processors to dispose of their products more effectively, George Peek and other proponents had promoted them as a panacea for the farm depression during much of the 1920s. After Peek became the first head of the Agricultural Adjustment Administration, he tried to push marketing agreements through rapidly. Agriculture Department officials argued at the Memphis hearing that regulation of the cottonseed industry under a marketing agreement that authorized the secretary of agriculture to license mills in compliance with its provisions would result in the greatest possible reduction in operating costs, which would benefit farmers and ginners by enabling processors to pay more for their raw materials.[46]

The labor provisions of the proposed cottonseed code included eight-hour shifts, a maximum forty-eight-hour work week, an hourly minimum wage of twenty-two and a half cents, and the right of mill workers to bargain collectively. Many crushers attending the hearing in Memphis objected to the proposed minimum wage, but they could not agree on an acceptable alternative. The proposal to require significant wage increases upset cotton producers and aggravated traditional tensions between crushers and representatives of the integrated companies. In many small southeastern and Mississippi Valley communities where planters and crushers competed for labor, farmers paying workers forty to fifty cents a day plus housing protested that wages higher than twelve and a half to fifteen cents an hour for mill labor would upset farming operations. Farm labor was exempt, by presidential proclamation, from wage regulation. Some oil men believed that refiner-controlled companies were willing to pay higher wages in order to eliminate struggling mills. A Buckeye official who supported the minimum wage argued that exceptions to it would protect less-efficient mills and perpetuate overcapacity.[47]

Following the Memphis hearing, AAA and NRA staff members collected information on wages in the cottonseed industry. Based on their findings that average hourly pay for unskilled laborers during the previous year had ranged from eight cents in the East to fourteen cents in the West, they decided to divide the Cotton Belt into four zones, the Southeast, the Central Region, the Southwest, and the Far West. In towns with populations of less than five thousand, where living costs were presumably lower and competition with farmers for labor was most prevalent, two- and three-press mills in zone one, the Southeast, as well as in Louisiana and Mississippi, were to be permitted to pay a lower minimum wage. Government and industry eventually compromised on minimum wages of eighteen, twenty, twenty-five, and thirty cents in the four zones and fifteen cents for "cotton-patch" mills.[48]

By mid-October of 1933 the committee representing the National Cottonseed Products Association agreed to accept the maximum hours and minimum wages proposed by NRA officials rather than risk having a higher wage schedule imposed on the industry. Numerous crushers continued to object to the proposed wage levels. Although a top Buckeye executive urged that the NRA labor code be put into effect without delay, most oil men insisted that labor provisions had to be coupled with an acceptable code or marketing agreement. Like other businessmen, cottonseed processors considered a "reasonable" profit only "just," in view of the increased wages and shorter hours mandated by the NRA.[49]

AAA officials felt obliged to hold a second public hearing at the end of November 1933, because the cottonseed code had been rewritten as a "Proposed Marketing Agreement for the Cotton Seed Crushing Industry." In the main, the agreement restated provisions of earlier fair-trade codes and incorporated features of the First World War stabilization program of the Food Administration. The agreement authorized mill operators in each state to select state committees and a national committee to administer the regulations.

The state committees, subject to approval of the national committee, had the authority to set the minimum and maximum range between the value of cottonseed products and the price of cottonseed. This provision incorporated the World War I guaranteed spread adopted by the Food Administration in 1917 and 1918. Anything less than the minimum spread would be considered evidence of a company purchasing seed at a loss to the detriment of its competitors, and anything greater than the maximum spread would be interpreted as excess profit gained at the expense of producers.[50]

Under the proposed marketing agreement, new mills were not to be constructed nor dormant mills activated, and additions or changes of location had to be approved by the national committee. Where overcapacity existed, the state committees could take steps to reduce it if 75 percent of the mills in a state and the national committee consented. All records had to be made available to officers of the national committee. To finance the administration of the agreement, mills were to be assessed according to the number of tons of seed they crushed.

Collection and publication of prices was to be the first duty of the state committees under the marketing agreement. That had also been the top priority of the FTC code adopted in 1928. Publicity helped stabilize raw-material costs by narrowing the range of prices paid for seed. Allowing prices bid for cottonseed to be included in price publication restored an item desired by the crushing industry that the Justice Department had forced processors to delete from the 1928 rules.

Most of the provisions covering contracts in the marketing agreement had been part of the 1928 code and prohibited practices crushers had used in the past to make contracts "elastic." Other rules condemned subterfuges employed by mills to pay more than the "open" price for cottonseed, that is, bonuses and rebates of all kinds. Uniform contracts and a prohibition on secret bonuses and rebates were standard requirements of all NRA codes.[51]

A provision that truck rates had to be based on the shortest distance between a mill and a seed collection point was included to prevent inflated transportation allowances from being used as bonuses to seed sellers. Since 1928, when processors had been too divided to adopt a uniform hauling rule, agreements had been reached in different states that permitted greater standardization of hauling allowances.

Under the proposed agreement, oil mills had to have the approval of their state committees in order to make new loans to ginners and cottonseed sellers. Current loans were to be terminated as soon as possible and no future loans made without adequate security and payment of "a fair rate" of interest. In 1933, as in 1928, processors remained too divided on the subject of gin loans to ban them, but the effects of the Depression made stricter control of loans desirable. After 1929 companies had to carry over many loans from year to year, and shrinking real estate values left mills without adequate security. Loans that before the Depression had been roughly 50 percent of a gin's value and payable out of profits within two or three years often amounted to considerably more than the property's market value following the crash, and hard times left many gins without sufficient income even to pay interest.[52]

Other rules in the proposed marketing agreement covered grading, provided deductions for excess trash, and forbade ginners to store cottonseed for farmers free of charge. Finally, the agreement explicitly prohibited the purchase of seed "at a price that will incur loss to a mill" and thus damage other mills in the area. That, as well as the uniform spread provision, was aimed at large processing companies that sometimes paid more for seed than they could crush at a profit in order to get the volume of crude oil they desired for manufacturing purposes.[53]

Objections to the draft agreement came from many quarters. Manufacturers of mill machinery protested the proposed ban on new mills in the marketing agreement. They argued that it was poor policy to destroy the market for machinery at a time when the country needed to create more jobs. Many farmers demanded that cottonseed sampling and grading be done by men with no connection to the crushing industry. Some crushers argued that making their records available to state and national committee members would enable competitors to know too much about their business.[54]

Early in the new year the proposed marketing agreement had to be redrafted as a code of fair-trade practices. Following George Peek's ouster as head of the Agricultural Adjustment Administration in December 1933, Agriculture Department officials abandoned marketing agreements. Secretary of Agriculture Henry Wallace placed more faith in production controls than in marketing agreements, and AAA administrators charged with protecting the rights of consumers and laborers viewed marketing agreements as primarily beneficial to processors.[55]

As code negotiations dragged on, an increasingly adversarial relationship developed between Department of Agriculture officials and representatives of the cottonseed industry. Placing the interests of farmers first, department members resisted proposals that threatened to erode farm income. In an era of interest-group politics, cottonseed processors numbering in the hundreds and employing a relatively small work force lacked the influence of cotton farmers. The prohibition against buying seed at a loss, a provision considered essential by many cottonseed processors if they were to pay higher wages, was eliminated from the redrafted code.[56]

At the May 1934 convention of the National Cottonseed Products Association, president J. Ross Richardson voiced the disappointment felt by processors:

It was thought by some that a marketing agreement for the cottonseed crushing industry would prove to be the Santa Claus to fill the empty stocking. Indeed, some of us journeyed to last year's Convention with thoughts of an arrangement that might lead to a repetition of the good old days under the food administration. Fixed prices for seed and products, with a good spread for working costs and profits, allocation of tonnage, and such other things as would cure all the economic and financial ills of the industry. What a sad awakening for those of us who had such thoughts.

A majority of the members attending the convention, nonetheless, voted in favor of adopting a code, and, despite much dissatisfaction with the negotiating committee for making unpopular wage concessions, asked the nine men to continue working with federal officials to get the most satisfactory regulations they could.[57]

Further code negotiations between industry representatives and NRA and AAA staff members were interrupted when the Federal Trade Commission issued a formal complaint against cottonseed processors in the summer of 1934. The commission had been about to take legal action against the trade associations a year earlier, but delayed when the Roosevelt administration indicated a willingness to suspend antitrust statutes in the interest of economic recovery. "We certainly don't want to issue a complaint charging the industry with practices which are approved under your code," an FTC official stated after examining the proposed cottonseed-industry code in 1933. By 1934 growing numbers of federal administrators involved in code activities had become disillusioned with curbs on competition and less tolerant of moderating antitrust laws. AAA officials assured the FTC that a "Complaint" against crushers for limiting competition for seed would not "embarrass" code negotiations.[58]

The FTC's action ended any hope of adopting a code that could go into effect during the 1934–35 crushing season. The Justice Department also launched an investigation of alleged antitrust violations and notified the NRA that approval of a code of trade practices for the cottonseed industry would weaken the government's case. The NRA pressed for immediate adoption of the code's labor provisions, but crushers persisted in their refusal to accept labor regulations unless they were part of a fair-trade code.[59]

In early September the Justice Department withdrew its objections to code negotiations after an investigation revealed insufficient evidence of "present illegal activities." The FTC also dropped its proceedings against officers of the National Cottonseed Products Association and of the independent Texas and Oklahoma associations. Negotiations on the cottonseed code resumed, but AAA officials eliminated provisions they believed might prejudice any future action brought against the industry by the Federal Trade Commission. Secretary Henry Wallace actually encouraged the FTC chairman to reinstitute proceedings in order to protect farmers in the sale of their cottonseed.[60]

Because the code proposed in late 1934 differed so materially from the marketing agreement drafted the previous year, the AAA considered it advisable to have a public hearing at Memphis in October. At that time it became evident that there was little agreement on key issues. Federal officials wanted increases in minimum wages and the elimination of the pay differential for two- and three-press mills, which small crushers and farmers considered unacceptable. Many processors objected to the requirement that they open their books and records to code authorities on request. Although a feature of earlier drafts, the "books and records clause" became a major stumbling block to adoption of the code in late 1934. Crushers insisted, as they always had, on the publication of prices bid for cottonseed in addition to those actually paid, but unlike the 1933 marketing agreement, the Code of Fair Competition debated in the fall of 1934 contained no provision for reporting and publicizing bids. Instead of mandating grading and price reporting throughout the Cotton Belt as the 1933 agreement had proposed, the 1934 version gave state committees the option of making grading and price reporting mandatory. In the light of FTC charges of past abuses, AAA officials advocated direct government supervision of those activities, as well as the institution of a market-reporting service by the Department of Agriculture. Compulsory grading had strong supporters, and equally vocal opponents among farmers, ginners, and crushers.[61]

When the United States Supreme Court struck down the National Industrial Recovery Act on 27 May 1935, representatives of the cottonseed-processing industry had been seeking some kind of enforceable self-regulatory agreement with the AAA and NRA for nearly two years without success. Bureaucratic regulations and changing ideas among government employees and agencies had retarded the course of negotiations. Those problems, plus the difficulties of negotiating with two agencies and of trying to resolve differences within the cottonseed industry and between processors and federal administrators, had been insurmountable. Officials of the National Cottonseed Products Association announced that the association would draw up its own "self-controling code," but the matter soon died.[62]

Because seed price reporting and grading remained important goals for many industry leaders, and achieving them through a federally enforced code had ceased to be a possibility, another strategy became necessary. Association leaders renewed their support for efforts to secure federal legislation that would provide reporting and grading services. For at least a decade southern congressmen had been trying to secure funds to enable the Department of Agriculture to publicize cottonseed prices. They supported price reporting primarily as a service to cotton farmers. In 1930 Representative Marvin Jones and Senator Morris Sheppard of Texas introduced a bill that would have authorized the department to gather and publish cottonseed and product prices. Senators Pat Harrison of Mississippi and Kenneth McKeller of Tennessee tried to persuade Congress to appropriate money for the reporting service. The National Cottonseed Products Association charged that opposition from the Federal Trade Commission caused Congress to remove funds from bills that would have enabled the Department of Agriculture to include cottonseed in its crop-reporting service.[63]

In 1938, following the passage of a measure introduced two years earlier, federal supervision of voluntary cottonseed sampling and grading and publication of the farm prices of cottonseed went into effect in the Valley Division of the National Cottonseed Products Association. By September, 83 percent of the mills in that division, which included Tennessee, Arkansas, Illinois, and northern Louisiana, were thought to be buying on grade. The Department of Agriculture gathered seed prices daily and published a weekly bulletin during the crushing season, which it sent free of charge to all interested parties. Crushers in the southeastern states requested the service, but the department could not expand its coverage until Congress made more funds available. Western processors had less interest in grading, because they did not have a problem with high moisture content.[64]

On the eve of the Second World War the industry had achieved some of the goals its representatives had set following World War I. It had failed to attain other objectives, largely because of aggressive competition for seed among oil mills and festering distrust between crushers and refiners. Processors created a stronger national trade association between the wars, although not as powerful an organization as some had envisioned. By the late 1930s, voluntary seed grading and publication of cottonseed prices paid to farmers had been implemented in the Mississippi Valley Division under Department of Agriculture supervision, and grading standards would gradually be extended to the southeastern states, Oklahoma, and much of Texas. The industrywide campaign to moderate competition by outlawing "unfair" business practices, which began in 1927 and went on almost continuously until 1935, ended un-successfully. "Fair competition is merely a resounding and illusory phrase," concluded a board reviewing the National Recovery Administration in 1934; "all competition is savage, wolfish, and relentless," it added, "and can be nothing else." Various cottonseed companies individually and cooperatively eliminated some excess crushing capacity, but the prob-lem of underutilization of oil mills remained a serious one.[65]

Beginning with America's involvement in World War I, federal inter-vention had an increasing impact on the cottonseed industry. During the 1920s the Departments of Commerce and Agriculture and the Federal Trade Commission assisted the industry in developing grading standards and framing rules of fair trade to stabilize seed buying. Changing per-sonnel and policies within the Federal Trade Commission, the National Recovery Administration, and the Agricultural Adjustment Administration hampered efforts by cottonseed-oil men during the early years of the De-pression to relax antitrust laws and moderate competition for seed. The fed-eral government's greatest impact on the cottonseed industry would come from the unintended consequences of New Deal measures designed to raise the incomes of industrial wage earners and southern cotton farmers.

CHAPTER 10

End of the Hydraulic Era

This government has got us all by the umbilicus.

Pat Geoghegan,
president, Wesson Oil &
Snowdrift Company, 1939

New Deal cotton-crop restrictions, federal minimum-wage laws, and competition from other vegetable oils after the mid-1930s accelerated the transition of cottonseed processing from an industry composed of hundreds of labor-intensive hydraulic-press mills, many of them quite small, to one with fewer and larger plants that employed labor-saving solvent and screw-press extraction. Increased labor costs and competition from soybean oil were the principal catalysts of change. Gradually, cottonseed processors closed or modernized the hydraulic mills scattered across the Cotton Belt until crushing took place in large and efficient continuous-process plants. With more and more cotton being produced in the Far West, processors in that region took the lead in adopting new methods. At the end of the twentieth century only two of the old hydraulic mills remain as relics of the first century of cottonseed processing, and cottonseed oil is just one among many vegetable oils on the American market.

New Deal programs to reduce production of cotton, corn, and hogs had an immediate impact on the crushing industry. As an emergency measure, the Agricultural Adjustment Administration paid farmers in 1933 to plow up cotton and kill pigs. The Commodity Credit Corporation, the federal agency whose primary function was to support the prices of farmers' crops, loaned money to farmers who stored their cotton instead of putting it on the market at the time of harvest. Mandatory cotton acreage allotments went into effect the following year. Between 1933 and 1936 smaller cotton crops and the drought in Texas and Oklahoma caused production of cottonseed and cottonseed oil to decline. At the same time, less corn and fewer hogs meant higher lard prices. That in turn strengthened the value of cottonseed oil, after refiners exhausted the large supplies they had on hand in 1933, because manufacturers had always priced it below lard. An excise tax on Philippine copra and coconut oil in the Revenue Act of May 1934 plugged the last major gap in the tariff barrier that had been erected in 1921–22 against foreign oils and oleaginous materials. Manufacturers substituted cottonseed oil for coconut oil in many products. In contrast, smaller supplies and increased prices had an adverse effect on demand for linters; the rapidly expanding cellulose industry began to make much greater use of wood pulp.[1]

In January 1936 the Supreme Court declared the processing tax of the Agricultural Adjustment Act unconstitutional, and Congress repealed the Bankhead Cotton Control Act of 1934, which had replaced voluntary cotton-crop controls with compulsory ones. To fill the gap, Congress passed a soil-conservation measure that authorized payments to farmers who voluntarily withdrew land from staple-crop cultivation and put it into legumes. The lifting of mandatory acreage restrictions resulted in record cotton crops and cottonseed-oil production in 1937 and 1938. The largest amount of cottonseed ever produced was in 1938, and only the oil yields of 1914 and 1927 surpassed those of the late 1930s. Cottonseed-product prices plummeted as a result of the increased production of all animal and vegetable fats. Moreover, lard lost its export market permanently after the hog reduction program of 1933–36 increased lard prices.

Under pressure from farmers, Congress passed a second Agricultural Adjustment Act in early 1938. Among its provisions was authorization for the secretary of agriculture to impose marketing quotas, although not mandatory acreage allotments, if two-thirds of the growers of a staple crop approved. Only farmers who limited the acreage they put into staple-crop cultivation were eligible for soil-conservation payments. In a one-sided vote, cotton farmers called for the imposition of mandatory marketing quotas. Those who exceeded their quotas would be penalized. By reducing cotton production and encouraging staple farmers to grow more soil-conserving crops, the second Agricultural Adjustment Act had a profound impact on the cottonseed industry.[2]

The tremendous productivity of southern cotton farmers limited the effectiveness of New Deal crop controls. During the 1930s the federal government reduced cotton acreage 43 percent, yet the amount of seed declined only 17 percent. Cottonseed-oil production actually increased slightly as the proportion of seed going to oil mills increased from about 77 percent in the 1920s to 84 percent during the late 1930s. Farmers boosted cotton yields by putting their least-fertile land into soil conservation, applying more fertilizers to their best fields, mechanizing their operations, and controlling boll weevil damage. Cottonseed production rose from about three hundred pounds per acre during the 1920s to nearly four hundred pounds per acre between 1935 and 1939.[3]

Before the Great Depression cottonseed oil had been the only American vegetable oil produced in significant quantities. By taxing Philippine coconut oil in 1934 and reducing the cottonseed available for processing through acreage control, federal policies caused vegetable-oil prices to rise for a time. Soil-conservation programs of the late 1930s encouraged farmers to put more of their land into soybeans, peanuts, and other plants that would improve the soil and fewer acres into surplus staple crops such as wheat, corn, and cotton. Because cottonseed oil could not satisfy domestic demand for inexpensive vegetable oils, it faced serious competition from soybean, corn, and peanut oils by the eve of World War II, when consumers began to have more money to spend for food.[4]

Soybean production in the United States expanded from about five million bushels in 1934 to eighty-seven million in 1939. At first, most of the soybean oil manufactured in the United States went into paints. When New Deal programs reduced supplies of shortening made with cottonseed oil, manufacturers became interested in soybean oil. By the end of the 1930s soybean oil sold for a penny a pound less than cottonseed oil and in many cases could be substituted for cottonseed oil in food products. Although soybean oil did not yet match the quality of cottonseed oil, processing improved sufficiently to make it acceptable. During the 1930s the American shortening industry increased the amount of soybean oil in its products from 1 to 18 percent. Soybean prices were supported during the war as part of the effort to increase domestic supplies of fats and oils. In the 1950s soybean acreage underwent "an explosive expansion," particularly in the southern states, where soybeans filled much of the gap left by shrinking cotton acreage.[5]

Located in the Midwest, the major center of soybean cultivation, the soybean-processing industry had the advantages of paying less for freight and of being closer to large population centers. Other factors made soybean oil cheaper than cottonseed oil. Solvent extraction worked well on soybeans and required less labor than the hydraulic presses employed by most cottonseed-oil mills. Implementation of minimum-wage legislation at the end of the 1930s erased the low-wage advantage of southern cottonseed processors. Also, soybeans could be stored with less risk of deterioration, which enabled processors to spread their production and marketing more evenly throughout the year. Sales of soybean oil soared, and soybean meal began to displace cottonseed meal in the northern states, where it had long been purchased for cattle feed. By 1944 more soybean oil than cottonseed oil was being produced in the United States.[6]

Because soybeans were raised solely to produce oil and meal, soybean acreage could be expanded in response to demand. As a by-product of cotton lint, the tonnage of cottonseed did not increase in response to higher vegetable-oil prices. Factors beyond the control of cottonseed processors affected the amount of seed available for crushing each year. Efforts to develop cottonseed with a higher oil content that could be raised just for the seed ended at the experimental stage on the eve of the Second World War.[7]

Large stocks of cottonseed oil and stronger competition from lard and soybean products during the 1930s caused cottonseed processors to seek ways of increasing domestic demand for cottonseed products. The trade association redoubled its efforts to expand the market for cottonseed oil as an ingredient in margarine, which involved working with margarine manufacturers to get prohibitory taxes lifted. During the late nineteenth century, rising margarine consumption had alarmed dairy farmers and butter manufacturers, and at their urging, Congress in 1886 required dealers to buy expensive licenses and placed a tax of two cents a pound on margarine. Despite the tax, sales of margarine grew steadily. In 1902 Congress levied a tax of ten cents a pound on colored margarine, which crippled the industry for a few years but did not destroy it.[8]

After the Spanish-American War, cheaper coconut oil from the Philippines began to replace cottonseed oil in American margarine. By the 1920s coconut and peanut oils dominated margarine manufacture, and producers referred to their products as "nut margarines." When the Institute of Margarine Manufacturers mounted a campaign against antimargarine legislation in 1924, there was so little cottonseed oil in its product that the institute could not get the active support of cottonseed processors and southern organizations until one of its member companies marketed an all-cottonseed-oil margarine. The excise tax placed on imported Philippine coconut oil in the Revenue Act of 1934 increased demand for domestic vegetable oils. The amount of cottonseed oil in margarine surpassed one hundred million pounds in 1936, nearly five times the amount used annually between 1920 and 1933.[9]

More than half the states either taxed margarine, in addition to federal taxation, or barred the manufacture or sale of colored margarine in the 1930s. The army, navy, and other federal agencies were prohibited from serving margarine as a table spread. At the urging of trade-association officials, Congress included cottonseed oil in the food-stamp program along with surplus butter and lard in 1937, but opposition from the dairy lobby caused cottonseed oil to be dropped the following year from the list of fats going to states for distribution among the poor. So powerful was the dairy lobby that efforts by cottonseed processors, southern legislators, and chambers of commerce to secure the repeal of federal and state taxes on margarine failed in all but a few instances.[10]

The war years brought increased production of margarine, and the quantity of cottonseed oil consumed by margarine makers in the late 1940s was more than double that used during the previous decade. When Congress finally removed discriminatory federal taxes on colored margarine in 1950, consumption soared. Unfortunately for cottonseed processors, cheaper soybean oil soon captured most of the margarine market.[11]

The cottonseed industry also sought to expand markets for cottonseed meal. The long campaign to eradicate Texas Fever by eliminating cattle ticks had made it safe to raise cows and operate dairies in most of the southern states by the early 1930s, and New Deal cotton acreage reductions provided an incentive for diversification. There were some gains in southern livestock production, but cottonseed meal encountered stiff competition from soybean processors seeking to supply northern animal breeders with a high-protein feed. State and national trade associations made greater efforts to promote the use of cottonseed meal in southern states. Texas A&M, the Universities of Tennessee and Oklahoma, and other southern agricultural colleges tested cottonseed meal and provided feeding schedules for different animals.[12]

Loss of oil and meal markets to soybean products, the first serious competition from another oil seed experienced by the American cottonseed industry, prompted cottonseed processors to provide more money for research. One of the problems engineers worked on was the application of solvent extraction to cottonseed processing. The use of continuous-process techniques had facilitated rapid growth in the American soybean-oil industry during the 1930s. Because cottonseed flakes tended to decompose when exposed to solvents, that and other technical problems had to be overcome before solvent extraction could be used in cottonseed processing. Despite its drawbacks, hydraulic pressing still produced the best grade of cottonseed oil.[13]

At the end of the 1930s, cottonseed-oil mills experienced great instability, in large measure because of new federal policies. Following passage of the second Agricultural Adjustment Act in 1938, incentives to take cotton land out of production resulted in the smallest cotton acreage on record. Believing that a reduced crop would mean less seed and higher oil prices, processors paid more for seed during the 1938 harvest than they had in recent years. That proved to be a bad guess, because intensive cultivation counteracted acreage restrictions. At the same time, a very large corn crop caused increased hog and lard production, which depressed the prices of all fats. Cottonseed processors not only had more oil to sell than they had expected, but lard and soybean oil provided formidable competition.[14]

Federal crop restrictions reduced the amount of cottonseed available for crushing during the 1939–40 season, however, and boll weevil damage further reduced seed supplies. Oil makers feared they would not be able to acquire enough seed for profitable operation. The outbreak of the Second World War brought the increased consumption of fats and oils that cottonseed processors had sought throughout the 1930s. Although domestic supplies of animal fats and vegetable oils multiplied, they still fell short of demand. In 1942 the Department of Agriculture announced a price support program for oil seeds, and in response, farmers planted many more acres of soybeans, peanuts, and flaxseed. Because of control programs, the production of cottonseed dropped slightly. To induce the 447 active cottonseed-oil mills to process a variety of oil seeds, the Commodity Credit Corporation (CCC) agreed in 1942 to buy any crude oil and meal that could not be sold through normal channels at prices set by the Office of Price Administration.[15]

Postwar federal policies designed to aid cotton farmers caused difficulties for cottonseed processors at a time when they faced increasingly strong competition from soybean oil and meal. Acreage restrictions had been lifted in 1944–45, because wartime labor shortages and conversion of some cotton land to other uses made them unnecessary, but increased cotton production led to the reimposition of allotments in 1950. Improved demand and significant reductions in cotton acreage caused the lifting of restrictions the following year. The Department of Agriculture resumed cotton allotments in 1954, and put the soil-bank program into effect two years later. The result of the two programs was a 40 percent cut in cotton acreage between 1948 and 1957, which reduced the supply of raw materials available to oil mills by 22 percent.[16]

Revival of the federal cottonseed price-support program in 1949 adversely affected cottonseed processors by making their products more expensive than other vegetable oils and meals. Oil-seed price supports had been implemented in 1942 to induce processors to increase their production of vegetable fats, but in 1949 the purpose was to shore up sagging farm income. "We have seen what happens to the entire national economy when farm prices drop too low," the head of the Commodity Credit Corporation said in 1950. "The agricultural producer may suffer first, but the down-pull of his lost buying power inevitably hits the rest of our business and industry."[17]

The price of cottonseed had declined from nearly eighty-six dollars a ton in 1947 to sixty-seven dollars in 1948 and was expected to drop to about thirty-five dollars in 1949. In August of that year, the CCC loaned money to farmers who stored their seed and sold it at a later date, after the glut had ended, to take advantage of higher prices. When officials discovered that too few farm and commercial storage facilities existed, the CCC agreed to purchase seed at the support price of $46.50 per ton. Oil mills contracted to crush the seed for a fee and turn over the oil, meal, and linters to the corporation for marketing. Only the Korean War saved the agency from heavy losses on the cottonseed products in its possession.[18]

The Commodity Credit Corporation had acquired about 12 percent of the cottonseed produced in 1949, and in the Southeast much of the seed deteriorated in storage. For that reason the agency decided not to store seed in the future as a means of increasing prices. Instead, CCC officials planned to set minimum seed prices that ginners would be encouraged to pay farmers and that processors would be asked to pay ginners in return for guaranteed price supports for cottonseed products.[19]

The small size of the cotton crop made cottonseed price supports unnecessary in 1950. Between 1951 and 1954 the Commodity Credit Corporation bought oil, meal, and linters at fixed prices from oil mills that paid gins the support price or higher for cottonseed. Much of the cottonseed meal was used for drought relief, but the CCC sustained large losses in disposing of linters and oil during the period. The agency "dumped" millions of pounds of cottonseed oil overseas at low prices. Soybean oil replaced much cottonseed oil at home, particularly in the manufacture of margarine and shortening.

In 1953 the National Cottonseed Products Association requested that cottonseed not be included in the price-support program, because the industry was losing its domestic markets. Higher cottonseed-oil, meal, and linters prices made them less competitive than soybean products. Legislation passed in 1956 sought to put the two oils on an equal footing by requiring that whenever price supports went into effect they had to apply to both cottonseed and soybeans and be at levels that would make products of the two competitive. After trying different means of supporting cottonseed prices, a 1959 Department of Agriculture appraisal concluded that none of them was completely satisfactory. Conceding that oil mills would have been financially better off without government intervention in 1958, the author justified price supports for their benefits to farmers.[20]

The Social Security Act of 1935, which required employers to pay payroll and other taxes on all their employees, and, to an even greater extent, the minimum-wage law of 1938 ended decades of cheap labor in the industry. When National Recovery Administration officials sought higher wages for oil-mill workers during the unsuccessful code negotiations of 1933 and 1934, a crusher speculated on what the result of such a policy might be: "Cottonseed oil mills, because of low rates of pay, have been very backward about installing labor saving machinery. However, if the rates of pay are increased too much there will undoubtedly be an immediate installation of a great deal of such machinery with the result that much labor will be displaced and more unemployment result."[21] As predicted, New Deal legislation raising hourly wages caused processors to look for new ways to cut the number of workers they employed.

Despite strong opposition from cottonseed processors and representatives of other southern industries, Congress enacted the Black-Connery minimum-wage bill. Going into effect in October 1938, the Fair Labor Standards Act, as the law was entitled, set a minimum wage and maximum working hours for people engaged in commerce and industry. Beginning at twenty-five cents an hour, minimum wages went up to thirty cents in 1939 and forty cents in 1945. As a seasonal industry, cottonseed crushing was exempted from the hourly provisions of the law.[22]

Industries in the South employed more unskilled laborers than those in other regions of the United States, but southern wage scales varied greatly. In 1938 the iron and steel, petroleum refining, and cement industries of the South reportedly paid all workers the minimum wage of twenty-five cents an hour or more. In the cotton goods industry, the beginning wage of 11 percent of its "common laborers" fell below the minimum. Comparable figures for several other southern industries were: fertilizer manufacturing, 17 percent; brick and tile making, 27 percent; and saw milling, 43 percent. The cottonseed-crushing industry, employing a large number of unskilled black workers, paid approximately 55 percent of all its workers less than twenty-five cents an hour in 1937–38.[23]

The Fair Labor Standards Act thus had a major impact on cottonseed-oil mills. Average hourly wages went up 30 percent between the crushing seasons of 1937–38 and 1939–40. In the southeastern states, where mill labor had always been paid less than in other sections of the South, hourly wages jumped 43 percent. They rose 36 percent in the Mississippi Valley region and 17 percent in the Southwest. Overall labor costs did not increase to the same extent because of a 19-percent reduction in the mill labor force during the two crushing seasons following enactment of the minimum-wage law. Although wages rose for unskilled workers, cooks and other skilled mill laborers did not see a comparable rise.[24]

Labor efficiency had not been a high priority with oil mills as long as they could employ workers at low wages. Hydraulic mills processed cottonseed in batches rather than continuously. Press-room workers had little to do between loading and unloading the presses, which in the smaller mills took only about half of their time. Few industries employed as many laborers per value of product as the crushing industry. Being a seasonal, low-wage industry, it had never paid mill owners to invest in expensive labor-saving machinery and methods. After the minimum-wage law went into effect, many milling companies purchased machinery to replace workers, because reduced labor costs more than compensated for larger capital investments.[25]

Small mills suffered more than large mills from the effects of the minimum-wage law, because they could not take advantage of economies of scale. Per ton processing and marketing costs declined as the volume of a mill's crush increased. It was difficult and expensive for small hydraulic mills to make the kinds of changes that would permit them to use labor more efficiently. The higher labor and power costs of small mills accelerated the trend toward consolidation that had been underway since the end of the First World War and contributed to the eventual disappearance of labor-intensive hydraulic mills. In 1940 researchers estimated that forty or fifty continuous-process plants of the screw or solvent type with the capacity to handle three to four hundred tons of seed daily could crush the entire crop of seed in three hundred days. A postwar study showed that oil mills remaining in business crushed an average of twelve thousand tons of cottonseed annually, compared to dormant mills that had processed an average of six thousand tons a season.[26]

By 1946 several screw-press mills were in operation and the first solvent-extraction plants were being built. The new extraction technologies required less labor and removed more oil from the seed than hydraulic presses. In the 1950s it was estimated that hydraulic mills required two and a half to three times more labor than other types of mills, and by 1958 the minimum wage had risen to one dollar an hour. Prepressing seed and then treating it with a solvent removed all but .9 percent of the oil. Solvent extraction alone removed all but 1.3 percent of the oil. In comparison, screw presses left 4.2 percent of the oil and hydraulic presses left 5.2 percent.[27]

The postwar geographical shift in cotton growing accelerated both the consolidation of the cottonseed industry and the building of more-efficient processing plants. The movement of cotton cultivation away from the rolling, upland areas of the South to dryer and more level lands in the West meant that many crushers in the Southeast, the East Texas prairies, and some other parts of the Cotton Belt could not find enough raw materials to remain in business. Cotton production in the southeastern states fell from 32 percent of the total in the early 1920s to 12 percent in 1958. Production in the lower Mississippi Valley during those years ranged from 25 percent in the early 1920s, when boll weevil destruction had not been brought under control, to a high of 42 percent in 1948, and back down to 25 percent a decade later. Southwestern production declined from 42 percent of the total cotton harvested in the early 1920s to a low of 24 percent in 1948, but by 1958 it accounted for 40 percent of the crop. The dramatic expansion in cotton growing took place in the Far West, which in the early 1920s harvested only 1 percent of the crop but by 1959 produced 23 percent.[28]

The magnet pulling cotton westward was cheaper production costs on large mechanized and irrigated farms in dryer areas less subject to boll weevil damage. The availability of relatively cheap synthetic fertilizers and water for irrigation made it possible after the Second World War to extend cotton growing to large tracts of flat, previously unproductive, western land suitable for tractors, cotton pickers, and other machines.

Irrigation and mechanization of much western cotton cultivation, in addition to intensive fertilization, substantially increased cottonseed yields. The per acre average during the 1920s had been three hundred pounds of seed; by 1959 the average yield exceeded eight hundred pounds. As oil mills closed in older sections of the Cotton Belt, new ones had to be built

in the West to accommodate the increased supplies of cottonseed produced there. Western processors took the lead in building modern plants.
Squeezed by rising labor, freight, and fuel costs at a time when product
prices remained the same or declined, western companies erected screw-
press and solvent-extraction mills in order to process seed as efficiently
as possible. Plant modernization helped to minimize drops in cottonseed-
oil production in the face of declining seed supplies. The large investment necessary to build continuous-process facilities contributed to mill
consolidation because a limited number of companies had sufficient
financial resources to make the transition. Unfortunately for the industry,
the westward movement of oil mills took processing plants farther from
the large consuming centers of the Northeast and Midwest, which gave
soybean oil and meal a further advantage.[29]

Cheaper freight rates and a more-extensive transportation network
also aided mill consolidation and modernization at mid-century. The
crushing industry had expanded in the early days of poor roads and high
transportation costs by crushing in many small units located near the cotton fields and in larger terminal facilities served by multiple rail lines.
Mass production of gas-powered vehicles and federal and state road-
building programs between the world wars made a shift to trucks possible. Their cheaper rates and greater flexibility enabled them to squeeze
out the railway companies, which had been the principal carriers of cottonseed and cottonseed products since the 1880s. Operators of interior
mills in states with adequate roads had been the first to realize the advantages of using trucks. As terminal mills turned more and more to truck
transport, the interior mills lost their advantage in the contest for seed.
By 1941 three-quarters of the cottonseed crushed was being moved by
trucks. A decade later mills received about 98 percent of their raw materials by truck.[30]

During most of the industry's first century, the need to crush cottonseed as quickly as possible to prevent it from deteriorating had given
small interior mills another advantage. Damp seed in masses could become too hot to touch within a few hours and needed to be processed
very rapidly, which country mills were able to do because their seed
tended to come from the surrounding territory. Improvements in preserv-
ing cottonseed made it less important to crush seed quickly and thus
close to the place where the cotton grew. Most of the steel seed houses
in use during the 1930s had cooling systems. Research into drying techniques accelerated following the 1937 Mississippi River flood, which left

much damp cottonseed at harvest time. In studies done over the next two decades, the U.S. Department of Agriculture found that drying and cooling seed at gins improved their quality by delaying the development of free fatty acids and removing trash and moisture. During the 1940s oil mills generally sucked or blew air through their stored seed, but they could use heat or chemicals to destroy the enzymes that formed in moist, hot seed. Despite these advances, cottonseed remained a semiperishable commodity. In addition to advances made in drying cottonseed, more and more seed was being produced in arid western regions, where it could be kept for months on the ground in large piles. Western oil mills could thus spread their operations over a longer period of time than had been possible earlier.[31]

New Deal crop control, soil conservation, and wage policies, as well as revolutionary technological changes in the cultivation of cotton, hastened the transformation of the old decentralized system of hydraulic mills into the modern, highly concentrated cottonseed-processing industry of today. The trend began after the First World War, when mills found it harder to protect themselves from aggressive competition because fixing prices and dividing seed were clearly illegal. On the eve of World War II, smaller supplies of cottonseed, higher labor costs, and competition from soybeans and other oil seeds forced cottonseed crushers to operate more efficiently, and that ultimately meant continuous processing, which could operate with fewer man hours and for more months of the year. A 30-percent reduction took place in the number of cottonseed-oil mills between 1947–48 and 1957–58, and in the latter year, only 13 percent of the seed was processed in the aging hydraulic-press mills concentrated in the Southeast and lower Mississippi Valley.[32] Cheaper and more-flexible transportation, improved storage methods, and the shift of cotton production to dryer, flatter areas of the Far West facilitated the consolidation of processing. By the 1950s, a century after commercial processing had begun in the United States, a distinctive period in the industry's history was coming to an end. The story of cottonseed processing during the hydraulic era had paralleled that of the "first New South," which was also vanishing.

CHAPTER 11

The New Industry
and the New South

The rise of the cottonseed industry has been a phenomenon among phenomena that have made the United States the premier industrial nation of the world. It has dotted the South from the Roanoke to the Rio Grande with 618 separate mills utilizing in an intricate and costly manufacturing process what forty years ago was a nuisance that required for its control the enactment of legislation. The economic significance of this injection of industrial blood into the anaemic veins of a body laid prostrate by a great internecine struggle does not escape the student of social conditions.

Leebert Lloyd Lamborn, 1904

Important as the cottonseed industry is in the national economy as a whole, it must be clear that this industry has a particular significance for the cotton belt. There has perhaps been a tendency to underrate this significance, because cotton itself has so long dominated the agricultural scene in this region.

Georges Minch Weber,
"The Economic Development of the
American Cottonseed Oil Industry," 1933

The disappearance of hundreds of small cottonseed mills during the middle decades of the twentieth century coincided with the demise of small cotton farms and tenant farming. The heyday of decentralized cotton growing and cottonseed processing had been from the 1880s to the 1920s, when cotton production expanded and tightened its grip on the economy. The southern environment shaped the cottonseed-products industry in numerous ways, and cottonseed milling in turn had a widespread impact on the people and places of the Cotton Belt for more than half a century before the Second World War.

The position of cottonseed crushing among the leading southern industries between 1890 and 1930 strengthens the image of the South before the mid-twentieth century as a predominantly rural region in the initial stages of industrialization. Measured by the value of its products, cottonseed milling during the early twentieth century ranked among the top five or six industries in the ten major cotton-producing states, yet the crushing industry was insignificant compared to American manufacturing overall. Nonetheless, as a widespread industrial activity with links to every sector of the cotton economy, crushing is an important part of the region's past.[1]

The history of cottonseed crushing also reinforces the general picture of New South industry as one that made up for inadequate capital, skilled labor, and technology by developing the region's rich natural resources. Oil mills processed a raw material found in abundance, but made crude, undifferentiated products that added little value to the seed. A largely unskilled black work force, poorly paid even by southern industrial-wage standards, made the adoption of labor-saving machinery uneconomical.

Expansion of the South's cottonseed-crushing industry depended on the progress of oil refining and manufacturing and marketing of name-brand products, which yielded greater profits than primary processing and took place to a large extent outside the Cotton Belt during the late nineteenth century. The northern cottonseed, soap-making, and meat-packing companies that developed and sold high-quality differentiated cottonseed-oil products influenced the southern crushing industry through their ownership of large numbers of oil mills.

A scarcity of capital in the South following the abolition of slavery and lags in scientific knowledge and managerial experience account in part for the geographical separation of the primary and secondary phases of cottonseed processing. The postbellum South's small market for vegetable oils and shortenings also delayed the development of cottonseed-oil refining and manufacturing in the region. The largely rural population made much of its own lard for home consumption, and the lower wages of southern agricultural and industrial workers left less disposable income for shortenings than the better pay of most residents of large, industrial cities in the North.

Technological dependence on the North also characterized the industry. The few southern companies that manufactured oil-mill machinery managed to capture only a small part of the market, despite the excellence of some of their products. Companies in antebellum New York and Ohio developed mill machinery to serve the linseed-oil industry and expanded during the late nineteenth century to supply cottonseed-oil mills. Southern textile mills likewise acquired machinery from established companies in the North.[2]

Not all southern industries had to go outside the region for equipment. Most cotton-gin machinery came from southern companies that got a head start in the early nineteenth century and retained their dominance. New Orleans foundries supplied Louisiana sugar mills with much of their machinery after the 1850s, even though northern foundries had previously monopolized the market. The Cardwell Machine Company of Richmond manufactured machinery for tobacco factories. In the case of cottonseed crushing, southern manufacturers of oil-mill machinery could not overcome their northern competitors' early start, greater capital, and proximity to a strong machine-tool industry.[3]

The first stage in the processing of most southern crops lasted only part of each year and left plants idle the remaining months. Cottonseed, sugar, and rice milling, as well as cotton ginning, were seasonal industries. Closing plants for several months of the year and releasing most laborers undermined the efficiency of basic processing. Additionally, seasonal industries generated fewer resources for investment in upgrading plant and equipment.

Compared to the lumber and textile industries, and tobacco manufacturing after World War I, cottonseed crushing and all other New South industries lagged far behind the leaders in the value of their products and the value added to their raw materials by manufacturing (see table 3). In 1922 cottonseed milling had the lowest percentage of value added by manufacturing (10.26 percent) among more than 250 industries surveyed by the Census Bureau.[4]

Although southern textile manufacturing outdistanced cottonseed processing by every measure and went on year round, the two activities had much in common that made them typical of industry in the first New South. In both cases, relatively little capital was required to start a mill, and the two industries expanded rapidly in the years after 1880. A large number of southern cotton mills, in common with cottonseed-crushing mills, were comparatively small operations that manufactured "coarse

Table 3
Value Added for Selected Southern
Industries, 1909, 1919, and 1929

Industry	1909 ($1,000)	1919 ($1,000)	1929 ($1,000)
Lumber[a]	235,351 (1)	464,574 (1)	394,312 (2)
Cotton goods	79,176 (2)	350,850 (2)	365,117 (3)
Tobacco	50,021 (3)	195,177 (3)	488,994 (1)
Cars	32,518 (4)	126,265 (4)	112,248 (5)
Foundry	26,854 (5)	51,795 (8)	81,181 (6)
Cottonseed	25,810 (6)	78,890 (6)	44,951 (9)
Fertilizer	19,060 (7)	58,755 (7)	41,822 (10)
Flour-Grist	16,504 (8)	35,108 (10)	31,384 (12)
Sugar Refining	11,473 (9)	22,509 (13)	10,081 (15)
Ice making	10,974 (10)	20,630 (14)	56,261 (8)
Furniture	9,026 (11)	30,227 (11)	40,517 (11)
Iron/Steel	8,002 (12)	40,595 (9)	73,438 (7)
Slaughtering and meat packing	6,358 (13)	23,900 (12)	21,576 (13)
Rice polishing	2,578 (14)	10,346 (15)	8,184 (16)
Petroleum	NA	97,823 (5)	120,896 (4)
Livestock feed NA	NA	12,866 (14)	
Vegetable oils and shortenings	NA	NA	7,095 (17)
Poultry	NA	NA	2,816 (18)

[a]Lumber includes timber and planing.
SOURCES: Computed from statistics for former Confederate states and Oklahoma in Bureau of the Census, *Census of Manufactures,* Reports by States, 1909, 1919, 1929.

goods" on which they earned modest profits. Dependent on the same crop, fluctuating raw-material prices frustrated textile manufacturers as well as cottonseed crushers. With overproduction a serious problem and no brand names to distinguish the output of one cotton mill from another, companies competed aggressively among themselves and kept labor costs, their principal expenditure, as low as possible in the struggle for market share. "Cutthroat" competition also characterized cottonseed milling, but it took place in the area of raw-materials acquisition, the major cost of cottonseed milling, rather than in product sales. Analysts advocated diversification and vertical integration for the ailing southern textile industry, but the cost of going into sales and other lines of production was prohibitive for all but a handful of companies. The same could be said of the cottonseed industry; whereas northern refining and manufacturing companies added crushing facilities to their holdings at comparatively low cost, most southern oil-mill companies lacked the necessary capital to move into refining, manufacturing, and sales.[5]

Despite real progress in the industrial sector, agriculture continued to dominate the South's economy well after it declined in importance elsewhere in the United States. As farmers shifted more and more from corn to cotton cultivation following the Civil War, larger areas of the South became part of the one-crop economy. As late as 1949 some sixteen million southern people drew most of their income from cotton. Few economic enterprises in the cotton-producing states were unrelated to cotton. Besides its cultivation, cotton had to be ginned, marketed, financed, stored, transported, and fabricated. Other people in the cotton-growing South provided goods and services required by those directly involved in growing and handling cotton. By transforming a by-product of cotton for which there had been no commercial demand into an "economic Cinderella," the cottonseed-crushing industry became an integral part of the network of cotton-based enterprises in the New South.[6]

Southern cotton growers as a group received the largest return from cottonseed crushing. The rapid spread of oil milling after 1880 made cottonseed the second most valuable cash crop in the former Confederate states and Oklahoma until tobacco pushed cottonseed into third place during the late 1930s, when demand for smoking tobacco increased and cotton acreage declined (see table 4). In 1943 cottonseed stood eighth in value among all crops in the nation after cotton lint, wheat, corn, tobacco, potatoes, soybeans, apples, and oranges. The revenue from cottonseed was about twice that of rice in 1943, and soybeans had just moved ahead of cottonseed.[7]

Table 4
Farm Value of Cottonseed and Tobacco
in the Southern States

	1909 ($)	1919 ($)	1929 ($)	1939 ($)
Cottonseed	121,076,984	347,739,123	209,772,704	110,938,306
Tobacco	35,231,245	256,529,974	153,950,704	177,790,177

SOURCES: Bureau of the Census, *United States Census of Agriculture: 1935* 1:397, 447, 477, 493, 535, 593, 621, 643, 669, 695, 715, 741; *United States Census of Manufactures, 1939,* vol. 2, pt. 1, 758; *United States Census of Agriculture: 1945* 2:514. The farm value of tobacco in the former Confederate states was computed by adding the value given for each of those states. The total value of cottonseed reported in the census also includes seed grown in the Far West, and in areas such as southeastern Missouri.

In 1902 the Census Bureau reported that "no single industry, based on agriculture, has shown a more remarkable growth during the last quarter of the century than that which has characterized the cottonseed industry of the South." In *"The New South" in the New Economic Order,* published in 1919, Holland Thompson observed that cottonseed contributed "considerably to the income of every cotton grower." Between 1909 and 1940, the money paid to cotton farmers for their seed averaged 66.5 percent of the total value of cottonseed products.[8]

Cottonseed paid for harvesting, ginning, and baling most of the South's cotton crop, and brought producers the first cash of the season. For many small cotton farmers, cottonseed money was the only cash they received all year. That gave seed money and cottonseed prices a greater relative importance for many cotton growers than its actual value compared to lint.[9]

A Mississippi song of the late nineteenth century explains why cottonseed prices interested many small growers more than the value of lint:

Go to de big plantations
Whar de hawgs an' cattle feed;
De white man gets de cotton an' corn
De nigger gits de seed.

In 1930 a Tennessee ginner said that the price of seed was the first thing black farmers asked about when they brought cotton to be ginned. "We get the seed and the white man gets the cotton," they reportedly said, so "we are more interested in this seed than we are in the cotton." H. L. Mitchell, cofounder during the Depression of the Southern Tenant Farmers Union, told of black Arkansas sharecroppers being heard to say on their way to the gin: "Git that white man's cotton off my seed."[10]

Under the lien laws passed in the southern states after the Civil War, cottonseed could have been taken for debt. The North Carolina crop mortgage, for example, covered "all that is cropped, cut or gathered." In a few cases, cottonseed was credited to farmers' accounts, but during the late nineteenth century, the custom developed of letting tenants and sharecroppers who received "furnish" through the planting and growing season keep seed money to live on while picking their crop. At the end of the 1930s, Oscar Johnson, president of the Cotton Council and manager of the largest cotton plantation in Mississippi, described cottonseed as "the only unmortgaged asset" of cotton farmers. "It supports the producer during the harvest season and the money is more widely distributed than is the money paid for lint."[11]

Most farmers realized modest sums from the sale of cottonseed. Sharecropping agreements usually specified that the seed be divided between croppers and landowners. In a study of cottonseed prices, George Marshall calculated that between 1923 and 1936 the cash realized by sharecroppers from cottonseed averaged twenty-five dollars a year. Yearly averages for the period reveal tremendous variations in sharecroppers' income from seed money, ranging from a high of $44.77 in 1923 to a low of $1.05 in 1931. In the latter year, small farmers sometimes went home empty handed, because the cottonseed did not cover the cost of ginning their cotton.[12]

Cotton farms in the 1920s produced an average of slightly more than four tons of seed. A grower had to sell twenty or more tons of seed or the equivalent of forty or more bales of cotton to receive the higher price mills paid gins for railway carloads or truckloads of cottonseed. Eighty-five percent of cotton farms produced less than ten bales of cotton in 1941. Even though about two-thirds of the value of cottonseed products went to cotton growers and landowners in payment for seed, the majority of cotton farmers lived a marginal existence.[13]

Even so, the crushing industry may have propped up the sharecropping system and other traditional production and credit arrangements by providing a market for cottonseed. Lint prices steadily declined during the last two decades of the nineteenth century as world supplies outgrew demand. More and more cotton producers became mired in debt. It is hard to imagine that tens of thousands of small farmers would have labored year in and year out growing cotton without some cash return. Had there been no seed money to partially compensate for low lint prices, it is conceivable that the agrarian protest movement mounted by cotton growers at the end of the century would have been strong enough to force some of the changes demanded by its leaders.

A small minority of substantial planters derived far greater benefits from the sale of cottonseed than the average cotton farmer. An Arkansas farmer-ginner-merchant called oil mills "one of the greatest blessings to cotton producers of nearly everything except the railroads." In the Mississippi Delta, the Arkansas and St. Francis Deltas, the Red River Valley of Louisiana, and a few other areas, there were plantations that controlled thousands of acres of land. Owners operated one or more gins primarily to process the cotton grown on their land. Sharecroppers received the farm or wagon price for seed, but large farmer-ginners collected the mill or carlot price. Any price increases occurring between the time of settlement with the tenants and the sale of seed to the oil mills generally went to the planter. Landowners frequently used cottonseed money to hire wage laborers to pick the cotton on the acreage under their direct control and supervision. In 1931 the *Cotton Oil Press* reported that the Memphis seed-loan office did not require farmers to pledge their cottonseed as security, but allowed them to keep seed money to defray the costs of picking and ginning their cotton. Other farmers counted on trading seed for meal to be used as fertilizer or cattle feed.[14]

Seed money assumed great importance for all producers, but complaints to state and federal representatives and agencies about low prices came primarily from large landowners, ginners, seed buyers, and brokers. The dissatisfaction of seed producers and sellers made cottonseed prices a "political football" for more than half a century. Wesson Oil's president recalled in 1939 that since he had entered the business early in the century, there had been at least thirty state and federal investigations into the "cottonseed-oil trust." The great fluctuation in cottonseed prices more than anything else caused dissatisfaction and provoked suspicion and antitrust investigations. Table 5 shows the variable return to farmers from cottonseed in the first half of the twentieth century.[15]

The cottonseed-milling industry had a profound impact on cotton ginning following the Civil War. After ginners became the major suppliers

Table 5
Southern Farm Earnings
from Cottonseed, 1909–1940

Year	Average Farm Price per Ton	Tons of Seed Crushed	Total Earned by Farmers
1909–10	$24.34	3,269,000	$79,730,910
1910–11	26.11	4,106,000	107,207,660
1911–12	17.18	4,921,073	78,675,947
1912–13	18.36	4,579,508	84,079,766
1913–14	21.96	4,847,628	106,453,910
1914–15	15.51	5,779,665	89,642,604
1915–16	30.15	4,202,313	126,699,730
1916–17	45.63	4,479,176	204,384,800
1917–18	64.28	4,251,680	273,297,990
1918–19	65.23	4,473,508	291,806,920
1919–20	65.79	4,012,704	263,995,790
1920–21	25.65	4,068,166	104,374,100
1921–22	29.14	3,077,717	89,684,730
1922–23	30.42	3,241,557	98,608,163
1923–24	41.23	3,307,598	136,372,260
1924–25	33.25	4,605,227	153,123,790
1925–26	31.59	5,558,243	175,584,890
1926–27	22.04	6,305,775	138,979,280
1927–28	34.83	4,654,017	162,099,410
1928–29	34.13	5,061,058	172,733,900
1929–30	30.95	5,015,714	155,236,340
1930–31	22.05	4,715,148	103,969,010
1931–32	8.96	5,328,014	47,739,005
1932–33	10.32	4,620,558	47,684,158
1933–34	12.89	4,156,911	53,582,582
1934–35	33.09	3,549,891	117,465,890

Table 5. (cont.)

Year	Average Farm Price per Ton	Tons of Seed Crushed	Total Earned by Farmers
1935–36	30.54	3,817,751	116,594,110
1936–37	33.41	4,498,321	150,288,900
1937–38	19.52	6,325,733	123,478,300
1938–39	21.80	4,470,516	97,457,480
1939–40	21.20	4,150,755	87,996,006
1940–41	21.72	4,398,011	95,524,798

SOURCES: Total farm income from cottonseed was calculated by multiplying the average farm price per ton reported by the USDA in "Cottonseed: Marketing Spreads between Price Received by Farmers and Value of Products at Crushing Mills," 5, by the total annual crush statistics in Cox, *The Cottonseed Crushing Industry of Texas in Its National Setting* (Austin: Univ. of Texas Press, 1949), 277–78.

of seed to the oil mills, crushers acquired gins and employed commission contracts, loans, and other methods of obligating ginners to sell them seed. In order to maximize their incomes, ginners were involved in the buying and selling of cottonseed in a variety of ways. Seasonal by nature, cotton ginning went on in conjunction with a number of other activities, and the whole business might be profitable even when the gin lost money. By the First World War a company needed to gin approximately one thousand bales of cotton in a season to operate profitably; therefore, gins competed strenuously for business. To attract customers, some cotton ginners reduced their rates for ginning and offset the losses by speculating in cottonseed. Other ginners offered high prices for cottonseed or cotton lint to bring in ginning business. Whether ginners relied on seed and lint transactions to keep their operations in the black or offered high prices for cottonseed and lint as inducements to farmers to gin with them, cottonseed buying and selling constituted a very important part of the cotton ginning industry.[16]

Southern merchants and businessmen also had a keen interest in cottonseed prices. Writing in the late 1880s, M. B. Hillyard stated in *The New South* that cottonseed was "an article of barter at country stores." In nonplantation areas of the Cotton Belt, merchants at crossroads and in small towns furnished supplies to farmers in return for crop mortgages. Sometimes they offered more than the going rate for seed and credited the sale to a customer's account in order to reduce his debt. Merchants at times paid higher prices for cottonseed than gins or mills to attract business. Seed money spent in stores and other local enterprises affected the total economy of the cotton-growing states. "In the deep South, retailers, wholesalers, and all banking and business houses are feeling acutely this season's lack of seed-money," reported *Business Week* in 1937. "Cottonseed is down from $42 a ton in 1936 to $18 a ton."[17]

Banks in the Cotton Belt had a stake in the cottonseed-oil industry, because mills generally borrowed money to buy most of their seed for the entire crushing season in three or four months. During the early 1880s, when competition for seed caused prices to reach unprofitable levels, Memphis banks forced local oil mills to form seed pools before they would loan money for seed purchases. The financial difficulties experienced by many oil mills due to deflation and short crops after the First World War left a number of banks with oil-mill loans they could not collect. When oil mills failed to repay their loans for several consecutive years, banks had to foreclose. Commenting on the demise of oil mills in Texas after World War I, a prominent crusher observed that "many of them have been silently laid away with the usual obsequies and local banks as chief mourners." To help mills and banks in its territory, the Dallas Federal Reserve Bank collected information about the prices of cottonseed and cottonseed products and crushing costs from numerous processors and distributed it to interested mills and banks. Officials of the Federal Reserve Bank hoped that the information would enable banks to make more realistic loans and mills to operate more efficiently.[18]

Cottonseed milling, like other New South industries, did little to relieve the critical problem of rural overpopulation by providing a viable alternative to agriculture for a significant number of people. Although American cottonseed-oil mills were more labor intensive than their European counterparts during the first half of the twentieth century, cottonseed crushing required comparatively few workers, and paid "common laborers" little more than the agricultural wage. It ranked eighth among the top dozen southern industries in number of workers employed industrywide in 1880 and in 1910 and twelfth in 1930, but southern manufacturing enterprises during those years, apart from lumber and cotton goods, had small work forces (see table 6). Crushing mills averaged 11,007 employees in 1899; 17,071 in 1909; and 14,242 in 1933. The maximum number of laborers would have been larger, but "temporary" laborers, who unloaded and stored cottonseed, could have counted on

Table 6
Cottonseed-Oil Mills, Wage Earners,
and Wages, 1859–1958

Date	Mills	Average Number of Wage Earners	Wages
1859	7	183	$76,950
1869	26	664	292,032
1879	45	3,319	880,836
1889	119	5,906	1,493,780
1899	369	11,007	3,143,459
1904	715	15,540	4,837,694
1909	817	17,071	5,835,249
1914	882	21,810	8,490,000
1919	711	26,766	20,615,000
1921	610	16,163	12,339,895
1923	511	12,745	7,908,305
1925	535	16,215	11,411,354
1927	547	18,434	14,259,555
1929	553	15,825	11,203,227
1931	504	12,268	8,335,459
1933	475	14,242	5,376,000
1935	458	13,226	5,912,000
1937	447	16,583	8,552,000
1939	447	15,191	8,939,000
1947	315	12,136	22,560,000
1954	286	11,082	29,831,000
1958	214	6,310	20,006,000

SOURCES: Statistics for 1859–1909, Bureau of the Census, *Census of Manufactures, 1909* 8:449. Statistics for 1914–58, Bureau of the Census, *Census of Manufactures, 1958* 2:20H-4.

Table 7
Cost of Cottonseed, Value of Oil-Mill Products,
and Value Added, 1859–1958

Date	Cost of Materials	Value of Products	Value Added
1859	$498,000	$741,000	$243,000
1869	1,333,631	2,205,610	871,979
1879	5,091,251	7,690,921	2,599,670
1889	14,363,126	19,335,947	4,972,821
1899	45,165,823	58,726,632	13,560,809
1904	80,029,863	96,407,621	16,377,758
1909	119,833,475	147,867,894	28,034,419
1914	180,976,000	212,217,000	31,151,000
1919	495,192,000	581,245,000	86,053,000
1921	194,864,000	217,225,000	22,361,000
1923	199,515,000	226,388,000	28,873,000
1925	244,315,000	295,685,000	51,370,000
1927	220,038,000	276,388,000	56,300,000
1929	249,020,000	298,376,000	49,356,000
1931	147,165,000	181,347,000	34,182,000
1933	78,229,000	104,212,000	25,983,000
1935	160,552,000	187,887,000	27,335,000
1937	195,747,000	242,043,000	46,296,000
1939	138,764,000	171,476,000	32,712,000
1947	413,488,000	518,091,000	104,603,000
1954	487,726,000	592,298,000	111,734,000
1958	348,580,000	420,649,000	63,587,000

SOURCES: Statistics for 1859–1909, Bureau of the Census, *Census of Manufactures, 1909* 8:44. Statistics for 1914–58, Bureau of the Census, *Census of Manufactures, 1958* 2:20H-4.

only a few months of work. The lumber and cotton-goods industries employed several hundred thousand workers annually, but the average number of workers hired by the other leading southern industries was approximately twenty-three thousand in 1910 and thirty-one thousand in 1930.[19]

Although the South remained a predominantly rural and agricultural region after the Civil War, interior towns multiplied, and cottonseed milling contributed to their rapid growth between 1880 and 1920. Putting postbellum town building into perspective, Harold Woodman emphasized that the forces of industrialization and urbanization transforming the Northeast and Midwest had little impact on the South. More than 80 percent of southerners lived in rural areas in 1900, compared to slightly less than 50 percent of the northern population. In the same year the value of manufacturing capital in the South was less than 10 percent of the nation's total.

Attributing the enormous post–Civil War increase in the number and size of southern towns primarily to changes in the financing and marketing of cotton, Woodman called the crossroads town "the New South's most significant 'urban' development." Also emphasizing the primacy of cotton in spurring the growth of southern towns but focusing on a different category of urban places, Kenneth Weiher called attention to the importance of cottonseed processing and cotton compressing in the multiplication of towns with populations of four to fifteen thousand.[20]

Urbanization lagged in the South for decades, but during the half century after 1880, southern towns and cities grew at twice the rate of those in other regions of the United States. Weiher believes that central-place theory, which links the growth of an urban place to the expansion of its market area, explains the rise of towns with populations of four to fifteen thousand. In central-place theory towns and cities function as part of an interdependent system. "Each city provides those services which have minimum market areas no larger than its own," Weiher wrote, but cities must look to a higher-order place to supply those services whose cost is so great they require larger market areas.

Entrepreneurs located cottonseed-oil mills and cotton compresses in towns along the expanding rail lines of the Cotton Belt. Although there were cottonseed-oil mills in all types and sizes of communities from small towns to metropolises, the majority were located in towns of four to fifteen thousand people. Weiher found that places with oil mills and presses had their periods of greatest growth in the decade following the establishment of those enterprises. By 1930 oil mills and compresses had ceased to be significant factors in southern urban growth. These findings fit the picture of an industry that expanded rapidly between 1880 and the First World War and then began to consolidate during the 1920s and 1930s.

The process of town building began with businessmen seeking industry to promote the economic well-being of themselves and their towns. David Carlton's observation that small-town merchants invested in textile mills to "enhance the civic wealth, power, and glory" of their towns applies equally to cottonseed-oil mills. "If every small town at the South can't raise sufficient capital to build a 10,000 spindle cotton mill," stated a South Carolinian in 1895, "such towns can at least raise sufficient of the needful to build a cottonseed-oil mill and ginnery." Three decades later a Georgian commented that "local civic pride" had been an important factor in the establishment of oil mills.[21]

Although cottonseed crushing became more and more concentrated in larger mills after 1920, most oil mills remained in the towns and smaller cities. "In small towns, where a majority of the mills are located, the mill's sprawling buildings and storage tanks are the biggest thing in town," wrote the author of an article on the Wesson Oil & Snowdrift Company in 1939. "Indeed," he continued, "the cottonseed crushing mill is as natural a characteristic of the southern landscape as a grain elevator in Saskatchewan, or a hydraulic power plant in the Sierras."[22]

It is impossible to determine the profitability of cottonseed-oil mills to investors in southern communities and elsewhere. Earnings varied from year to year depending on seed and product prices and from place to place according to local conditions and the managerial and technical skills of operators. Henry Hammond commented in 1896 that many poorly constructed or inefficiently managed mills had failed, but that other mills had earned profits of 30 percent or more. Writing shortly before World War I, Luther A. Ransom stated that oil-mill earnings were "very small," averaging less than those of other manufacturing industries. The narrow spread between raw material costs and product prices caused the American Cotton Oil Company management during the First World War to propose that its mills crush cottonseed for producers for a fee or toll instead of buying seed and milling them. English and European oil mills also found it difficult to earn money. In 1922–23, crushing mills in only four states earned a profit, and during the following year mills in every state lost money, according to a U.S. Tariff Commission report. Trade-association statistics for 1927–32 show that from the average net revenue earned on each ton of cottonseed processed, seed merchants received 14.6 percent and oil mills only 4 percent. Hugh Humphreys, a Memphis cottonseed-meal broker, owner of an oil mill in Mississippi, and first head of the Cottonseed Division of the Food Administration, reflected in 1930 on the poor earnings of cottonseed crushers during his long association with the industry: "During these 33 years I feel safe in saying that for all of their efforts and investment, the industry has been operated at a loss to the investors in the enterprise. The record is one of disaster and ruin to those engaged in the crushing of cottonseed, and I think the entire cause is the ruthless, reckless competition in buying cottonseed. . . . I cannot recall at this time any man who has amassed a fortune from the crushing of cottonseed."[23]

Some mills reportedly earned profits of 10 percent or better during the 1920s. Because they often kept only one set of books for all of their activities, even oil men did not always know whether their profits had been earned from crushing or auxiliary businesses. Various people described cottonseed-processing margins as more in the nature of "tolls" or "charges for the performance of standard services" than profits because crushers had little opportunity to earn higher prices by producing superior products. The only thing that can be said with confidence about the profitability of American cottonseed crushing before the Second World War is that the highly competitive industry had many ups and downs, and during periods of financial distress, oil mills changed hands frequently and at depressed prices.[24]

Despite its generally modest economic performance, the cottonseed-crushing industry did have multiplier effects in the South. The proliferation of cottonseed-oil mills during the last two decades of the nineteenth century contributed to the expansion of the southern fertilizer industry. With the abolition of slavery, few farmers in the South Atlantic states could afford to clear new land as they frequently had in the past when old fields became unproductive. Massive applications of fertilizer to depleted and marginal land made the Southeast one of the largest fertilizer-consuming areas in the nation during the late nineteenth century.

Fertilizer manufacturers depended on organic sources of nitrogen until the early twentieth century. Peruvian guano, introduced into the United States in the 1840s, improved soils by the addition of nitrogen and phosphate, but guano was expensive and supplies decreased after the peak year of 1875. During the late 1880s, studies by chemists in Germany and France called attention to the importance of using a "complete fertilizer" that contained nitrogen, phosphate, and potash. By itself, cottonseed meal is close to being a complete fertilizer, but it is a particularly rich source of nitrogen. With the coming of cottonseed-oil mills to the southeastern states in the 1880s, farmers used the meal on a large scale to fertilize cotton and tobacco fields, generally mixing it with acid phosphate and potash.

George Washington Scott pioneered the use of cottonseed meal as an ammoniate in commercial fertilizers. A native of Pennsylvania, Scott moved to Florida in 1851 and prospered as a cotton and commission merchant in Tallahassee. He acquired phosphate lands and first used cottonseed meal in fertilizer in 1866. Following a move to Decatur, Georgia, in about 1878, Scott established a fertilizer plant and ordered cottonseed meal from an oil mill in Montgomery, Alabama. Marketed as "Scott's Gossypium Phospho," the fertilizer was named for its two major ingredients. Farmers liked the new fertilizer, because it did not smell bad and was easy to handle.

Following Scott's lead, other manufacturers began to use cottonseed meal as a source of nitrogen in some of their fertilizers. Many cottonseed-oil mills in the Southeast produced balanced fertilizers as a sideline. The Virginia-Carolina Chemical Company, commonly referred to as the "fertilizer trust," acquired the Southern Cotton Oil Company in 1901 and bought a large number of additional oil mills in order to control as much of the fertilizer business in the South as possible and to insure plentiful supplies of cottonseed meal for its products.

In the 1909 *Census of Manufactures,* cottonseed meal was called "one of the best ammoniates" and "an important ingredient in the manufacture of fertilizers." According to the *Cotton Oil Magazine,* 170 oil mills produced commercial fertilizers valued at more than $8.5 million in 1913–14. Of those mills, 62 were in Georgia, 30 in South Carolina, 26 in North Carolina, 23 in Alabama, 9 in Mississippi, 8 in Arkansas, 6 in Louisiana, and 1 in Florida. These statistics indicate that on the eve of the First World War, 30 to 40 percent of all oil mills in the South Atlantic states made fertilizer from cottonseed meal. Writing at the close of the war, Holland Thompson said that the fertilizer industry depended "largely" on cottonseed meal.

Inorganic forms of nitrogen gradually replaced organic sources during the early decades of the twentieth century. First mined in Chile in 1880, saltpeter, or nitrate of soda, was being used as a top dressing for cotton by progressive farmers in North Carolina during the opening decade of the century and as an ingredient in many commercial fertilizers.

On the eve of World War I, fertilizer formulas worked out for various truck crops by the North Carolina Agricultural Experiment Station called for two or three times as much cottonseed meal as nitrate of soda. By 1930 nitrate of soda had become the preferred source of nitrogen in the southeastern states.[25]

Cottonseed meal brought higher prices when sold as an animal feed rather than a fertilizer. Livestock production declined in the Southeast after the Civil War, and although it began to recover during the 1930s, it did not become commercially important until after the Second World War. In Texas, on the other hand, the number of cattle increased. A good market existed in the Southwest for high-protein cottonseed meal as a supplement, or, mixed with hulls, as a balanced livestock feed. In the early twentieth century, several southern states had small feed-mixing industries, and some oil mills sold mixed feeds as a sideline, but statistics on production and materials are lacking. Although considerable meal was exported or sold to northern dairymen, a number of early cottonseed-oil mills operated feedlots as a way of using cottonseed meal produced in excess of local demand. Favorable reports on the feeding value of cottonseed meal by southern state agricultural departments and experiment stations and the educational services of the national trade association helped to develop southern demand for cottonseed meal. Exports practically ceased in the 1930s, and by the end of the decade almost 70 percent of the cottonseed meal was being consumed in the southern states. This was in part a result of the loss of northern markets to soybean meal, but the effectiveness of the campaign to persuade southern farmers to feed more cottonseed meal to their animals also played a role. As demand for meal and hulls grew, cattle feeding at oil mills became less important.[26]

The most significant spin-off of the cottonseed-crushing industry was the manufacture of vegetable shortening and oil. During the late nineteenth century, cottonseed-oil refining and manufacturing went on primarily in Cincinnati, Chicago, Bayonne, New Jersey, and other northern cities. In the twentieth century, manufacturers of cottonseed oils and shortenings established plants below the Mason-Dixon line, and more southern-owned companies made edible fats from cottonseed oil. In 1929 the leading states in the production of vegetable shortenings were Texas (17 percent), Tennessee (12 percent), Illinois (percentage unknown), Georgia (8 percent), and Louisiana (approximately 8 percent). The Southern Cotton Oil Company, majority southern owned following its reorganization in 1925, produced Snowdrift and Wesson Oil. Although trade figures were closely guarded secrets, a 1939 estimate placed the company's annual earnings from Snowdrift at about $5 million, compared to some $25 million for Procter & Gamble's Crisco and $20 million for Lever Brothers' Spry, which had been introduced in 1936 and aggressively marketed.[27]

The crushing industry had its greatest impact on the Cotton Belt between 1880 and 1940. For more than half a century cottonseed processing was an important part of the cotton-based economy of the New South. Federal crop-reduction and soil-conservation measures first enacted during the New Deal had the long-term effect of reducing cottonseed supplies and stimulating soybean production. Minimum-wage legislation forced oil mills to operate more efficiently, which speeded up the trend toward large-scale processing. Radios, improved roads, and trucks helped to end the isolation that had once characterized the Cotton Belt. Market reports kept farmers informed about cottonseed prices, and better transportation made it unnecessary for gins and oil mills to be located as close to the cotton fields as in earlier years.

Hydraulic-press mills that once filled the air of many southern towns with a distinctive fried-ham odor during the crushing season have all but disappeared, along with hundreds of thousands of sharecroppers, tenants, and other small farmers who produced much of the seed processed by the mills. For the past several decades cottonseed has barely defrayed ginning costs, with little or no cash left over for producers. A few large corporations do most of the processing today, and cottonseed oil's minor status among the wide variety of fats and shortenings available to consumers has obscured its role as the pioneer of the edible vegetable-oil industry in the United States. By tracing the history of cottonseed processing from the raw materials to the finished products, I hope that there will be renewed appreciation for an industry that put money into the pockets of cotton farmers in the South and entrepreneurs in many parts of the United States by making "something from nothing."

Appendix

Cotton Production and Cottonseed Oil Mills, 1880–1950

Year	Bales of Cotton	(% of total)	Oil Mills[a]	(% of total)
Alabama				
1880	699,654	12.2	2	4.3
1890	915,210	12.2	9	7.6
1900	1,106,840	11.6	28	7.6
1910	1,129,527	10.6	71	8.7
1920[b]	718,163	6.3	47	6.6
1930	1,312,963	9.0	34	6.4
1940	772,711	6.7	28	6.3
1950	824,290	5.3	21	6.1
Arkansas				
1880	608,256	10.6	4	8.9
1890	619,494	9.3	8	6.7
1900	709,880	7.5	20	5.4
1910	776,879	7.3	71	8.7
1920	869,350	7.6	47	6.6
1930[c]	1,398,475	9.6	34	6.1
1940	1,351,209	11.8	28	6.3
1950	1,584,307	10.3	21	6.7

Cinderella of the New South

Year	Bales of Cotton	(% of total)	Oil Mills[a]	(% of total)
Georgia				
1880	814,441	14.1	0[d]	0.0
1890	1,191,846	15.9	17	14.3
1900	1,287,992	13.5	43	11.7
1910	1,992,408	18.7	142	17.4
1920	1,681,907	14.8	116	16.3
1930	1,344,488	9.2	61	11.0
1940	905,088	7.9	51	11.4
1950	609,967	3.9	27	8.6
Louisiana				
1880	508,569	8.8	12	26.7
1890	659,180	8.8	7	5.9
1900	709,041	7.4	24	6.5
1910	268,909	2.5	43	5.3
1920	306,791	2.7	28	3.9
1930	798,828	5.5	23	4.2
1940	717,713	6.2	21	4.7
1950	607,186	3.9	14	4.4
Mississippi				
1880	963,111	16.7	8	17.8
1890	1,154,725	15.5	13	11.0
1900	1,313,798	13.8	41	11.1
1910	1,127,156	10.6	87	10.6
1920	957,527	8.4	49	6.9
1930	1,875,108	12.9	50	9.0
1940	1,533,092	13.3	41	9.2
1950	1,496,902	9.7	39	12.4
North Carolina				
1880	389,598	6.8	0	0.0
1890	336,261	4.5	11	9.2
1900	459,707	4.8	21	5.7
1910	665,132	6.2	53	6.5

Year	Bales of Cotton	(% of total)	Oil Mills[a]	(% of total)
1920	858,406	7.5	62	8.7
1930	764,328	5.2	49	8.9
1940	458,146	4.0	37	8.3
1950	472,389	3.1	25	7.9
Oklahoma				
1880	NA	0.0	0	0.0
1890	425	0.0	0	0.0
1900	225,525	2.3	12	3.2
1910	555,742	5.2	39	4.8
1920	1,006,242	8.8	51	7.2
1930	1,130,415	7.7	45	8.1
1940	520,591	4.5	29	6.5
1950	567,792	3.7	18	5.7
South Carolina				
1880	522,548	9.1	0	0.0
1890	747,190	10.0	17	14.3
1900	881,422	9.2	50	13.6
1910	1,279,866	12.0	103	12.6
1920	1,476,645	13.0	81	11.4
1930	835,963	5.7	38	6.9
1940	849,982	7.4	30	6.7
1950	543,936	3.5	27	8.6
Tennessee				
1880	320,621	5.7	9	20.0
1890	190,579	2.5	15	12.7
1900	234,592	2.5	17	4.6
1910	264,562	2.5	20	2.4
1920	306,974	2.7	22	3.1
1930	503,816	3.4	20	3.6
1940	436,126	3.8	15	3.4
1950	616,742	4.0	12	3.5

Year	Bales of Cotton	(% of total)	Oil Mills[a]	(% of total)
Texas				
1880	805,284	14.0	4	8.9
1890	1,471,242	19.7	13	10.9
1900	2,506,212	26.3	103	27.9
1910	2,455,174	23.0	194	23.7
1920	2,971,757	26.1	200	28.1
1930	3,793,392	26.0	176	31.8
1940	2,724,442	23.7	144	32.2
1950	5,549,667	36.0	95	30.1

[a]Number of mills is given for 1879, 1889, 1899, 1909, 1919, 1929, 1939, and 1947.
[b]In 1920 a number of mills were dormant because of short crops.
[c]Planters drained and cultivated extensive acreages in eastern Arkansas.
[d]An oil mill in Augusta, Georgia, began operations in the late 1870s.
Sources: Bales of cotton produced and percentage of the total crop are from Donald B. Dodd and Wynelle S. Dodd, *Historical Statistics of the South* (University: University of Alabama Press, 1973), 5, 9, 21, 29, 37, 41, 45, 49, 53, 57; number of mills is from table 4, Maurice R. Cooper, "History of Cotton and the United States Cottonseed Industry," in *Cottonseed and Cottonseed Products: Their Chemistry and Chemical Technology,* ed. Alton E. Bailey (New York: Interscience Publishers, New York, 1948), 24 and *Census of Manufactures, 1947.*
Caveat: Number and percentage of mills cannot be equated with crushing capacity.

Notes

Abbreviations

COP	*Cotton Oil Press*
C&COP	*Cotton and Cotton Oil Press*
DAT, CPL	D. A. Tompkins Papers, Charlotte (North Carolina) Public Library
DAT, DU	D. A. Tompkins Papers, Duke University Library, Durham, North Carolina
DU	Perkins Library, Duke University, Durham, North Carolina
ECU	East Carolina University Library, Greenville, North Carolina
FGT	Francis G. Thomason Papers, Mitchell Memorial Library, Mississippi State University, Starkville
MSA	Mississippi State Archives, Jackson
MSU	Mississippi State University Library, Starkville
NA	National Archives, Washington, D.C.
NAL	National Agricultural Library, Beltsville, Maryland
OPD	*Oil, Paint and Drug Reporter*
RGD	R. G. Dun & Company Collection. Baker Library, Harvard University Graduate School of Business Administration.
SC	South Caroliniana Library, University of South Carolina, Columbia
UA	University of Alabama Library, University, Alabama
USFA	United States Food Administration
ZP	E. V. Zoeller Papers, Southern Historical Collection, Wilson Library, University of North Carolina, Chapel Hill

Abbreviations for Record Group 302, Archives Division, Texas State Library, Austin:

AGC	Attorney General Correspondence, 1898–1914
SNB1	Stenographer's Notebook, 24 October–1 November 1913
SNB2	Stenographer's Notebook, 5–15 November 1913

SPF/CCO   S. P. Freeling v. Choctaw Cotton Oil Company
T/MCO   Texas v. Mansfield Cotton Oil Company

Introduction

Both epigraphs are from the minutes of the Interstate Cotton Seed Crushers' Association. The association, formed in 1897, published the minutes of its annual conventions after 1902. The Memphis Public Library and the National Agricultural Library have incomplete series of the *Proceedings of the Interstate Cotton Seed Crushers' Association* through 1916. Beginning in 1917 the new journal of the association, the *Cotton Oil Press,* included the full proceedings of its conventions in every June issue.

1. Edward Atkinson, *Cheap Cotton by Free Labor* (Boston: A. Williams, 1861), 38; Joseph B. Killebrew et al., *Introduction to the Resources of Tennessee* (Nashville: Tavel, Eastman & Howell, 1874), 102–3; M. B. Hillyard, *The New South* (Baltimore: *Manufacturers' Record,* 1887), 34; Census Office, *Twelfth Census of the United States: 1900,* vol. 9, *Manufactures,* pt. 3, *Special Reports on Selected Industries,* "Cottonseed Products," by Daniel C. Roper (Washington, D.C., 1902), 588; C. W. Burkett and C. H. Poe, "Cotton Seed: Once an Outcast Now a Prince," *Cotton* (New York: Doubleday, Page, 1906), 275–81; "That Old Georgia Law," *Cotton Oil Press* 15 (Apr. 1932): 29 (hereafter cited as *COP*); B. F. Taylor, *Early History of the Cotton Oil Industry in America* (Columbia, S.C.: privately printed, 1936), 16.

2. "Editorial," *COP* 4 (Oct. 1920): 33; George F. Deasy, "Geography of the United States Cottonseed Oil Industry," *Economic Geography* 17 (Oct. 1941): 347; James E. Boyle, "New Orleans and Memphis Exchanges for Cottonseed Products," *Commerce and Finance* 18 (25 Sept. 1929): 2065; A. L. Ward, "Cottonseed—'Farm Cinderella,'" *Manufacturers' Record* 105 (July 1936): 32–33; A. G. Hopkins, "Cotton's Future as a Leading Source of Essential Fat," in *Proceedings of the Fifth Cotton Research Congress* (n.p.: Statewide Cotton Committee of Texas, 1944), 91.

3. Thomas R. Chaney, "The Cotton-Seed-Oil Industry," in *One Hundred Years of American Commerce,* ed. Chauncey M. Depew (New York: D. O. Haynes, 1895), 454–55; Matthew Brown Hammond, *The Cotton Industry: An Essay in American Economic History* (Ithaca, N.Y., 1897), 171; *Proceedings of the Seventh Cotton Research Congress* (n.p.: Statewide Cotton Committee of Texas, 1946), 73; Dept. of Agriculture, Bureau of Agricultural Economics, "Cottonseed: Marketing Spreads between Price Received by Farmers and Value of Products at Crushing Mills," by Kathryn Parr and Richard O. Been (Washington, D.C., 1942), 2, in the National Agricultural Library, Beltsville, Maryland (hereafter cited as NAL).

4. Pete Daniel, *Breaking the Land: The Transformation of Cotton, Tobacco, and Rice Cultures since 1880* (Urbana: Univ. of Illinois Press, 1985); Gavin Wright, *Old South, New South* (New York: Basic Books, 1986).

5. Calculations of comparative value of products and value added by manufacturing for different southern industries were derived from statistics re-

ported in the *United States Census of Manufactures* for the relevant years, and Georges Minch Weber, "The Economic Development of the American Cottonseed Oil Industry" (Ph.D. diss., Univ. of California, 1933), 32a.

6. Emory Q. Hawk, *Economic History of the South* (New York: Prentice-Hall, 1934; Westport, Conn.: Greenwood Press, 1973), 298, 453; C. Vann Woodward, *Origins of the New South* (Baton Rouge: Louisiana State Univ. Press, 1951), 126–31, 135; George B. Tindall, *The Emergence of the New South* (Baton Rouge: Louisiana State Univ. Press, 1967), 87–88; David C. Roller and Robert W. Twyman, eds., *The Encyclopedia of Southern History* (Baton Rouge: Louisiana State Univ. Press, 1979), 375; Charles Reagan Wilson and William Ferris, eds., *Encyclopedia of Southern Culture* (Chapel Hill: Univ. of North Carolina Press, 1989), 36; Harold D. Woodman, *King Cotton and His Retainers* (Lexington: Univ. of Kentucky Press, 1968; Columbia: Univ. of South Carolina Press, 1990).

7. Bennett H. Wall, "Breaking Out: What Is Not in Southern History, 1918–1988," *Journal of Southern History* 55 (Feb. 1989): 3–20; W. J. Matherly, "North Carolina's Position in Cottonseed Industry," *North Carolina Commerce and Industry,* 3 (Nov. 1925): 1; "Wesson," *Fortune* 20 (Sept. 1939): 66; Daniel, *Breaking the Land,* xv.

8. Victor S. Clark, *History of Manufactures in the United States,* 2 vols. (Washington, D.C.: Carnegie Institute, 1929; New York: Peter Smith, 1949), vol. 2: 186; Luther A. Ransom, *The Great Cottonseed Industry of the South* (New York: Oil, Paint and Drug Reporter, 1911), 53.

9. Woodward, *Origins of the New South,* ix, 112; Tindall, *Emergence of the New South,* x; Howard N. Rabinowitz, *The First New South, 1865–1920* (Arlington Heights, Ill.: Harlan Davidson, 1992), 183–86.

10. Harvey S. Perloff with Vera W. Dobbs, *How a Region Grows* (New York: Committee for Economic Development, 1963), 43–44.

11. Dept. of Agriculture, Agricultural Marketing Service, *A Study of Practices Affecting the Use of Major Vegetable Oils for Refining and Processing,* by William Emory and Jack S. Wolf (Washington, D.C., 1960), 6, Francis G. Thomason Papers, "Publications," Mitchell Memorial Library, Mississippi State University, Starkville (hereafter cited as FGT).

12. Dept. of Agriculture, Division of Statistics, Misc. Series, Bulletin No. 16, "The Cost of Cotton Production," by John Hyde and James L. Watkins (Washington, D.C., 1899), 30; D. A. Tompkins Company, *Ginneries, Oil Mills, Fertilizer Works, Cost of Plants, Operation, Etc.* (rpt. from the *Manufacturers' Record,* 1889–90), 1, D. A. Tompkins Papers, Robinson-Spangler Room, Charlotte (North Carolina) Public Library (hereafter cited as DAT, CPL).

1. Beginnings of the American Cottonseed Industry

1. Louis Edgar Andes, *Vegetable Fats and Oils,* 4th English ed. (London: Scott, Greenwood & Son, 1925), iii, 2–3; Dept. of Agriculture, "Some American Vegetable Food Oils, Their Sources and Methods of Production,"

Yearbook, 1916, by H. S. Bailey (Washington, D.C., 1917), 159; Harold W. Brace, *History of Seed Crushing in Great Britain* (London: Land Books, 1960), 9–22.

2. Brace, *History of Seed Crushing in Great Britain,* 37; W. G. Hoffman, "100 Years of the Margarine Industry," in *Margarine,* ed. J. H. Van Stuyvenberg (Liverpool: Liverpool Univ. Press, 1969), 9–11; Fernand Braudel, *The Structures of Everyday Life* (New York: Harper & Row, 1981), 212; Charles Wilson, *The History of Unilever,* 3 vols. (London: Cassell, 1954; New York: Frederick A. Praeger, 1968), vol. 2: 24–26, vol. 3: 17.

3. *Niles' Register* 26 (15 May 1824): 178, 47 (29 Nov. 1834): 198; J. Leander Bishop, *A History of American Manufactures from 1608 to 1860,* 3 vols. (Philadelphia: Edward Young, 1868; New York: August M. Kelley, 1966), vol. 2: 81 n. 1; Whitney Eastman, *The History of the Linseed Oil Industry in the United States* (Minneapolis: T. S. Denison, 1968), 18; Carter Litchfield et al., *The Bethlehem Oil Mill 1745–1934: German Technology in Early Pennsylvania* (Kemblesville, Pa.: Olearius Editions, 1984), 51.

4. Bishop, *History of American Manufactures* 2:81 n. 1.

5. Edward Rutledge, Charleston, to Phineas Miller (near Savannah), 21 Aug. 1790, Edward Rutledge Papers, Manuscript Division, Perkins Library, Duke University, Durham, North Carolina (hereafter cited as DU).

6. Denison Olmsted, *Memoir of Eli Whitney, Esq.* (New Haven, Conn.: Durrie & Peck, 1846; New York: Arno Press, 1972), 15–47; Constance McLaughlin Green, *Eli Whitney and the Birth of American Technology* (Boston: Little, Brown, 1956), 40–96.

7. James L. Watkins, *King Cotton: A Historical and Statistical Review, 1790–1908* (New York: James L. Watkins & Sons, 1908), 163; "William Dunbar," in Roller and Twyman, *Encyclopedia of Southern History,* 374.

8. John Drayton, *A View of South Carolina* (Charleston: W. P. Young, 1802), 153, 212; Taylor, *Early History of the Cotton Oil Industry,* 9–10.

9. H. C. Nixon, "The Rise of the American Cottonseed Oil Industry," *Journal of Political Economy* 38 (Feb.–Dec. 1930): 74; *A Guide to the Manuscript Collection of the South Caroliniana Library, University of South Carolina* (Columbia: Univ. of South Carolina, 1982), 236.

10. Bishop, *History of American Manufactures* 2:81; Patent Office, Jabez Smith's Hulling Machine, Patent No. 5673, patented 28 Dec. 1829, vol. 9, 21; Patent Office, Jabez Smith, of Petersburg, Virginia, Improvement in Machines for Hulling Cotton-Seed, Patent No. 3951, dated 15 Mar. 1845; David R. Williams, Society Hill, S.C., to Col. James Chesnut, near Camden, S.C., 27 Dec. 1829, 25 Mar., 11 Apr. 1830, typed copies of correspondence, Manuscript Dept., Baker Library, Harvard Graduate School of Business Administration; A Cotton Planter to the *Columbia (S.C.) Telescope* in *Niles' Register* 37 (3 Oct. 1829): 96.

11. J. Kelly Turner and John L. Bridgers Jr., *History of Edgecombe County, North Carolina* (Raleigh, N.C.: Edwards & Broughton Printing, 1920), 343; A. S. Clayton to the *Athens (Ga.) Southern Banner,* 30 July 1833, in *Niles' Register* 45 (7 Sept. 1833): 30.

12. "Can Cotton-Seed Oil or Rosin Oil Be Manufactured with Advantage in

Alabama," *DeBow's Review* 19 (Nov. 1855): 601; Litchfield et al., *Bethlehem Oil Mill,* 48–50.

13. Brace, *History of Seed Crushing in Great Britain,* 30–48; Bishop, *History of American Manufactures* 3:194; Andes, *Vegetable Fats and Oils,* 3.

14. A Cotton Planter to the *Columbia (S.C.) Telescope* in *Niles' Register* 37 (3 Oct. 1829): 96, 45 (7 Sept. 1833): 30; Nixon, "Rise of the American Cotton-seed Oil Industry," 75; Williams Haynes, *American Chemical Industry,* 6 vols. (New York: D. Van Nostrand, 1954), vol. 1: 126.

15. J. Carlyle Sitterson, *Sugar Country* (Univ. of Kentucky Press), 32–33; Watkins, *King Cotton,* 170.

16. J. Woolridge, *History of Nashville, Tenn.* (Nashville: Publishing House of the Methodist Episcopal Church, South, 1890), 221; David Rattray, *The City of Natchez* (Natchez, Miss.: Democrat Book and Job Print, 1881), 20; Peter J. Hamilton, *Colonial Mobile* (1897; Mobile: First National Bank of Mobile, 1952, rpt. of 1910 rev. ed.), 358; Nixon, "Rise of the American Cottonseed Oil Industry," 76; Paul Wayne Taylor, "Mobile: 1818–1859, as Her Newspapers Pictured Her" (Master's thesis, Univ. of Alabama, 1951), 37; Communication from *New Orleans Louisiana Advertiser* in *Niles' Register* 48 (16 May 1835): 186.

17. Patent Office, *Report of 1844,* no. 42, 431–33; A. S. Clayton to the *Athens (Ga.) Southern Banner,* 30 July 1883, in *Niles' Register* 45 (7 Sept. 1833): 30; "Can Cotton-Seed Oil or Rosin Oil Be Manufactured with Advantage in Alabama," 601; Patent Office, Jabez Smith, Improvement in Machines for Hulling Cotton-Seed, Patent No. 3951.

18. John F. Moloney, "The Marketing of Cottonseed, a Report Prepared in Connection with Project II, Postwar Agricultural and Economic Problems of the Cotton Belt" (Memphis: National Cottonseed Products Association [1945?]); D. A. Tompkins, *Cotton and Cotton Oil* (Charlotte, N.C.: privately printed, 1901), 204–5; Census Office, "Cottonseed Products," 589; David Wesson, "Pictorial Description of the Cotton Oil Industry," *Chemical and Metallurgical Engineering* 22 (10 Mar. 1920): 470; Roscoe C. Clark, "The Cottonseed Products Industry," *Journal of Accountancy* 54 (Sept. 1932): 178; Dept. of Agriculture, "Cottonseed: Marketing Spreads," 3.

19. La., vol. 9, 247, R. G. Dun & Company Collection, Baker Library, Harvard University Graduate School of Business Administration (hereafter cited as RGD); Leebert Lloyd Lamborn, *Cottonseed Products* (New York: D. Van Nostrand, 1904), 19; Brace, *History of Seed Crushing in Great Britain,* picture of press facing p. 96.

20. Charles W. Bradbury Papers, Southern Historical Collection, Wilson Library, University of North Carolina, Chapel Hill (hereafter cited as SHC); *DeBow's Review* 16 (Feb. 1854): 203–4; La., vol. 7, 269, vol. 13, 295, RGD; Henry V. Ogden, *Cotton-Seed Oil and Cotton-Seed Oil Mills* (Atlanta: Constitution Print, 1880), 5; Chaney, "Cotton-Seed-Oil Industry," 451; William T. Brannt, *A Practical Treatise on Animal and Vegetable Fats and Oils,* 2 vols. (Philadelphia: Henry Carey Baird, 1896), vol. 1: 445.

21. R.I., vol. 7, 163, La., vol. 11, 289, vol. 14, 89, RGD; M. K. Thornton, *Cottonseed Products* (Wharton, Tex.: Oil Mill Gazetteer, 1932), 14; Nixon,

"Rise of the American Cottonseed Oil Industry," 78; Bishop, *History of American Manufactures* 3:376.

22. J. R. Sypher, "Cotton Seed, Cotton Seed Oil, Cotton Seed Cake," in *Cotton Culture,* by Joseph B. Lyman (New York: Orange, Judd, 1868), 181; Lamborn, *Cottonseed Products,* 19; J. Thomas Scharf, *History of Saint Louis City and County,* 2 vols. (Philadelphia: Louis H. Everts, 1883), vol. 2: 1291; Taylor, *Early History of the Cotton Oil Industry,* 15.

23. Patent Office, W. R. Fee, Cotton Seed Huller, Patent No. 17,961, patented 11 Aug. 1857; Ohio, vol. 79, 149, RGD; Atkinson, *Cheap Cotton by Free Labor,* 17; John F. Moloney, "Cottonseed Oil—A Typical American Indus-try," in *Proceedings of the First Cotton Research Congress* (n.p.: Statewide Cotton Committee of Texas, 1940), 232–33; Charles Cist, "Cotton-Seed Oil," *DeBow's Review* 27 (July 1859): 111–12, 27 (Aug. 1859): 220–22; Charles Cist, *Sketches and Statistics of Cincinnati in 1859* [Cincinnati: n.p., 1859?], 311–13.

24. Sypher, "Cotton Seed, Cotton Seed Oil," 181.

25. St. Louis city directory, 1860, 50, 1872, 65; "Cottonseed Crushing Before the Civil War," *COP* 14 (Dec. 1930): 38; Alan Smith Thompson, "Mobile, Alabama, 1850–1861: Economic, Political, Physical, and Population Char-acteristics" (Ph.D. diss., Univ. of Alabama, 1979), 113.

26. "Cottonseed Crushing Before the Civil War," 38.

2. Expansion of Cottonseed Milling in the South

The first epigraph is from the *Proceedings of the Cotton Seed Crusher's Associa-tion.* Organized in 1878, the association published the *Proceedings* of its annual meetings from 1879 through 1883. Those for 1879–82 are at the Cincinnati His-torical Society and the 1883 minutes are at the NAL.

1. *Proceedings of the Cotton Seed Crushers' Association,* 1879, 35; "Cotton-Seed Oil—Its Manufacture and Uses," *New York Times,* 26 Mar. 1877, p. 2.

2. "Cotton-Seed Oil," *Hunt's Merchants' Magazine and Commercial Review,* Mar. 1857, 386.

3. Sypher, "Cotton Seed, Cotton Seed Oil," 184, 187.

4. Atkinson, *Cheap Cotton by Free Labor,* 17; Sypher, "Cotton Seed, Cotton Seed Oil," 188; Interstate Cotton Seed Crushers' Association, *Bulletin* 1 (1906): back page, in South Caroliniana Library, University of South Caro-lina, Columbia (hereafter cited as SC); Weber, "Economic Development," 20–24.

5. *Proceedings of the Cotton Seed Crushers' Association,* 1881, 14–15.

6. "Cottonseed Crushing Before the Civil War," 37; Lamborn, *Cottonseed Products,* 23; "Cottonseed Oil Men on a Tour," *Oil, Paint and Drug Re-porter* 25 (16 Apr. 1884): 8 (hereafter cited as *OPD*); *Proceedings of the Cotton Seed Crushers' Association,* 1883, 71; *Proceedings of the Interstate Cotton Seed Crushers' Association,* 1913, 53.

7. *New Orleans Deutsche Zeitung,* 24 Apr. 1857, p. 2; "Cottonseed Crushing Before the Civil War," 39; Andrew Morrison, *The Industries of New Orleans* (New Orleans: J. M. Elstner & Co., 1885), 63; Henry B. Moore, "Pioneer in Marketing Cotton Seed Meal," *COP* 1 (June 1917): 27–28.

8. Sitterson, *Sugar Country,* 273–74; "Death of F. W. Brode," *COP* 15 (Oct. 1931): 11.

9. "Edward Flash Retires from Business," *COP* 15 (June 1931): 83–84; *Cotton-Oil,* 5th ed. (New York: Aspegren & Co., 1913), 6; Wilson, *History of Unilever* 2:36.

10. William C. Stubbs, *Cotton and Its Products,* Bulletin No. 13, Louisiana State Experiment Station [Baton Rouge: 1887?]; Oklahoma Agricultural and Mechanical College, Agricultural Experiment Station, *Report, 1898–1899,* 68; Dept. of Agriculture, Office of Experiment Stations, Bulletin No. 80, *The Agricultural Experiment Stations in the United States,* by A. C. True and V. A. Clark (Washington, D.C., 1900), 141, 193, 355, 357, 401, 411, 416, 419, 511, 514, 517, 519, 565; Oklahoma Agricultural Experiment Station, Bulletin No. 51, "Feeding Cottonseed Meal to Hogs," by F. C. Burtis and J. S. Malone (Stillwater, Okla., 1901, 3–15; *The Value of Cotton-Seed Products in the Feeding of Farm Animals, as a Human Food and as a Fertilizer* (Dallas: Bureau of Publicity of the Interstate Cotton Seed Crushers' Association, 1913).

11. Ledgers of the Tar River Oil Company, Henry Clark Bridgers Papers, East Carolina Manuscript Collection, East Carolina University Library, Greenville, North Carolina (hereafter cited as ECU); F. C. Dunn, Kinston, N.C., to J. Havens, Washington, N.C., 28 Oct. 1905, William Blount Rodman Papers, ECU; Dept. of Agriculture, Agricultural Information Bulletin No. 79, "Cottonseed Oil Mill Characteristics and Marketing Practices" (Washington, D.C., 1951), 32; *Cotton Oil,* 6; Dept. of Agriculture, Commodity Exchange Authority, "The Cottonseed Oil Futures Market" (Washington, D.C., 1949), 11–12. The New Orleans Cotton Exchange organized a futures market in cottonseed oil in 1925, but New York remained the dominant market. Boyle, "New Orleans and Memphis Exchanges," 2065, 2067.

12. Tenn., vol. 30, 232, 287, RGD.

13. Tenn., vol. 7, 244, 402, RGD; Census of Manufactures, 1870, MS, Tennessee: Anderson to Lewis Counties, DU; *Proceedings of the Interstate Cotton Seed Crushers' Association,* 1905, 79, 1907, 64, 1914, 89–90.

14. Ala., vol. 10, 112, RGD; D. A. Tompkins Company, *Cotton Seed Oil Mills, Cotton Oil Refineries, Cotton Factories, Sulphur Acid Chambers, Acid Phosphate Works, Electric Lighting* (Charlotte, N.C.: R. B. Elam Print, 1893), 4, in DAT, CPL (hereafter cited as D. A. Tompkins Co., *Catalog*).

15. Ohio, vol. 85, 108, Mo., vol. 47, 206, Miss., vol. 12, 435, RGD.

16. Weber, "Economic Development," 27a; Woodward, *Origins of the New South,* 113.

17. Wright, *Old South, New South,* 107–11.

18. John L. Stover, *The Railroads of the South, 1865–1900: A Study in Finance and Control.* (Chapel Hill: Univ. of North Carolina Press, 1955), 186–87, 189–90.

19. "Cotton Seed Oil Mills," *Manufacturers' Record* 8 (19 Sept. 1885): 178; Hillyard, *New South,* 35.

20. Walter B. Moore, "Oldest Cotton Oil Mill Has Had Unique History," *Cotton*

Gin & Oil Mill Press 56 (3 Dec. 1955): 12–13, 30; Tenn., vol. 31, 338, RGD.

21. James C. Cobb, *Industrialization and Southern Society* (Chicago: Dorsey Press, 1984), 18, 19, 24.

22. "South Carolina Cotton-Seed Oil Industry," *OPD* 46 (5 Nov. 1894): 8; "New Southern Cotton-Seed Mills," *OPD* 56 (28 Aug. 1899): 9; Interstate Cotton Seed Crushers' Association, *Bulletin* 1:2.

23. E. N. Hinson, "The Financial End of the Oil Milling Business," *OPD* 57 (25 June 1900): 28 E.

24. Minutes of the Beech Island [S.C.] Agricultural Club, 7 Nov. 1885, 5 May 1894, 3 Oct. 1896, sent to the author by Frank W. Atkinson of Beech Island; *Aiken Journal and Review,* 25 Mar., 8 Apr., 6 May, 24 June, 29 July, 7 Oct. 1896; Kathwood Manufacturing Corporation, Return of Corporations to the Secretary of State, 27 July 1896; President to Daniel Pratt Gin Co., 6 July 1897; unsigned to Northington-Munger-Pratt Co., 29 July 1897; Harry Hammond to Henry [C. Hammond], 23 July 1901, Kathwood Manufacturing Company Papers, SC; Carol Bleser, ed, *The Hammonds of Redcliffe* (New York: Oxford Univ. Press, 1981), 139, 326–27, 340–41.

25. "Cotton Seed Oil Mills," 178; "Outlook for the Cotton Seed Industry," *OPD* 50 (20 July 1896): 5; Henry Hammond, "The Cotton Seed Industry," *OPD* 50 (12 Oct. 1896): 25; "Growing Competition in the Cottonseed Industry," *OPD* 54 (4 July 1898): 5; W. B. Kilgore, "The Cottonseed Oil Industry," *OPD* 55 (26 June 1899): 26 H; *Report of the Federal Trade Commission on the Cotton-Seed Industry,* 71st Cong., 2d sess., S. Docs., pt. 8, Texas, 8219 (hereafter cited as *Report of the Federal Trade Commission* [followed by state]); Dept. of Agriculture, "Cottonseed Oil Mill Characteristics and Marketing Practices," 35.

26. "Small Cotton-Seed Oil Mills," a booklet published by the Cardwell Machine Company c. 1890 and rpt. in *Cotton and Cotton Oil Press* 41 (21 Dec. 1940): A-4, A-5, A-7 (hereafter cited as *C&COP*); Charles W. Dabney, "A Plea for Small Cotton Seed Oil Mills," *OPD* 21 (17 May 1882): 934; "Farm Cottonseed Oil Mills," *OPD* 25 (6 Feb. 1884): 13.

27. Tompkins, *Cotton and Cotton Oil,* 227–28, 231; D. A. Tompkins, *Cotton Seed and Its Products* (machinery catalog with no publication information, 1900), 5, DAT, CPL; "Address of President B. F. Taylor," *Proceedings of the Interstate Cotton Seed Crushers' Association,* 1912, 33.

28. Kilgore, "Cottonseed Oil Industry," 26 G; Hammond, "Cotton Seed Industry," 25; J. J. Culbertson, "History of Cottonseed Crushing in Texas," *COP* 15 (Oct. 1931): 26.

29. Bureau of the Census, *Thirteenth Census of the United States: 1910,* vol. 9, *Manufactures: 1909, Reports by States* (Washington, D.C., 1912), 27, 227, 427, 627, 909, 1010, 1149, 1185, 1210; Burkett and Poe, *Cotton,* 285.

30. "Proceedings of the Interstate Cotton Seed Crushers' Association, 1921," *COP* 5 (June 1921): 104; A. B. Cox, *The Cottonseed Crushing Industry of Texas in Its National Setting* (Austin: Univ. of Texas Press, 1949), 66, 177.

31. "Address of President B. F. Taylor," 33; *Cotton Seed Oil Magazine* 28 (Jan. 1917): 17.

32. Tariff Commission, "Survey of the American Cotton Oil Industry," in *Tariff Information Surveys*, rev. ed. (Washington, D.C., 1921), 103.

3. Cottonseed Buying and Selling

1. Cox, *Cottonseed Crushing Industry of Texas*, 166.
2. Minutes of the Monticello Conference, 24 Sept. 1903, Zoeller Papers, Southern Historical Collection, University of North Carolina, Chapel Hill (hereafter cited as ZP); "Cottonseed Crushing Before the Civil War," 39; Edwin L. Jewell, *Jewell's Crescent City Illustrated* (New Orleans, 1873), 39; "Rural View," *OPD* 28 (9 Dec. 1885): 19; Chaney, "Cotton-Seed-Oil Industry," 452.
3. Prof. Myers, "Cottonseed, Its Uses and Products," *OPD* 25 (25 June 1884): 33.
4. Dept. of Agriculture, Office of Experiment Stations, Bulletin No. 33, "The Handling and Uses of Cotton," by Henry Hammond, in *The Cotton Plant: Its History, Botany, Chemistry, Culture, Enemies, and Uses*, ed. Charles W. Dabney (Washington, D.C., 1896), 354–60; D. A. Tompkins, "The Cultivation, Picking, Baling and Manufacturing of Cotton, from a Southern Standpoint, a Paper Read at the Meeting of the New England Cotton Manufacturers' Association, at Atlanta, Ga., Oct. 25, 1895," DAT, CPL; Charles S. Aiken, "The Evolution of Cotton Ginning in the Southeastern United States," *Geographical Review* 63 (Apr. 1973): 199–202, 205; John Hebron Moore, *The Emergence of the Cotton Kingdom in the Old Southwest* (Baton Rouge: Louisiana State Univ. Press, 1988), 57–64.
5. William Wallace, *Prospectus of Proposed Cotton Seed Oil Mill* [1868?], SC; D. A. Tompkins, "The Cotton Oil Industry in America," rpt. of an article in *Cassier's Magazine* [1900?]: 2–3, North Carolina Room, Wilson Library, Univ. of North Carolina, Chapel Hill; *New York Times*, 26 Mar. 1877, p. 2; Aiken, "Evolution of Cotton Ginning," 209–10.
6. Chaney, "Cotton-Seed-Oil Industry," 452, 454; "Proceedings of the Interstate Cotton Seed Crushers' Association, 1926, *COP* 10 (June 1926): 55; Woodman, *King Cotton and His Retainers*, 269–94.
7. Chaney, "Cotton-Seed-Oil Industry," 454; *Proceedings of the Texas Cotton Seed Crushers' Association*, 1901, 4, NAL.
8. *Mobile: Seaport and Trade Center, her Relations to the New South, 1887–88* (Mobile: Metropolitan and Star Publishing, 1888), 74; *Proceedings of the Cotton Seed Crushers' Association*, 1882, 128.
9. Chaney, "Cotton-Seed-Oil Industry," 454; *Proceedings of the Cotton Seed Crushers' Association*, 1883, 75–79.
10. W. D. Shue, "The Cotton Oil Industry," *Mississippi Historical Society Publications* 8 (1904): 260; Circular No. 3 from C. L. Ives, New Bern, N.C., 22 Sept. 1906; [E. V. Zoeller] to C. L. Ives, 11 July 1907, ZP; Memphis Merchants' Exchange, *Annual Statement of the Trade and Commerce of Memphis, Tenn., for the Year 1896*, 23, Memphis–Shelby County Public Library (hereafter cited as Memphis Merchants' Exchange *Report*, [followed by year]).
11. Dept. of Agriculture, "Handling and Uses of Cotton," 357–60; Lamborn,

Cottonseed Products, 4–8; Charles S. Aiken, "Cotton Gins," in Wilson and Ferris, *Encyclopedia of Southern Culture,* 568–69; Aiken, "Evolution of Cotton Ginning," 205–9.

12. Shue, "Cotton Oil Industry," 260; Cox, *Cottonseed Crushing Industry of Texas,* 160, 166, 265; "Cotton Oil Milling Industry Is Exonerated," *COP* 11 (Apr. 1928): 22; *Cottonseed and Its Products,* 8th ed. (Memphis: National Cottonseed Products Assn., 1978), 11; testimony of a farmer and an independent seed buyer at Lawton, Okla., 14 Jan. 1918; testimony of farmer-ginners at Mangum, Okla., 16 Jan. 1918; S. P. Freeling, attorney general, v. Choctaw Cotton Oil Company et al., Attorney General Correspondence, July 1898–Aug. 1914, RG 302, Archives Division, Texas State Library, Austin (hereafter cited as SPF/CCO).

13. *Report of the Federal Trade Commission,* pt. 9, Okla., 11357, 11365; pt. 3, Ga., 1255; pt. 4, Ala., 2520, 2584, 2637, 2676–77, 3072; pt. 5, N.C., 3469; pt. 7, Miss., 7096, 7246; pt. 11, Ark., 13513, 13564, 13566; pt. 13, summary, 15743; Deasy, "Geography of the United States Cottonseed Oil Industry," 347; James C. Cobb, *The Most Southern Place on Earth* (New York: Oxford Univ. Press, 1992), 103; Eugene Allen Smith, "Report on the Cotton Production of the State of Alabama," extract from the U.S. Census, 1880, 154, Univ. of Alabama, Tuscaloosa; George Marshall, "Cottonseed—Joint Products and Pyramidal Control," in *Price and Price Policies,* ed. Walton Hamilton (New York: McGraw-Hill, 1938), 216, 224–26; copy of a cottonseed receipt furnished to the Texas attorney general's office by W. J. Croom, Wharton, Tex., Tex. v. Mansfield Cotton Oil Company, RG 302, Archives Division, Texas State Library, Austin (hereafter cited as T/MCO).

14. *Report of the Federal Trade Commission,* pt. 7, Miss., 6949, 7206; pt. 10, La., 12397; pt. 11, Ark., 13511–12.

15. Testimony of feed yard operator and cottonseed buyer, Lawton, Okla., 14 Jan. 1918, SPF/CCO; *Report of the Federal Trade Commission,* pt. 3, Ga., 958; pt. 9, Okla., 11109, 11385; pt. 10, La., 12025; Tompkins, *Cotton and Cotton Oil,* 206.

16. W. G. McNair, Jackson, Miss., to K. C. Hall (Laurel, Miss.), 12 Dec. 1907, State of Miss., Ex. Rel., Ross A. Collins, attorney general, vol. 7237 American Cotton Oil Company et al., RG 48, vol. 32, Mississippi State Archives (hereafter cited as RG 48, vol. no., MSA); testimony of farmer-ginner, Mangum, Okla., 16 Jan. 1918; testimony of independent seed buyer, Lawton, Okla., 14 Jan. 1918, SPF/CCO; testimony of C. E. Herod and A. L. Thompson, seed buyers, Grosbeck, Tex., 3 Nov. 1913; testimony of L. M. Morgan, J. H. Snowden, and C. J. Kling, seed buyers, Kasse, Tex., 3 Nov. 1913; Stenographer's Notebook, 24 Oct.–1 Nov. 1913, RG 302, Archives Division, Texas State Library, Austin (hereafter cited as SNB1), J. T. Bogard to Attorney General B. F. Looney, 18 Oct. 1917, T/MCO; *Report of the Federal Trade Commission,* pt. 3, Ga., 1103, 1232, 1234, 1241, 1248, 1489; pt. 4, Ala., 2480; pt. 9, Okla., 11359, 11385, 11405.

17. Interstate Cotton Seed Crushers' Association, *Bulletin* 3 (1907): 5, SC; J. M. Macdonald, Buckeye Cotton Oil Co., Cincinnati, to S. N. Malone, Jackson, Miss., 31 Oct. 1906; J. M. Macdonald to W. G. McNair, Jackson, Miss., 29

Aug. 1912, RG 48, vol. 35, MSA; *Minutes of the Annual Meeting of the Alabama Cotton Seed Crushers Association,* 1913, 31–33, Manuscript Collection, University of Alabama Library, University, Alabama (hereafter cited as UA); C. Wood Davis, "Corn and Cotton-Seed: Why the Price for Corn Is Low," *Forum* 24 (1898): 730–43.

18. C. L. Ives, New Bern, N.C., to E. V. Zoeller, Tarboro, N.C., 14 Sept. 1903, ZP; testimony of cottonseed buyer, Timpson, Tex., T/MCO; *Report of the Federal Trade Commission,* pt. 3, Ga., 1035, 1084; pt. 5, N.C., 3619; pt. 7, Miss., 6818.

19. *Report of the Federal Trade Commission,* pt. 12, Tenn., 14924. (The FTC interviewed witnesses from eastern Arkansas in Memphis.)

20. *Report of the Federal Trade Commission,* pt. 3, Ga., 1603; pt. 8, Tex., 8447–48; Lillington [N.C.] Oil Mill Company Papers, 1913–1923, 10-C, 29 Sept. 1915, 49, DU.

21. Testimony of three ginners, Altus, Okla., 15 Jan. 1918; testimony of five ginners, Mangum, Okla., 16 Jan. 1918; testimony of four ginners and an independent seed buyer, Lawton, Okla., 14 Jan. 1918, SPF/CCO; "Monthly Letter of Secretary Cleaver," *COP* 3 (Nov. 1919): 20; *Report of the Federal Trade Commission,* pt. 3, Ga., 1439, 1443; pt. 11, Ark., 12608, 12648, 12650; pt. 12, Tenn., 14587; Marshall, "Cottonseed—Joint Products," 231.

22. *Manufacturers' Record* 24 (6 Oct. 1893): 167, 24 (13 Oct. 1893): 183; [G. L. Keith], Mt. Pleasant, Tex., to D. C. Harrington, Texarkana, Tex., 7 Sept. 1913; testimony of C. E. Herod, Grosbeck, Tex., SNB1; testimony of ginners H. T. Ashcraft and J. A. Ashcraft, Rogers, Tex., 5 Nov. 1913; testimony of ginner A. N. Weems, Cameron, Tex., 5 Nov. 1913; undated stenographer's notebook, RG 302, Texas State Library, Austin.

23. *Proceedings of the Third Annual Session of the South Carolina Cotton Seed Crushers' Association,* 23 June 1908, 32, NAL; A. M. DuMay, Washington, N.C., to E. V. Zoeller, Tarboro, N.C., 16 Oct. 1912; [E. V. Zoeller] to A. M. DuMay, 17 Oct. 1912; A. M. DuMay to E. V. Zoeller, 1 Nov. 1912, ZP; F. W. Hobbs, "The Cotton Seed Oil Industry with Particular Reference to the Farmers and Ginners' Cotton Oil Company" (Bachelor's thesis, [1919], Barker Texas History Center, Univ. of Texas, Austin), n.p.; Tariff Commission, "Survey of America's Cottonseed Oil Industry," *COP* 4 (Feb. 1921): 49; "Financing Cotton Oil Mills," *COP* 8 (Nov. 1924): 45.

24. Ledgers of the Tar River Oil Company, Henry Clark Bridgers Jr. Papers, ECU; minutes of Monticello Hotel Conference, 24 Sept. 1903, ZP; "Wesson," 109; *Report of the Federal Trade Commission,* pt. 8, Tex., 8340–41; "Proceedings of the Interstate Cotton Seed Crushers' Association, 1917," *COP* 1 (June 1917): 55; "Address of Mr. Oscar Wells, President of the First National Bank of Birmingham, Alabama," *COP* 8 (June 1924): 19; W. J. Evans, "Banking Relations in Cotton Oil Milling," *COP* 8 (Aug. 1924): 33.

25. *Proceedings of the Third Annual Session of the South Carolina Cotton Seed Crushers' Association,* 1908, 28, NAL; E. V. Zoeller, Tarboro, N.C., to H. E. Wells, Columbia, S.C., 30 Dec. 1903; Jonathan Havens, Washington, N.C., to E. V. Zoeller, 16 Jan. 1905; C. L. Ives, New Bern, N.C., to E. V. Zoeller, 6 Mar. 1906; Jonathan Havens to E. V. Zoeller, 14 Apr. 1906, ZP; *Report of*

the Federal Trade Commission, pt. 3, Ga., 1086; pt. 7, Miss., 7461; pt. 13, summary, 15780; Dept. of Agriculture, "Cottonseed Oil Mill Characteristics and Marketing Practices," 31–32.

26. Manager, Buckeye Cotton Oil Co. mill, Jackson, Miss., to Buckeye Cotton Oil Co., Cincinnati, 2 July 1907, RG 48, vol. 35, MSA; *Minutes of the Annual Meeting of the Alabama Cotton Seed Crushers Association,* 1913, 38, 40, UA; testimony of R. J. F. Morris, ginner, Palestine, Tex., 1 Oct. 1915, testimony of Day, manager of Lockart Oil Mill, Luling, Tex., 16 Aug. 1915, statement by Emil Buescher, president, Smithville [Tex.] Cotton Oil Co., 13 Oct. 1917, printed contracts for salaried and commission buyers, Fidelity Cotton Oil Co., Houston, c. World War I, T/MCO; *Report of the Federal Trade Commission,* pt. 13, summary, 15756.

27. Harry Hammond to Henry [C. Hammond], 23 July 1901; James D. Dawson, district manager, Southern Cotton Oil Co. to C. C. F. Hammond, 6 June 1904, Kathwood Manufacturing Company Papers, SC; Tompkins, *Cotton and Cotton Oil,* 205; minutes of the Monticello Conference, 24 Sept. 1903, ZP; [K. C. Hall], Laurel, Miss., to J. M. Wilson, Meridian, Miss., 8 Oct. 1907; E. M. Durham, Vicksburg, Miss., to K. C. Hall, 21 Oct. 1909; form letter from L. Foote, Canton, Miss., 18 Sept. 1911, RG 48, vol. 32, MSA; E. H. Cahn, Meridian, Miss., to L. M. Porter, Aberdeen, Miss., 29 Aug. 1907; E. H. Cahn to Ernest Lamar, Selma, Ala., 15 Oct. 1907; Ernest Lamar to 7 mills, 25 Aug. 1908, RG 48, vol. 34, MSA; testimony of W. A. Webb, ginner, Teague, Tex.; testimony of C. J. Kling, ginner, Kasse, Tex., SNB1, G. L. Keith, Mt. Pleasant, Tex., to P. A. Norris, Ada, Okla., 13 Sept. 1913, RG 302, TSL-A; T. F. Justiss, "Statement to Cotton Ginners and Cottonseed Buyers, 38-H-3," undated; T. F. Justiss, "To All Buyers and Sellers of Cotton Seed, Circular No. 40," 14 June 1918, U.S. Food Administration Papers (hereafter cited as USFA), RG 4, National Archives (hereafter cited as RG 4, NA); *Report of the Federal Trade Commission,* pt. 4, Ala., 2457; pt. 6, S.C., 4884; pt. 8, Tex., 8194; pt. 13, summary, 15757; J. C. Munden, Elizabeth City, N.C., to C. A. Johnson, Tarboro, N.C., 19 Aug. 1934, F. S. Royster Mercantile Company, Inc. Records, ECU.

28. S. P. Alexander, Clarksdale, Miss., to USFA, 6 Dec. 1917, RG 4, NA; *Report of the Federal Trade Commission,* pt. 3 Ga., 1032, 1452; pt. 4. Ala., 2456; pt. 5, N.C., 3552; pt. 6, S.C., 4883, 4898; pt. 12, Tenn., 14583, 14650, 14935.

29. *Report of the Federal Trade Commission,* pt. 3, Ga., 1333–37, 1380, 1389; pt. 4, Ala., 2430–33.

30. F. L. Hogan, Starkville, Miss., to E. Cahn, Aberdeen, Miss., 28 Sept. 1906, RG 48, vol. 34, MSA; S. S. Dale & Son, Prentiss, Miss., to K. C. Hall, Laurel, Miss., 5 Sept. 1908, RG 48, vol. 32, MSA; C. L. Ives, New Bern, N.C., to E. V. Zoeller, Tarboro, N.C., 5 Oct. 1904; J. Havens, Washington, N.C., to E. V. Zoeller, 28 Oct. 1904; form letter from H. E. Wells, Columbia, S.C., 30 Dec. 1904; circular letter from J. Havens, 2 Jan. 1905; C. L. Ives to E. V. Zoeller, 12 Jan. 1905, ZP; *Report of the Federal Trade Commission,* pt. 8, Tex., 8088.

31. Tompkins, *Cotton and Cotton Oil,* 205; *Report of the Federal Trade Com-*

mission, pt. 3, Ga., 1194; pt. 7, Miss., 7341–42; testimony of ginner, Mangum, Okla., 16 Jan. 1918, SPF/CCO; E. Cahn, Meridian, Miss., to L. M. Porter, Aberdeen, Miss., 25 July 1907, RG 48, vol. 34, MSA; H. C. Forrester, Meridian, Miss., to K. C. Hall, Laurel, Miss., 10 Sept. 1907; [K. C. Hall] to W. B. Gowdy and W. G. McNair, Jackson, Miss., 23 June 1909; W. B. Gowdy to K. C. Hall, 21 Aug. 1909, RG 48, vol. 32, MSA.

32. *Minutes of the Annual Meeting of the Alabama Cotton Seed Crushers Association,* 1913, 38, UA; Buckeye Cotton Oil Co., Cincinnati, to Buckeye Cotton Oil Co., Jackson, Miss., 4 Oct. 1907, and other letters in RG 48, vol. 35, MSA; [K. C. Hall] to J. T. Hunter, Decatur, Miss., 18 Oct. 1909, RG 48, vol. 32, MSA; *Report of the Federal Trade Commission,* pt. 3, Ga., 1064.

33. Testimony of J. F. Wilson, manager, Rockwell County [Tex.] Oil Co., 25 Sept. 1913, [Texas] Attorney General Correspondence, July 1898–Aug. 1914, RG 302, Archives Division, Texas State Library, Austin (hereafter cited as AGC); testimony of gin manager, Altus, Okla., SPF/CCO; testimony of R. J. F. Morris, ginner, Palestine, Tex., 1 Jan. 1915; testimony of ginner, Luling, Tex., 16 Aug., 1915, T/MCO; testimony of ginner C. J. Kling, SNB1; "Commission Buyer's Contract," Fidelity Cotton Oil Company, RG 302, TSL-A; K. C. Hall, Laurel, Miss., to H. C. Forrester, Meridian, Miss., 9 Oct. 1909, RG 48, vol. 32, MSA; *Report of the Federal Trade Commission,* pt. 4, Ala., 2563.

34. J. M. Macdonald, Cincinnati, to S. N. Malone, Jackson, Miss., 12 Nov. 1906, RG 48, vol. 35; E. M. Durham, Vicksburg, Miss., to E. Cahn, Meridian, Miss., 12 Oct. 1907; form letter from Ernest Lamar, Selma, Ala., 19 Sept. 1910, RG 48, V. 34; Brookhaven Cotton Oil Co. to K. C. Hall, Laurel, Miss., and E. L. Robbins, Hattisburg, Miss., 5 Feb. 1908; K. C. Hall to H. C. Forrester, Meridian, Miss., 9 Oct. 1909, RG 48, vol. 32, MSA; Shue, "Cotton Oil Industry," 285; *Minutes of the Annual Meeting of the Alabama Cotton Seed Crushers Association,* 1913, 17, UA; *Proceedings of the Third Annual Session of the South Carolina Cotton Seed Crushers' Association,* 1908, 32, NAL; *Report of the Federal Trade Commission,* pt. 3, Ga., 1497, 1577, 1974, 1979, 2006.

35. Circular from Selma, Ala., 23 Oct. 1907; W. C. McClure, Columbus, Miss., to E. Cahn, Meridian, Miss., 14 Oct. 1908, RG 48, vol. 34, MSA; W. A. Reynolds, "Some Evils in Seed Buying," *Proceedings of the Interstate Cotton Seed Crushers' Association,* 1912, 62–63; statement of Emil Buescher, president, Smithville [Tex.] Oil Co. to R. V. Nichols, special agent, 13 Oct. 1917, T/MCO; *Report of the Federal Trade Commission,* pt. 3, Ga., 1060; pt. 5, N.C., 3467.

36. Testimony of S. B. Guynes, ginner, Calvert, Tex., SNB1; P. A. Norris, Ada, Okla., to George L. Keith, Mt. Pleasant, Tex., 15 Sept. 1913; testimony of J. L. Hudgins, manager, Industrial Cotton Oil Co., Houston, 22 Nov. 1913, RG 302, TSL-A; *Report of the Federal Trade Commission,* pt. 3, Ga., 1050, 1504; pt. 4, Ala., 2360, 2564; pt. 8, Tex., 8087, 8432, 8498, 8499, 8663–64, 9043; pt. 12, Tenn., 14725; pt. 13, summary, x, 15756.

37. Frank M. Hunt, Newton, Miss., to H. C. Forrester, Meridian, Miss., 5 Oct. 1910; unsigned to L. Foot, Canton, Miss., 14 Sept. 1911, RG 48, vol.

32; E. Cahn, Meridian, Miss., to M. Frank, [Atlanta], 28 Jan. 1907; S. N. Malone, Natchez, Miss., to E. Cahn, 17 Nov. 1910, RG 48, vol. 34, MSA; *Report of the Federal Trade Commission,* pt. 8, Tex., 9691, 9696, 9700.

38. Testimony of independent buyer, Altus, Okla., 15 Jan. 1918, SPF/CCO; *Minutes of the Annual Meeting of the Alabama Cotton Seed Crushers Association,* 1913, 17, UA; "Past Presidents Send Their Greetings," *COP* 1 (May 1917): 30; "Proceedings of the Interstate Cotton Seed Crushers' Association, 1919," *COP* 3 (June 1919): 84–85, 94; *Report of the Federal Trade Commission,* pt. 3, Ga., 1080, 1407; pt. 7, Miss., 7109; pt. 8, Tex., 9419, 10089–90; National Cottonseed Products Association, "Economic Survey of the Cottonseed Products Industry," 15 Jan. 1931, table 8, NAL.

39. "Proceedings of the Interstate Cotton Seed Crushers' Association, 1919," *COP* 3 (June 1919): 92; *Report of the Federal Trade Commission,* pt. 3, Ga., 1075, 1206, 1219; pt. 6, S.C., 5424; pt. 13, summary, 15744–46.

40. *Report of the Federal Trade Commission,* pt. 3, Ga., 975, 1102, 1336; pt. 6, S.C., 5407; pt. 11, Ark., 13703; pt. 5, Miss., 7167.

41. W. B. Gowdey, Jackson, Miss., to K. C. Hall, Laurel, Miss., 11 Jan. 1907, RG 48, vol. 32, MSA; testimony of ginner and farmer, Luling, Tex., 16 Aug. 1915, T/MCO; testimony of oil miller, Mangum, Okla., 16 Jan. 1918; testimony of ginner and of independent cottonseed buyer, Altus, Okla., 15 Jan. 1918, SPF/CCO.

42. C. A. Sweeton, assistant attorney general, to Attorney General B. F. Looney, 21 Oct. 1913; testimony of F. Brady, ginner, Waxahachie, Tex., 3 Nov. 1913, SNB1; statement of H. T. Ashcraft, gin owner, Rogers, Tex., 5 Nov. 1913, Stenographer's Note Book dated 3 Nov.–15 Nov. 1913, RG 302, Archives Division, Texas State Library, Austin (hereafter cited as SNB2); testimony of manager, Farmers' Union Gin and Warehouse Co., Bastrop County, Tex.; testimony of McNeal and Neill, farmers, and of J. M. Rector, independent seed buyer, Luling, Tex., 16 Aug. 1915, T/MCO; *Report of the Federal Trade Commission,* pt. 8, Tex., 9410–11.

43. Daniel Clifford Roper, "Census Office Cotton Report and the Significant Development of the Cottonseed-Oil Industry," *South Atlantic Quarterly* 2 (Jan. to Oct. 1903): 239; D. A. Tompkins Co., *Catalog,* 5, DAT, CPL; Dept. of Agriculture, "Handling and Uses of Cotton," 364; E. Cahn, Meridian, Miss., to E. M. Durham, Vicksburg, Miss., 7 Oct. 1907; E. M. Durham to E. Cahn, 23 July 1906; E. Cahn to E. M. Durham, 20 Dec. 1909, RG 48, vol. 34, MSA; *Proceedings of the Interstate Cotton Seed Crushers' Association,* 1903, 28, 1910, 109; William Bragaw & Co., Washington, N.C., to E. V. Zoeller of Tarboro, N.C., 26 Aug., 2 Sept. 1904, ZP; Cox, *Cottonseed Crushing Industry of Texas,* 65; L. Tuffly Ellis, "The Round Bale Cotton Controversy," *Southwestern Historical Quarterly* 71 (Oct. 1967): 221; Howard B. Clay, "Daniel Augustus Tompkins and Industrial Revival in the South," *East Carolina College Publications in History* 2 (1965): 126; Kathwood Manufacturing Company Papers, SC; Lillington Oil Mill Company, "President's Report," 3 June 1916, DU; *Report of the Federal Trade Commission,* pt. 11, Ark., 13677.

44. "The Murray Company and Its History," *Cotton Seed Oil Magazine* 28 (Jan.

1917): 46; "Cotton Gins and Ginners Problems," *COP* 12 (Feb. 1929): 21; Aiken, "Evolution of Cotton Ginning," 208, 210; J. L. Benton, Monticello, Georgia, to T. F. Justiss, USFA, 17 Apr. 1918; F. C. Weinert, commissioner of Tex. Markets and Warehouse Dept., to E. A. Peden, federal food administrator for Tex., 8 May 1918; R. F. Abbay, Commerce, Miss., to G. H. Denny, USFA, 11 May 1918; W. L. Carmack, Opelika, Ala., to Geo. H. Denney, 6 June 1918, RG 4, NA.

45. R. G. Walton, manager, Clay County [Tex.] Cotton Oil Co. to B. F. Looney, attorney general, Austin, 9 July, 1913; C. A. Sweeton, assistant attorney general, Austin, to B. F. Looney, 21 Oct. 1913, AGC; *Report of the Federal Trade Commission,* pt. 7, Miss., 6239, 7410–12; pt. 8, Tex., 8132; pt. 9, Okla., 11154; pt. 13, summary, xi, 15752; *Laws of the State of Mississippi* . . . (Memphis, Tenn.: Press of E. H. Clarke & Bro., 1914), chap. 162; "Monthly Letter of Secretary Gibson," *COP* 4 (Oct. 1920): 27; Michael R. Green to Lynette B. Wrenn, 1 July 1991, regarding a search of the 36th, 37th, and 38th Legislatures by the reference archivist of the Texas State Library and Archives which revealed no laws related to cottonseed-oil mills and cotton gins.

46. *Report of the Federal Trade Commission,* preliminary report, 2; pt. 13, summary, x.

47. Lerona Rosamond Morris, *Oklahoma: Yesterday, Today, Tomorrow* (Guthrie, Okla.: Cooperative Publishing, 1930), vol. 1: 718, 752–54; *Report of the Federal Trade Commission,* pt. 8, Tex., 8146, 8152; "J. W. Simmons Empire Builder," *COP* 8 (Dec. 1924): 35.

48. *Report of the Federal Trade Commission,* pt. 12, Tenn., 14323, 14435, 14499, 14505, 14540, 14593, 15555.

49. *Report of the Federal Trade Commission,* pt. 7, Miss., 7365, 7410; pt. 12, Tenn., 15165.

50. O. M. Tabb, manager, Farmers Union Clearing House, Titus County, Tex., to Attorney General Dave Looney, 9 Sept. 1913; testimony of manager of Farmers & Ginners Oil Co., Sulphur Springs, Tex., 11 Oct. 1913; testimony of S. F. McCarley before C. A. Sweeton, assistant attorney general, 14 Oct. 1913, AGC; *Report of the Federal Trade Commission,* pt. 3, Ga., 1064; pt. 8, Tex., 8367; pt. 11, Ark., 13052–53; Delta and Pine Land Company Records, Box 22, "Financial Records: Inventories; Gin Operation," 1935, 1938, MSU; "Proceedings of the Interstate Cotton Seed Crushers' Association, 1918," *COP* 2 (June 1918): 77; form letter from E. M. Durham, Vicksburg, Miss., 2 May 1908, RG 48, vol. 32, MSA; D. B. Brown, Arkadelphia, Ark., to J. T. Fargarson, Memphis, 18 May, 1918; Haiwatha Manufacturing Co., Jackson, Miss., "Profit and Loss Account—Ginning Department, Season 1917–1918"; W. B. West, Columbia, S.C. Cotton Seed Crushers' Association, to Hugh Humphreys, head of Cotton Seed Division of USFA, 12 Feb. 1918, RG 4, NA.

51. Alfred Lief, *"It Floats": The Story of Procter & Gamble* (New York: Rinehart, 1958), 283; Manager, Buckeye Cotton Oil Co., Jackson, Miss., to Buckeye Cotton Oil Co., Cincinnati, 2 July 1907; J. M. Macdonald to Buckeye Cotton Oil Co., Jackson, Miss., 3 Aug. 1908, RG 48, vol. 35, MSA; *Report of the Federal Trade Commission,* pt. 3, Ga., 1121; pt. 4., Ala., 2910; pt. 8, Tex., 8366; pt. 11, Ark., 12873; "Wesson," 102.

52. *Report of the Federal Trade Commission,* pt. 3, Ga., 1130–31; pt. 7, Miss., 6439–42, 7195, 7257–58, 7289; pt. 11, Ark., 12906–7, 13669.

53. Testimony of ginner, Mangum, Okla., 16 Jan. 1918; testimony of two ginners, Lawton, Okla., 14 Jan. 1918, SPF/CCO; *Report of the Federal Trade Commission,* pt. 8, Tex., 8153, 8500–8501, 8645; pt. 12, Tenn., 14542, 14645, 14651; "Elimination of Mill Loan Gin Control," *COP* 17 (Oct. 1933): 8.

54. *Report of the Federal Trade Commission,* pt. 7, Miss., 6241, 6668; pt. 11, Ark., 12544, 12549, 12981–82, 13104; pt. 13, summary, 15762–63; "Cotton Gins and Ginners Problems," *COP* 13 (May 1929): 21.

55. *Report of the Federal Trade Commission,* pt. 4, Ala., 2505; pt. 7, Miss., 6444, 7229; pt. 8, Tex., 8152–56, 8503; pt. 9, Okla., 10970; pt. 13 summary, 15766; Woodman, *King Cotton and His Retainers,* 348–50.

56. *Report of the Federal Trade Commission,* pt. 3. Ga., 1456–59, 1580–81, 1733–34, 1960–62; pt. 5, N.C., 3751–52; pt. 12, Tenn., 14438–41, 14576–77, 14596, 14645.

57. Minutes of the Monticello Conference, 24 Sept. 1903, ZP; Dept. of Agriculture, Office of Markets and Rural Organization, Farmers' Bulletin No. 764, *Cotton Ginning Information for Farmers,* by Fred Taylor, D. C. Griffith, and C. E. Atkinson, 31 Oct. 1916, 4; *Report of the Federal Trade Commission,* pt. 3, Ga., 1443; pt. 4, Ala., 2388, 2414; pt. 5, N.C., 3488–89; pt. 9, Okla., 11007, 11094–96; pt. 10, La., 11762–63.

58. "Wesson," 68; Thomas D. Clark, *Pills, Petticoats, and Plows: The Southern Country Store* (Norman: Univ. of Oklahoma Press, 1964), 109; *Report of the Federal Trade Commission,* pt. 3, Ga., 952; pt. 4, Ala., 2418; pt. 5, N.C., 3992; pt. 12, Tenn., 14929.

59. G. P. Kilpatrick, secy. and treas., Burke County Oil and Fertilizer Co., Waynesboro, Ga., to USFA, 20 Nov. 1917, RG 4, NA; *Report of the Federal Trade Commission,* pt. 6, S.C., 4934; pt. 8, Tex., 9445, 9710; Moloney, "Marketing of Cottonseed," 3.

60. *OPD* 28 (4 Nov. 1885): 5; [K. C. Hall] to N. Smith-Vaniz, Brookhaven, Miss., 1 Oct. 1908, RG 48, vol. 32, MSA; *Report of the Federal Trade Commission,* pt. 3, Ga., 1981; pt. 4, Ala., 2486; pt. 5, N.C., 3470, 3721, 3796; pt. 12, Tenn., 14604; printed form sent to seed buyers by New Bern Cotton Oil and Fertilizer Co., 14 Sept. 1903, ZP.

61. Lillington Oil Mill Company Papers, Minutes of Directors' Meeting, 3 Oct. 1917, DU; *Report of the Federal Trade Commission,* pt. 5, N.C., 3820; pt. 7, Miss., 6681; pt. 11, Ark., 13510; testimony of independent oil miller, Mangum, Okla., 16 Jan. 1918, SPF/CCO.

62. Testimony of oil-mill manager, Mangum, Okla., 16 Jan. 1918, SPF/CCO; R. P. Thompson, Brenham [Tex.] Compress, Oil & Mfg. Co. to Food Administration, 26 Dec. 1917, RG 4, NA; *Report of the Federal Trade Commission,* pt. 8, Tex., 8416; pt. 10, La., 11762; "Proposed Cotton Ginners' Code of Fair Competition," 22 Aug. 1933, National Recovery Administration Records, RG 9, National Archives (hereafter cited as RG 9, NA); National Cottonseed Products Association, *Facts about a Great Exclusively Southern Industry—Cottonseed,* table 3, 18, RG 9, NA.

63. *Proceedings of the Texas Cotton Seed Crushers' Association,* 1901, 23 C; 1908, 65; 1911, 63; 1912, 40, NAL; *Minutes of the Annual Meeting of the Alabama Cotton Seed Crushers Association,* 1913, 17, 24, 28, UA; "Proceedings of the Interstate Cotton Seed Crushers' Association, 1917," *COP* 1 (June 1917): 36, 43; "Editorial," *COP* 1 (Dec. 1917): 25; "Proceedings of the Interstate Cotton Seed Crushers' Association, 1918," *COP* 2 (June 1918): 69; "Tri-State Superintendents' Meeting," *COP* 10 (Aug. 1926): 18; *Report of the Federal Trade Commission,* pt. 3, Ga., 1056–57; pt. 4, Ala., 2553, 3075.

64. *Report of the Federal Trade Commission,* pt. 12, Tenn., 14487–89; "Cotton Seed Trading Center Opened in Memphis," *Commercial and Financial Chronicle* 128 (26 Jan. 1929): 487–88; "The Memphis Hedge Market in Cottonseed and Cottonseed Meal," *COP* 13 (May 1929): 36; E. T. Allen, "Report of Committee on Future Trading," *COP* 15 (June 1931): 60; C. B. Stout, "Relation of Future Trading to Cottonseed," *COP* 15 (Aug. 1931): 25; "Editorial," *COP* 16 (Jan. 1933): 16.

65. *Report of the Federal Trade Commission,* pt. 13, summary, viii–ix; "Will Clayton's Cotton," *Fortune* 32 (Nov. 1945): 138–47, 231–38; vol. 32: (Dec. 1945): 159–63, 231–42.

4. Cottonseed Crushing

1. Cobb, *Industrialization and Southern Society,* 5–6; Wright, *Old South, New South,* 160–97; Weber, "Economic Development," 64.

2. Henry C. Dethloff, *A History of the American Rice Industry, 1685–1985* (College Station: Texas A&M Univ. Press, 1988), 32–33; Greville Bathe and Dorothy Bathe, *Oliver Evans: A Chronicle of Early American Engineering* (Philadelphia: Historical Society of Pennsylvania, 1925; New York: Arno Press, 1972), 11–12.

3. Hammond, "The Cotton Seed Industry," 25; *Cottonseed and Its Products,* 14; *Report of the Federal Trade Commission,* pt. 10, La., 12191; A. L. Durand, Chickasha [Okla.] Cotton Oil Co. to L. E. Kline, NRA assistant deputy administrator, 3 May 1934; L. E. Kline, "Partial History of the Proposed Code of Fair Competition for the Cottonseed Crushing Industry," 7 Sept. 1935, 2, RG 9, NA; *Texas Cottonseed Crushing Mills and Their Products, 1965–66 Season* (Cotton Research Committee of Texas, Univ. of Texas, Austin, 1967), 31–32; E. T. George, "Fifty-Seven Years with Mr. Cottonseed," *C&COP* 40 (8–10 May 1939): 5.

4. George S. Jamieson, *Vegetable Fats and Oils,* 2d ed. (New York: Reinhold, 1943), 194–95; *Cottonseed and Linseed Oil Machinery* (Dayton, Ohio: Stilwell–Bierce & Smith–Vaile, 1895), 5, DAT, CPL; A. J. O'Connor, Memphis Trades and Labor Council, to Hon. Wm. Green, president, American Federation of Labor, Washington, D.C., 28 Nov. 1933, RG 9, NA.

5. Dethloff, *American Rice Industry,* 34; Bathe and Bathe, *Oliver Evans,* 11, 14; Thornton, *Cottonseed Products,* 40; Louis C. Hunter, *A History of Industrial Power in the United States, 1780–1930,* vol. 2: *Steam Power* (Charlottesville: Univ. Press of Virginia, 1985), 34; Culbertson, "History of Cottonseed Crushing in Texas," 25.

6. *Cottonseed and Linseed Oil Machinery,* 5–6.

7. Hunter, *Steam Power,* xxi; G. Hoffman, "How and Why We Burn Cotton-Seed Hulls," *Power* 77 (Sept. 1933): 462–63.

8. There are statistics on motive power in the cottonseed crushing industry for 1914, 1919, 1925, 1927, and 1929 in Bureau of the Census, *Fifteenth Census of the United States: 1930, Manufactures: 1929,* vol. 2, *Reports by Industries,* 709–12, and in Bureau of the Census, *Sixteenth Census of the United States: 1940, Manufactures: 1939,* vol. 2, pt. 1, *Reports by Industries, Groups 1 to 10,* 760.

9. P. R. Lamar, "Discussion of Twelve-Hour Operation," *COP* 8 (July 1924): 27; H. M. French, "Motors and Control for Cotton Gins and Cottonseed-Oil Mills," *Melliand Textile Monthly* 4 (Sept. 1932): 357–59, (Oct. 1932): 424–25; "Diesel Engines in the Cotton Oil Industry," *Power* 76 (Oct. 1932): 211; Nathan Rosenberg, *Technology and American Economic Growth* (New York: Harper Torchbooks, 1972), 161–62.

10. John Leahy, "Cottonseed Processing Links Agriculture and Industry Profitably," *Southern Power & Industry* (Oct. 1939): 40; Taylor, *Early History of the Cotton Oil Industry,* 18; "Editorial," *COP* 3 (Aug. 1919): 26.

11. "Past Presidents Send Greetings," *COP* 1 (May 1917): 30; Henry J. Parrish, "Oil Milling in Memphis in 1881," *COP* 11 (May 1927): 53; J. B. Nealey, "Making Cottonseed Oil and Its Products," *Manufacturers' Record* 103 (Feb. 1934): 18; Clark, "Cottonseed Products Industry," 180.

12. "Wesson," 71; Ogden, *Cotton-Seed Oil,* 13–14.

13. Fee Patent, 11 Aug. 1857; Arthur Coleman, "Marvelous Story of Cottonseed Products," *COP* 13 (Jan. 1930): 33; Maurice R. Cooper, "History of Cotton and the United States Cottonseed Industry," in *Cottonseed and Cottonseed Products: Their Chemistry and Chemical Technology,* ed. Alton E. Bailey (New York: Interscience Publishers, 1948), 21; Cist, "Cotton-Seed Oil," 220–21.

14. Patent Office, F. A. Wells, Cotton Seed Hulling Machine, No. 96,177, 26 Oct. 1869; Moloney, "Cottonseed Oil—A Typical American Industry," 233; Thornton, *Cottonseed Products,* 15, 94, 102; "Cottonseed Crushing Before the Civil War," 37; *Cottonseed and Linseed Oil Machinery,* 20; M. E. Karsten, "Fifty Years of Oil Mill Operating," *COP* 16 (July 1932): 25; Lamborn, *Cottonseed Products,* 51; *Pioneering in Kiowa County* (Hobart, Okla.: Kiowa County Historical Society, 1982), vol 6: 246.

15. Lamborn, *Cottonseed Products,* 55; "Cottonseed Crushing Before the Civil War," 39; Culbertson, "History of Cottonseed Crushing in Texas," 25; Karsten, "Fifty Years of Oil Mill Operating," 25; Thornton, *Cottonseed Products,* 123.

16. Thornton, *Cottonseed Products,* 126–27; Lamborn, *Cottonseed Products,* 35, 63–67, 74; *Practical Points for Oil Mill Managers and Superintendents* (Dayton, Ohio: Buckeye Iron & Brass Works, n.d., but stamped 3 Apr. 1920), 17; Tompkins, *Cotton and Cotton Oil,* 284; *Cottonseed and Linseed Oil Machinery,* 7; O. H. Alderks, "Cooking of Meats and Recovery of the Oil," in Bailey, *Cottonseed and Cottonseed Products,* 617.

17. *Cottonseed and Linseed Oil Machinery*, 7.

18. E. L. Carpenter and Leo Holdredge, "The Cottonseed-Oil Industry, Its History, Economics, Processes, and Problems," *Mechanical Engineering* 53 (May 1931): 357; Leahy, "Cottonseed Processing Links Agriculture and Industry," 42; Alderks, "Cooking of Meats and Recovery of Oil," 615–25.

19. Leahy, "Cottonseed Processing Links Agriculture and Industry," 42; W. L. Woolrich, "Cottonseed Processing Research," *Mechanical Engineering* 61 (Feb. 1939): 133; C. A. Perkins and R. Brooks Taylor, "Cotton Seed Oil Pressing Costs Cut," *Food Industries* 9 (Aug. 1937): 435–37, 472; *Business Week*, 21 Jan. 1939, 31–32.

20. "Cottonseed Crushing Before the Civil War," 39; Culbertson, "History of Cottonseed Crushing in Texas," 25; *New York Times*, 26 Mar. 1877, p. 2; Moore, "Oldest Cotton Oil Mill," 13; description of cottonseed milling from the *Handbook of Augusta [Georgia]*, 1878, quoted in the Historic American Engineering Record, GA-8, 1, Heritage, Conservation and Recreation Service, Library of Congress.

21. Parrish, "Oil Milling in Memphis in 1881," 53; Karsten, "Fifty Years of Oil Mill Operating," 25; Charles V. Rother, "Looking Back Fifty Years," *COP* 15 (June 1931): 92; Ogden, *Cotton-Seed Oil*, 8.

22. Brace, *History of Seed Crushing in Great Britain*, 50–51; Culbertson, "History of Cottonseed Crushing in Texas," 26; Thornton, *Cottonseed Products*, 137.

23. Lamborn, *Cottonseed Products*, 88, 91–92; Tompkins, *Cotton and Cotton Oil*, 335; Grace Lockhart, "Tons of Human Hair," *Scientific American*, 144 (June 1931): 386–87; Erwin W. Thompson, "Press Cloth from Human Hair," *Oil Miller* 2 (Aug. 1913): 27.

24. Culbertson, "History of Cottonseed Crushing in Texas," 25; Brace, *History of Seed Crushing in Great Britain*, 42–49.

25. Tompkins, *Cotton and Cotton Oil*, 330; Parrish, "Oil Milling in Memphis in 1881," 53; Karsten, "Fifty Years of Oil Mill Operating," 25; Rother, "Looking Back Fifty Years," 92; Brace, *History of Seed Crushing in Great Britain*, 74–76; Jamieson, *Vegetable Fats and Oils*, 203; A. J. O'Connor, Memphis, to Hon. Wm. Green, Washington, D.C., 28 Nov. 1933, RG 9, NA.

26. *Cottonseed and Linseed Oil Machinery*, 36; Leahy, "Cottonseed Processing Links Agriculture and Industry," 43; Dept. of Agriculture, "Handling and Uses of Cotton," 366; J. C. Gilbert, "Expanding Uses for Cotton Seed and Linters," *Commerce and Finance* 17 (8 Feb. 1928): 356–57; Karsten, "Fifty Years of Oil Mill Operating," 25; Rother, "Looking Back Fifty Years," 92.

27. Jamieson, *Vegetable Fats and Oils*, 203–4; Lamborn, *Cottonseed Products*, 89; *Proceedings of the Interstate Cotton Seed Crushers' Association*, 1911, 60; David Wesson, "History and Development of the Cottonseed Oil Industry," *Chemical and Metallurgical Engineering* 21 (26 Nov.–3 Dec. 1919): 662; W. D. Harris, "Solvent Extraction of Cottonseed Oil," *Bulletin of the Agricultural and Mechanical College of Texas* 12 (15 Sept. 1941): 7; "Inefficient Cotton Oil Mill Methods," *COP* 3 (Mar. 1920): 31; "Proceedings of the Cotton Seed Crushers' Association, 1886," *OPD* 29 (12 May 1886):

10; *Proceedings of the Texas Cotton Seed Crushers' Association,* 1908, 44, NAL.

28. Thornton, *Cottonseed Products,* 122–23, 138, 144; Leahy, "Cottonseed Processing Links Agriculture and Industry," 43; Kline, "Partial History of the Proposed Code of Fair Competition," 3; "Official Report of Proceedings, Hearing on Proposed Code of Fair Competition for the Cotton-Seed Crushing Industry, Memphis," 15 Oct. 1934, RG 9, NA.

29. Karsten, "Fifty Years of Oil Mill Operating," 25; Tompkins, *Cotton and Cotton Oil,* 335–36; Lamborn, *Cottonseed Products,* 106; Jamieson, *Vegetable Fats and Oils,* 205.

30. Brace, *History of Seed Crushing in Great Britain,* 79, 164; "Proceedings of the Interstate Cotton Seed Crushers' Association, 1923," *COP* 16 (May 1923): 58; Ogden, *Cotton-Seed Oil,* 10–11; Markley, "The Cotton Processing Industry," A-4, A-5; W. E. Worth, Wilmington, N.C., to *Oil Mill Gazetteer,* Brownsville, Tex., 11 Nov. 1906; W. E. Worth to G. A. Darby, New York City, 14 Nov. 1906, Worth Family Papers, DU; *Proceedings of the Cotton Seed Crushers' Association,* 1883, 82; David Wesson, "Solvent Extractions—The New and Better Way," *Oil & Fat Industry* 7 (1930): 258; Leahy, "Cottonseed Processing Links Agriculture and Industry," 44.

31. Brace, *History of Seed Crushing in Great Britain,* 164; Alderks, "Cooking of Meats," 641–45.

32. "Anderson Oil Expeller," *Oil Miller* 1 (Sept. 1912): 19–20; "Anderson Expeller Cotton Seed Oil Mills—Cold Pressed System," *Oil Miller* 2 (Jan. 1913): 14–15; *Proceedings of the Interstate Cotton Seed Crushers' Association,* 1913, 65; *Pioneering in Kiowa County* 6:247; Thornton, *Cottonseed Products,* 233; Brace, *History of Seed Crushing in Great Britain,* 95–98; interview with Brian Lundgren of the Elgin [Tex.] Oil Mill, 16 Sept. 1992.

33. J. Lewkowitsch, *Chemical Technology and Analysis of Oils, Fats, and Waxes,* 3 vols. (London: Macmillan, 1909), vol. 2: 15; Jamieson, *Vegetable Fats and Oils,* 201–2; Harris, "Solvent Extraction of Cottonseed Oil," 6, 7, 9; R. D. Ryan, "Economical Value of the Expeller," *Cotton Gin and Oil Mill Press* 48 (12 July 1947): A-3; Fred Bailey, "USDA Announces Development of New Solvent Extraction Method," *C&COP* 48 (8 Mar. 1947): A-3; Leahy, "Cottonseed Processing Links Agriculture and Industry," 44.

34. John Alfred Heitmann, *The Modernization of the Louisiana Sugar Industry* (Baton Rouge: Louisiana State Univ. Press, 1987), 45; Thornton, *Cottonseed Products,* 94; Hobbs, "Cotton Seed Oil Industry," n.p.; Nathan Rosenberg, "Technological Change in the Machine Tool Industry, 1840–1910," *Journal of Economic History* 23 (Dec. 1963): 414–43.

35. *OPD* 31 (9 Feb. 1887): 10; Taylor, *Early History of the Cotton Oil Industry,* 17; M. C. McMillan, "The Manufacture of Cotton Gins, a Southern Industry, 1793–1860" (Prattville, Ala.: distributed by Continental Eagle Corporation, n.d.).

36. Eastman, *History of the Linseed Oil Industry,* 18, 25, 26, 31, 108; *Half-Century's Progress of the City of Brooklyn: The City's Leading Manufacturers and Merchants* (1886), 237, Brooklyn Public Library; Henry Stiles, *His-*

tory of Kings County and the City of Brooklyn (1884), 684–87, Brooklyn Public Library; *Proceedings of the Cotton Seed Crushers' Association,* 1883, 82–83; "Cotton Seed Crushers' Convention," *OPD* 27 (29 Apr. 1885): 9; "Small Cotton-Seed Oil Mills," A-4, A-5; Nannie Mae Tilley, *The Bright Tobacco Industry, 1860–1929* (Chapel Hill: Univ. of North Carolina Press, 1948), 496; Buckeye Iron & Brass Works, *Practical Points for Oil Mill Managers and Superintendents.*

37. Culbertson, "History of Cottonseed Crushing in Texas," 26; Taylor, *Early History of the Cotton Oil Industry,* 19; *The Plan and Scope of the Alabama Alliance Oil Company, to Be Located at Demopolis, Alabama,* (Mobile: Mobile Stationery Co. Power Print, 1889), UA.

38. *Fort Worth (Tex.) Gazette,* 11 Mar. 1892, printed in Federal Writers Project, *Research Data: Fort Worth and Tarrant County* (Fort Worth, Tex.: Fort Worth Public Library, 1941), vol. 5: 1854; "Cottonseed Oil," *Manufacturers' Record* 23 (31 Mar. 1893): 86; "Cottonseed Oil," *Manufacturers' Record* 24 (15 Sept. 1893): 113; Dallas City Directories, 1886–1897; "Murray Company and Its History," *Cotton Seed Oil Magazine* 28 (Jan. 1917): 46.

39. Brace, *History of Seed Crushing in Great Britain,* 160–66; Culbertson, "History of Cottonseed Crushing in Texas," 26.

40. *Nashville* (Tenn.) *American,* 17 July 1897, p. 5; "French Oil Mill Machinery Company," *Cotton Seed Oil Magazine* 29 (May 1917): 41; "Oil Mill Machinery Men Organize," *COP* 2 (Nov. 1918): 30; "Sudden Death of A. W. French," *COP* 9 (May 1925): 18; "Pioneers in Oil Mill Engineering," *COP* 15 (May 1931): 20.

41. D. A. Tompkins, "Cotton-Seed Oil," *Manufacturers' Record* 11 (12 Mar. 1887): 160.

42. Tompkins, *Cotton and Cotton Oil,* 213; Tompkins, "Cotton-Seed Oil," 160; Alfred Dupont Chandler Jr., *The Visible Hand* (Cambridge: Belknap Press, Harvard Univ. Press, 1977), 259–62; George Tayloe Winston, *A Builder of the New South, Being The Story of the Life Work of Daniel Augustus Tompkins* (1920; Freeport, N.Y.: Books for Libraries Press, 1972), 28–80, 95–96; D. A. Tompkins Company, *The Scope and Character of its Work in Developing the Industrial Resources of the South* (Charlotte Observer Printing and Publishing House, 1895), 5, DAT, CPL; Clay, "Daniel Augustus Tompkins," 126, 141, 144.

43. Karsten, "Fifty Years of Oil Mill Operating," 25; "Average Report—Mill Work—Sept. 15th to Nov. 1st, 1917," Barrow-Agee Laboratories, Memphis, Tennessee; "To Our Oil Mill Friends from Barrow-Agee Laboratories," 16 Oct. 1917, RG 4, NA; Thomas C. Law, "Service of Cotton Products Chemists," *COP* 1 (May 1917): 33–34; G. S. Fraps, "Scientific Investigation in the Oil Industry," *COP* 3 (Apr. 1920): 45; A. A. French, "The Problems of the Oil Mill Superintendent," *COP* 7 (May 1923): 53; "Chemical Analysis Fundamental in Oil Milling," *COP* 12 (Oct. 1924): 28; *Report of the Federal Trade Commission,* pt. 11, Ark., 13262–63, and pt. 12, Tenn., 14472–73.

44. "The Millions in the Cotton Seed Oil Business," *OPD* 20 (27 July 1881): 132; "Profits of Cotton Seed Oil Manufacturing," *OPD* 20 (21 Dec. 1881):

1116; "The Southern Company," *OPD* 34 (11 July 1888): 5; "New Southern Cotton Seed Oil Mills," *OPD* 56 (18 Dec. 1899): 12; Tompkins, "Cotton-Seed Oil," 160; William E. Laird and James R. Rinehart, "Deflation, Agriculture, and Southern Development," *Agricultural History* 42 (Apr. 1968): 116. During the period used by Laird, 1879–97, average cotton prices declined about one-third, from 9.83 cents per pound to 6.68 cents. Cotton prices are from Robert Sigafoos, *Cotton Row to Beale Street* (Memphis: Memphis State Univ. Press, 1979), 347–48.

45. "Cotton Seed Oil Business in Texas," *OPD* 19 (4 May 1881): 591; Kilgore, "Cottonseed Oil Industry," 26 H; Hammond, "The Cotton Seed Industry," 50; George H. Denny to All Crushers of Cottonseed, Circular No. 47, USFA, Washington, D.C., 22 Aug. 1918, RG 4, NA; *Facts About a Great Exclusively Southern Industry—Cottonseed,* 25.

46. Holland Thompson, *The New South in the New Economic Order* (New Haven: Yale Univ. Press, 1919), 106; Tilley, *Bright Tobacco Industry,* 318, 515; Wright, *Old South, New South* 177–79; Dept. of Labor, Bureau of Labor Statistics, "Wages and Hours of Labor in Cottonseed Oil Mills," *Monthly Labor Review* 27 (July 1928): 109–20.

47. Dept. of Labor, "Wages and Hours of Labor in Cottonseed Oil Mills," 109; "Wesson," 71; Wright, *Old South, New South,* 179–80.

48. Ledgers of the Tar River Oil Company, Tarboro, N.C., for 1895–1917 show that wages accounted for only 4.3 to 6.7 percent of annual operating costs compared to 62 to 81 percent for seed purchases, Henry Clark Bridgers Jr. Papers, ECU. *Thirteenth Census of the United States: 1910, Manufactures: 1909,* shows that in state after state labor's share of oil-mill operating expenses in 1909 ranged from 2.4 to 5.8 percent. The Wesson Oil Company's cost of labor in 1939 was less than 6 percent of its operating costs. "Wesson," 104; Dept. of Labor, Wage and Hour and Public Contracts Divisions, "Economic Factors Bearing on the Establishment of Minimum Wages in the Cottonseed and Peanut Crushing Industry" (Washington, D.C., 1943), 29, NAL.

49. "Millions in the Cotton Seed Oil Business," *OPD* 20 (27 July 1881): 132; "Profits of Cotton Seed Oil Manufacturing," *OPD* 20 (21 Dec. 1881): 1116; "Cottonseed Oil Manufacture," *OPD* 21 (29 Mar. 1882): 605; Rother, "Looking Back Fifty Years," 92; Manuscript Census of Manufactures, Shelby County, Tennessee, 1880, 37, DU; Statement of J. L. Benton, Monticello, Ga., 29 Nov. 1933, RG 9, NA; David L. Carlton, *Mill and Town in South Carolina* (Baton Rouge: Louisiana State Univ. Press, 1982), 85; Woodward, *Origins of the New South,* 207.

50. Hammond, "The Cotton Seed Industry," 25; Woodward, *Origins of the New South,* 224–26; Hobbs, "Cotton Seed Oil Industry," n.p.; Dept. of Labor, "Wages and Hours of Labor in Cottonseed Oil Mills," 109; A. J. O'Connor, Memphis, to Hon. Wm. Green, Washington, D.C., 28 Nov. 1933; A. L. Durand, Chickasha [Okla.] Cottonseed Oil Co. to C. H. Cunningham, NRA deputy assistant administrator, 4 Dec. 1933, RG 9, NA; J. R. Arnold, NRA Division of Economic Research and Planning, "The Cottonseed Crushing Industry," 12 Jan. 1934, RG 9, NA; "Wesson," 104.

51. M. W. Newman, Hollis, Okla., to Hugh S. Johnson, Washington, D.C., 9 July 1933; W. W. Ramsey, Colorado, Tex., to Hugh S. Johnson, 22 July 1933; R. B. Maples, Rock Hill, S.C., to President Franklin D. Roosevelt, 3 Aug. 1933; D. S. Egan, Southern Cotton Oil Co., Little Rock, Ark., to Hugh S. Johnson, 12 Aug. 1933; unsigned from Savannah, Ga., to Hugh Johnson, 10 Sept. 1933; W. C. Beam, Sweetwater, Tex., to Hon. Hugh Johnson, 3 Oct. 1933; W. C. Beam to Charles H. Cunningham, asst. deputy administrator, NRA, 23 Nov. 1933; Carl Halstead, Stroud, Okla., to C. C. Farrington, Processing and Marketing Section, AAA, undated but received 13 Dec. 1933; unsigned from Ft. Smith, Ark., to Gen. Hugh S. Johnson, 8 Jan. 1934; Hamblin [Tex.] Working Men's Association to Hugh S. Johnson, 17 Dec. 1933; B. B. Ashlock, Hobart, Okla., to Honorable Franklin Roosevelt, 18 Jan. 1934; unsigned from employee of Birmingham [Ala.] Cotton Oil Co. to Hugh Johnson, [?] Feb. 1934; P. J. Burnett, Oklahoma City, to Hugh Johnson, 21 Feb. 1934; Frank Ford, Talladega, Ala., to Hugh Johnson, 19 Feb. 1934; Oral Gordon, Guthrie, Okla., to Hugh Johnson, 10 Mar. 1934; undated petition from Altus [Okla.] Cotton Oil Co. employees to Honorable Franklin D. Roosevelt; E. A. Blair, Elberton, Ga., to Francis Perkins, 24 Sept. 1934; J. R. Kay, Honea Path, S.C., to Mr. Roosevelt, 4 Oct. 1934; unsigned from Montgomery, Ala., 19 Nov. 1934, RG 9, NA.
52. Brace, *History of Seed Crushing in Great Britain,* 69; John R. Arnold, Div. of Research and Planning, NRA to C. H. Cunningham, asst. deputy administrator, NRA, 5 Dec. 1933; Kline, "Partial History of the Proposed Code of Fair Competition," 3; Ray K. Powell et al. to Hon. Hugh S. Johnson, 15 Sept. 1933; W. E. Hudmon, Sylvania, Ga., to M. H. Pettit, deputy administrator, NRA, Washington, D.C., 20 Sept. 1933; A. L. Durand, Chickasha [Okla.] Cotton Oil Co. to C. H. Cunningham, Washington, D.C., 4 Dec. 1933, RG 9, NA.
53. Bureau of the Census, *Manufactures: 1909,* vol. 9: 218; T. C. Taliaferro, "Fire Records of Cottonseed Oil Mills," *COP* 9 (Sept. 1925): 26; J. P. Dickinson, "Why Oil Mills Cannot Get Good Young White Men in the Mills to Learn the Business," *COP* 11 (May 1927): 55.
54. Hobbs, "Cotton Seed Oil Industry," n.p.; "Progress of the Cottonseed Oil Industry," *OPD* 28 (23 Sept. 1885): 32; *Cotton Seed Oil Magazine* 25 (Oct. 1915): 11, NAL; "1833–1983: 150 Years in Oktibbeha County," *Starkville (Miss.) Daily News.*
55. J. J. Culbertson, "The Alarming Increase in Cost of Crushing Seed," *COP* 1 (July 1917): 23; "Monthly Letter of President Wallace," *COP* 1 (Oct. 1917): 14; "Monthly Letter of President Wallace," *COP* 1 (Apr. 1918): 16; "Proceedings of the Interstate Cotton Seed Crushers' Association, 1918," *COP* 2 (June 1918): 46; "President Montgomery's Monthly Letter," *COP* 2 (Aug. 1918): 18; "President Montgomery's Monthly Letter," *COP* 2 (Nov. 1918): 18; "Conference on Oil Mill Labor Shortage," *COP* 2 (Nov. 1918): 23. I have seen only one reference to labor in pre–World War I oil-mill publications, a statement in the *Proceedings of the Interstate Cotton Seed Crushers' Association* for 1906 that "labor conditions have added to the increased cost of production."

56. *Memphis Avalanche*, 18 Aug. 1882, 18 Oct. 1882; Peter Gottlieb, *Making Their Own Way* (Urbana: Univ. of Illinois Press, 1987), 12, 23, 26; D. M. Black, textile organizer, Rome, Ga., to William Green, president, American Federation of Labor, Washington, D.C., 7 Sept. 1933; J. H. Gore, Helena, Ark., to Frank Morrison, Washington, D.C., 3 Feb. 1933; W. C. Beam, president, Federal Union No. 19136, Sweetwater, Tex., to Frank Morrison, secy., American Federation of Labor, 15 Jan. 1934; R. G. Smith, Tyronza, Ark., to Hon. William Green, 10 Jan. 1934, RG 9, NA; Gary M. Fink, ed., *Labor Unions* (Westport, Conn.: Greenwood Press, 1977), 106–9; *New Orleans States*, 29 Aug. 1949, 2; F. Ray Marshall, *Labor in the South* (Cambridge: Harvard Univ. Press, 1967), 240; Dept. of Labor, Bureau of Labor Statistics, Bulletin No. 836, *Labor Unionism in American Agriculture*, by Stuart M. Jamieson (Washington, D.C., 1945), 323.

57. G. W. Covington, "Greater Efficiency in Mill Work," *COP* 5 (June 1921): 89; O. T. Joslin & Co. (engineering firm of New York and Cincinnati with "a summer School of Technology") to Farmers' Co-operative Mfg. Co., Tarboro, N.C., 12 June 1895, ZP; W. B. West, "B. F. Taylor, Secretary South Carolina Cotton Seed Crushers' Association," *Oil Miller* 3 (Feb. 1914): 25; *Report of the Federal Trade Commission*, pt. 7, Miss., 6682. Obituaries of oil-mill managers and officials, which appeared regularly in trade publications, told of men being promoted from one job to another within the industry but never that they had taken special oil-mill training courses.

58. *Proceedings of the Interstate Cotton Seed Crushers' Association*, 1911, 57–58; Covington, "Greater Efficiency in Mill Work," *COP* 5 (June 1921): 89; "Address of A. T. Madra," *COP* 7 (May 1923): 48; E. E. Randolph, North Carolina State College, "Engineering College Course in Oil Industry," *COP* 8 (Sept. 1924): 30–31; Harris, "Solvent Extraction of Cottonseed Oil," 6.

59. Dickinson, "Why Oil Mills Cannot Get Good Young White Men," 55.

5. Cottonseed-Oil Refining and Manufacturing

1. Lamborn, *Cottonseed Products*, 127; Hillyard, *New South*, 35.

2. "Who Does the Refining of Oil?," *Cotton Seed Oil Magazine* 27 (June 1916): 12, NAL; Weber, "Economic Development," 77; *Report of the Federal Trade Commission*, pt. 8, Tex., 8487–88; Burkett and Poe, *Cotton*, 285.

3. Heitmann, *Modernization of the Louisiana Sugar Industry;* "Cottonseed Crushing Before the Civil War," 39; Lamborn, *Cottonseed Products*, 21; Andes, *Vegetable Fats and Oils*, 285; Ogden, *Cotton-Seed Oil*, 9; Wesson, "History and Development of the Cottonseed Oil Industry," 661.

4. Cooper, "History of Cotton," 34–35; T. C. to Mr. Editor, *Niles' Register* 37 (3 Oct. 1829): 96; Howard C. Black, "Edible Cottonseed Oil Products," in Bailey, *Cottonseed and Cottonseed Products*, 732; G. M. Weber and C. L. Alsberg, *The American Vegetable-Shortening Industry* (Palo Alto, Calif.: Food Research Institute, Stanford Univ., 1934), 232.

5. Patent Office, *Report of 1844*, 431–33; Bishop, *History of American Manufactures* 2:443; Weber and Alsberg, *American Vegetable-Shortening Industry*, 251.

6. Lamborn, *Cottonseed Products,* 36, 127–29, 135–38; Jamieson, *Vegetable Fats and Oils,* 206–7; Edward M. James, "Processing of Cottonseed Oil," in Bailey, *Cottonseed and Cottonseed Products,* 691–731.

7. Wesson, "Pictorial Description," 470; *Proceedings of the Cotton Seed Crushers' Association,* 1882, 95–97; Weber, "Economic Development," 78; *Memphis Daily Appeal,* 5 Mar. 1886; *Proceedings of the Interstate Cotton Seed Crushers' Association,* 1914, 86.

8. David Wesson, "Contributions of the Chemist to the Cotton-Seed Oil Industry," *Journal of Industrial and Engineering Chemistry* 7 (Apr. 1915): 276–77; Wesson, "History and Development of the Cottonseed Oil Industry," 661–62; Chandler, *Visible Hand,* 243; James, "Processing of Cottonseed Oil," 693.

9. George, "Fifty-Seven Years with Mr. Cottonseed," 5; Wesson, "History and Development of the Cottonseed Oil Industry," 661–62.

10. Lamborn, *Cottonseed Products,* 127–33; Tompkins, *Cotton and Cotton Oil,* 346–56; Wesson, "Pictorial Description," 468.

11. "Cotton Seed—Its Uses and Manufacture," *OPD* 19 (1 June 1881): 780; E. L. Johnson, New York, to E. V. Zoeller, Tarboro, N.C., 1 Sept. 1892, J. T. E. Thornhill, Mutual Refining Co., Charleston, to E. V. Zoeller, 14 Sept. 1892, ZP; Wesson, "History and Development of the Cottonseed Oil Industry," 662.

12. "Cotton Seed—Its Uses and Manufacture," *OPD* 19 (1 June 1881): 780.

13. Sypher, "Cotton Seed, Cotton Seed Oil," 184–85; Wesson, "History and Development of the Cottonseed Oil Industry," 662; Weber, "Economic Development," 23.

14. Richard L. Bushman and Claudia L. Bushman, "The Early History of Cleanliness in America," *Journal of American History* 74 (Mar. 1988): 1213–38; Oscar Schisgall, *Eyes on Tomorrow: The Evolution of Procter & Gamble* (Chicago: J. G. Ferguson Publishing, 1981), 24–25; "The American Cotton Oil Company, Annual Report for the Fiscal Year Ending August 31, 1891," *Commercial and Financial Chronicle* 53 (7 Nov. 1891): 53; Wilson, *History of Unilever* 1:31.

15. Weber and Alsberg, *American Vegetable-Shortening Industry,* 1–2, 5–6, 8, 59, 194–95.

16. Parrish, "Oil Milling in Memphis in 1881," 53; Davis, "Corn and Cotton-Seed," 731–32; Weber and Alsberg, *American Vegetable-Shortening Industry,* 37–38.

17. James Harvey Young, *Pure Food* (Princeton: Princeton Univ. Press, 1989); Weber and Alsberg, *American Vegetable-Shortening Industry,* 29; 40–57, 73.

18. *Proceedings of the Cotton Seed Crushers' Association,* 1882, 92–96; Culbertson, "History of Cottonseed Crushing in Texas," 27.

19. Brannt, *Practical Treatise* 2:227–29; J. H. Van Stuyvenberg, ed, *Margarine* (Liverpool: Liverpool Univ. Press, 1969), 5–7; Wilson, *History of Unilever* 2:8, 30–31.

20. Weber and Alsberg, *American Vegetable-Shortening Industry,* 253–54; Black, "Edible Cottonseed Oil Products," 733.

21. Rudolf Clemen, *By-Products in the Packing Industry* (Chicago: Univ. of Chicago Press, 1927), 86–88; Weber and Alsberg, *American Vegetable-Shortening Industry,* 9–12; Gene Holcomb, "Chemistry's Contribution to the Cottonseed Industry," *Chemical & Engineering News* 20 (10 Apr. 1942): 440–42.

22. Brace, *History of Seed Crushing in Great Britain,* 161; Weber and Alsberg, *American Vegetable-Shortening Industry,* 256; Cooper, "History of Cotton," 35.

23. Thornton, *Cottonseed Products,* 173; W. B. Allbright, "How Cottonseed Oil Became a Food Product," *COP* 8 (June 1924): 52; Weber and Alsberg, *American Vegetable-Shortening Industry,* 20; Wilson, *History of Unilever* 2:29, 57; David Wesson, "Historical Aspects of Vegetable Oil Refining," *COP* 13 (Jan. 1930): 22.

24. Clemen, *By-Products in the Packing Industry,* 77; Wesson, "Pictorial Description," 468; James, "Processing of Cottonseed Oil," 709–10.

25. Weber and Alsberg, *American Vegetable-Shortening Industry,* 249–51.

26. Dept. of Agriculture, "Some American Vegetable Food Oils," 167–70; Wesson, "History and Development of the Cottonseed Oil Industry," 662; Weber and Alsberg, *American Vegetable-Shortening Industry,* 258–59; Clemen, *By-Products of the Packing Industry,* 164; John P. Harris and Alexander B. McKechnie, "Modern Deodorizing Methods," *COP* 11 (Dec. 1927): 27.

27. Weber and Alsberg, *American Vegetable-Shortening Industry,* 231; Clemen, *By-Products in the Packing Industry,* 77–79; Thornton, *Cottonseed Products,* 168; Wilson, *History of Unilever* 1:127, 2:101.

28. J. H. Shroder, "Hydrogenation Case Adjudged," *COP* 4 (Jan. 1921): 34, 53; Weber and Alsberg, *American Vegetable-Shortening Industry,* 93; Black, "Edible Cottonseed Oil Products," 733–38, Wilson, *History of Unilever* 2:357.

29. Clemen, *By-Products of the Packing Industry,* 129–30, 150; P. M. Jarvis, "Industry Makes Markets for Cottonseed," *Proceedings of the Seventh Cotton Research Congress* (n.p.: Statewide Cotton Committee of Texas, 1946), 79; Black, "Edible Cottonseed Oil Products," 744–46; Weber and Alsberg, *American Vegetable-Shortening Industry,* 206.

30. "David Wesson," *National Cyclopedia of American Biography,* vol. 27, 79–80; "David Wesson," *Encyclopedia of American Biography,* vol. 4, 101–2; David Wesson, "The Dixie Olive, Address Before the Ottawa Section of the American Institute of Chemical Engineers," *COP* 9 (Oct. 1925): 21.

31. Wesson, "Contributions of the Chemist," 276–77; Holcomb, "Chemistry's Contribution to the Cottonseed Industry," 440–42.

32. Heitmann, *Modernization of the Louisiana Sugar Industry,* 266–67; A. Hunter Dupree, *Science in the Federal Government* (Cambridge: Belknap Press, Harvard Univ. Press, 1957), 337; Rosenberg, *Technology and American Economic Growth,* 117–18.

33. K. S. Markley and D. F. J. Lynch, "The Technology of the Cottonseed Crushing Industry," in *Proceedings of the First Cotton Research Congress* (n.p.: Statewide Cotton Committee of Texas, 1940), 217–20; *Commodity*

Year Book 1941 (New York: Commodity Research Bureau, 1941), 210; John Moloney, "Trends in the Industrial Use of Cottonseed Products," in *Proceedings of the Second Cotton Research Congress* (n.p.: Statewide Cotton Committee of Texas, 1941), 77–78; James, "Processing of Cottonseed Oil," 702; Dept. of Agriculture, *Study of Practices Affecting the Use of Major Vegetable Oils,* 28–29, 37.

6. Organization of the Cottonseed Industry

Proceedings of the conventions of the Cotton Seed Crushers' Association for 1879–81 are preserved by the Cincinnati Historical Society and those for 1882 and 1883 by the NAL. The *Oil, Paint and Drug Reporter* gave detailed coverage of the 1885 convention and a full transcription of convention proceedings in 1886. *OPD* 25 (7 May 1884): 10, 27 (15 Apr. 1885): 5, 27 (29 Apr. 1885): 8, 29 (12 May 1886): 9–14, 31 (25 May 1887): 27.

1. Glenn Porter, *The Rise of Big Business* (New York: Thomas Y. Crowell, 1973), 55–56, 61–62, 64–65.
2. Cox, *Cottonseed Crushing Industry of Texas,* 54.
3. *Proceedings of the Cotton Seed Crushers' Association,* 1879, 33, 1882, 87–88.
4. *Proceedings of the Cotton Seed Crushers' Association,* 1879, 35, 1880, 21, 1881, 154, 1882, 85, 1883, 1–2, 82–83.
5. Louis Galambos, *Competition & Cooperation* (Baltimore: Johns Hopkins Press, 1966), 3–9.
6. "Cotton Seed Crushers' Association Formed," *OPD* 52 (26 July 1897): 26; James E. Fickle, *The New South and the "New Competition"* (Urbana: Univ. of Illinois Press, 1980), 16; *Proceedings of the Cotton Seed Crushers' Association,* 1883, 44.
7. *Proceedings of the Cotton Seed Crushers' Association,* 1881, 2, 1882, 88, 1883, 4; "Cotton Seed Oil Mills," 178–79; Weber, "Economic Development," 55; *Art Supplement to the Greater Memphis Edition of the Evening Scimitar,* Apr. 1899, 7–8; Memphis Merchants' Exchange, *Report,* 1884, 17.
8. *Proceedings of the Cotton Seed Crushers' Association,* 1881, 8; *State of Louisiana vs. American Cotton Oil Trust,* Civil District Court, Argument of Thomas J. Semmes, 12 Mar. 1889, 61, Tulane University Library, New Orleans; *New York Times,* 15 Feb. 1890, p. 1; George, "Fifty-Seven Years with Mr. Cottonseed," 6.
9. *The War of the Rebellion: A Compilation of the Official Records of the Union and Confederate Armies,* prepared by Col. Robert N. Scott (Washington, D.C., 1889), series I, vol. 26, pt. 1, 909; vol. 30, 170; vol. 31, pt. 3, 133; vol. 32, pt. 2, 167; vol. 47, pt. 2, 219, 222, 259, 262–63, 280–82; *Memphis City Directory,* 1866; J. B. Smith, Dayton, Ohio, to E. V. Zoeller, Tarboro, N.C., 11 Nov. 1891, ZP.
10. *New York Times,* 15 Feb. 1890, p. 5; Allbright, "How Cottonseed Oil Became a Food Product," 52; "Death of Major Robert Gibson," *COP* 11 (July 1927): 17; *Proceedings of the Cotton Seed Crushers' Association,* 1881, 2;

Proceedings of the Interstate Cotton Seed Crushers' Association, 1907, 60; George, "Fifty-Seven Years with Mr. Cottonseed," 6.

11. Chandler, *Visible Hand,* 285–87; Patrick G. Porter, "Origins of the American Tobacco Company," *Business History Review* 43 (Spring, 1969): 59–76.

12. Porter, *The Rise of Big Business,* 56–57, 62.

13. Naomi R. Lamoreaux, *The Great Merger Movement in American Business, 1895–1904,* (Cambridge: Cambridge Univ. Press, 1985), 11, 45–46, 98.

14. Chandler, *Visible Hand,* 317–19; Lamoreaux, *The Great Merger Movement,* 115; "A Pool in Cottonseed Oil," *New York Times,* 2 Mar. 1886, p. 3, 25 Feb. 1888, p. 8, 7 July 1891, p. 8.

15. *Fort Worth Gazette,* 11 Mar. 1892, *Research Data: Fort Worth and Tarrant County* 5: 2829.

16. *Memphis Daily Appeal* 2, 5 Mar. 1886; Memphis Merchants' Exchange, *Report,* 1886, 57.

17. Weber, "Economic Development," 68–69; "Cotton Seed Crushers' Convention," *OPD* 31 (25 May 1887): 27.

18. "State of Louisiana vs. American Cotton Oil Trust, Arguments of Thomas J. Semmes," 63; Memphis Merchants' Exchange, *Report,* 1886, 58–59; *Art Supplement to the Greater Memphis Edition of the Evening Scimitar,* Apr. 1899, 8.

19. Reported in the *Memphis Daily Appeal,* 5 Mar. 1886; *New York Times,* 25 Feb. 1888, p. 8; Memphis Merchants' Exchange, *Report,* 1886, 59.

20. *New York Times,* 8 Mar. 1887, p. 1.

21. Tompkins, "Cotton-Seed Oil," 160; Lamoreaux, *The Great Merger Movement,* 139; Chandler, *Visible Hand,* 334; Clay, "Daniel August Tompkins," 123–24.

22. *New.York Times,* 1 Mar. 1887, p. 1, 6 Mar. 1887, p. 1, 7 Mar. 1887, p. 2, 8 Mar. 1887, p. 1; "The New Oil Mills," *Manufacturers' Record,* 7 (26 Mar. 1887): 239.

23. *New York Times,* 28 Apr. 1887, p. 5, 2 July 1887, p. 8, 3 July 1887, p. 5.

24. *Memphis Daily Appeal,* 5 Mar. 1886; *New York Times,* 7 Mar. 1887, p. 2.

25. D. A. Tompkins Co., *Catalog,* 5; "The Cottonseed Oil Trust," *New York Times,* 25 Oct. 1887, p. 9; *New York Times* 28 Oct. 1887, p. 3; Chandler, *Visible Hand,* 166, 321; City Directories of Boston and Cincinnati; military pension records of John V. Lewis, NA; Lynette B. Wrenn, "Cincinnati and the Cottonseed Industry," *Queen City Heritage,* 48 (Fall 1990): 18–23 n. 19, 31.

26. Chandler, *Visible Hand,* 330; *New York Times,* 1 Oct. 1889, p. 9, 19 Oct. 1889, p. 1, 25 Oct. 1889, p. 9.

27. *New York Times,* 1 Nov. 1889, p. 1; 2 Nov. 1889, p. 1; 7 Nov. 1889, p. 5; 2 July 1890, p. 8; 3 July 1890, p. 8.

28. *New York Times,* 15 Feb. 1890, p. 5; 23 Apr. 1890, p. 8. Chandler, *Visible Hand,* 425. "Edward Dean Adams," *National Cyclopedia of American Biography* 10:419.

29. Chandler, *Visible Hand,* 179, 424–25; *New York Times,* 9 Apr. 1892, p. 5.

30. *Proceedings of the Interstate Cotton Seed Crushers' Association,* 1903, 28.

New York Times, 2 Nov. 1894, p. 9; 7 Nov. 1895, p. 14. Chandler, *Visible Hand,* 368.

31. "Plans of the American Cotton Oil Co.," *Manufacturers' Record* 23 (24 Nov. 1893): 288; George, "Fifty-Seven Years with Mr. Cottonseed," 5.

32. "American Cotton Oil Company," *OPD* 40 (9 Nov. 1891): 7; *New York Times,* 21 Apr. 1896, p. 8; Chandler, *Visible Hand,* 298–99.

33. Shue, "Cotton Oil Industry," 286; Chaney, "Cotton-Seed-Oil Industry," 451–55; Chandler, *Visible Hand,* 503–12.

34. Southern Cotton Oil Company, "Balance Sheet May 31, 1907," "Balance Sheet May 31, 1908," Benjamin Newton Duke Papers, DU; *Illustrated Philadelphia: Its Wealth and Industries* (New York: American Publishing and Engraving, 1889), 143; Culbertson, "History of Cottonseed Crushing in Texas," 27; Clay, "Daniel Augustus Tompkins," 124; Winston, *Builder of the New South,* 101.

35. Tompkins, "Cotton-Seed Oil," 160–61; Winston, *Builder of the New South,* 95–100; Tompkins, *Cotton and Cotton Oil,* 216–20; "The Southern Company," *OPD* 34 (11 July 1888): 5; "Southern Cotton Oil Company Report," *OPD* 39 (24 June 1891): 5.

36. D. A. Tompkins Co., *Catalog,* 4; *Manufacturers' Record* 12 (24 Sept. 1887): 277; Winston, *Builder of the New South,* 101; *New York Times* 13 Mar. 1887, p. 14, 18 Mar. 1887, p. 1; "The Southern Company," *OPD* 34 (11 July 1888): 5; Culbertson, "History of Cottonseed Crushing in Texas," 27; Lamoreaux, *The Great Merger Movement,* 155.

37. Tilley, *Bright Tobacco Industry,* 160–61.

38. *Commercial & Financial Chronicle* 75 (6 Sept. 1902): 496, 81 (22 July 1905): 263; Taylor, *Early History of the Cotton Oil Industry,* 19; *Poor's Manual of Industrials,* 1914, 2334.

39. "Statement by John Doe Pertaining to the Cotton Seed Oil Industry of Texas & Elsewhere," AGC; Shue, "Cotton Oil Industry," 286; *Proceedings of the Interstate Cotton Seed Crushers' Association,* 1907, 106, 1910, 153; *Report of the Federal Trade Commission,* pt. 8, Tex., 8482.

40. *New York Times,* 12 Sept. 1902, p. 1; "State of Texas v. Swift & Co. et al." (1915–23), RG 302, TSL-A.

41. *The Oil Miller* 3 (Feb. 1914): 25; *Report of the Federal Trade Commission,* pt. 13, summary, ix, 15742; pt. 3, Ga., 1171; United Packinghouse Workers of America, Soap Workers Organizing Committee, "Inter-Relations Between Meat Packing, Soap and Cottonseed Oil Industries," 1943, Pamphlets in American History on microfiche.

42. Lief, *"It Floats,"* 4–6, 31, 49–50; Schisgall, *Eyes on Tomorrow,* viii, 22–28; Bushman and Bushman, "Early History of Cleanliness," 1213–38.

43. Lief, *"It Floats,"* 102; Schisgall, *Eyes on Tomorrow,* 66; "The Buckeye Cotton Oil Company," *Chemical and Engineering News* 20 (10 Apr. 1942): 438.

44. Lief, *"It Floats,"* 102–5; Schisgall, *Eyes on Tomorrow,* 67–74; compilation of seed purchases, the Buckeye Cotton Oil Company, [1918?], RG 4, NA.

45. Wilson, *History of Unilever* 1:184–85, 302, 2:323, 395, 3:163–65, 235; Marshall, "Cottonseed—Joint Products," 272.

46. Weber, "Economic Development," 68–69; "Outlook for the Cotton Seed Industry," *OPD* 50 (20 June 1896): 5; *Proceedings of the Interstate Cotton Seed Crushers' Association,* 1910, 87.

47. "Texas Cottonseed Oil Interests," *OPD* 46 (13 Aug. 1894): 7.

48. *Nashville (Tenn.) American,* 16, 17, 18 July 1897; *Proceedings of the Interstate Cotton Seed Crushers' Association,* 1910, 43.

49. "Past Presidents Send Greetings," *COP* 1 (May 1927): 29; *Report of the Federal Trade Commission,* pt. 3, Ga., 945, 1484, 1486; pt. 5, N.C., 3617; pt. 8, Tex., 8419; WHJ [W. H. Jasspon], manager, Perkins Oil Mill, Memphis, to Stanley Posner, NRA Compliance Board, 18 Nov. 1933, RG 9, NA.

50. *Proceedings of the Interstate Cotton Seed Crushers' Association,* 1905, 33, 1913, 70; *Minutes of the Annual Meeting of the Alabama Cotton Seed Crushers Association,* 1913, 6, 43, UA; *Report of the Proceedings of the Thirteenth Annual Convention of the Cotton Seed Crushers' Association of Georgia,* 1917, cover, NAL; *Proceedings of the Third Annual Session of the South Carolina Cotton Seed Crushers' Association,* 1908, 2, NAL; C. L. Ives, New Bern, N.C., to E. V. Zoeller, Tarboro, N.C., 21 May 1906, ZP; *New Orleans Daily Picayune,* 27 July 1906, p. 8; *Proceedings of the First Annual Convention of the Mississippi Cotton Seed Crushers Association,* 1912, cover, NAL; H. C. Brown, district manager, Southern Cotton Oil Co., Augusta, Ga., to Hugh Humphreys, USFA, 5 Mar. 1918; *Report of the Federal Trade Commission,* pt. 12, Tenn., 14501–2.

51. "Members of the Interstate Cotton Seed Crushers' Association, 1907–1908," *Proceedings of the Interstate Cotton Seed Crushers' Association,* 1907, 108–10.

52. John F. Moloney, "A Half Century of Progress, the Story of the National Cottonseed Products Association, 1897–1946," *C&COP* 47 (4 May 1946): 16.

53. "Cotton Seed Crushers' Meeting," *OPD* 56 (7 Aug. 1899): 5; *Proceedings of the Interstate Cotton Seed Crushers' Association,* 1902, 18; "Special Rules and Regulations for the Cotton Seed Product Trade as Adopted by the Dealers of Memphis and Approved by the Memphis Merchants Exchange, February 20, 1883," Memphis Merchants' Exchange, *Report,* 1883, 99–104; *Report of the Federal Trade Commission,* pt. 12, Tenn., 14750.

54. *Proceedings of the Interstate Cotton Seed Crushers' Association,* 1911, 33, 1913, 72–77; Moloney, "Half Century of Progress," 11, 20.

55. *Proceedings of the Interstate Cotton Seed Crushers' Association,* 1906, 34–36, 44, 1908, 15, 1911, 47, 100, 1912, 44; Interstate Cotton Seed Crushers' Association, Publicity Bureau, *Bulletins 1–13 (Nov. 1906–Jan. 1911),* of Interstate Cotton Seed Crushers' Association, NAL.

56. *Proceedings of the Interstate Cotton Seed Crushers' Association,* 1911, 38; "Proceedings of the Interstate Cotton Seed Crushers' Association, 1917," *COP* 1 (June 1917): 45; "Proceedings of the Interstate Cotton Seed Crushers' Association, 1918," *COP* 2 (June 1919): 45; *Investigation of the Cotton Seed Industry,* pt. 3, Ga., 945.

7. Cottonseed Price Fixing and Politics

1. Hammond, "The Cotton Seed Industry," 25; Bureau of the Census, "Cottonseed Products," 594; *Proceedings of the Interstate Cotton Seed Crushers' Association,* 1910, 107; Dept. of Agriculture, "Cottonseed: Marketing Spreads," 2, 5.

2. Weber, "Economic Development," 56–57; Thomas C. Cochran, *Business in American Life* (New York: McGraw-Hill, 1972), 152–53; Porter, *The Rise of Big Business,* 37, 61–62.

3. "Crushers' Views on the Cotton Seed Industry," *OPD* 50 (24 Aug. 1896): 25; "The Cottonseed Outlook," *OPD* 50 (7 Sept. 1896): 8; "Cotton Seed Crushers Association Formed," *OPD* 52 (26 July 1897): 26; W. R. Smith-Vaniz, Brookhaven, Miss., to Buckeye Cotton Oil Co. managers, 10 Feb. 1911, RG 48, vol. 32, MSA.

4. Cox, *Cottonseed Crushing Industry of Texas,* 65.

5. John E. Land, *Pen Illustrations of New Orleans, 1881–82* (New Orleans: privately printed, 1882), 75; "Cotton Seed—Its Uses and Manufacture," *OPD* 19 (1 June 1881): 779; *Proceedings of the Cotton Seed Crushers' Association,* 1879, 33, 1882, 125; Dept. of Interior, Census Office, *Tenth Census of the United States, 1880, Census of Agriculture,* pt. 1, *Mississippi Valley and South Western States,* "Report on Cotton Production in the United States," by Eugene W. Hilgard (Washington, D.C., 1884), 98.

6. "Litigation in New Orleans," *OPD* 31 (13 Apr. 1887): 29.

7. *Proceedings of the Cotton Seed Crushers' Association,* 1883, 44, 70; Weber, "Economic Development," 105.

8. "Cotton Seed Crushers' Association Convention," *OPD* 26 (14 May 1884): 10; "Combination in Cotton Seed Oil Industry," *OPD* 26 (19 Nov. 1884): 5; "The Cottonseed Pool," *OPD* 27 (18 Feb. 1885): 5.

9. "The Mississippi Valley Cottonseed Pool," *OPD* 27 (6 May 1885): 5.

10. Memphis Merchants' Exchange, *Report,* 1885, 150; *Memphis Daily Appeal,* 5 Mar. 1886.

11. *New York Times,* 15 Apr. 1887, p. 5, 21 June 1888, p. 1; "State of Louisiana vs. American Cotton Oil Trust," Tulane Univ.; "Termination of Cotton Oil Suit in New Orleans," *OPD* 35 (26 June 1889): 9.

12. "Cottonseed Oil," *Manufacturers' Record* 23 (24 Nov. 1893): 288; D. A. Tompkins Co., *Catalog,* 4–5; Clay, "Daniel Augustus Tompkins," 125; *Plan and Scope of the Alabama Alliance Oil Company,* n.p.

13. "Cottonseed Oil," *Manufacturers' Record* 23 (31 Mar. 1893): 163; "Plans of American Cotton Oil Co.," *Manufacturers' Record* 24 (24 Nov. 1893): 288; "Letter from Corsicana Cotton Oil Company," *Manufacturers' Record* 24 (1 Dec. 1893): 305.

14. James Curtis Ballagh, *The South in the Building of the Nation,* vol. 6 (Richmond, Va.: Southern Historical Publication Society, 1909), 290; "Fixing the Price of Seed in Tennessee," *Manufacturers' Record* 24 (3 Nov. 1893): 232, 251; "Georgia Farmers Will Fix Seed Prices," *Manufacturers' Record* 24 (17 Nov. 1893); 269; "Tennessee Suit Filed in Cotton Seed Cases," *OPD* 46 (19 Nov. 1894): 9.

15. Culbertson, "History of Cottonseed Crushing in Texas," 27; "State of Texas v. Swift & Co.," RG 302, TSL-A; *Manufacturers' Record* 24 (6 Oct. 1893): 167, 24 (13 Oct. 1893): 183, 24 (20 Oct. 1893): 202; "Statement by John Doe Pertaining to the Cotton Seed Oil Industry of Texas and Elsewhere," [1913], AGC.

16. "Texas Cottonseed Oil Interests," *OPD* 45 (13 Aug. 1894): 7; "Fixing the Price on Cottonseed," *OPD* 45 (24 Sept. 1894): 5; "Decree in the Texas Case," *OPD* 49 (13 Apr. 1896): 24A; Ballagh, *South in the Building of the Nation* 6:290; testimony of H. W. Meisner, manager, Temple [Tex.] Cotton Oil Mill, 3 Nov. 1913, AGC; statement of Emil Buescher, president, Smithville [Tex.] Oil Co., 13 Oct. 1917, T/MCO.

17. "Southern Views on the Situation," *OPD* 45 (8 Jan. 1894): 9; "Situation in Cotton Seed Industry," *OPD* 50 (21 Sept. 1896): 7; "Cotton Oil Men Meet at Chattanooga," *OPD* 51 (28 June 1897): 7; "Cotton Seed Crushers' Association Formed," *OPD* 52 (26 July 1897): 26; "Meeting of Cotton Oil Men," *OPD* 53 (9 May 1898): 5; "Cotton Seed Crushers' Meet," *OPD* 53 (16 May 1898): 5; "Cotton Seed Crushers' Convention in Chattanooga," *OPD* 53 (23 May 1898): 8; *Progressive Farmer,* 13, 20 Nov. 1900, 10 Sept. 1901.

18. "Lime" [H. E. Wells, Columbia, S.C.] to E. V. Zoeller, Tarboro, N.C., 26 Sept. 1903, minutes of Monticello Conference, 2 Oct. 1903, ZP; Lynette B. Wrenn, "Cottonseed Price-Fixing in Eastern North Carolina, 1903–1907," *North Carolina Historical Review* 67 (Oct. 1990): 411–37.

19. Gibson Gin & Oil Co. [Calvert, Tex.] to J. W. Allison, Dallas, AGC.

20. Statement of John W. Fitzhugh, seed buyer, Arlington, Tex., Oct. 1913; C. A. Sweeton, asst. attorney general, to R. V. Nichols, special agent, 11 Oct. 1915; testimony of Fred Psencik, cottonseed buyer, Smithville, Tex., undated; J. M. Collins, farmer, Childress, Tex., to B. F. Looney, attorney general, 26 Sept. 1916; J. T. Bogard, farmer and state legislator, to B. F. Looney, 18 Oct. 1917, T/MCO; testimony of J. L. Hudgins, general manager, Industrial Cotton Oil Co. to C. A. Sweeton, 22 Nov. 1913; statement of H. M. Wade, county attorney, Rockwell County, Tex., to B. F. Looney, 17 Apr. 1913; *Farmers' Fireside Bulletin,* [Arlington, Tex.], 6 Aug. 1913; William Bacon to C. A. Sweeton, 12 Nov. 1913; statement of the president of the Texas Dairymen's Association to C. A. Sweeton, 6 Sept. 1913; statement of H. C. Greer, cottonseed buyer, Austin, Tex., undated; statement of Henry Erle Keys, former oil-mill manager, to C. A. Sweeton, 27 Oct. 1915, AGC; statement of D. M. Seybold, ginner, Temple, Tex., 3 Nov. 1913; statement of E. B. Greathouse, ginner, Temple, Tex., undated; statement of L. L. Shields, seed buyer, Santa Anna, Texas, 3 Sept. 1913; statement of H. T. Ashcraft, ginner, Rogers, Texas, 5 Nov. 1913, SNB2.

21. W. B. Gowdey, Jackson, Miss., to E. Cahn, Meridian, Miss., 2 Feb. 1906; E. M. Durham, Vicksburg, Miss., to E. Cahn, 25 July 1906, RG 48, vol. 34, MSA.

22. H. C. Forrester, Meridian, Miss., to K. C. Hall, Laurel, Miss., 10 Sept. 1907; Unsigned to J. W. McRaven, Newton, Miss., 16 Sept. 1907; W. B. Gowdey, Jackson, Miss., to K. C. Hall, 11 Nov. 1907; K. C. Hall to W. B. Gowdey

and W. G. McNair, Jackson, Miss., 23 June 1909; W. B. Gowdey to K. C. Hall, 21 Aug. 1909, RG 48, vol. 32, MSA.

23. *Houston Chronicle,* 25 Oct. [1914?], RG 302, TSL-A.

24. "Correspondence from the South," *OPD* 30 (27 Oct. 1886): 7; "The Season's Cotton Seed Prospects," *OPD* 40 (24 Aug. 1891): 7; *Progressive Farmer,* 5 June 1900; Dept. of Agriculture, Office of Experiment Stations, Bulletin No. 33, "The Feeding Value of Cotton-Seed Products" by B. W. Kilgore, in Dabney, *Cotton Plant,* 385–421.

25. "Convention," *OPD* 25 (14 May 1884): 10; "Communication from *New Orleans Times Democrat,*" *OPD* 30 (8 Sept. 1886): 32.

26. Robert C. McMath Jr., *Populist Vanguard* (Chapel Hill: Univ. of North Carolina Press, 1975), 20; Michael Schwartz, *Radical Protest and Social Structure* (Chicago: Univ. of Chicago Press, 1976), 266; Willard Range, *A Century of Georgia Agriculture, 1850–1950* (Athens: Univ. of Georgia Press, 1954), 141.

27. *Farmers' Co-operative Manufacturing Company* (Tarboro, N.C.: C. G. Bradley, 1888), 5, J. Bryan Grimes Papers, ECU; Book of Incorporations, Edgecombe County, 5 Mar. 1888; State of North Carolina, Dept. of the Secretary of State, "Articles of Incorporation of Farmers Cooperative Manufacturing Company," 13 Jan. 1889.

28. *Plan and Scope of the Alabama Alliance Oil Company;* Lawrence Goodwyn, *Democratic Promise* (New York: Oxford Univ. Press, 1976), 123; Leder Oil Company, Demopolis, Alabama, listed in *Proceedings of the Interstate Cotton Seed Crushers' Association,* 1907, 98.

29. Dept. of Agriculture, Farm Credit Administration, Cooperative Research and Service Division, Circular No. C-114, "Crushing Cottonseed Cooperatively," by John S. Burgess Jr., June 1939, NAL; Dept. of Agriculture, Farm Credit Administration, Circular No. 30, "Crushing Cottonseed Cooperatively," by Elmer J. Perdue, Mar. 1962, NAL.

30. "The Season's Cotton Seed Prospects," OPD 40 (24 Aug. 1891): 7; "The Cotton Seed Oil Outlook," *OPD* 45 (8 Jan. 1894): 7; "Fixing the Price on Cotton Seed," *OPD* 46 (24 Sept. 1894): 5; "The Cottonseed Outlook," *OPD* 50 (24 Aug. 1896): 5; "Reports from Cotton Seed Crushers," *OPD* 50 (23 Nov. 1896): 25; J. Havens, Washington, N.C., to Wells, Columbia, S.C., Borden, Goldsboro, N.C., Ives, New Bern, N.C., Dunn, Kinston, N.C., Zoeller, Tarboro, N.C., 27 Oct. 1903, ZP; Wright, *Old South, New South,* 114–15.

31. *Proceedings of the Annual Convention of the Mississippi Valley Cotton Planters' Association Embracing the States of Alabama, Arkansas, Louisiana, Mississippi and Tennessee,* 1880, 14, MSA; "Cotton Seed Crushers and the Planters," *OPD* 21 (22 Nov. 1882): 1126; *Manufacturers' Record* 30 (30 Oct. 1896): 225.

32. *Manufacturers' Record* 24 (3 Nov. 1893): 251; "Georgia Farmers Will Fix Seed Prices," *Manufacturers' Record* 24 (17 Nov. 1893): 269.

33. J. M. Macdonald, Buckeye Cotton Oil Co., Cincinnati, to Buckeye Cotton Oil Co., Jackson, Miss., 21 Sept. 1907; W. G. McNair, Jackson, Miss., to

J. M. Macdonald, 19 Oct. 1907, RG 48, vol. 35, MSA; George Locke Robson, "The Farmers' Union in Mississippi" (Master's thesis, Mississippi State Univ., Starkville, 1963), MSA; *Report of the Federal Trade Commission,* pt. 9, Okla., 11370–84; pt. 11, Ark., 13275–85.

34. *Progressive Farmer,* 23 Oct. 1900.

35. *Progressive Farmer,* 5 June 1900, 27 Aug., 3 Sept., 1 Oct. 1901; "To Cotton Farmers and Growers" (clipping from unidentified newspaper), 25 Sept. 1901, J. Bryan Grimes Papers, ECU; H. E. Wells, Columbia, S.C., to E. V. Zoeller, Tarboro, N.C., 9 Nov. 1903, ZP.

36. *Proceedings of a Special Convention of the Interstate Cotton Seed Crushers' Association,* 1907, 52–56; 1908, 13; Interstate Cotton Seed Crushers' Association, *Bulletin* 6 (1907): 5, in *Bulletins 1–13* (Nov. 1906–Jan. 1911), NAL.

37. "Wesson," 104; *Proceedings of the Interstate Cotton Seed Crushers' Association,* 1915, 131; "It Will Lead to Bloodshed," editorial, *Jackson (Miss.) Daily News,* 15 Sept. 1931, rpt. in *COP* 15 (Oct. 1931): 8; *Report of the Federal Trade Commission,* pt. 3, Ga., 1085.

38. Shue, "Cotton Oil Industry," 285–86; *Progressive Farmer,* 16 Oct., 20 Nov. 1900; *Commercial and Financial Chronicle,* 99 (15 Aug. 1914): 47, 113 (23 July 1921): 420; *New York Times,* 20 Apr. 1913, p. 6, 25 Jan. 1914, pt. 2, p. 1, 19 May 1914, p. 12; "Mississippi Cotton Oil Case," *Cotton Seed Oil Magazine* 25 (Sept. 1915): 41; "Verdict Favors Seed Dealers," *Cotton Seed Oil Magazine* 25 (Oct. 1915): 45; W. G. Mann, speech to oil-mill superintendents, *Cotton Seed Oil Magazine* 26 (Nov. 1915): 32; "Investigating Cottonseed Prices," *Cotton Seed Oil Magazine* 27 (Sept. 1916): 38–39, NAL; J. M. Macdonald, Cincinnati, to S. N. Malone, Jackson, Miss., 16 Apr. 1907, RG 48, vol. 35, MSA; "Southern Expects to Return to Texas," *COP* 3 (Sept. 1919): 34; records related to the prosecution of Oklahoma oil mills in 1917 and numerous indictments of Texas cottonseed-oil mills for price fixing on the eve of World War I are preserved in RG 302, TSL-A.

39. "Sons of Plato Are Described as Oath-Bound Society Whose Purpose is Fixing Price and Dividing Seed Territory," *Houston Chronicle,* 25 Oct. [1914], RG 302, TSL-A; *Proceedings of the First Annual Convention of the Mississippi Cotton Seed Crushers Association,* 1912, 14, NAL.

40. Henry C. Hammond, "Cotton Seed Meal as a Food for Work Stock," *Bulletin* 10, in Interstate Cotton Seed Crushers' Association, *Bulletins 1–13 (Nov. 1906–Jan. 1911),* 3, NAL; *Report of the Federal Trade Commission,* pt. 9, Okla., 11398.

41. *Proceedings of the First Annual Convention of the Mississippi Cotton Seed Crushers Association,* 1912, 4–5, NAL; J. W. McLean, Darlington, La., to USFA, 19 July 1918, RG 4, NA; *Progressive Farmer,* 2, 16 Aug. 1919, 11 Oct. 1919, 39, 8 Nov. 1919, 30, 15 Oct. 1927, 4; Kent Osband, "The Boll Weevil Versus 'King Cotton,'" *Journal of Economic History* 45 (Sept. 1985): 627–43; *Proceedings of the Alabama Cotton Seed Crushers Association,* 1913, 44, UAL.

42. Cox, *Cottonseed Crushing Industry of Texas,* table 2, "Growth of the Cottonseed Industry in Texas and United States, 1899 to 1939," 5.

43. *Cotton Seed Oil Magazine* 27 (Oct. 1916): 25–26, 28 (Nov. 1916): 28–29.

8. World War I and Postwar Shocks

1. Cooper, "History of Cotton," 24; Bureau of the Census, *United States Census of Manufactures: 1958,* vol. 2, *Industry Statistics,* pt. 1, *Major Groups 20 to 28* (Washington, D.C., 1961), 20H-6.

2. Culbertson, "Alarming Increase in Cost of Crushing Seed," 23; "Monthly Letter of President Wallace," *COP* 1 (Apr. 1918): 16; "Proceedings of the Interstate Cotton Seed Crushers' Association, 1918," 42; "President Montgomery's Monthly Letter," *COP* 2 (Nov. 1918): 18; "Conference on Oil Mill Labor Shortage," 23; "President Montgomery's Monthly Letter," *COP* 2 (Dec. 1918):18; G. D. Miller, Sherman, Tex., to the American Livestock & Loan Co., Denver, 1 Nov. 1917; W. D. Claybrooke, Albertville, Ala., to R. M. Hobbie, Alabama state food administrator, 24 Dec. 1917; R. P. Thompson, Brenham, Tex., to USFA, 26 Dec. 1917; R. L. McMath, Americus, Ga., to J. L. Benton, USFA, 1 Jan. 1918; USFA to M. J. Allen, Richfield, Kans., 20 Feb. 1920; John Aspegren, Portsmouth [Va.] Cotton Oil Refining Corp. to Hugh Humphreys, USFA, 25 Mar. 1918; Rap Walker, traffic manager, American Cotton Oil Co. to USFA, 25 Mar. 1918; W. B. West, Columbia, to South Carolina Cotton Seed Crushers' Association, 20, 30 Mar. 1918, RG 4, NA.

3. *Preliminary Inventory of the Records of the United States Food Administration, 1917–1920, Part I: The Headquarters Organization* (Washington, D.C., 1943), ix, 184, RG 4, NA; Murray R. Benedict, *Farm Policies of the United States, 1790–1950* (New York: Twentieth Century Fund, 1953; New York: Octagon Books, 1966), 162; "Monthly Letter of President Wallace," *COP* 1 (Aug. 1917): 11–12; "Proceedings of the Interstate Cotton Seed Crushers' Association, 1918," *COP* 2 (June 1918): 40; Moloney, "Half Century of Progress," 19–20.

4. William O. Thompson, New York, president, American Cotton Oil Co. to David H. Pyle, USFA, 1 Oct. 1917; P. F. Jones, Marion, S.C., cottonseed dealer to Mr. [T. F.] Justice, head of cotton ginning section, n. d.; USFA to Aliceville [Ala.] Oil & Manufacturing Co., 13 Dec. 1917; R. M. Hobbie, food administrator for Ala., to Buckeye Cotton Oil Co., Selma, Ala., 25 Jan. 1918; USFA to S. K. Asken, Edwards, Miss., 15 Feb. 1918, RG 4, NA.

5. "Rules for Cottonseed Products," *National Provisioner* 57 (10 Nov. 1917): 27, RG 4, NA; "Monthly Letter of President Wallace," *COP* 1 (Nov. 1917): 14.

6. "Editorial," *COP* 1 (Dec. 1917): 25; "Proceedings of the Interstate Cotton Seed Crushers' Association, 1918," 70.

7. President C. C. Littleton, Fort Worth, to the Members of the Texas Cotton Seed Crushers' Association, 27 Sept. 1917, Russell Acree, Darlington, president of the S.C. Cotton Seed Crushers' Association, to J. L. Benton, USFA, 16 Nov. 1917, RG 4, NA; "Cost of Cotton Seed by States for Five Years," *COP* 1 (Nov. 1917): 27; "Monthly Letter of President Wallace," *COP* 1 (Jan. 1918): 15; David Wesson, "The Cotton Oil Industry," *COP* 1 (Apr. 1918): 19.

8. W. F. Bridewell to Hugh Humphreys, USFA, 5 Dec. 1917; W. A. Thompson, N.Y., to M. L. Requa, USFA, 12 Dec. 1917; W. B. West, Columbia, to S.C. Cotton Seed Crushers' Association, 13 Dec. 1917; USFA to Braxton Beachem, food administrator for Fla., 13, 14 Dec. 1917, Braxton Beachem

to Hugh Humphreys, 27 Dec. 1917; C. E. McCord, secy., Alabama Cotton-seed Crushers Association, to USFA, 26 Dec. 1917; C. F. Nelson, manager, Eastern Division, Union Seed & Fertilizer Co. (American Cotton Oil Co. subsidiary), to William Elliot, food administrator for S.C., 17 Jan. 1918; David Pyle, USFA, to Hon. Sydney Anderson, House Office Bldg., 28 Jan. 1918; USFA to Refiners and Lard Substitute Manufacturers, 16-H-1, 5 Jan. 1918; "Valuation [of seed, oil, meal, lint, hulls] of Dec. 21, 1917," telegram from Humphreys to Dr. Stratton D. Brooks, food administrator for Okla., 23 Jan. 1918; undated "Amendments and Additions to Special Regulations for Licensees Engaged in the Business of Ginning, Crushing, Refining and Dealing in Cottonseed, Cotton Seed Oil, Cotton Seed Meal, Cotton Seed Cake, Peanut Oil, Soya Bean Oil, Palm Oil and Copra Oil, Peanut Meal and Soya Bean Meal, that Were Promulgated on Nov. 1, 1917," *Flour & Feed* (Jan. 1918): 58, RG 4, NA; "Monthly Letter of President Wallace," *COP* 1 (Oct. 1917): 13–14; Benedict, *Farm Policies of the United States,* 163.

9. Telegram, USFA to J. D. Lewis, president, Union Seed & Fertilizer Co. (American Cotton Oil Co. subsidiary), 9 Nov. 1917; Interoffice Memorandum, [Hugh] Humphreys to Gutterson, 14 Dec. 1917; Bryan Bell, secy., Louisiana Cottonseed Crushers' Association to Hugh Humphreys, 26 Dec. 1917; I. L. Hathaway, Pine Bluff, Ark., to Hamp Williams, food administrator for Ark., 19 Jan. 1918; R. M. Hobbie, food administrator for Ala., to Buckeye Cotton Oil Co., Selma, Ala., 25 Jan. 1918; R. M. Hobbie to Union Seed & Fertilizer Co., 25 Jan. 1918; "Statement to Cotton Ginners and Cottonseed Buyers," from T. F. Justiss, USFA, 38-H-3, undated (38-H was dated Apr. 1918); mimeographed bulletin sent to members of the Texas Cotton Seed Crushers' Association by the Bureau of Publicity, 2 Feb. 1918, RG 4, NA.

10. H. C. Brown, district manager, Southern Cotton Oil Co., Augusta, Ga., to Hugh Humphreys, USFA, 11 Mar. 1918; USFA to Cotton Seed Crushers, 38-H, 9 Apr. 1918; C. H. Benceni, Brownwood, Tex., to Hugh Humphreys, 16 Jan. 1918; Orin Ashton, Chickasha, Okla., to Stratton D. Brooks, food administrator for Okla., 8 Jan. 1918; Stratton Brooks to Hugh Humphreys, 19 Jan. 1918; Home Oil Mill, Decatur, Ala., to USFA, 31 May 1918; R. F. Franklin, Adairsville, Ga., to Herbert Hoover, 8 Nov. 1917; Bryan Bell, secy., Louisiana Cotton Seed Crushers' Association, to USFA, 20 Dec. 1917; W. W. Abbot, Louisville, Ga., to G. H. Denny, USFA, 6 Apr. 1918; *Flour & Feed* (Jan. 1918): 30, RG 4, NA.

11. W. B. West, Columbia, secy., S.C. Cotton Seed Crushers' Association, to Cotton Seed Division, USFA, 12 Feb., 20, 30 Mar. 1918; H. C. Brown, district manager, Southern Cotton Oil Co., Augusta, Ga., to Hugh Humphreys, USFA, 5 Mar. 1918; USFA Circular No. 26 to Cotton Seed Crushers, 19 Apr. 1918; T. F. Justiss to Ginners and Seed Merchants, Circular Letter no. 32, 15 May 1918; Washington County Warehouse Co., Brenham, Tex., to T. F. Justiss, USFA, 23 May 1918; T. F. Justiss to All Buyers and Sellers of Cotton Seed, Circular No. 40, 14 June 1918; USFA Circu-

lar No. 47 to All Crushers of Cottonseed, 22 Aug. 1918; USFA Circular No. 49 to All Crushers of Cottonseed and the Purchasers of the Products Thereof, 7 Sept. 1918, RG 4, NA; "President Montgomery's Monthly Letter," *COP* 2 (Sept. 1918): 18; "Editorial," *COP* 3 (Dec. 1919): 25; *Report of the Federal Trade Commission,* pt. 9, Okla., 10974–75.

12. USFA Circular No. 60 to Licensees of the Cottonseed Industry, 11 Feb. 1919; report of meeting of government and industry representatives, 29 Apr. 1919; Louis N. Geldert, Memphis, secy. of War Service Committee (of cottonseed crushers) to Cottonseed Division, USFA, 24 May 1919, RG 4, NA; "Editorial," *COP* 2 (Jan. 1919): 29; "Editorial," *COP* 2 (Apr. 1919): 25–26; "Editorial," *COP* 3 (June 1919): 25.

13. Bernard M. Baruch, *American Industry in the War: A Report of the War Industries Board* (New York: Prentice-Hall, 1941), 165, 181–83; "President Wallace's Address," *COP* 2 (June 1918): 43, 46–48; J. J. Lawton, "Special Linter Committee Report," *COP* 3 (June 1919): 53–56; Williams Haynes, *Cellulose: The Chemical that Grows* (New York: Southern Horizons, 1946; Garden City, N.Y.: Doubleday, 1953), 64–66.

14. Baruch, *American Industry in the War,* 183.

15. "President Montgomery's Monthly Letter," *COP* 3 (May 1919): 18–19; "Proceedings of the Interstate Cotton Seed Crushers' Association, 1919," *COP* 3 (June 1919): 42, 53–57, 77; "Dangerous Delays," *COP* 3 (Oct. 1919): 26.

16. "Editorial," *COP* 3 (July 1919): 25; "Monthly Letter of President DuBose," *COP* 3 (Jan. 1920): 17; "Decision of Secretary of War Baker on Appeal of Linter Claims," *COP* 4 (June 1920): 27.

17. "Adverse Decision in Linter Cases," *COP* 9 (Aug. 1925): 18; "From General Counsel Benet," *COP* 14 (July 1930): 17–18; "Editorial," *COP* 14 (Oct. 1930): 23; "Another Linter Claims Victory," *COP* 16 (Dec. 1932): 15.

18. "Address of George C. Speir," *COP* 9 (May 1923): 55; Haynes, *Cellulose,* 67–72.

19. A. K. Burrow, "Report of Linter Grading Committee," *COP* 10 (June 1926): 42; "Proceedings of the Interstate Cotton Seed Crushers' Association, 1928," *COP* 12 (June 1928): 23; Peter Van Wyck, "Cotton Linters," in Bailey, *Cottonseed and Cottonseed Products,* 899; Haynes, *Cellulose,* 256–94.

20. "War Service Committee Report," *COP* 3 (June 1919): 68; "Monthly Letter of Secretary Cleaver," *COP* 3 (Sept. 1919): 19; "Co-operation in Seed Marketing," *COP* 3 (Sept. 1919): 21; "Editorial," *COP* 3 (Oct. 1919): 17; "Monthly Letter of President DuBose," *COP* 3 (Oct. 1919): 27.

21. *Report of the Federal Trade Commission,* pt. 6, Miss., 7498; pt. 11, Ark., 12557; pt. 12, Tenn., 14991.

22. "Monthly Letter of President Lawton," *COP* 4 (Sept. 1920): 26; "Monthly Letter of President Lawton," *COP* 4 (Nov. 1920): 25; "Major Brode and His Friends," *COP* 4 (Apr. 1921): 36; Wright, *Old South, New South,* 154; Benedict, *Farm Policies of the United States,* 168, 174; Weber, "Economic Development," table 4a, "Value of Crude Products of the Cottonseed

Crushing Industry in the United States, Annually from 1875," 287; Dept. of Agriculture, "Cottonseed: Marketing Spreads," 5.

23. Benedict, *Farm Policies of the United States,* 170, 192.

24. "Monthly Letter of President DuBose," *COP* 3 (Oct. 1919): 17; "Monthly Letter of President DuBose," *COP* 4 (May 1920): 22; "Monthly Letter of President Lawton," *COP* 4 (Sept. 1920): 25; "The Future of Cottonseed Oil," *COP* 4 (Dec. 1920): 39; Weber, "Economic Development," table 15, "World Cottonseed Oil Exports by Principal Countries, 1901–1931," 300; Georges Minch Weber, "Legislative Weapons in Inter-industry Competition—Oils and Fats," *Harvard Business Review* 13 (Oct. 1934): 72–73; L. W. Haskell, vice president, Southern Cotton Oil Co., to USFA, 18 Feb. 1918; N. B. Ware, Atlanta Oil & Fertilizer Co., to USFA, 23 Jan. 1918; USFA Circular No. 60 to Licensees of the Cottonseed Industry, 11 Feb. 1919, RG 4, NA.

25. *Progressive Farmer,* 5 July 1919, 28; Philip Green Wright, *The American Tariff and Oriental Trade* (Chicago: Univ. of Chicago Press, 1931), 100–102.

26. "Monthly Letter of President Lawton," *COP* 4 (Jan. 1921): 25; "Protest Vegetable-Oil Tariff," *COP* 4 (Jan. 1921): 58; "Survey of America's Cottonseed Oil Industry by the United States Tariff Commission," *COP* 4 (Feb. 1921): 50; "Argument for Vegetable Oil Tariff," *COP* 4 (Mar. 1921): 52; John Aspegren, "Economic Conditions in the Cotton Seed Oil Industry," *Chemical Age* 32 (June 1924): 259–61; Geoffrey Perrett, *America in the Twenties: A History* (New York: Simon and Schuster, 1982): 26–27.

27. "Special Meeting of Association," *COP* 5 (Jan. 1922): 17; *Report of the Federal Trade Commission,* pt. 9, Okla., 10776–77.

28. "Crushers' Association Opposes Tariff," *COP* 5 (Feb. 1922): 17–18; "Editorial," *COP* 6 (May 1922): 26–27; "Editorial," *COP* 6 (Oct. 1922): 23; *Report of the Federal Trade Commission,* pt. 8, Tex., 8092; Wilson, *History of Unilever* 1:304.

29. Edwin G. Nourse, *American Agriculture and the European Market* (New York: McGraw-Hill, 1924); Benedict, *Farm Policies of the United States,* 169, 202–4, 233, 236; Theodore Saloutos, *The American Farmer and the New Deal* (Ames: Iowa State Univ. Press, 1982), 5, 10, 140, 148.

30. E. C. DeSegundo, "Some Cotton Seed Products in Their Relation to Present-Day Needs," *Scientific American Supplement* 86 (14 Dec. 1918): 383; "Address of Dr. Francis M. Turner," *COP* 7 (May 1923): 59; Markley, "The Cotton Processing Industry," A-4; Nourse, *American Agriculture and the European Market,* 195; Weber and Alsberg, *American Vegetable-Shortening Industry,* 155; Wilson, *History of Unilever* 2:104, 156, 176, 199.

31. Wilson, *History of Unilever* 1:245, 278–79; "The Vegetable Oil Trade of Great Britain," *COP* 3 (Dec. 1919): 28; "The Tariff on Vegetable Oils and Its Effects on the Foreign Trade in Cottonseed Oils," *Monthly Business Review* (Dallas: Federal Reserve Board), rpt. in *COP* 9 (June 1925): 90–91.

32. Weber, "Economic Development," 144–57.

33. Henry I. Richards, *Cotton and the AAA* (Washington, D.C.: Brookings Institution, 1936), 12; William H. Jasspon, "What Is Wrong with the Cotton Oil

Industry?," *Commerce and Finance* 13 (9 Jan. 1924): 119; William H. Jasspon, "Too Many Bulls Still in Cotton Seed," *Commerce and Finance* 14 (4 Mar. 1925): 431–32; William H. Jasspon, "The Cotton Oil Industry— Looking Forward," *Commerce and Finance* 15 (13 Jan. 1926): 135; William H. Jasspon, "What a Large Crop Does to the Cotton Oil Industry," *Commerce and Finance* 16 (12 Jan. 1927): 119, 121.

34. R. F. Abbay, Commerce, Miss., to Dr. G. H. Denny, director, Cotton-Seed Dept. of USFA, 11 May 1918, RG 4, NA; *Report of the Federal Trade Commission,* pt. 10, La., 12190, 12318.

35. "American Cotton Oil Stops Crushing Mills," *New York Times,* 13 June 1923, p. 29; *Commercial and Financial Chronicle* 113 (5 Nov. 1921): 1992, 115 (25 Nov. 1922): 237, 116 (14 Apr. 1923): 2769, 2996, 117 (25 Aug. 1923): 896, 117 (15 Sept. 1923): 1238, 117 (29 Sept. 1923): 1464, 117 (27 Oct. 1923): 1888, 117 (10 Nov. 1923): 2112; 118 (5 Jan. 1924): 87; "World's Largest Cottonseed Oil Mill," *COP* 4 (Feb. 1921): 30; "American Ceases Crushing Operations," *COP* 7 (July 1923): 21; "Breaking Up of American's Mill Organization," *COP* 7 (Aug. 1923): 25; "American Cotton Oil Company Reorganizes," *COP* 7 (Oct. 1923): 20; "Dixie Company's New Memphis Oil Mill," *COP* 7 (Nov. 1923): 33; *Capital Changes Reporter* 1:347; Aspegren, "Economic Conditions in the Cotton Seed Oil Industry," 260.

36. *Commercial and Financial Chronicle* 115 (9 Sept. 1922): 1206, 120 (21 Feb. 1925): 970; "Southern Cotton Oil Co. Receivership," *COP* 7 (Apr. 1924): 29; "The Southern Cotton Oil Company," *COP* 8 (Mar. 1925): 18; "Ambrose Dromgoole Geoghegan," *National Cyclopedia of American Biography* 33:520–21; "Wesson," 70, 102; *Capital Changes Reporter* 6:140.

37. John B. Gordon, "Consumption of Industrial Oils and Fats Exceeded Production," *Chemical & Metallurgical Engineering* 36 (Jan. 1929): 54–55; "Editorial," *COP* 8 (Aug. 1923): 25–27; "Covington-Perry Mill Group," *COP* 10 (Sept. 1926)): 19; "Merger of Thirteen Mississippi Oil Mills," *COP* 11 (Nov. 1927): 19; *Report of the Federal Trade Commission,* pt. 13, summary, 15723–24.

38. "Growth of Kershaw Mill Interests," *COP* 8 (Nov. 1924): 33.

39. *Report of the Federal Trade Commission,* pt. 11, Ark., 13339, 13341, 13343; *Memphis Commercial Appeal,* 6 Apr., 16 May, 22 June 1935; "National Buys Phoenix Mills," *COP* (Aug. 1925): 19.

40. Carpenter and Holdredge, "Cottonseed-Oil Industry," 354; *Investigation of the Cottonseed Industry,* pt. 13, summary, xv, 15719–23.

41. *Report of the Federal Trade Commission,* pt. 13, summary, 15735–36.

42. *Report of the Federal Trade Commission,* pt. 13, summary, 15724–31.

43. *Report of the Federal Trade Commission,* pt. 13, summary, 15732, 15735.

44. *Report of the Federal Trade Commission,* pt. 13, summary, viii–ix.

45. French, "Problems of the Oil Mill Superintendent," *COP* 7 (May 1923): 53; "Proceedings of the Interstate Cotton Seed Crushers' Association," *COP* 12 (June 1928): 70.

9. Competition and Cooperation
between the World Wars

1. "Address of John Aspegren," *COP* 3 (June 1919): 81.
2. Culbertson, "History of Cottonseed Crushing in Texas," 27; "Cotton Industry Official Survey," *COP* 15 (Jan. 1932): 27; Arthur R. Burns, *The Decline of Competition* (New York: Columbia Univ. Press, 1936), 507.
3. *Report of the Federal Trade Commission,* pt. 9, Okla., 10776–77.
4. Thomas S. Kenan Jr., Atlanta Cotton Oil Co., to Herbert Hoover, 17 Nov. 1917, RG 4, NA; *Report of the Federal Trade Commission,* pt. 3, Ga., 965, 1077; pt. 5, N.C., 3821; pt. 11, Ark., 13413–14; Memorandum from M. J. Harron, NRA Legal Division, to Blackwell Smith, NRA Legal Division, 18 Oct. 1933, RG 9, NA.
5. Arthur Jerome Eddy, *The New Competition* (New York: D. Appleton, 1912); H. R. Tosdal, "Open Price Associations," *American Economic Review* 7 (June 1917): 331–52; Gabriel Kolko, *The Triumph of Conservatism* (New York: Free Press of Glencoe, 1963), 63, 174–75, 180–81, 267; Samuel Haber, *Efficiency and Uplift* (Chicago: Univ. of Chicago Press, 1964), 72; Robert F. Himmelberg, *The Origins of the National Recovery Administration* (New York: Fordham Univ. Press, 1976); Dupree, *Science in the Federal Government,* 338–39.
6. Moloney, "Half Century of Progress," 16, 23–25; Galambos, *Competition & Cooperation,* 55.
7. "Open Competition Upheld," *COP* 5 (Jan. 1922): 24; "Proceedings of the Interstate Cotton Seed Crushers' Association, 1922," *COP* 5 (July 1922): 84; Himmelberg, *Origins of the National Recovery Administration,* 16–21, 26–40; M. Browning Carrott, "The Supreme Court and American Trade Associations, 1921–1925," *Business History Review* 44 (Autumn 1970): 320–38; "Outline of New Administration Plans," *COP* 9 (Oct. 1925): 17.
8. *Report of the Federal Trade Commission,* pt. 13, summary, 15783–94; Burns, *Decline of Competition,* 52.
9. Wrenn, "Cottonseed Price-Fixing in Eastern North Carolina," 435–37.
10. *Report of the Federal Trade Commission,* pt. 8, Tex., 8797; pt. 13, summary, xi–xii
11. Himmelberg, *Origins of the National Recovery Administration,* 10; "State Secretaries' Letters," *COP* 5 (July 1921): 19; "Monthly Letter of President Kahn," *COP* 6 (Sept. 1922): 17; Burns, *Decline of Competition,* 47–48.
12. "Report of Uniform Cost Accountancy Committee," *COP* 7 (May 1923): 45; "Report of Committee on Uniform Cost Accountancy," *COP* 8 (June 1924): 35; Clark, "Cottonseed Products Industry," 170–91; K. Y. Siddall, "Determining the Purchase Price of Cottonseed," *National Association of Cost Accountants* 16 (15 Dec. 1934): 421–33.
13. "Executive Secretary's New Year Message," *COP* 14 (Jan. 1931): 17–18; G. S. Meloy, head of Cottonseed Grading and Market News, Agricultural Marketing Service, Dept. of Agriculture, "The Evolution of Cottonseed Marketing Practices," Address, Ginners Conference, Stoneville, Miss., June 3, 1941, NAL; Dept. of Agriculture, Production and Marketing Administra-

tion, Cotton Branch, Agriculture Information Bulletin No. 39, "The Grading of Cottonseed," Washington, D.C., 1951.

14. *Report of the Federal Trade Commission,* pt. 3, Ga., 1789; "Editorial, Buying Seed on Analysis," *COP* 12 (Oct. 1928): 23.
15. *Report of the Federal Trade Commission,* pt. 3, Ga., 1570–71; pt. 6, S.C., 5403; pt. 7, Miss., 7453; pt. 8, Tex., 8840, 9420–38; pt. 10, La., 12365; pt. 11, Ark., 13525–26; pt. 12, Tenn., 14381.
16. *Report of the Federal Trade Commission,* pt. 7, Miss., 6948, 6995, 7020, 7204, 7210; pt. 10, La., 11999; pt. 11, Ark., 13531, 13615.
17. *Report of the Federal Trade Commission,* pt. 3, Ga., 1638; pt. 5, N.C., 3516; pt. 11, Ark., 12903, 13502; pt. 12, Tenn., 14482, 15055; Moloney, "Marketing of Cottonseed," 5.
18. *Report of the Federal Trade Commission,* pt. 3, Ga., 1250, 1253; pt. 5, N.C., 3513, 3521.
19. "Editorial, Time to Halt and Take Counsel Together," *COP* 14 (Oct. 1930): 24; "Cottonseed Crushers to Seek More Harmonious Relations with Planters," *OPD* 119 (25 May 1931): 17; Dept. of Agriculture, "Grading of Cottonseed," 33.
20. "Editorial," *COP* 11 (Nov. 1927): 17–18; Himmelberg, *Origins of the National Recovery Administration,* 51.
21. *Report of the Federal Trade Commission,* pt. 3, Ga., 1787; pt. 6, S.C., 4900.
22. *Cottonseed Industry, Letter from the Chairman of the Federal Trade Commission Transmitting a Report of the Federal Trade Commission on the Cottonseed Industry, Submitted in Pursuance of House Resolution No. 439, Sixty-Ninth Congress* (Washington, D.C., 1928), 16; "Proposed Code of Business Conduct Principles," *COP* 11 (Apr. 1928): 17–18.
23. *Report of the Federal Trade Commission,* pt. 4, Ala., 2253–54; pt. 5, N.C., 3488; pt. 7, Miss., 6923, 6959, 7897.
24. *Report of the Federal Trade Commission,* pt. 4, Ala., 2746–47, 2816–17; pt. 7, Miss., 6882; pt. 10, La., 11781.
25. "National Association President W. A. Sherman Sends New Year's Greetings to the Industry," *COP* 14 (Jan. 1931): 23.
26. Interstate Commerce Commission, Rate Structure Investigation, No. 17000, "Cottonseed, Its Products and Related Articles," by John T. Money and George Esch (Washington, D.C., 1931), 42, 253; "Cottonseed Milling-In-Transit Recommended," *COP* 15 (July 1931): 7, "Editorial," *COP* 15 (July 1931): 15; *Report of the Federal Trade Commission,* pt. 3, Ga., 1052; pt. 5, N.C., 3829; pt. 7, Miss., 6298, 6300–301, 6305, 6309, 6692, 6808, 6938, 7214, 7327, 7341; pt. 8, Tex., 8219, 8255, 8371, 8509; pt. 10, La., 11798, 11926, 12009, 12267; Siddall, "Determining the Purchase Price of Cottonseed," 426; Moloney, "Marketing of Cottonseed," 9.
27. *Report of the Federal Trade Commission,* pt. 7, Miss., 6793.
28. H. C. Brown, district manager, Southern Cotton Oil Co., Augusta, Ga., to J. L. Benton., USFA, 28 Jan. 1918, RG 4, NA; "Letter from Christie Benet," *COP* 12 (May 1928): 19; "Editorial, The Time for United Action Has Arrived," *COP* 12 (May 1928): 34; *Report of the Federal Trade Commission,*

pt. 4, Ala., 2257, 2348; pt. 6, S.C., 4935; pt. 8, Tex., 8690; Moloney, "Marketing of Cottonseed," 10.

29. "Proceedings of the Interstate Cotton Seed Crushers' Association, 1928," *COP* 12 (June 1928): 22, 28, 37–40, 63; "Code of Business Ethics Adopted at Trade Practice Conference," *COP* 12 (Aug. 1928): 21–22.

30. Jasspon, "What Is Wrong with the Cotton Oil Industry?" 119; *Facts About a Great Exclusively Southern Industry—Cottonseed,* 10.

31. *Report of the Federal Trade Commission,* pt. 7, Miss., 6673; pt. 13, summary, 15767, 15769.

32. "Code of Business Ethics Adopted at Trade Practice Conference," *COP* 12 (Aug. 1928): 21–23; "Editorial," *COP* 12 (Aug. 1928): 27; "Putting the New Code Into Practice," *COP* 12 (Sept. 1928): 19–20; *Report of the Federal Trade Commission,* pt. 7, Miss., 7458.

33. "New Year Message from President Byram," *COP* 12 (Jan. 1929): 17; "Present Problems of the Oil Mill Industry," *COP* 13 (May 1929): 19; "Proceedings of the Interstate Cotton Seed Crushers' Association, 1929," *COP* 13 (June 1929): 20, 24; "Editorial, Operations Under the Code," *COP* 13 (Oct. 1929): 25; "Editorial, The Oil Mill Act of Emancipation," *COP* 13 (Mar. 1930): 25; "Cottonseed Industry's Latest AAA-NRA Code Hearing," *COP* 18 (Oct. 1934): 12; *Report of the Federal Trade Commission,* pt. 7, Miss., 6517, 6542; pt. 8, Tex., 8105, 8159, 8252, 8267, 8284, 8392–93, 8454; pt. 9, Okla., 10842, 10972, 11170; pt. 10, La., 11872, 12053, 12057–58; pt. 11, Ark., 12543, 12727, 13261, 13326.

34. Himmelberg, *Origins of the National Recovery Administration,* 75–76; Moloney, "Half Century of Progress," 16, 24–25; *Report of the Federal Trade Commission,* pt. 3, Ga., 945; pt. 8, Tex., 8005; pt. 9, Okla., 10807, 11464–65; pt. 11, Ark., 12811; pt. 13, summary, 15739–42.

35. "State Groups of National Association Members Organize," *COP* 13 (Sept. 1929): 17–18; "Code of Trade Practices in Operation," *COP* 13 (Oct. 1929): 19.

36. "General Counsel Benet Reviews Situation to Date," *COP* 13 (Dec. 1929): 17–18; *Report of the Federal Trade Commission,* pt. 8, Tex., 8419.

37. *Report of the Federal Trade Commission,* pt. 3, Ga., 1205, 1246; pt. 4, Ala., 2615, 2769, 2858–59; pt. 7, Miss., 6242, 6295, 6297, 6329, 6517, 6662, 6741, 6743, 6865, 7007, 7273, 7894–95; "Tonnage Complex—Greed for Tonnage," *COP* 16 (Mar. 1933): 16–17.

38. "General Counsel Benet Vigorously Refutes the Charges of Law Violation by Cottonseed Industry," *COP* 13 (Nov. 1929): 17; "Proceedings of the National Cottonseed Products Association, 1930," *COP* 14 (June 1930): 23; *Report of the Federal Trade Commission,* Preliminary Report, 6 Jan. 1930, 1–2; pt. 4, Ala., 2308, 2407, 2448; pt. 7. Miss., 7920.

39. Himmelberg, *Origins of the National Recovery Administration,* 90, 92–93, 96; "Address of General Counsel Christie Benet," *COP* 13 (June 1929): 24; "Editorial, National Convention Faces Serious Problems," *COP* 15 (May 1931): 25; "Proceedings of the National Cottonseed Products Association, 1931," *COP* 15 (June 1931): 26; "National Association Plans for New Season," *COP* 15 (Aug. 1931): 8; "Editorial," *COP* 15 (Feb. 1932): 22.

40. Memorandum from Sidney C. Sufrin, NRA Labor Advisory Board, to J. D. Kennedy, 9 July 1934; Memorandum on the Complaint of the Federal Trade Commission against the National Cottonseed Products Association from T. O. Asbury, vice president, Southern Cotton Oil Co., 31 July 1934; "For Release to the Newspapers of Friday Morning" (by the National Cottonseed Products Association), 17 Aug. 1934, RG 9, NA; "Answer of National Cottonseed Products Association to the Complaint of the Federal Trade Commission, 15 August 1934," *COP* 18 (Aug. 1934): 11–21; H. A. Wallace, secy. of agriculture, to Hon. Ewin L. Davis, chairman, Federal Trade Commission, 23 Jan. 1935, RG 145, Agricultural Stabilization and Conservation Service, National Archives (hereafter cited as RG 145, NA).

41. "Proceedings of the National Cottonseed Products Association, 1930," *COP* 14 (June 1930): 19; "It Will Lead to Bloodshed," *COP* 15 (Oct. 1931): 8; "Editorial, The Economics of the Oil Mill Situation," *COP* 15 (Nov. 1931): 18; "Cottonseed Oil Foods Institute," *COP* 16 (Sept. 1932): 13; E. C. McInnis, "The Cotton Oil Industry and the South," *COP* 16 (Oct. 1932): 29; "Economic Survey Completed for Five Years," *COP* 13 (Jan. 1933): 13; *Report of the Federal Trade Commission,* pt. 10, La., 12390; pt. 11, Ark., 13522; pt. 12, Tenn., 14917.

42. "Proceedings of the National Cottonseed Products Association, 1933," *COP* 17 (June 1933): 21; "Marketing Agreement Submitted to Washington," *COP* 17 (July 1933): 9–12.

43. Himmelberg, *Origins of the National Recovery Administration,* 1, 4, 181–212; William E. Leuchtenburg, *Franklin D. Roosevelt and the New Deal,* (New York: Harper & Row, 1963), 55–58.

44. Cotton Seed Conference, 13 June 1933; Informal Conference, Cottonseed Industry, 3 July 1933; Informal Conference of Representatives of National Cottonseed Products Association, Inc., 6 July 1933; Conference with Representatives of the Federal Trade Commission in Regard to the Proposed Cottonseed Agreement and Code and the Relation Thereof to the Complaints Brought by the Federal Trade Commission Against the Industries, 15 July 1933; "Code of Fair Competition for the Cottonseed Crushing Industry," 3 Aug. 1933; Informal Conference, The Cotton Industry, 11 Aug. 1933, RG 9, NA.

45. "The Public Hearing on Cottonseed Code," *COP* 17 (Oct. 1933): 11–15.

46. "Cottonseed Code Hearing Develops Needed Change," *OPD* 124 (25 Sept. 1933): 49; Benedict, *Farm Policies of the United States,* 304.

47. W. H. Jasspon, Perkins Cotton Oil Mill, Memphis, to Stanley Posner, Compliance Board, NRA, 18 Nov. 1933; B. J. Gantt, Buckeye Cotton Oil Co., Cincinnati, to Harry A. Lindsay, deputy administrator, NRA, 1 Dec. 1933; numerous telegrams from farmers, oil millers, and other businessmen to W. E. Hudman, president, Screven Oil Mill, Silvania, Ga., and representative of small town cottonseed-oil mills of the Southeast, 11 Oct. 1933; W. E. Hudman to M. H. Pettit, NRA deputy administrator, 20 Sept. 1933; E. J. Broughton, Eastern Cotton Oil Co., Hertford, N.C., to Edward F. McGrady, asst. secy. of labor, 21 Oct. 1933; D. S. Murph, chief, Cotton

Processing and Marketing Section, USDA to M. H. Pettit, 26 Oct. 1933, RG 9, NA; *Report of the Federal Trade Commission,* pt. 4, Ala., 2865.

48. A. L. Durand, Chickasha [Okla.] Cotton Oil Co., to C. H. Cunningham, NRA asst. deputy administrator, 4 Dec. 1933; Memorandum from H. B. Lindsay, NRA Division for AAA Codes, to C. H. Cunningham, 14 Nov. 1933; "Code of Labor Provisions for the Cottonseed Crushing Industry" (penciled in, "Text used at supplementary hearing, 11-29-33"), RG 9, NA; "Proceedings of the National Cottonseed Products Association, 1934," *COP* 18 (June 1934): 62.

49. J. V. Champion and J. H. Leroy Sr., receivers for Eastern Cotton Oil Co. [Norfolk, Va.], to H. B. Lindsay, deputy, NRA Legal Division, 5 Dec. 1933; Farmers Cotton Oil Co., Wilson, N.C., to H. B. Lindsay, 5 Dec. 1933; [Ga. senator] Walter F. George to H. B. Lindsay, 4, 6 Dec. 1933; Freemont [N.C.] Oil Mill Co. to [N.C. senator] Hon. Josiah Bailey, 5 Dec. 1933; Central Oil & Fertz. Co., Clayton, N.C., to Senator Josiah Bailey, 5 Dec. 1933; Consolidated Cotton Oil Co., Statesville, N.C., to Senator Josiah Bailey, 5 Dec. 1933; B. J. Gantt, Buckeye Cotton Oil Co., Cincinnati, to Harry A. Lindsay, Industrial Adviser on Cottonseed Crushing Code, 1 Dec. 1933; R. F. Crow, Houston, to L. E. Kline, asst. deputy director, NRA, 13 Aug. 1934, RG 9, NA; "Editorial, Public Hearing on Ginners' and Oil Mill Codes," *COP* 17 (Sept. 1933): 11; "Editorial, AAA and NRA Control Not Yet But Soon," *COP* 17 (Dec. 1933): 5; "Oil Millers Marketing Agreement Prospects," *COP* 17 (Jan. 1934): 9–12; Burns, *Decline of Competition,* 465.

50. G. S. Meloy, Dept. of Agriculture, to F. A. Stewart, vice president, San Joaquin [Calif.] Cotton Oil Co., 15 Dec. 1933, RG 145, NA.

51. *Report of the Federal Trade Commission,* pt. 8, Tex., 8689; Burns, *Decline of Competition,* 500.

52. *Report of the Federal Trade Commission,* pt. 3, Ga., 1202; pt. 5, N.C., 3752; pt. 7, Miss., 7289; pt. 9, Okla., 11089, 11091; pt. 10, La., 11781.

53. Dept. of Agriculture, Agricultural Adjustment Administration, "Proposed Marketing Agreement for the Cotton Seed Crushing Industry, 4 Nov. 1933," NAL.

54. John W. O'Leary, president, Machinery and Allied Products Institute, to Hon. Henry W. Wallace, 10 Nov. 1933; D. S. Murph, chief, Cotton Processing and Marketing Section, to C. B. Upton, vice president, French Oil Mill Machinery Co., 27 Dec. 1933; Ralph C. Roudebush, Memphis, to Hon. K. D. McKellar [Tenn. senator], 17 Jan. 1934; C. B. L. Arner, senior economic expert, Cotton Processing and Marketing Section, AAA, to Hon. Kenneth McKellar, 22 Jan. 1934; Hugh M. Brinkley, Bruins, Ark., representing East Arkansas Cotton Planters, to D. S. Murph, 8 Jan. 1934; F. A. Stewart, San Joaquin [Calif.] Cotton Oil Co., to James A. Kennedy, deputy administrator, AAA, 4 Dec. 1933, RG 145, NA.

55. "Editorial," *COP* 17 (Jan. 1934): 7; Kline, "Partial History of the Proposed Code of Fair Competition"; Saloutos, *American Farmer and the New Deal,* 58–64, 80, 87–90.

56. "Editorial, "Industry Still in Air after Latest Code Conference," *COP* 17

(Mar. 1934): 5–7; "Committee Considering Latest Draft of Code," *COP* 18
(Apr. 1934): 7–8; "Address of Dr. George B. L. Arner of AAA," *COP* 18
(June 1934): 50–51; C. C. Farrington, asst. chief, Cotton Processing and
Marketing Section, to Fred W. Burruss, editor, *Oil Miller & Cotton Ginner,*
13 Feb. 1934; C. A. Cobb, chief, Cotton Production Section, AAA, to Ernest
E. Scholl, acting director, Extension Service, Oklahoma A&M College, 9
Mar. 1934; Lawrence Myers, acting in charge, Cotton Processing and Marketing Section, to R. F. Crow, Houston, South Texas Cotton Oil Co. (head
of NCPA code committee), 2 Apr. 1934; G. B. L. Arner, senior economic
expert, Cotton Processing and Marketing Section, to R. F. Crow, 2 May
1934, RG 145, NA.

57. "Address of President J. Ross Richardson" [Anderson, Clayton Co.], *COP* 18
(June 1934): 12.

58. "Conference with Representatives of the Federal Trade Commission in Re-
gard to the Proposed Cottonseed Agreement and Code and the Relation
Thereof to the Complaints Brought by the Federal Trade Commission
Against the Industries, 15 July 1933," RG 9, NA; Memorandum from
Jerome N. Frank, General Counsel, AAA, to Mr. [C. C.] Davis, 11 Apr. 1934,
RG 145, NA; "Federal Trade Commission Threw a Bomb," *COP* 18 (June
1934): 95–97, 99; "Cottonseed Crushers Lose F. T. C. Code," *OPD* 123 (22
May 1933): 17.

59. M. L. Wilson to Hon. Harold M. Stephens, asst. attorney general, 25 July
1934; H. A. Wallace to Attorney General, 8 Sept. 1934, RG 145, NA.

60. Homer Cummings, attorney general, to Hon. Henry A. Wallace, 19 Dec.
1934; Lawrence Myers, acting chief, Cotton Processing, and Marketing Section, Memorandum to the Administrator [C. C. Davis], 4 Feb. 1935, RG 145,
NA. Also see this chapter, note 41.

61. Memorandum from Griffin Barry to Richard Eldridge, 25 Oct. 1934, RG 9,
NA; "Cottonseed Industry's Latest AAA-NRA Code Hearing," *COP* 18 (Oct.
1934): 7–12; "Editorial, the Cottonseed Code Situation to Date," *COP* 18
(Nov. 1934): 13; "Anticipating Promulgation of Code," *COP* 18 (Feb. 1935):
27; Lawrence Myers, Cotton Processing and Marketing Section, to Hon.
Marvin Jones, chairman, House Committee on Agriculture, 2 Oct. 1934;
Homer D. Wade, exec. secy., Texas Co-operative Council and Texas Cooperative Ginners' Ass'n, and C. K. Bullard, attorney, Texas Cotton Cooperative Ass'n and Texas Cotton Growers Gin Company, To: National
Recovery Administration, and Hon. Henry A. Wallace, n.d. (stamped received 11 Oct. 1934); H. A. Wallace to Hon. Garland S. Ferguson Jr., chairman, Federal Trade Commission, 23 Nov. 1934; Lawrence Myers, acting
chief, Cotton Processing and Marketing Section, to R. F. Crow, Houston,
chairman, Code Committee, 4 Dec. 1934, RG 145, NA; "Proposed Code of
Fair Competition for the Cottonseed Crushing Industry," 12 Sept. 1934, RG
9, NA.

62. Kline, "Partial History of the Proposed Code of Fair Competition"; "Report
of Code Committee," *COP* 19 (June 1935): 59; "Editorial, Again the Problem of Self-Governing Industries," *COP* 19 (June 1935): 73; Cover, *COP* 19
(July 1935).

63. "Daily Cottonseed Price Reports Proposed," *COP* 7 (Mar. 1924): 26; "Address of General Counsel," *COP* 14 (June 1930): 24–25; "Cottonseed Price Reporting," *COP* 14 (July 1930): 39; "Executive Secretary's New Year Message," *COP* 14 (Jan. 1931): 18; "Pass the Jones Bill for Cottonseed Grading," *COP* 15 (Dec. 31, 1931): 18; "Cottonseed Industry's Latest AAA-NRA Code Hearing," *COP* 18 (Oct. 1934): 8; "Memorandum on the Complaint of the Federal Trade Commission against the National Cottonseed Products Association, 31 July 1934," RG 9, NA.

64. "Report of the President," *C&COP* 37 (1–3 June 1936): 4; L. T. Stone, "What Does the Trade Think of Seed Grading?" *C&COP* 39 (12 Mar. 1938): 3; "Address of G. S. Meloy," *C&COP* 39 (16–18 May 1938): 33–34; "83 Per Cent of All Mills in Seven States to Buy Seed on Grade This Season," *C&COP* 39 (10 Sept. 1938): 6; "H. R. 8642 . . . The Seed Grading Bill," *C&COP* 41 (13 Apr. 1940): 7; "Proceedings of the National Cottonseed Products Association, 1940," *C&COP* 41 (13–14 May 1940): 22; Guy S. Meloy, "Grading and Evaluation of Cottonseed," in Bailey, *Cottonseed and Cottonseed Products,* 520, 522–23.

65. Burns, *Decline of Competition,* 518; Dept. of Agriculture, "Grading of Cottonseed," 5; Dept. of Agriculture, Production and Marketing Administration, "Further Development in Cotton Standardization and Related Activities," Service and Regulatory Announcement No. 165, (Washington, D.C., 1953), 23, FGT.

10. End of the Hydraulic Era

1. Otto Wilson, "Government Policies Affect Vegetable-Oil Output," *Industrial and Engineering Chemistry* 12 (20 Nov. 1934): 406–7; Haynes, *Cellulose,* 286.

2. Leuchtenburg, *Franklin D. Roosevelt and the New Deal,* 73–75, 170–72, 255–56; Tindall, *Emergence of the New South,* 393–94, 396, 404–7; Wayne D. Rasmussen and Gladys L. Baker, *The Department of Agriculture* (New York: Praeger, 1972), 23–30.

3. *Commodity Year Book,* 207; Dept. of Agriculture, *Study of Practices Affecting the Use of Major Vegetable Oils,* 5.

4. Saloutos, *American Farmer and the New Deal,* 257–59; C. E. Lund, "These Versatile Fats and Oils," *C&COP* 40 (13 May 1939): 7, 25; Jack Blackwell, "Factors Causing Declines in Cottonseed Value," *C&COP* 40 (19 Aug. 1939): 7; Moloney, "Cottonseed Oil—A Typical American Industry," 238.

5. T. H. Gregory, "Lets Face Our Problems Squarely," *C&COP* 41 (27 Apr. 1940): 11; "Report of the President," *C&COP* 41 (13–14 May 1940): 4–5; "Farm Chemurgy," *Newsweek* 13 (10 Apr. 1939): 45; Moloney, "Trends in the Industrial Use," 75; Dept. of Agriculture, *Study of Practices Affecting the Use of Major Vegetable Oils,* summary, n.p.; Harry D. Fornari, "The Big Change: Cotton to Soybeans," *Agricultural History* 53 (Jan. 1979): 245–53.

6. Dept. of Agriculture, Agricultural Marketing Service, Marketing Research Report No. 58, "Processing the Three Major Oil Seeds" (Washington, D.C., 1954), 15; "The Soybean Takes Root—Grows in Importance," *C&COP* 40 (5

Aug. 1939): 6; Hopkins, "Cotton's Future as a Leading Source of Essential Fat," 95; Charles E. Lund, "Production and Consumption of Cottonseed and Cottonseed Products," in Bailey, *Cottonseed and Cottonseed Products,* 63.

7. *Commodity Year Book, 1941,* 207.

8. H. C. Pirrung, "Butterine, Its Origin, History and Laws from a Manufacturer's Viewpoint of Twenty-five Years Experience," *Bulletin 13* (Interstate Cotton Seed Crushers' Association, Jan. 1911): 8–15; S. F. Riepma, *The Story of Margarine* (Washington, D.C.: Public Affairs Press, 1970), 113–16, 120–23; R. Alton Lee, *A History of Regulatory Taxation* (Lexington: Univ. Press of Kentucky, 1973), 14, 18, 22, 27; "Big Strides in Oleo Production," *COP* 3 (Sept. 1919): 34.

9. "Editorial, Margarine Wins Victory in Northwest," *COP* 8 (Dec. 1924): 24–25; "The Oil Mills' Competitive Products," *COP* 8 (Jan. 1925): 36; "Editorial," *COP* 8 (Mar. 1925): 25; "Editorial, Cotton Oil's Progress in the Country's Food Program," *COP* 17 (May 1933): 8–10; "Address by C. O. Moser," *COP* 19 (June 1935): 22; A. L. Ward, "Margarine—A Major Outlet for Southern Vegetable Fats and Oils," *Manufacturers' Record* 106 (Apr. 1937): 42, 69–70.

10. "Cottonseed Slump Hurts South," *Business Week,* 6 Nov. 1937, 45; "Conspicuously Successful Texas Convention," *COP* 16 (July 1932): 11; "New Oils and Fats Promotional Organization," *COP* 17 (Nov. 1933): 11; "More 100% Cotton Oil Margarine," *COP* 17 (Nov. 1933): 13; "One Hundred Per Cent Domestic Oil Margarine," *COP* 17 (Jan. 1934): 6; "Address by C. O. Moser," *COP* 19 (June 1935): 21; "Lets Face Our Problems Squarely," *C&COP* 41 (27 Apr. 1940): 26; Benedict, *Farm Policies of the United States,* 380; Weber, "Legislative Weapons in Inter-industry Competition," 74; Riepma, *Story of Margarine,* 124.

11. Dept. of Agriculture, "Cottonseed Oil Futures Market," 6; N. R. Whitney, "Domestic Markets for Cottonseed and Cottonseed Products," in *Proceedings of the Ninth Cotton Research Congress* (n.p.: Statewide Cotton Committee of Texas, 1948), 52; Dept. of Agriculture, *Study of Practices Affecting the Use of Major Vegetable Oils,* 62.

12. Ward, "Cottonseed—'Farm Cinderella,'" 32–33; A. L. Ward, "A Brief Survey of Recent Trends Influencing the Use of Cottonseed Products," in *Proceedings of the Second Cotton Research Congress* (n.p.: Statewide Cotton Committee of Texas, 1941), 51; S. M. Harmon, "Cottonseed Industry 1939," *Manufacturers' Record* 109 (Jan. 1940): 46; Tindall, *Emergence of the New South,* 124–25; Range, *Century of Georgia Agriculture,* 198–207; Dept. of Agriculture, *Study of Practices Affecting the Use of Major Vegetable Oils,* 28.

13. A. Cecil Wamble, "New Opportunities Through Research," *Proceedings of the Seventh Cotton Research Congress* (n.p.: Statewide Cotton Committee of Texas), 87–88.

14. Rasmussen and Baker, *Department of Agriculture,* 29–30; "Wesson," 109; Harmon, "Cottonseed Industry 1939," 46.

15. L. T. Stone, "The Bill of the Boll Weevil," *C&COP* 41 (6 Jan. 1940): 5; "Report of the President," *C&COP* 41 (13–14 May 1940): 4–5; "Wanted: Cot-

tonseed," *Newsweek* 13 (22 May 1939): 46; Wamble, "New Opportunities Through Research," 84–85; Dept. of Agriculture, press release, "Pricing-Marketing-Processing Program for Four Oil Crops Announced by USDA," 28 Aug. 1942, Notebook, Cottonseed Program Origin, FGT; Dept. of Labor, "Economic Factors Bearing on the Establishment of Minimum Wages in the Cottonseed and Peanut Crushing Industry," 11–14, NAL.

16. Dept. of Agriculture, *Study of Practices Affecting the Use of Major Vegetable Oils,* 4–6.

17. Talk by Ralph S. Trigg, president of the Commodity Credit Corporation, at a meeting of the Texas Cotton Ginners' Association, Dallas, 3 Apr. 1950, 2, FGT.

18. Dept. of Agriculture, Commodity Credit Corporation, "1949—Crop Cottonseed Purchase and Loan Program, June 1951," 1–2, FGT.

19. Latham White to Walter W. Sikes, 11 Sept. 1951, "Brief Comparison of 1949 and 1950 Cottonseed Programs," 30 Jan. 1953, FGT.

20. National Cottonseed Products Association News Letter, No. 337, 30 Jan. 1953, No. 372, 15 Sept. 1954; "The Impact of Cottonseed Support Programs Upon Our Industry," remarks of C. J. Orr, Anderson, Clayton & Co., to the Mississippi Cottonseed Crushers Association, 16 June 1955; Dept. of Agriculture, "Appraisal of 1958 Crop Cottonseed Support Operations," 19 July 1959 [date added], FGT.

21. H. L. Durand, Chickasha [Okla.] Cotton Oil Co. to C. H. Cunningham, deputy asst. administrator, NRA, 4 Dec. 1933, RG 9, NA.

22. Resolution adopted at a joint meeting of North and South Carolina cottonseed crushers, *Proceedings of the Joint North and South Carolina Crushers' Association, June 21–22, 1937,* N.C. Dept. of Agriculture, Box 47, North Carolina Archives, Raleigh; John F. Moloney, "Some Effects of the Federal Fair Labor Standards Act upon Southern Industry," *Southern Economic Journal* 9 (1942): 15; "Wage and Hour Bill," *C&COP* 39 (25 June 1938): 3–4.

23. Moloney, "Some Effects of the Federal Fair Labor Standards Act," 17.

24. Wright, *Old South, New South,* 236; Moloney, "Some Effects of the Federal Fair Labor Standards Act," 19–20.

25. Moloney, "Trends in the Industrial Use," 72–73; "Wesson," 104.

26. Moloney, "Some Effects of the Federal Fair Labor Standards Act," 20; Markley and Lynch, "Technology of the Cottonseed Crushing Industry," 212–16, 224; Dept. of Agriculture, "Cottonseed Oil Mill Characteristics and Marketing Practices," 1; Dept. of Agriculture, Production and Marketing Administration, Fats and Oils Branch, "Marketing and Processing Costs of Cottonseed-Oil Mills in the Postwar Period, 1946–47 to 1950–51," by Calvin C. Spilsbury (Washington, D.C., 1952).

27. Wamble, "New Opportunities Through Research," 88; Dept. of Agriculture, Marketing Research Report No. 218, "Labor and Power Utilization at Cottonseed Oil Mills," by Julia A. Mitchell, Donald Jackson, and C. B. Gilliland (Washington, D.C., 1958), 1, 3, 67.

28. Dept. of Agriculture, *Study of Practices Affecting the Use of Major Vegetable Oils,* 6.

29. Merle Prunty Jr., "Recent Quantitative Changes in the Cotton Regions of the Southeastern States," *Economic Geography* 27 (July 1951): 189–208; Dept. of Agriculture, *Study of Practices Affecting the Use of Major Vegetable Oils,* 6–7, 27, 74; Rosenberg, *Technology and American Economic Growth,* 136–38.

30. Dept. of Agriculture, *Study of Practices Affecting the Use of Major Vegetable Oils,* 6, 13; Saloutos, *American Farmer and the New Deal,* 7; Benedict, *Farm Policies of the United States,* 237; *Report of the Federal Trade Commission,* pt. 5, N.C., 3829; *Commodity Yearbook, 1941,* 208; G. S. Meloy, "The Importance of Cottonseed Grading," *C&COP* 47 (24 Aug. 1946): 5; Dept. of Agriculture, "Farm-To-Mill Margins for Cottonseed and Cottonseed Products in Tennessee, Sept. 1946–July 1950," by A. R. Sabin, *Agricultural Economist* (1951): 5, NAL.

31. "Overcapacity Ruins the Profits," *Food Industries* 4 (Mar. 1932): 103; "Major Problems in Oil Mill Plant Efficiency," *COP* 16 (Apr. 1933): 7; Dept. of Agriculture, Agricultural Research Service, "Cottonseed Drying and Storage at Cotton Gins," Technical Bulletin No. 1262 (Washington, D.C., 1962), 6, 71–72; Dept. of Agriculture, Agricultural Research Service, "Cottonseed Handling at Gins," Production Research Report No. 66 (Washington, D.C., 1963), 19; Wamble, "New Opportunities Through Research," 86.

32. Dept. of Agriculture, *Study of Practices Affecting the Use of Major Vegetable Oils,* 13–14; Harris, "Solvent Extraction of Cottonseed Oil," 9.

11. The New Industry and the New South

1. Weber, "Economic Development," 33; Marshall, "Cottonseed—Joint Products," 201; John Samuel Ezell, *The South Since 1865* (New York: Macmillan, 1963), 153; Wright, *Old South, New South,* 227.

2. Carlton, *Mill and Town in South Carolina,* 63.

3. M. C. McMillan, "Daniel Pratt, Ante-bellum Southern Industrialist" (Prattville, Ala.: provided by the Continental Eagle Corporation, 1993); William H. Phillips, "Making a Business of It: The Evolution of Southern Cotton Gin Patenting, 1831–90" (paper read at the Cotton Gin Symposium, Auburn Univ., 7 May 1993); Rother, "Looking Back Fifty Years," 92; Heitmann, *Modernization of the Louisiana Sugar Industry,* 44–47; Tilley, *Bright Tobacco Industry,* 1948), 496.

4. "Editorial, Actual Conditions of Oil Milling Revealed," *COP* 7 (Jan. 1924): 26.

5. Brent D. Glass, *The Textile Industry in North Carolina* (Raleigh: Division of Archives and History, North Carolina Dept. of Cultural Resources, 1992), 60–62, 83–84; Galambos, *Competition & Cooperation,* 18, 42, 71.

6. Woodman, *King Cotton and His Retainers,* 319–33; Cobb, *Industrialization and Southern Society,* 5–26; Wright, *Old South, New South,* 81; Albert W. Niemi, "Structural Shifts in Southern Manufacturing, 1849–1879," *Business History Review* 45 (Spring 1971): 79–84.

7. Weber, "Economic Development," 33, 97; T. A. Hughston, "The Economic Significance of Cottonseed to the Southwest and the Nation," in *Proceedings of the Fifth Cotton Research Congress* (n.p.: Statewide Cotton Commit-

tee of Texas, 1944), 105; T. A. Hughston, "Merchandising Cottonseed and Cottonseed Products," in *Proceedings of the Eighth Cotton Research Congress* (n.p.: Statewide Cotton Committee of Texas, 1947), 61; "Cottonseed Products Association Told to Avoid Further Price Rises," *OPD* 139 (2 June 1941): 47; Moloney, "Marketing of Cottonseed," 1.

8. Bureau of the Census, *Twelfth Census of the United States, 1900,* vol. 6, *Agriculture,* pt. 2, *Crops and Irrigation* (Washington, D.C., 1902), 416; Shue, "Cotton Oil Industry," 253; Thompson, *"The New South" in the New Economic Order,* 100; Dept. of Agriculture, "Cottonseed: Marketing Spreads," 5.

9. "Cotton Seed Oil Outlook," *OPD* 45 (8 Jan. 1894): 9; Chaney, "Cotton-Seed-Oil Industry," 455; *Report of the Federal Trade Commission,* pt. 7, Miss., 7102, 7077; pt. 11, Ark., 13513; *Proceedings of the Interstate Cotton Seed Crushers' Association,* 1910, 107; E. L. Johnson, "A Plea for the New Cereal, The Cotton-Seed," *Forum* 30 (1900): 53; Deasy, "Geography of the United States Cottonseed Oil Industry," 347.

10. Shue, "Cotton Oil Industry," 265; *Report of the Federal Trade Commission,* pt. 12, Tenn., 15055; H. L. Mitchell, *Mean Things Happening in This Land* (Montclair: Allanheld, Osmun, 1979), 21.

11. *The North Carolina Code of 1939,* section 2355, 1014; Hammond, *Cotton Industry,* 148; "Council Moves to Improve Fats and Oils Situation," *C&COP* 40 (5 Aug. 1939): 12; *Report of the Federal Trade Commission,* pt. 4, Ala., 2676; pt. 7, Miss., 7246, 7096; pt. 11, Ark., 13522, 13563, 13566; Works Progress Administration, Division of Social Research, Research Monograph 22, *The Plantation South, 1934–1937,* by William C. Holley, Ellen Winston, and T. J. Woofter Jr. (Washington, D.C., 1940; New York: Da Capo Press, 1971), 26; Cobb, *Most Southern Place on Earth,* 103; Leahy, "Cottonseed Processing Links Agriculture and Industry," 38.

12. Daniel, *Breaking the Land,* 166; Marshall, "Cottonseed—Joint Products," 225.

13. Interstate Commerce Commission, "Cottonseed, Its Products and Related Articles," 249–50; Lund, "Production and Consumption," 62; "Tenants' Acreages, Production and Earnings, 1933–1944," Box 18, Delta & Pine Land Company Records, MSU.

14. *Report of the Federal Trade Commission,* pt. 11, Ark., 13626; Works Progress Administration, *Plantation South, 1934–1937,* 39–40; "Cottonseed Exempt Under Seed Loans," *COP* 15 (July 1931): 9.

15. Marshall, "Cottonseed—Joint Products," 227; "Wesson," 104; Interstate Commerce Commission, "Cottonseed, Its Products and Related Articles," 250.

16. Aiken, "Evolution of Cotton Ginning," 220; testimony of ginner, Altus, Okla., 15 Jan. 1918; testimony of ginner, Mangum, Okla., 16 Jan. 1918, SPF/CCO; A. G. Fulkerson, gin manager, Anadarko [Okla.] Cotton Oil Co. to USFA, 11 Mar. 1918; Hiawatha Manufacturing Company, "Profit and Loss Account—Ginning Department, Season 1916–1917"; C. F. Sherrod Jr., Jackson, Miss., to Herbert Hoover, 7 June 1918; W. L. Carmack, Opelika,

Ala., to Geo. H. Denney, USFA, 6 June 1918, RG 4, NA; *Report of the Federal Trade Commission,* pt. 3, Ga., 1258, 1416; pt. 4, Ala., 2456, 2508, 2519; pt. 7, Miss., 7077, 7427–29; pt. 11, Ark., 13481, 13560; "Status of Ginners' Marketing Agreement," *COP* 17 (Oct. 1933): 8; The Agricultural Experiment Station of the N.C. State College of Agriculture and Engineering and N.C. Dept. of Agriculture, Technical Bulletin No. 71, "A Preliminary Study of Cotton Ginning Costs in North Carolina," June 1942, 5–6, DAT, CPL; Cox, *Cottonseed Crushing Industry of Texas,* 168; Moloney, "Economics of Cottonseed Crushing," 684; Moloney, "Marketing of Cottonseed," 9–10; Dept. of Agriculture, "Cotton and Cottonseed Marketing, Related Production Practices Among Negro Farmers in Red River Delta Area of Louisiana, 1951," by Frederick C. Temple (Washington, D.C., 1953), 50.

17. Hillyard, *New South* 310; testimony of W. L. Morgan, cottonseed buyer, Kasse, Tex., SNB1; *Report of the Federal Trade Commission,* pt. 5, N.C., 3469; pt. 7, Miss., 7193, 7201; pt. 10, La., 11989; "Cottonseed Slump Hurts South," 45; *C&COP* 40 (5 Aug. 1939): 12.

18. "Mississippi Valley Cottonseed Pool," *OPD* 27 (6 May 1885): 5; Culbertson, "History of Cottonseed Crushing in Texas," 26; *Report of the Federal Trade Commission,* pt. 8, Tex., 8330–54.

19. Bureau of the Census, *Sixteenth Census of the United States: 1940, Manufactures: 1939,* vol. 2, *Reports by Industries,* pt. 1, *Groups 1–10* (Washington, D.C., 1942), 758. Bureau of the Census, *Census of Manufactures: 1947,* vol. 2, *Statistics by Industry* (Washington, D.C., 1949), 429. Wright, *Old South, New South,* table 6.2, "Leading Southern Manufacturing Industries, 1880, 1910, and 1930," 160–62. Informal Conference, Cottonseed Industry, 3 July 1933, RG 9, NA.

20. Kenneth Weiher, "The Cotton Industry and Southern Urbanization, 1880–1930," *Explorations in Economic History* 14 (1977): 120–39; Woodman, *King Cotton and His Retainers,* 326–28; Rudolf Heberle, "The Mainsprings of Southern Urbanization," in *The Urban South,* ed. Rupert B. Vance and Nicholas Demereth (Chapel Hill: Univ. of North Carolina Press, 1954), 7–13; Perrett, *America in the Twenties,* 117.

21. Carlton, *Mill and Town in South Carolina,* 13, 21, 23; Tompkins, "Cotton-Seed Oil," 160; "Correspondent from Blacksburg, S.C.," *Manufacturers' Record* 27 (19 Apr. 1895): 188; *Report of the Federal Trade Commission,* pt. 3, Ga., 962.

22. "Wesson," 66, 68.

23. "Tentative Working Plan Co-operative Crushing," 15 Feb. 1918; W. W. Abbott, Louisville, Ga., to Dr. Geo. H. Denney, USFA, 6 Apr. 1918, RG 4, NA; Dept. of Agriculture, "Handling and Uses of Cotton," 374–75; Ransom, *Great Cottonseed Industry,* 52; National Cottonseed Products Association, "Economic Survey of the Cottonseed Products Industry"; Wilson, *History of Unilever* 2:248; *Report of the Federal Trade Commission,* pt. 12, Tenn., 14624–25.

24. WHJ [Jasspon], Memphis, to Stanley Posner, NRA Compliance Board, 18 Nov. 1933, RG 9, NA; Cox, *Cottonseed Crushing Industry of Texas,* 265;

Report of the Federal Trade Commission, pt. 5, N.C., 3830; pt. 7, Miss., 7614; pt. 8, Tex., 8378; pt. 9, Okla., 10981–83, 11114; Marshall, "Cotton-seed—Joint Products," 1272.

25. *Proceedings of the Cotton Seed Crushers' Association,* 1881, 16–17; Hammond, *Cotton Industry,* 135–36; Lamborn, *Cottonseed Products,* 221–23; George W. Scott files at the DeKalb County Historical Society, Decatur, Georgia; Bureau of the Census, *Thirteenth Census of the United States: 1910,* vol. 9, *Manufactures: 1909, Reports by States* (Washington, D.C., 1912), 215, 227, 1141; Bureau of the Census, *Thirteenth Census of the United States: 1910,* vol. 10, *Manufactures: 1909, Reports for Principal Industries* (Washington, D.C., 1912), 575; "Census Report," *Cotton Oil Magazine* 26 (Feb. 1916): 24; Thompson, *"The New South" in the New Economic Order,* 100; Rosser H. Taylor, "Fertilizers and Farming in the Southeast, 1840–1950," *North Carolina Historical Review* 30 (July 1953): 305–28, 30 (Oct. 1953): 483–523; Richard C. Sheridan, "Chemical Fertilizers in Southern Agriculture," *Agricultural History* 53 (Jan. 1979): 308–18.

26. *The Value of Cotton-Seed Products in the Feeding of Farm Animals;* "The Story of G. C. Street," *C&COP* 39 (23 July 1938): 5; John F. Moloney, "Markets for Cottonseed Cake and Meal," *C&COP* 39 (24 Sept. 1938), 3; Cox, *Cottonseed Crushing Industry of Texas,* 96–102, 203.

27. Weber and Alsberg, *American Vegetable-Shortening Industry,* 150; "Wesson," 106; Cox, *Cottonseed Crushing Industry of Texas,* 131.

Bibliography

Books

Andes, Louis Edgar. *Vegetable Fats and Oils*. London: Scott, Greenwood & Son, 1925.

Atkinson, Edward. *Cheap Cotton by Free Labor*. Boston: A. Williams, 1861.

Ayers, Edward L. *The Promise of the New South: Life after Reconstruction*. New York: Oxford Univ. Press, 1992.

Bailey, Alton E., ed. *Cottonseed and Cottonseed Products: Their Chemistry and Chemical Technology*. New York: Interscience Publishers, 1948.

Ballagh, James Curtis. *The South in the Building of the Nation,* vol 6. Richmond, Va.: Southern Historical Publication Society, 1909.

Baruch, Bernard M. *American Industry in the War: A Report of the War Industries Board*. New York: Prentice-Hall, 1941.

Bathe, Greville, and Dorothy Bathe. *Oliver Evans: A Chronicle of Early American Engineering*. Philadelphia: Historical Society of Pennsylvania, 1935; New York: Arno Press, 1972.

Benedict, Murray R. *Farm Policies of the United States, 1790–1950*. New York: Twentieth Century Fund, 1953; New York: Octagon Books, 1966.

Bishop, J. Leander. *A History of American Manufactures from 1608 to 1860*. 3 vols. Philadelphia: Edward Young, 1868; New York: August M. Kelley, 1966.

Brace, Harold W. *History of Seed Crushing in Great Britain*. London: Land Books, 1960.

Brannt, William T. *A Practical Treatise on Animal and Vegetable Fats and Oils*. 2 vols. Philadelphia: Henry Carey Baird, 1896.

Burkett, C. W., and C. H. Poe. *Cotton: Its Cultivation, Marketing, Manufacture, and the Problems of the Cotton World*. New York: Doubleday, Page, 1906.

Burns, Arthur R. *The Decline of Competition*. New York: Columbia Univ. Press, 1936.

Capital Changes Reporter. 6 vols. N. J.: Commerce Clearing House, 1985.

Carlton, David L. *Mill and Town in South Carolina, 1880–1920*. Baton Rouge: Louisiana State Univ. Press, 1982.

Chandler, Alfred Dupont, Jr. *The Visible Hand: The Managerial Revolution in American Business*. Cambridge: Belknap Press, Harvard Univ. Press, 1977.

Cist, Charles. *Sketches and Statistics of Cincinnati in 1859.* [Cincinnati: n.p., 1859?]

Clark, Victor S. *History of Manufactures in the United States.* 3 vols. Washington, D.C.: Carnegie Institute, 1929; New York: Peter Smith, 1949.

Clemen, Rudolf. *By-Products in the Packing Industry.* Chicago: Univ. of Chicago Press, 1927.

Cobb, James C. *Industrialization and Southern Society, 1877–1984.* Chicago: Dorsey Press, 1984.

———. *The Most Southern Place on Earth.* New York: Oxford Univ. Press, 1992.

Cochran, Thomas C. *Business in American Life: A History.* New York: McGraw-Hill, 1972.

Commodity Year Book, 1941. New York: Commodity Research Bureau, 1941.

Cox, A. B. *The Cottonseed Crushing Industry of Texas in Its National Setting.* Austin: Univ. of Texas Press, 1949.

Daniel, Pete. *Breaking the Land: The Transformation of Cotton, Tobacco, and Rice Cultures since 1880.* Urbana: Univ. of Illinois Press, 1985.

Dethloff, Henry C. *A History of the American Rice Industry, 1865–1985.* College Station: Texas A&M Univ. Press, 1988.

Drayton, John. *A View of South Carolina, as Respects Her Natural and Civil Concerns.* Charleston: W. P. Young, 1802.

Dupree, A. Hunter. *Science in the Federal Government: A History of Policies and Activities to 1940.* Cambridge: Belknap Press, Harvard Univ. Press, 1957.

Eastman, Whitney. *The History of the Linseed Oil Industry in the United States.* Minneapolis: T. S. Denison, 1968.

Eddy, Arthur Jerome. *The New Competition.* New York: D. Appleton, 1912.

Ezell, John Samuel. *The South Since 1865.* New York: Macmillan, 1963.

Fickle, James E. *The New South and the "New Competition": Trade Association Development in the Southern Pine Industry.* Urbana: for the Forest History Society by the Univ. of Illinois Press, 1980.

Galambos, Louis. *Competition & Cooperation: The Emergence of a National Trade Association.* Baltimore: John Hopkins Press, 1966.

Goodwyn, Lawrence. *Democratic Promise: The Populist Movement in America.* New York: Oxford Univ. Press, 1976.

Gottlieb, Peter. *Making Their Own Way: Southern Blacks' Migration to Pittsburgh, 1916–1930.* Urbana: Univ. of Illinois Press, 1987.

Green, Constance McLaughlin. *Eli Whitney and the Birth of American Technology.* Boston: Little, Brown, 1956.

Hamilton, Peter J. *Colonial Mobile.* 1897. Rpt. of 1910 rev. ed., Mobile, Ala.: First National Bank of Mobile, 1952.

Hammond, Matthew Brown. *The Cotton Industry: An Essay in American Economic History.* Ithaca, N.Y., 1897.

Hawk, Emory Q. *Economic History of the South.* New York: Prentice-Hall, 1934; Westport, Conn.: Greenwood Press, 1973.

Haynes, Williams. *American Chemical Industry.* 6 vols. New York: D. Van Nostrand, 1954.

———. *Cellulose: The Chemical that Grows.* New York: Southern Horizons, 1946; Garden City, N.Y.: Doubleday, 1953.

Heitmann, John Alfred. *The Modernization of the Louisiana Sugar Industry, 1830–1910*. Baton Rouge: Louisiana State Univ. Press, 1987.

Hillyard, M. B. *The New South*. Baltimore: *Manufacturers' Record*, 1887.

Himmelberg, Robert F. *The Origins of the National Recovery Administration: Business, Government, and the Trade Association Issue, 1921–1933*. New York: Fordham Univ. Press, 1976.

Hunter, Louis C. *Steam Power: A History of Industrial Power in the United States, 1780–1930*. Vol. 2, *Steam Power*. Charlottesville: Univ. Press of Virginia, 1985.

Jamieson, George S. *Vegetable Fats and Oils, Their Chemistry, Production and Utilization for Edible, Medicinal and Technical Purposes*. 2d ed. New York: Reinhold Publishing, 1943.

Jewell, Edwin L. *Jewell's Crescent City Illustrated*. New Orleans, 1873.

Kolko, Gabriel. *The Triumph of Conservatism: A Reinterpretation of American History, 1900–1916*. New York: Free Press of Glencoe, 1963.

Lamborn, Leebert Lloyd. *Cottonseed Products: A Manual of the Treatment of Cottonseed for Its Products and Their Utilization in the Arts*. New York: D. Van Nostrand, 1904.

Lamoreaux, Naomi R. *The Great Merger Movement in American Business, 1895–1905*. Cambridge: Cambridge Univ. Press, 1985.

Land, John E. *Pen Illustrations of New Orleans, 1881–1882*. New Orleans: privately published, 1882.

Lee, R. Alton. *A History of Regulatory Taxation*. Lexington: Univ. Press of Kentucky, 1973.

Leuchtenburg, William E. *Franklin D. Roosevelt and the New Deal, 1932–1940*. New York: Harper & Row, 1963.

Lewkowitsch, J. *Chemical Technology and Analysis of Oils, Fats, and Waxes*. 3 vols. London: Macmillan, 1909.

Lief, Alfred. *"It Floats": The Story of Procter & Gamble*. New York: Rinehart, 1985.

Litchfield, Carter, Hans-Joachim Finke, Stephen G. Young, and Karen Zerbe Huetter. *The Bethlehem Oil Mill , 1745–1934: German Technology in Early Pennsylvania*. Kemblesville, Pa.: Olearius Editions, 1984.

Marshall, F. Ray. *Labor in the South*. Cambridge: Harvard Univ. Press, 1967.

McMath, Robert C. *Populist Vanguard: A History of the Southern Farmers' Alliance*. Chapel Hill: Univ. of North Carolina Press, 1975.

Mobile: Seaport and Trade Center, Her Relations to the New South. Mobile: Metropolitan and Star Publishing, 1888.

Moore, John Hebron. *The Emergence of the Cotton Kingdom in the Old Southwest*. Baton Rouge: Louisiana State Univ. Press, 1988.

Morris, Lerona Rosamond. *Oklahoma: Yesterday, Today, Tomorrow*. 2 vols. Guthrie, Okla.: Cooperative Publishing, 1930.

Morrison, Andrew. *The Industries of New Orleans*. New Orleans: J. M. Elstner & Co., 1885.

Nourse, Edwin G. *American Agriculture and the European Market*. New York: McGraw-Hill, 1924.

Olmstead, Dennis. *Memoirs of Eli Whitney, Esq.* New Haven, Conn.: Durrie & Peck, 1846; New York: Arno Press, 1972.

Perloff, Harvey S., and Vera W. Dodds. *How a Region Grows: Area Development in the U.S. Economy.* New York: Committee for Economic Development, 1963.

Perrett, Geoffrey. *America in the Twenties: A History.* New York: Simon and Schuster, 1982.

Pioneering in Kiowa County, vol. 6. Hobart, Okla.: Kiowa County Historical Society, 1982.

Porter, Glenn. *The Rise of Big Business, 1860–1910.* New York: Thomas Y. Crowell, 1973.

Rabinowitz, Howard N. *The First New South, 1865–1920.* Arlington Heights, Ill.: Harlan Davidson, 1992.

Range, Willard. *A Century of Georgia Agriculture, 1850–1950.* Athens: Univ. of Georgia Press, 1954.

Ransom, Luther A. *The Great Cottonseed Industry of the South.* New York: Oil, Paint and Drug Reporter, 1911.

Rasmussen, Wayne D., and Gladys L. Baker. *The Department of Agriculture.* New York: Praeger, 1972.

Rattray, David. *The City of Natchez.* Natchez, Miss.: Democrat Book and Job Print, 1881.

Richards, Henry I. *Cotton and the AAA.* Washington, D.C.: Brookings Institution, 1936.

Riepma, S. F. *The Story of Margarine.* Washington, D.C.: Public Affairs Press, 1970.

Rightor, Henry, ed. *Standard History of New Orleans.* Chicago: Lewis Publishing, 1900.

Rosenberg, Nathan. *Technology and American Economic Growth.* New York: Harper Torchbooks, 1972.

Saloutos, Theodore. *The American Farmer and the New Deal.* Ames: Iowa State Univ. Press, 1982.

Scharf, J. Thomas. *History of Saint Louis City and County.* 2 vols. Philadelphia: Louis H. Everts, 1883.

Schisgall, Oscar. *Eyes on Tomorrow: The Evolution of Procter & Gamble.* Chicago: J. G. Ferguson, 1981.

Schwartz, Michael. *Radical Protest and Social Structure.* Chicago: Univ. of Chicago Press, 1976.

Sigafoos, Robert. *Cotton Row to Beale Street: A Business History of Memphis.* Memphis: Memphis State Univ. Press, 1979.

Sitterson, J. Carlyle. *Sugar Country: The Cane Sugar Industry in the South, 1753–1950.* Lexington: Univ. of Kentucky Press, 1953.

Stover, John F. *The Railroads of the South, 1865–1900: A Study in Finance and Control.* Chapel Hill: Univ. of North Carolina Press, 1955.

Taylor, B. F. *Early History of the Cotton Oil Industry in America.* Columbia, S.C.: privately published, 1936.

Texas Cottonseed Crushing Mills and Their Products, 1965–1966 Season. Austin: Univ. of Texas Press, 1967.

Thompson, Holland. *"The New South" in the New Economic Order*. New Haven, Conn.: Yale Univ. Press, 1919.

Thornton, M. K. *Cottonseed Products*. Wharton, Texas: *Oil Mill Gazetteer*, 1932.

Tilley, Nannie May. *The Bright Tobacco Industry, 1860–1929*. Chapel Hill: Univ. of North Carolina Press, 1948.

Tindall, George Brown. *The Emergence of the New South, 1913–1945*. Baton Rouge: Louisiana State Univ. Press, 1967.

Tompkins, D. A. *Cotton and Cotton Oil*. Charlotte, N.C.: privately published, 1901.

Turner, J. Kelly, and John L. Bridgers Jr. *History of Edgecombe County, North Carolina*. Raleigh, N.C.: Edwards & Broughton Printing, 1920.

Van Stuyvenberg, J. H., ed. *Margarine: An Economic, Social and Scientific History, 1869–1969*. Liverpool: Liverpool Univ. Press, 1969.

Watkins, James L. *King Cotton: A Historical and Statistical Review, 1790–1908*. New York: James L. Watkins & Sons, 1908.

Weber, G. M., and C. L. Alsberg. *The American Vegetable- Shortening Industry, Its Origin and Development*. Palo Alto, Calif.: Food Research Institute, Stanford Univ., 1934.

Wilson, Charles. *The History of Unilever: A Study in Economic Growth and Social Change*. 3 vols. London: Cassell, 1954; New York: Frederick A. Praeger, 1968.

Winston, George Tayloe. *A Builder of the New South: Being the Story of the Life Work of Daniel Augustus Tompkins*. 1920. Freeport, N.Y.: Books for Libraries Press, 1972.

Woodman, Harold D. *King Cotton and His Retainers: Financing and Marketing the Cotton Crop of the South, 1800–1925*. Lexington: Univ. of Kentucky Press, 1968; Columbia: Univ. of South Carolina Press, 1990.

Woodward, C. Vann. *Origins of the New South, 1877–1914*. Baton Rouge: Louisiana State Univ. Press, 1951.

Wright, Gavin. *Old South, New South: Revolutions in the Southern Economy Since the Civil War*. New York: Basic Books, 1986.

Wright, Philip Green. *The American Tariff and Oriental Trade*. Chicago: University of Chicago Press, 1931.

Young, James Harvey. *Pure Food: Securing the Federal Food and Drug Acts of 1906*. Princeton: Princeton Univ. Press, 1989.

Articles, Bulletins, Pamphlets, Reports, Chapters, Speeches, Booklets, and Proceedings

Aiken, Charles S. "Cotton Gins." In *Encyclopedia of Southern Culture*, ed. Charles Reagan Wilson and William Ferris. Chapel Hill: Univ. of North Carolina Press, 1989.

———. "The Evolution of Cotton Ginning in the Southeastern United States." *Geographical Review* 63 (Apr. 1973): 196–224.

Alderks, O. H. "Cooking of Meats and Recovery of Oil." In *Cotton and Cottonseed Products*, ed. Alton E. Bailey, 615–50. New York: Interscience Publishers, 1948.

Allbright, W. B. "How Cottonseed Oil Became a Food Product." *Cotton Oil Press* 8 (June 1924): 52–53.

"American Cotton Oil Company, Annual Reports, Year Ending August 31." *Commercial and Financial Chronicle* 53 (7 Nov. 1891): 676–79, 55 (5 Nov. 1892): 766–69, 57 (4 Nov. 1893): 766–68.

"Answer of the National Cottonseed Products Association to the Complaint of the Federal Trade Commission, 15 August 1934." *Cotton Oil Press* 18 (Aug. 1934): 3–16.

Aspegren, John. "Economic Conditions in the Cotton Seed Oil Industry." *Chemical Age* 32 (June 1924): 259–61.

Black, Howard C. "Edible Cottonseed Oil Products. In *Cotton and Cottonseed Products,* ed. Alton E. Bailey, 732–62. New York: Interscience Publishers, 1948.

Blackwell, C. P. *Applying Science to Agriculture.* Oklahoma A. and M. College Agricultural Experiment Station, Report for 1 July 1932 to 30 June 1934.

Bowld, W. F. "Development of the Chemical Cotton Cellulose Industry." *Proceedings of the First Cotton Research Congress.* Statewide Cotton Committee of Texas, 1944.

Boyle, James E. "New Orleans and Memphis Exchanges for Cottonseed Products." *Commerce and Finance* 39 (25 Sept. 1929): 2065, 2067.

"The Buckeye Cotton Oil Company." *Chemical and Engineering News* 20 (10 Apr. 1942): 438.

Bushman, Richard L., and Claudia L. Bushman. "The Early History of Cleanliness in America." *Journal of American History* 74 (Mar. 1988): 1213–38.

Carpenter, E. L., and Leo Holdredge. "The Cottonseed-Oil Industry." *Mechanical Engineering* 53 (May 1931): 353–59.

Carrott, M. Browning. "The Supreme Court and American Trade Associations, 1921–1925." *Business History Review* 44 (Autumn 1970): 320–38.

Chaney, Thomas R. "The Cotton-Seed-Oil Industry." In *One Hundred Years of American Commerce,* ed. Chauncey M. Depew, 451–55. New York: D. O. Haynes, 1895.

Cist, Charles. "Cotton-Seed Oil." *DeBow's Review* 27 (July 1859): 111–12, 27 (Aug. 1859): 220–22.

Clark, Roscoe C. "The Cottonseed Products Industry." *Journal of Accountancy* 54 (Sept. 1932): 170–91.

Clay, Howard B. "Daniel Augustus Tompkins and Industrial Revival in the South." *East Carolina College Publications in History* 2 (1965): 114–45.

Cooper, Maurice. "History of Cotton and the United States Cottonseed Industry." In *Cotton and Cottonseed Products,* ed. Alton E. Bailey, 51–101. New York: Interscience Publishers, 1948.

Cotton Oil, 5th ed. New York: Aspegren & Co., 1913.

Cottonseed and Its Products. 8th ed. Memphis: National Cottonseed Products Association, 1978.

Cottonseed and Linseed Oil Machinery. Dayton, Ohio: Stilwell-Bierce & Smith-Vaile, 1895. DAT, CPL.

"Cottonseed Crushing Before the Civil War." *Cotton Oil Press* 14 (Dec. 1930): 37, 39.

"Cotton Seed Oil Mills." *Manufacturers' Record* 8 (19 Sept. 1885): 178–79.

"Cottonseed Slump Hurts South." *Business Week*, 6 Nov. 1937, 45–46.

Culbertson, J. J. "History of Cottonseed Crushing in Texas." *Cotton Oil Press* 15 (Oct. 1931): 25–29.

The D. A. Tompkins Company, the Scope and Character of Its Work in Developing the Industrial Resources of the South. Charlotte, N.C.: Charlotte Observer Printing and Publishing House, 1895. DAT, CPL

Dabney, Charles W. "A Plea for Small Cotton Seed Oil Mills." *Oil, Paint and Drug Reporter* 21 (17 May 1882): 934.

Davis, C. Wood. "Corn and Cotton-Seed: Why the Price for Corn Is Low." *Forum* 24 (1898): 731–32.

Deasy, George F. "Geography of the United States Cottonseed Oil Industry." *Economic Geography* 17 (Oct. 1941): 345–52.

DeSegundo, E. C. "Some Cotton Seed Products in Their Relation to Present-Day Needs." *Scientific American Supplement* 86 (14 Dec. 1918): 382–83.

Dickinson, J. P. "Why Oil Mills Cannot Get Good Young White Men in the Mills to Learn the Business." *Cotton Oil Press* (May 1927): 55–56.

"Diesel Engines in the Cotton Oil Industry." *Power* 76 (Oct. 1932): 211.

Dobbs, Philip. "Vegetable Oil Processing Industry." *Magazine of Wall Street* 20 (Jan. 1945): 426–27, 439–40.

"Economic Survey of the Cottonseed Products Industry." Memphis: National Cottonseed Products Association, 15 Jan. 1931. NAL.

"1833–1983: 150 Years in Oktibbeha County." *Starkville Daily News*, 1983.

"Edward Flash Retires from Business." *Cotton Oil Press* 15 (June 1931): 83–84.

Facts about a Great Exclusively Southern Industry—Cottonseed. Memphis: National Cottonseed Products Association, 1931. RG 9, National Archives, Washington, D.C.

"Farm Chemurgy." *Newsweek* 13 (10 Apr. 1939): 45.

Farmers Cooperative Manufacturing Company. Tarboro, N.C.: C. G. Bradley, 1888. J. Bryan Grimes Papers, ECU.

"Federal Trade Commission Threw a Bomb." *Cotton Oil Press* 18 (June 1934): 95–97.

Fornari, Harry D. "The Big Change: Cotton to Soybeans." *Agricultural History* 53 (Jan. 1979): 245–53.

French, H. M. "Motors and Control for Cotton Gins and Cottonseed-Oil Mills." *Melliand Textile Monthly* 4 (Sept. 1932): 357–59; vol. 4 (Oct. 1932): 424–25.

George, E. T. "Fifty-Seven Years with Mr. Cottonseed." *Cotton and Cotton Oil Press* 40 (8–10 May 1939): 5–6.

Gilbert, J. C. "Expanding Uses for Cotton Seed and Linters." *Commerce and Finance* 17 (8 Feb. 1928): 356–57.

Gordon, John B. "Consumption of Industrial Oils and Fats Exceeded Production." *Chemical & Metallurgical Engineering* 36 (Jan. 1929): 54–55.

Hammond, Henry C. "Cotton Seed Meal as a Food for Work Stock." *Bulletin, Number 10.* In *Bulletins 1–13 (Nov. 1906–Jan. 1911) of Interstate Cotton Seed Crushers' Association.* NAL.

Hammond, Henry. "The Cotton Seed Industry." *Oil, Paint and Drug Reporter* 50 (12 Oct. 1896): 25–26.

Harmon, S. M. "Cottonseed Industry 1939." *Manufacturers' Record* 109 (Jan. 1940): 46, 62.

Harris, John P., and Alexander B. McKechnie. "Modern Deodorizing Methods, the Key Process to Quality Edible Oils." *Cotton Oil Press* 8 (Dec. 1927): 27–30.

Harris, W. D. "Solvent Extraction of Cottonseed Oil." *Bulletin of the Agricultural and Mechanical College of Texas.* 4th series. Vol. 12. No. 12 (15 Sept. 1941): 1–31.

Heberle, Rudolf. "The Mainsprings of Southern Urbanization." In *The Urban South,* ed. Rupert B. Vance and Nicholas Demereth, 6–23. Chapel Hill: Univ. of North Carolina Press, 1954.

Hoffman, G. "How and Why We Burn Cotton-Seed Hulls." *Power* 77 (Sept. 1933): 462–63.

Hoffman, W. G. "100 Years of the Margarine Industry." In *Margarine,* ed. J. H. Van Stuyvenberg, 9–36. Liverpool: Liverpool Univ. Press, 1969.

Holcomb, Gene. "Chemistry's Contribution to the Cottonseed Industry." *Chemical & Engineering News* 20 (10 Apr. 1942): 440–42.

Hopkins, A. G. "Cotton's Future as a Leading Source of Essential Fat." In *Proceedings of the Fifth Cotton Research Congress,* 91–103. N.p.: Statewide Cotton Committee of Texas, 1944.

Hughston, T. A. "The Economic Significance of Cottonseed to the Southwest and the Nation." *Proceedings of the Fifth Cotton Research Congress,* 104–6. N.p.: Statewide Cotton Committee of Texas, 1944.

———. "Merchandising Cottonseed and Cottonseed Products." In *Proceedings of the Eighth Cotton Research Congress,* 57–61. N.p.: Statewide Cotton Committee of Texas, 1947.

James, Edward M. "Processing of Cottonseed Oil." In *Cotton and Cottonseed Products,* ed. Alton E. Bailey, 691–731. New York: Interscience Publishers, 1948.

Jarvis, P. M. "Industry Makes Markets for Cottonseed." In *Proceedings of the Seventh Cotton Research Congress,* 76–82. N.p.: Statewide Cotton Committee of Texas, 1946.

Jasspon, William H. "The Cotton Oil Industry—Looking Forward." *Commerce and Finance* 15 (13 Jan. 1926): 135.

———. "Too Many Bulls Still in Cotton Seed." *Commerce and Finance* 14 (4 Mar. 1925): 119.

———. "What a Large Crop Does to the Cotton Oil Industry." *Commerce and Finance* 16 (12 Jan. 1927): 119, 121.

———. "What Is Wrong with the Cotton Oil Industry?" *Commerce and Finance* 13 (Jan. 1924): 431–32.

Johnson, Edwin Lehman. "A Plea for the New Cereal, the Cotton-Seed." *Forum* 30 (1900): 51–54.

Karsten, M. E. "Fifty Years of Oil Mill Operating." *Cotton Oil Press* 16 (July 1932): 25–26.

Kilgore, W. G. "The Cottonseed Oil Industry." *Oil, Paint and Drug Reporter* 55 (26 June 1899): 26H.

Laird, William E., and James R. Rinehart. "Deflation, Agriculture, and Southern Development." *Agricultural History* 42 (Apr. 1968): 115–24.

Lawton, J. J. "Special Linter Committee Report." *Cotton Oil Press* 3 (June 1919): 53–56.

Leahy, John. "Cottonseed Processing Links Agriculture and Industry Profitably." *Southern Power & Industry* (Oct. 1939): 37–44.

Lockhart, Grace. "Tons of Human Hair in Industry." *Scientific American* 144 (June 1931): 386–87.

Loggins, R. L. "Diesel Engines in the Cotton Oil Industry." *Power* 76 (Oct. 1932): 211.

Lund, Charles E. "Production and Consumption of Cottonseed and Cottonseed Products." In *Cotton and Cottonseed Products,* ed. Alton E. Bailey, 105–16. New York: Interscience Publishers, 1948.

Markley, K. S. "The Cotton Processing Industry." *Cotton and Cotton Oil Press* 47 (24 Aug. 1946): A-3–A-6.

Markley, K. S., and D. F. J. Lynch. "The Technology of the Cottonseed Crushing Industry." In *Proceedings of the First Cotton Research Congress,* 211–24. N.p.: Statewide Cotton Committee of Texas, 1940.

Marshall, George. "Cottonseed—Joint Products and Pyramidal Control." In *Price and Price Policies,* ed. Walton Hamilton, 201–97. New York: McGraw-Hill, 1938.

Matherly, W. J. "North Carolina's Position in Cottonseed Industry." *North Carolina Commerce and Industry* 3 (Nov. 1925): 1.

McMillan, M. C. "Daniel Pratt, Ante-bellum Southern Industrialist." Prattville, Ala.: Continental Eagle Corp., 1993.

———. "The Manufacture of Cotton Gins, 1793–1860." Continental Eagle Corp.

Meloy, Guy S. "The Evolution of Cottonseed Marketing Practices." Address, Ginners Conference, Stoneville, Miss., 3 June 1941. NAL.

———. "Grading and Evaluation of Cottonseed." In *Cottonseed and Cottonseed Products,* ed. Alton E. Bailey, 497–527. New York: Interscience Publishers, 1948.

Moloney, John F. "A Half Century of Progress, the Story of the National Cottonseed Products Association, 1897–1946." *Cotton Oil Press* 47 (4 May 1946): 9–31.

———. "Cottonseed Oil—A Typical American Industry." In *Proceedings of the First Cotton Research Congress,* 232–42. N.p.: Statewide Cotton Committee of Texas, 1940.

———. "Economics of Cottonseed Crushing." *In Cottonseed and Cottonseed Products,* ed. Alton E. Bailey, 651–88. New York: Interscience Publishers, 1948.

———. "The Marketing of Cottonseed, a Report Prepared in Connection with Project II, Postwar Agricultural and Economic Problems of the Cotton Belt." Memphis: National Cottonseed Products Association, [1945?].

———. "Markets for Cottonseed Cake and Meal." *Cotton and Cotton Oil Press* 39 (24 Sept. 1938): 3.

———. "Some Effects of the Federal Fair Labor Standards Act upon Southern Industry." *Southern Economic Journal* 9 (1942): 15–23.

———. "Trends in the Industrial Use of Cottonseed Products." In *Proceedings of the Second Cotton Research Congress,* 71–92. N.p.: Statewide Cotton Committee of Texas, 1941.

Moore, Walter B. "Oldest Cotton Oil Mill Has Had Unique History." *Cotton Gin & Oil Mill Press* 56 (3 Dec. 1955): 12–13, 30.

Nealey, J. B. "Making Cottonseed Oil and Its Products." *Manufacturers' Record* 103 (Feb. 1934): 18–19.

Niemi, Albert W. "Structural Shifts in Southern Manufacturing." *Business History Review* 45 (Spring 1971): 79–81.

Nixon, H. C. "The Rise of the American Cottonseed Oil Industry." *Journal of Political Economy* 38 (Feb.–Dec. 1930): 73–85.

Ogden, Henry V. *Cotton-Seed Oil and Cotton-Seed Oil Mills.* Atlanta: Constitution Print, 1880.

Osband, Kent. "The Boll Weevil Versus 'King Cotton.'" *Journal of Economic History* 45 (Sept. 1985): 627–43.

"Overcapacity Ruins the Profits." *Food Industries* 4 (Mar. 1932): 103–5.

Parrish, Henry J. "Oil Milling in Memphis in 1881." *Cotton Oil Press* 11 (May 1927): 53–54.

Perkins, C. A., and Taylor R. Brooks. "Cotton Seed Oil Pressing Costs Cut." *Food Industries* 9 (Aug. 1937): 435–37, 472.

Phillips, William H. "Making a Business of It." Paper presented at the Auburn University Cotton Gin Symposium, 5–7 May 1993.

Picard, Glenn H. "Edible Vegetable Oils." *Oil Miller* 8 (Mar. 1918): 30–31.

Pirrung, H. C. "Butterine, Its Origin, History and Laws from a Manufacturers' Viewpoint of Twenty-five Years Experience." *Bulletin* 13, 1911. In *Bulletins 1–13 (Nov. 1906–Jan 1911)* of Interstate Cotton Seed Crushers' Association, 8–15, NAL.

Porter, Patric G. "Origins of the American Tobacco Company." *Business History Review* 43 (1969): 58–76.

Practical Points for Oil Mill Managers and Superintendents. Dayton, Ohio: Buckeye Iron & Brass Works, n.d., but stamped 3 Apr. 1920.

"Proposed Code of Business Conduct Principles." *Cotton Oil Press* 11 (Apr. 1928): 17–18.

Prunty, Merle, Jr. "Recent Quantitative Changes in the Cotton Regions of the Southeastern States." *Economic Geography* 27 (July 1951): 189–208.

Prunty, Merle, Jr., and Charles S. Aiken, "The Demise of the Piedmont Cotton Region." *Annals of the Association of American Geographers* 62 (June 1972): 283–306.

Report, 1898–1899. Stillwater: Oklahoma Agricultural and Mechanical College, Agricultural Experiment Station, n.d.

Reynolds, W. A. "Some Evils in Seed Buying." *Proceedings of the Interstate Cotton Seed Crushers' Association,* 1912, 62–63.

Roper, Daniel Clifford. "Census Office Cotton Report and the Significant Development of the Cottonseed-Oil Industry." *South Atlantic Quarterly* 2 (Jan. to Oct. 1903): 237–45.

Rosenberg, Nathan. "Technological Change in the Machine Tool Industry, 1840–1910." *Journal of Economic History* 23 (Dec. 1963): 414–43.

Rother, Charles V. "Looking Back Fifty Years." *Cotton Oil Press* 15 (June 1931): 92.

Ryan, R. D. "Economical Value of the Expeller." *Cotton Gin and Oil Mill Press* 48 (12 July 1947): A-3–A-4.

Sheridan, Richard C. "Chemical Fertilizers in Southern Agriculture." *Agricultural History* 53 (Jan. 1979): 308–18.

Shue, W. D. "The Cotton Oil Industry." *Mississippi Historical Society Publications* 8 (1904): 253–92.

Siddall, K. Y. "Determining the Purchase Price of Cottonseed." *National Association of Cost Accountants* 16 (15 Dec. 1934): 421–33.

"Small Cotton-Seed Oil Mills." Cardwell Machine Company booklet c. 1890 rpt. in *Cotton and Cotton Oil Press* 41 (21 Dec. 1940): A-4, A-5, A-7.

Smith, Eugene Allen. "Report on the Cotton Production of the State of Alabama." Extract from the U.S. Census, 1880, UA.

Sypher, J. R. "Cotton Seed, Cotton Seed Oil, Cotton Seed Cake." In *Cotton Culture,* by Joseph B. Lyman, 180–89. New York: Orange, Judd, 1868.

Taylor, B. F. "Address of President." *Proceedings of the Interstate Cotton Seed Crushers' Association,* 1912, 32–40.

Taylor, Rosser H. "Fertilizers and Farming in the Southeast, 1840–1950." *North Carolina Historical Review* 30 (July 1953): 305–28, 30 (Oct. 1953): 483–523.

Thompson, Erwin W. "Press Cloth from Human Hair." *Oil Miller* 2 (Aug. 1913): 27–28.

Tompkins, D. A. "The Cotton Oil Industry in America." Rpt. of article in *Cassier's Magazine* [1900?], North Carolina Room, Wilson Library, University of North Carolina, Chapel Hill.

———. *Cotton Seed and Its Products.* D. A. Tompkins Company, Catalog, 1900. DAT, CPL.

———. "Cotton-Seed Oil." *Manufacturers' Record* 11 (12 Mar. 1887): 160.

———. *Cotton Seed Oil Mills, Cotton Oil Refineries, Cotton Factories, Sulphur Acid Chambers, Acid Phosphate Works, Electric Lighting.* Charlotte, N.C.: R. B. Elam Print, 1893. DAT, CPL.

———. "Cultivation, Baling and Manufacturing of Cotton from a Southern Standpoint, a Paper Read at the Meeting of the New England Cotton Manufacturers' Association, at Atlanta, Ga., Oct. 25, 1895." DAT, CPL.

———. "Ginneries, Oil Mills, Fertilizer Works, Cost of Plants, Operation, Etc." Rpt. from the *Manufacturers' Record.* Charlotte: D. A. Tompkins Company, [1899?]. DAT, CPL.

———. "Printed Address Delivered at the Annual Convention of the Interstate Cotton Seed Crushers' Association, June 14–15–16." DAT, CPL.

Tosdal, H. R. "Open Price Associations." *American Economic Review* 7 (June 1917): 331–52.

United Packinghouse Workers of America, Soap Workers Organizing Committee. "Inter-Relations Between Meat Packing, Soap and Cottonseed Oil Industries." Pamphlets in American History on Microfilm, 1943.

The Value of Cotton-Seed Products in the Feeding of Farm Animals, as a Human Food and as a Fertilizer. Dallas: Bureau of Publicity of the Interstate Cotton Seed Crushers' Association, 1913.

Van Wyck, Peter. "Cotton Linters." In *Cotton and Cottonseed Products,* ed. Alton E. Bailey, 894–905. New York: Interscience Publishers, 1948.

Wall, Bennett. "Breaking Out: What is Not in Southern History, 1918–1988." *Journal of Southern History* 55 (Feb. 1989): 3–20.

Wamble, A. Cecil. "New Opportunities Through Research." In *Proceedings of the Seventh Cotton Research Congress,* 83–88. N.p.: Statewide Cotton Committee of Texas, 1946.

"Wanted: Cottonseed." *Newsweek* 13 (22 May 1939): 46.

Ward, A. L. "A Brief Survey of Recent Trends Influencing the Use of Cottonseed Products." In *Proceedings of the Second Cotton Research Congress,* 48–63. N.p.: Statewide Cotton Committee of Texas, 1941.

———. "Cottonseed—'Farm Cinderella,' One-Time Step-Child of Southern Farms Now Second Most Valuable Cash Crop." *Manufacturers' Record* 105 (July 1936): 32–33.

———. "Margarine—A Major Outlet for Southern Vegetable Fats and Oils." *Manufacturers' Record* 106 (Apr. 1937): 42, 69.

Weber, Georges M. "Legislative Weapons in Inter-industry Competition—Oils and Fats." *Harvard Business Review* 13 (Oct. 1934): 72–81.

Weiher, Kenneth. "The Cotton Industry and Southern Urbanization, 1880–1930." *Explorations in Economic History* 14 (1977): 120–39.

"Wesson." *Fortune* 20 (Sept. 1939): 66–71, 102–8.

Wesson, David. "Application of Chemical Research to Cotton Oil Industry." *Chemical and Metallurgical Engineering* 26 (28 June 1922): 1219.

———. "Application of Modern Analytical Methods to Transactions in Cottonseed Products." *Oil, Paint and Drug Reporter* 111 (30 May 1927): 34.

———. "Contributions of the Chemist to the Cotton-Seed Oil Industry." *Journal of Industrial and Engineering Chemistry* 7 (Apr. 1915): 276–77.

———. "The Cotton Oil Industry." *Cotton Oil Press* 1 (Apr. 1918): 19.

———. "Cotton Oil Industry in the War." *Journal of Industrial and Engineering Chemistry* 10 (Nov. 1918): 930–31.

———. "The Dixie Olive, Address Before the Ottawa Section of the American Institute of Chemical Engineers." *Cotton Oil Press* 9 (Oct. 1925): 21.

———. "Historical Aspects of Vegetable Oil Refining, an Address Before the American Oil Chemists Society, 14 November 1929." *Cotton Oil Press* 13 (Jan. 1930): 22–23.

———. "History and Development of the Cottonseed Oil Industry." *Chemical and Metallurgical Engineering* 21 (26 Nov.–3 Dec. 1919): 661–62.

———. "Lard Substitutes, History of Its Manufacture from the Viewpoint of a Technical Chemist," Bulletin 13, 1911. In *Bulletins 1–13 (Nov. 1906–Jan. 1911) of Interstate Cotton Seed Crushers' Association,* 3–4, NAL.

———. "Pictorial Description of the Cotton Oil Industry." *Chemical and Metallurgical Engineering* 22 (10 Mar. 1920): 465–72.

———. "Solvent Extractions—The New and Better Way." *Oil & Fat Industry* 7 (1930): 258.

———. "Some Phases of Progress in Vegetable Oil Production." In *Twenty-Five Years of Chemical Engineering Progress,* ed. Sidney D. Kirkpatrick, 226–33.

N.p.: American Institute of Chemical Engineers, 1933; Freeport, N.Y.: Books for Libraries Press, 1968.

West, W. B. "B. F. Taylor, Secretary South Carolina Cotton Seed Crushers' Association." *Oil Miller* 3 (Feb. 1914): 25–26.

Whitney, R. R. "Domestic Markets for Cottonseed and Cottonseed Products." In *Proceedings of the Ninth Cotton Research Congress,* 49–56. N.p.: Statewide Cotton Committee of Texas, 1948.

"Will Clayton's Cotton." *Fortune* 32 (Nov. 1945): 138–47, 231–38, 32 (Dec. 1945): 159–63, 231–42.

Wilson, Otto. "Government Policies Affect Vegetable Oil Output." *Industrial and Engineering Chemistry* 12 (20 Nov., 1934): 406–7.

Woolrich, W. L. "Cottonseed Processing Research." *Mechanical Engineering* 61 (Feb. 1939): 131–35.

Wrenn, Lynette B. "Cincinnati and the Cottonseed Industry." *Queen City Heritage* 48 (Fall 1990): 15–32.

———. "Cottonseed Price-Fixing in Eastern North Carolina, 1903–1907." *North Carolina Historical Review* 67 (Oct. 1990): 411–37.

Government Publications

Agricultural Experiment Station of the North Carolina State College of Agriculture and Engineering and North Carolina Dept. of Agriculture. Technical Bulletin No. 71. "A Preliminary Study of Cotton Ginning Costs in North Carolina." Raleigh, 1942.

Interstate Commerce Commission. Rate Structure Investigation. No. 17000. "Cottonseed, Its Products and Related Articles," by John T. Money and George Esch. Washington, D.C., 1931.

Louisiana State Experiment Station. Bulletin No. 13. *Cotton and Its Products,* by William C. Stubbs. [Baton Rouge, 1887?]

Oklahoma Agricultural Experiment Station. Bulletin No. 51. "Feeding Cottonseed Meal to Hogs," by F. C. Burtis and J. S. Malone. Stillwater, 1901.

Texas Engineering Experiment Station. Bulletin No. 136. "Screw Pressing of Cottonseed," by Cecil A. Wamble and William B. Harris. College Station, 1954.

U.S. Congress. Senate. *Hearings Before the Committee on Agriculture and Forestry on S. 4208* (a bill for the prevention and removal of obstructions and burdens upon interstate commerce in cottonseed oil by regulating transactions on Future Exchanges and for other purposes), 69th Cong., 1st sess., 18, 26, 27 May 1926.

U.S. Congress. *Cottonseed Industry.* 70th Cong., 1st sess., 1928. H. Doc. 193.

U.S. Congress. Senate. *Report of Federal Trade Commission on Cotton-seed Industry* (13 reports issued at intervals, 1930–32), 71st Cong., 2d sess.

U.S. Dept. of Agriculture. Agricultural Marketing Service. *A Study of Practices Affecting the Use of Major Vegetable Oils for Refining and Processing,* by William Emory and Jack S. Wolf. Washington, D.C., 1960.

U.S. Dept. of Agriculture. Office of Experiment Stations. Bulletin No. 80. *The Agricultural Experiment Stations in the United States,* by A. C. True and V. A. Clark. Washington, D.C., 1900.

U.S. Dept. of Agriculture. "The Castor Oil Industry," by Charles M. Daugherty. In *Agricultural Yearbook, 1904,* 287–98.

U.S. Dept. of Agriculture. Division of Statistics. "The Cost of Cotton Production," by John Hyde and James L. Watkins. Misc. ser. Bulletin No. 16. Washington, D.C., 1899.

U.S. Dept. of Agriculture. Bureau of Agricultural Economics. "Cotton and Cottonseed Marketing, Related Production Practices among Negro Farmers in Red River Delta Area of Louisiana, 1951," by Frederick C. Temple. Washington, D.C., 1953.

U.S. Dept. of Agriculture. Office of Markets and Rural Organization. *Cotton Ginning Information for Farmers,* by Fred Taylor, D. C. Griffith, and C. E. Atkinson. Washington, D.C., 1916.

U.S. Dept. of Agriculture. Agricultural Research Service. "Cottonseed Drying and Storage at Cotton Gins." Technical Bulletin No. 1262. Washington, D.C., 1962.

U.S. Dept. of Agriculture. Agricultural Research Service. "Cottonseed Handling at Gins." Production Research Report No. 66. Washington, D.C., 1963.

U.S. Dept. of Agriculture. Bureau of Agricultural Economics. "Cottonseed: Marketing Spreads Between Price Received by Farmers and Value of Products at Crushing Mills," by Kathryn Parr and Richard O. Been. Washington, D.C., 1942.

U.S. Dept. of Agriculture. Commodity Exchange Authority. "The Cottonseed Oil Futures Market." Washington, D.C., 1949.

U.S. Dept. of Agriculture. Production and Marketing Administration, Fats and Oil Branch. "Cottonseed Oil Mill Characteristics and Marketing Practices." Agricultural Information Bulletin No. 79. Washington, D.C., 1951.

U.S. Dept. of Agriculture. Farm Credit Administration, Cooperative Research and Service Division. "Crushing Cottonseed Cooperatively," by John S. Burgess Jr. Circular No. C-114. Washington, D.C., 1939.

U.S. Dept. of Agriculture. "Crushing Cottonseed Cooperatively," by Elmer J. Perdue. FCS Circular No. 30. Washington, D.C., 1962.

U.S. Dept. of Agriculture. "Farm-To-Mill Margin for Cottonseed and Cottonseed Products in Tennessee, September 1946–July 1950," by A. R. Sabin. *Agricultural Economist.* Washington, D.C., 1951.

U.S. Dept. of Agriculture. Office of Experiment Stations. "The Feeding Value of Cotton-Seed Products," by B. W. Kilgore. In *The Cotton Plant: Its History, Botany, Chemistry, Culture, Enemies, and Uses,* ed. Charles W. Dabney, 385–421. Bulletin No. 33. Washington, D.C., 1896.

U.S. Dept. of Agriculture. Production and Marketing Administration, Cotton Branch. "The Grading of Cottonseed." Agricultural Information Bulletin No. 39. Washington, D.C., 1951.

U.S. Dept. of Agriculture. Office of Experiment Stations. "The Handling and Uses of Cotton," by Henry Hammond. In *The Cotton Plant: Its History, Botany, Chemistry, Culture, Enemies, and Uses,* ed. Charles W. Dabney, 351–84. Bulletin No. 33. Washington, D.C., 1896.

U.S. Dept. of Agriculture. Marketing Research Report No. 218. "Labor and Power Utilization at Cottonseed Oil Mills," by Julia A. Mitchell, Donald Jackson, and C. B. Gilliland. Washington, D.C., Feb. 1958.

U.S. Dept. of Agriculture. Production and Marketing Administration, Fats and Oils Branch. "Marketing and Processing Costs of Cottonseed-Oil Mills in the Postwar Period, 1946–47 to 1950–51," by Calvin C. Spilsbury. Washington, D.C., 1952.

U.S. Dept. of Agriculture. Agricultural Marketing Service. "Processing the Three Major Oil Seeds." Marketing Research Report No. 58. Washington, D.C., 1954.

U.S. Dept. of Agriculture. Agricultural Adjustment Administration. "Proposed Marketing Agreement for the Cotton Seed Crushing Industry." Washington, D.C., 1933. NAL.

U.S. Dept. of Agriculture. *Yearbook, 1916.* "Some American Vegetable Food Oils, Their Sources and Methods of Production," by H. S. Bailey. Washington, D.C., 1917.

U.S. Dept. of Commerce and Labor. Bureau of the Census. *Thirteenth Census of the United States: 1910.* Vol. 5. *Agriculture 1909 and 1910.* Washington, D.C., 1913.

U.S. Dept. of Commerce and Labor. Bureau of the Census. *Thirteenth Census of the United States: 1910.* Vol. 9. *Manufactures 1901, Reports by States.* Vol. 10. *Reports for Principal Industries.* Washington, D.C., 1912.

U.S. Dept. of Commerce. Bureau of the Census. *Fourteenth Census of the United States: 1920.* Vol. 9. *Manufactures 1919, Reports for States.* Washington, D.C., 1923.

U.S. Dept. of Commerce. Bureau of the Census. *Fifteenth Census of the United States: 1930. Manufactures: 1929.* Vol. 2. *Reports by Industries.* Vol. 3. *Reports by States.* Washington, D.C., 1933.

U.S. Dept. of Commerce. Bureau of the Census. *Sixteenth Census of the United States: 1940. Manufactures, 1939.* Vol 2. *Reports by Industries.* Pt. 1. *Groups 1 to 10.* Vol. 3. *Reports for States.* Washington, D.C., 1942.

U.S. Dept. of Commerce. Bureau of the Census. *Census of Manufactures: 1947.* Vol. 3. *Statistics by States.* Washington, D.C., 1949.

U.S. Dept. of Commerce. Bureau of the Census. *United States Census of Manufactures: 1958.* Vol. 2. *Industry Statistics.* Pt. 1. *Major Groups 20 to 28.* Washington, D.C., 1962.

U.S. Dept. of Labor. Wage and Hour and Public Contracts Divisions. "Economic Factors Bearing on the Establishment of Minimum Wages in the Cottonseed and Peanut Crushing Industry." Washington, D.C., 1943.

U.S. Dept. of Labor. Bureau of Labor Statistics. Bulletin No. 836. *Labor Unionism in American Agriculture,* by Stuart M. Jamieson. Washington, D.C., 1945.

U.S. Dept. of Labor. Bureau of Labor Statistics. "Wages and Hours of Labor in Cottonseed Oil Mills." *Monthly Labor Review* 27 (July 1928): 109–23.

U.S. Dept. of the Interior. Bureau of the Census. *Twelfth Census of the United States: 1900.* Vol 9. *Manufactures.* Pt. 3. *Special Reports on Selected Industries.* "Cottonseed Products," by Daniel C. Roper, 587–94. Washington, D.C., 1902.

U.S. Dept. of the Interior. Bureau of the Census. *Twelfth Census of the United States: 1900.* Vol. 6. *Agriculture.* Pt. 2. *Crops and Irrigation.* Washington, D.C. 1902.

U.S. Dept. of the Interior. Census Office. *Tenth Census of the United States, 1880, Census of Agriculture,* pt. 1, *Mississippi Valley and South Western States,* "Report on Cotton Production in the United States," by Eugene W. Hilgard. Washington, D.C., 1884.

U.S. Dept. of the Interior. Census Office. *Report on the Statistics of Agriculture in the United States at the Eleventh Census: 1890.* Washington, D.C., 1895.

U.S. Patent Office. *Report of 1844.* No. 42, 431–33.

U.S. Patent Office. Jabez Smith's Hulling Machine, Patent No. 5673, 28 Dec. 1829, vol. 9, 21.

U.S. Patent Office. Jabez Smith, of Petersburg, Virginia, Improvement in Machines for Hulling Cotton-Seed, Patent No. 3951, 15 Mar. 1845.

U.S. Patent Office. W. R. Fee, Cotton Seed Huller, Patent No. 17,961, 11 Aug. 1857.

U.S. Patent Office. F. A. Wells, Cotton Seed Hulling Machine, Patent No. 96,177, 26 Oct. 1869.

U.S. Tariff Commission. "Survey of the American Cotton Oil Industry." In *Tariff Information Surveys,* 90–118. Washington, D.C., 1921.

Works Progress Administration. Division of Social Research. Research Monograph 22. *The Plantation South, 1934–1937,* by William C. Holley, Ellen Winston, and T. J. Woofter Jr. Washington, D.C., 1940; New York: Da Capo Press, 1971.

Manuscripts and Archival Holdings

Alabama

Minutes of the Annual Meeting of the Alabama Cotton Seed Crushers' Association, 1913, Alabama Collection, W. Stanley Hoole Special Collections Library, University of Alabama, University, Alabama.

The Plan and Scope of the Alabama Alliance Oil Company. Mobile: Mobile Stationery, 1889. Alabama Collection, W. Stanley Hoole Special Collections Library, University of Alabama, University, Alabama.

Georgia

Report of Committee of Independent Cotton Seed Oil Mills in Regard to Establishing an Oil Refinery. Columbus, Georgia: Thomas Gilbert Printer, 1903, University of Georgia Library, Athens.

George W. Scott files, Kekalb County Historical Society, Decatur, Georgia.

Louisiana

"State of Louisiana vs. American Cotton Oil Trust," Civil District Court, Argument of Thomas J. Semmes, 12 Mar. 1889. Tulane University Library, New Orleans, Louisiana.

Massachusetts

R. G. Dun & Company Collection, Baker Library, Harvard Graduate School of Business Administration, Harvard University.

David R. Williams letters, 1829–30. Typed copies of originals in South Caroliniana Library, Columbia. Baker Library, Harvard Graduate School of Business Administration, Harvard University.

Mississippi

Delta & Pine Land Company Papers, Mitchell Memorial Library, Mississippi State University, Starkville.

Francis G. Thomason Papers, Mitchell Memorial Library, Mississippi State University, Starkville.

Records of the Attorney General, Record Group 48, Mississippi State Archives, Jackson.

Proceedings of the Annual Convention of the Mississippi Valley Cotton Planters' Association Embracing the States of Alabama, Arkansas, Louisiana, Mississippi and Tennessee, 1880. Mississippi State Archives, Jackson.

North Carolina

Charles W. Bradbury Papers, Wilson Library, Southern Historical Collection, University of North Carolina, Chapel Hill.

Henry Clark Bridgers Papers, J. Y. Joiner Library, East Carolina Manuscript Collection, East Carolina University, Greenville.

J. Bryan Grimes Papers, East Carolina Manuscript Collection, East Carolina University, Greenville.

Lillington Oil Mill Papers, Perkins Library, Duke University, Durham.

Manuscript Census of Manufactures, Shelby County, Tennessee, 1880. Manuscript Division, Perkins Library, Duke University, Durham.

William Blount Rodman Papers, East Carolina Manuscript Collection, East Carolina University, Greenville.

F. S. Royster Mercantile Co. Papers, East Carolina Manuscript Collection, East Carolina University, Greenville.

Edward Rutledge Papers, Manuscript Collection, Perkins Library, Duke University, Durham.

D. A. Tompkins Papers, Robinson-Spangler Room, Charlotte [North Carolina] Public Library.

D. A. Tompkins Papers, Manuscript Collection, Perkins Library, Duke University, Durham.

D. A. Tompkins Papers, Wilson Library, Southern Historical Collection, University of North Carolina, Chapel Hill.

Worth Family Papers, Manuscript Collection, Perkins Library, Duke University, Durham.

E. V. Zoeller Papers, Wilson Library, Southern Historical Collection, University of North Carolina, Chapel Hill.

Ohio

Proceedings of the Cotton Seed Crushers' Association, 1879–82, Cincinnati Historical Society.

South Carolina

Kathwood Manufacturing Company Papers, South Caroliniana Library, University of South Carolina, Columbia.

Proceedings of the Fourth Annual Session of the South Carolina Cotton Seed Crushers' Association, June 16 1909, South Caroliniana Library, University of South Carolina, Columbia.

William Wallace. *Prospectus of Proposed Cotton Seed Oil Mill.* ca 1868. South Caroliniana Library, University of South Carolina, Columbia.

Tennessee

Annual reports of the Memphis Chamber of Commerce, 1869, 1875, and of the Memphis Merchants' Exchange, 1883–88, 1894, 1896–97, 1900–1901, Memphis–Shelby County Public Library.

Proceedings of the Interstate Cotton Seed Crushers' Association, 1902–3, 1905, 1906–7, 1909–11, 1913–15, Memphis–Shelby County Public Library.

Texas

Records of the Attorney General, Record Group 302. Texas State Library and Archives, Austin.

National Agricultural Library

Proceedings of the Interstate Cotton Seed Crushers' Association, 1906, 1908, 1912, and others.

Proceedings of the First Annual Convention of the Mississippi Cotton Seed Crushers Association, June 25, 1912.

Proceedings of the Third Annual Session of the South Carolina Cotton Seed Crushers' Association, 1908.

Proceedings of the Cotton Seed Crushers' Association, 1879–83.

National Archives

Agricultural Stabilization and Conservation Service Papers, Record Group 145.

National Recovery Administration Records, Record Group 9.

U.S. Food Administration Records, Record Group 4.

Newspapers and Trade Journals

Art Supplement to the Greater Memphis Edition of the Evening Scimitar, Apr. 1899.

Baltimore Manufacturers' Record, 1885–87, 1893–97.

Commercial and Financial Chronicle, 1892–1930.

Cottonseed Oil Magazine, 1915–17.

Cotton Oil Press, 1917–35.

Cotton and Cotton Oil Press, 1936–40, 1946.

DeBow's Review, 1854–60.

Memphis Daily Appeal and *Memphis Daily Avalanche,* 1866–93.

Niles' Register, 1829, 1833.

Oil Miller, 1912–13.

Oil, Paint and Drug Reporter, 1880–1900.

Progressive Farmer, 1886–92, 1900–1901, 1903, 1919–20.

Theses and Dissertations

Hobbs, F. W. "The Cotton Seed Oil Industry with Particular Reference to the Farmers and Ginners Cotton Oil Company." B. A. thesis, University of Texas, Austin, ca 1919.

Robson, George Locke. "The Farmers' Union in Mississippi." Master's thesis, Mississippi State University, Starkville, 1963.

Taylor, Paul Wayne. "Mobile: 1818–1859, as Her News Papers Pictured Her." M.A. thesis, University of Alabama, 1951.

Thompson, Alan Smith. "Mobile, Alabama, 1850–1861: Economic, Political, Physical, and Population Characteristics." Ph.D. diss., University of Alabama, 1979.

Weber, Georges Minch. "The Economic Development of the American Cottonseed Oil Industry." Ph.D. diss., University of California, 1933.

Interviews

Allen Ater, Executive Secretary of the National Cottonseed Products Association, 26 July 1988.

James Kolar, Moulton, Texas, 16 Sept. 1992.

Brian Lundgren, Elgin Oil Mill, Elgin, Tex., 16 Sept. 1992.

A. J. Thurmond, Executive Vice President of the Mississippi Valley Oilseed Processors Association, 4 Aug. 1988.

Index